BIOGRAPHICAL DICTIONARY OF
AMERICAN CULT AND SECT LEADERS

GARLAND REFERENCE LIBRARY
OF SOCIAL SCIENCE
(VOL. 212)

BIOGRAPHICAL DICTIONARY OF
AMERICAN CULT AND SECT LEADERS

J. Gordon Melton

Garland Publishing, Inc.
New York & London
1986

Library of Congress Cataloging-in-Publication Data

Melton, J. Gordon.
  Biographical dictionary of American cult and sect
leaders.

  (Garland reference library of social science ; vol.
212)
  1. United States—Religion—Biography—Dictionaries.
I. Title. II. Series: Garland reference library of
social science ; v. 212.
BL2525.M448 1986   291.9'092'2 [B]   83-48226
ISBN 0-8240-9037-3 (alk. paper)

Cover design by Stan Rosinski

Printed on acid-free, 250-year-life paper
Manufactured in the United States of America

CONTENTS

CONTENTS

INTRODUCTION

Prior to this *Biographical Dictionary of American Cult and Sect Leaders*, no one had attempted in a single volume to assemble and correlate the historical material on the men and women who, as founders and leaders of the various minority religious and spiritual movements, are largely responsible for the extensive pluralism in American religion. With more than fifteen hundred separate denominations, ethnic church bodies, spiritual groups, occult organizations, and even a few atheistic associations in America, the variety of American religion has reached such proportions as to make America a microcosm of world religion.

This volume offers additional criteria for evaluating the effects religious leaders have had in molding and reflecting the religious thought and behavior of the country. Cult leaders represent the outermost example of individuals who gathered and taught a following and raised up new generations without directly considering the ideas of those people generally regarded as the leading religious thinkers of America. In a similar vein, sectarian leaders frequently built large followings by dissenting from the main currents of the religious thought of their day. The sectarian leaders are reminiscent of those obscure popular theologians who in the nineteenth century controlled and molded the life of the Methodists, the Baptists, and other growing denominations, and who had far more to do with shaping the American religious intellectual climate than did the small group of theologians whose direct influence was confined to the older Reformation churches. While educated New Englanders were reading Timothy Dwight, Nathanial Taylor, and Samuel Hopkins, Methodist circuit riders put John Watson's *Institutes* in their saddle bags and carried them across the frontier; and people like Alexander Campbell combined their theological and evangelistic chores while building the new denominations of middle America. The "best" theologians were rarely the ones to whom the majority of people and churches turned.

From the perspective of America's religious pluralism and the many popular religious currents, the title of this volume could be misleading. Few people, at least in the United States, think of themselves as sectarian or cultish. The terms *cult* and *sect* are labels placed on religious groups and their adherents by others, primarily their critics. Both terms carry negative connotations; groups that have been called cults have had to develop in the face of a militant anticult movement in recent decades. The 1970s witnessed repeated attacks upon so-called cults in the courts, through the legislatures, and by such direct actions as deprogramming. Because of the anticult movement, a more neutral term such as *alternative religion* should perhaps have been substituted.

On the other hand, the two terms as used in their more neutral sense by social scientists do indicate the two most prominent types of religious leaders upon which this volume concentrates. Sects have provided a continuing protest against the deficiencies found in the mainline churches. Although resembling these established churches, sects have dissented on issues of strictness of behavior (Holiness Movement), firm allegiance to doctrinal positions (Fundamentalism), and/or doctrinal innovations (Pentecostalism). Some sects eventually become churches in their own right and join the established order—such as the United Methodists and American Baptists—and they in turn become the breeding ground for new sects. Others, like the Amish, remain in heightened sectarian dissent for generations.

Cults do not deviate from established religion; rather they represent more radical religious innovation within a culture. They appear as a distinctly new religious/spiritual option. Some cults emerge from within the culture. In the past, Spiritualism, the Theosophical Society, Father Divine's Peace Mission, and the Nation of Islam arose as uniquely American religious alternatives. From the beginning of the Colonial period, most cults and most new religions have come from across the seas— Europe, the Middle East, India, Japan. A remarkable increase in Asian religion has occurred since immigration restrictions were lifted in 1965.

This volume presents biographical sketches of the founders and major leaders of the cults and sects of the United States. In some cases the founders of the new religious movements that gained a following in the United States lived and died in a foreign land, and in a few cases they never visited their American mission field. Such is the case with Swami Sivananda, Sri Ramakrishna, and Baha'u'llah. Others, such as Annie Besant, John Nelson Darby, and Swami Vivekananda, paid only occasional visits to their American followers.

To have been included in this volume, a person must have been the founder or a most outstanding leader (i.e., Annie Besant, George Winslow Plummer, Abdul-Baha) who contributed substantively to the growth and development of a religious group properly labeled a cult or a sect. Only persons whose deaths had occurred prior to January 1, 1983, have been included. For this reason many well-known cult and sect leaders such as L. Ron Hubbard, Carl McIntire, Sun Myung Moon, Victor P. Wierwille, and Herbert W. Armstrong, will not be found here.

Initially a list of more than one hundred names was compiled. It was submitted to the editorial board assembled for this volume for suggestions and then further enlarged. The list continued to grow throughout the months of writing. A few names about whom no substantive material could be found were deleted. This volume contains a total of 213 sketches and summarizes all the presently available biographical material on cult and sect founders.

In the preparation of this volume, it was quickly discovered that most of the people on the original list had never been written up in any standard reference work. Thus, a lesser criterion of inclusion in this volume became of necessity the availability of biographical material from which a sketch could be drawn. A special effort was made to locate materials on both women and nonwhite leaders, because their role in founding and leading dissenting movements has been more prominent than in the mainline churches. Racism and sexism have been contributing factors in the initiation of many sects and cults.

Each biographical sketch is preceded by a set of data—date and place of birth, date and place of death, marriages (with dates if known), and post–high-school education. In cases in which multiple marriages have occurred, except in the case of Joseph Smith, Jr., and Brigham Young, for obvious reasons, each spouse is listed along with the date and the cause of the dissolution of the marriage (by death or divorce). Each sketch attempts to outline in 300 to 500 words the major events in the person's life with special reference to their religious background, key religious experiences, and the individual's role in founding and developing a specific religious group or movement. In the case of several leaders, their relationship to new religious groups was largely ignored in the biographical sketches that had appeared in standard reference works. Paul Carus, for example, has been remembered as a philosopher and editor by people completely unaware of or unconcerned about his key role in the establishment of Buddhism in America. J. Gresham Machen is well known as an outstanding conservative Presbyterian theologian, but his last years as the founder and leader of a small Presbyterian sect and as the initiator of a chain of schismatic churches have been virtually forgotten.

After each sketch, two sets of source material will be found. The first set, primary works, lists selected works by the individual, such as autobiographical volumes, English translations (when the person wrote originally in a foreign language), sets of collected works (as in the case of Menno Simons and John Nelson Darby), and standard editions (as opposed to first editions) where such exist (as in the case of Emmanuel Swedenborg).

A subsequent set, secondary works, lists biographies of the person and other volumes containing significant biographical material about the person, such as histories of the groups s/he founded. In some cases no biographies exist. In other cases the biographies that do exist are of such poor quality that supplemental material from substantive periodical articles has been cited. In most cases the sources cited were by no means the only ones used in the compiling of the sketch. The Institute for the Study of American Religion, which this author directs, has accumulated files on all the religious groups in the United States, and those files were freely consulted. Frequently essential material about an individual could only be assembled by putting together bits of information from a number of brochures and other items published by a group.

The sources cited, however, should prove an adequate starting point for anyone wishing to explore the career of the individual at greater depth. In the case of highly controversial people, those with both strong critics and staunch defenders (Madame Blavatsky, Paul Twitchell, and Ellen G. White, to name a few), source material representative of the wide range of opinion has been cited.

As the author of this volume, I accept full responsibility for any of its deficiencies. I would, however, like to acknowledge the substantive assistance I received, without which this volume could never have been completed. I am particularly indebted to the many individuals who have, over the past two decades, contributed material that is currently housed in the Institute for the Study of American Religion, from which this volume is largely derived. They are far too many to mention, but I hope each will accept my thanks.

The prime word of gratitude must go to those who served on the editorial board for this volume: James V. Geisendorfer, Robert S. Ellwood, Jr., Charles Edwin Jones, Sulayman S. Nyang, Gordon Stein, and Donald Tinder. They made suggestions for inclusion in the volume and read selected portions of it, adding their comments. One editorial board member, Gordon Stein, also wrote the several biographies of the free thought and atheist leaders, the only items in the volume not written by me. James V. Geisendorfer, with whom I have worked for many years, was the most active board member. He gave continual imput and assistance throughout the project and read the entire text in its final draft. Almost all of his suggestions for improvement have been incorporated in the finished copy. I appreciate the efforts of each of the board members.

A number of people read and commented on the final sketches of people about whom they had special knowledge. David Christopher Lane edited the several items related to figures out of the Sant Mat Sikh tradition. So substantive were his additions that I incorporated them within the items on Jaimal Singh, Sawan Singh, and Shiv Dayal Singh. Other individuals who read and commented on particular entries include Jerry G. Bergman, Raymond Buckland, Randall K. Bunkett, C. Walter Driscoll, Sherrie Dupree, Lawrence Foster, Steven J. Gelberg, James Janisch, Connie Jones, Mrs. Clarence L. Jordan, Sulayman S. Nyang, William V. Rauscher, Archbishop Serena, Marian E. Shafer, Donald L. Waldrop, and Swami Yogeshananda. The Baha'i Office of Public Affairs assisted in the final editing of the entries on Baha'u'llah, Abdu'l-Baha, and Shoghi Effendi Rabbani; and the St. Germain Foundation assisted with the entries on Guy W. Ballard and Edna Ballard. Thank you all.

J. Gordon Melton
Chicago, February 1984

ABBREVIATIONS

DRB   Henry Warner Bowden, *Dictionary of American Religious Biography*. Westport, Conn.: Greenwood Press, 1977.

DAB   *Dictionary of American Biography*. New York: Charles S. Scribner's Sons, 1928–1977. 21 Volumes. 5 Supplements.

EOP   Leslie A. Shepard, ed., *Encyclopedia of Occultism and Parapsychology*. Detroit, Mich.: Gale Research, 1978. 2 Volumes.

EWM   Nolan B. Harmon, ed., *Encylopedia of World Methodism*. Nashville, Tenn.: United Methodist Publishing House, 1974. 2 Volumes.

ESB   *Encyclopedia of Southern Baptists*. Nashville, Tenn.: Broadman Press, 1958–82. 4 Volumes.

ME   *The Mennonite Encyclopedia*. Scottsdale, Penn.: Mennonite Publishing House, 1955–1959. 4 Volumes.

NAB   Edward T. James, ed., *Notable American Women*. Cambridge, Mass.: Belknap Press of Harvard University Press, 1971. 3 Volumes.

WWW   *Who Was Who in America*. Chicago: A. N. Marquis Company, 1942–1976. 6 Volumes.

WWWH   *Who Was Who in America, Historical Volume, 1607–1896*. Chicago: A. N. Marquis Company, 1963.

THE DICTIONARY

ABDU'L-BAHA (Abbas Effendi) (May 23, 1844, Teheran, Persia [Iran]—November 28, 1921, Haifa, Palestine [Israel]); married Fatima Munirih, 1873.

The person known as Abdu'l-Baha, the successor to Baha'u'llah, founder of the Baha'i World Faith, was born in Teheran as Abbas Effendi, the eldest son of Baha'u'llah. He grew up during the days of the movement founded by the Bab, a Persian prophet, who had announced his mission on May 23, 1844, the day Abbas Effendi was born. Baha'u'llah joined the Babis, as the Bab's followers were known, and Abbas Effendi had occasion as a child to visit his father in prison where he was being held with other Babis. Even before Baha'u'llah's declaration in 1866 that he was "Him Whom God shall make manifest," he recognized his father's mission and became his devoted follower. He accompanied the family into exile in 1853, after Baha'u'llah's release from prison, traveling first to Bagdad, then Adrianople (now Edirne, Turkey), and finally to Akka (now Acre) in Palestine. In 1886, at his father's direction, he wrote the first history of the Baha'i movement.

Baha'u'llah named Abbas Effendi his successor in his will, and he assumed that position in 1892. Soon after the succession, however, he faced the opposition of his half-brother, Mirza Mohammad Ali, who, along with other members of Baha'u'llah's family, challenged Abbas Effendi's authority. The Turkish authorities were brought into the dispute, and as a result, he was placed in strict confinement from 1901 to 1908. He was released only when the successful revolt of the Young Turks led to the release of political prisoners throughout the Ottoman Empire.

Abbas Effendi established his leadership of the Baha'is and defined his role with the title Abdu'l-Baha (Slave of Baha). He understood himself to be the Interpreter of Baha'u'llah and was called the Center of the Covenant. His writings are considered by Baha'is as scripture and stand with Baha'u'llah's in the authoritative books, *Baha'i Scriptures* (1923) and *Baha'i World Faith* (1943, rev. 1956). Abdu'l-Baha emphasized the universalist theme in Baha'u'llah and taught that all religions were one and that all the Great Manifestations (Prophets of God) taught the same faith. He summarized Baha'u'llah's essential teachings as ten principles of the Baha'i faith: (1) the independent investigation of truth; (2) the oneness of the human race; (3) the conformity of religion to science and reason; (4) the banishment of religious, racial, political, and patriotic prejudice; (5) the equality of men and women; (6) the working together of all classes of society in love and harmony; (7) the parliament of man as a court of last appeal in international questions; (8) universal education; and (9) a universal language.

When he took charge of his duties as leader of the Baha'is around the world, he directed his attention to the international spread of the faith. He oversaw the building of the first Baha'i temple, in Ishqabad, in Russian Turkistan. In 1911, when travel restrictions were discontinued and his health improved, he made his first foreign trip—to England, France, and Egypt.

Abdu'l-Baha encouraged the worldwide spread of the Baha'i faith. He sent missionaries to America (the first arrived in 1912) and received American followers who traveled to Acre. In 1912 he began a twenty-month tour that brought him to Europe and the United States. In Wilmette, Illinois, he dedicated the grounds on which the first North American temple was constructed. He returned to Palestine and settled in Haifa just before World War I began. Again the Turkish authorities confined him and even threatened to kill him, but he survived until the British took control.

After the war the British conferred a knighthood on Abdu'l-Baha in recognition of his work for the peace and prosperity of Palestine. He died at Haifa in 1921, naming his grandson, Shoghi Effendi, his successor.

Abdu'l-Baha (Abbas Effendi), *Paris Talks* (London, 1912).

———— , *The Secret of Divine Civilization* (Wilmette, 1918).

———— , *Some Answered Questions* (Wilmette, 1930).

———— , *Will and Testament* (Wilmette, 1927).

H. M. Balyuzi, *Abdu'l-Baha* (London, 1971).

Myron H. Phelps, *Abbas Effendi, His Life and Teachings* (New York, 1903).

William McElwee Miller, *The Baha'i Faith* (South Pasadena, Calif., 1974).

DRB, 5–6.

Romona Allen Brown, *Memories of Abdu'l-Baha* (Wilmette, 1980).

ADAMSKI, George (April 17, 1891, Poland—April 23, 1965, Washington, D.C.) married, Mary A. Shimbersky, December 25, 1917.

George Adamski, teacher of cosmic philosophy, was the first person to claim visitation by the space brothers who inhabit flying saucers. Little is known of his early life. He was born in Poland and came to the United States with his parents when he was two years of age. He developed an interest in the occult and first emerged into public light in 1936, when he founded the Royal Order of Tibet through which he taught a course in the mastery of life.

In the 1940s, while working in a café near Mt. Palomar, he became interested in flying saucers. He claimed as early as October 9, 1946 (almost a year before Kenneth Arnold's sightings of saucers over Mt. Rainier in Washington made flying saucers a popular topic) to have seen a large saucer near Mt. Palomar. In August 1947 he claimed to have seen 184 saucers flying in formation. He also began to write a novel, *Pioneers in Space*, which was published in 1949 and which invited readers to organize roundtable discussions and write the author with their questions. He called this activity the Advanced Thinkers Club.

The same year *Pioneers in Space* was published, Adamski was asked by some other people interested in flying saucers if he would keep a watch and take pictures of anything he saw. He took many pictures of what he claimed were spaceships. In March 1950 he gave his first lecture on his pictures, a lecture covered by a San Diego newspaper. In March 1951 an article about his pictures appeared in *Fate Magazine* and brought Adamski national attention.

After the *Fate* article, Adamski became acquainted with a broad group of people interested in flying saucers, and with these he began to speculate on the people or creatures that inhabited the saucers. The decisive event came on November 20, 1952, when he met and conversed telepathically with a man from Venus. On December 13 he had a return visit, at which time he was given a message in some indecipherable hieroglyphics. These visits became the subject of Adamski's next book (written jointly with Desmond Leslie), *Flying Saucers Have Landed*, which appeared in September 1953. This book made Adamski famous and he was invited to lecture around the country on his experiences and the message of the people from space.

His next book, *Inside the Space Ships* (actually ghostwritten by associate Charlotte Blob) quickly followed. This book contained further accounts of his adventures and claims about space and life on other planets. Adamski believed that all the planets were very much like earth and had life forms similar to earth's. He claimed there were twelve planets in the solar system and that the moon had a fertile far side.

For the many people who became enthusiastic about his claims, he organized the International Get Acquainted Program and encouraged his correspondents to organize group meetings and monthly study programs. In 1958 his telepathy course appeared and was widely circulated among his followers.

In 1959 Adamski made a round-the-world tour, during which he was received by Queen Juliana of the Netherlands, widely known in her own country for her interest in the occult. This tour filled most of Adamski's next book, *Flying Saucers Farewell* (1961).

In 1961 Adamski turned over much of the organizational work he had built up to C. A. Honey, who began to issue a monthly *Science Publications Newsletter* in January 1962 as the only authorized source of information from Adamski. Adamski moved on to a "new phase" as a full-time teacher of the subject of his latest book, *Cosmic Philosophy*.

Almost from the beginning of his career as a claimant to extraterrestrial contact, critical voices arose. As early as 1957 popular "ufologist" James Moseley published claims that Adamski faked his photographs and that the people who verified his contacts were his close friends. Editor Ray Palmer claimed that his account of meeting the Venusian had been submitted to him in 1944 as a science fiction story. Later the hieroglyphics were discovered to have come from an obscure anthropological work. In 1963 C. A. Honey broke with Adamski and published materials showing how Adamski had re-edited his Royal Order of Tibet material to make it appear as if his lessons had come from the space brothers.

Despite these exposés, numerous followers remained after Adamski's death to carry on his work and keep his writings in print. In 1965 his daughter Alice Wells formed the George Adamski Foundation in Vista, California. Former secretary Charlotte Blob founded the UFO Education Center headquartered in Valley Center, California. These two, as well as other independent groups, keep the Adamski claims alive and continue to circulate his occult teachings.

George Adamski, *Flying Saucers Farewell* (reprinted as *Behind the Flying Saucer Mystery*) (New York, 1961).

——— , *Inside the Space Ships* (reprinted as *Inside the Flying Saucers*) (New York, 1955).

——— , *Questions and Answers by the Royal Order of Tibet* (N.p., 1936).

——— , *Cosmic Philosophy* (Freeman, S. D., 1972).

"Memorial Issue," *The Controversial Phenomena Bulletin*, May–June 1965.

"Special Adamski Expose Issue," *Saucer News*, No. 27, October 1957.

Brad Steiger, *The Aquarian Revelations* (New York, 1971).

Lou Zinsstag and Timothy Good, *George Adamski, The Untold Story*, (Beckenham, Kent, 1983).

The Adamski Documents (Clarksburg, W.V., n.d.).

Ronald D. Story, ed., *The Encyclopedia of UFOs* (Garden City, N.Y., 1980), 2–4.

EOP, 4.

ADLER, Felix (August 13, 1851, Alzey, Germany—April 24, 1933, New York, New York); married Helen Goldmark, May 24, 1880; education: Columbia College, BA, 1870; University of Berlin, Heidelberg University, Ph.D., 1873.

Felix Adler, founder of the Ethical Culture Society and the American Ethical Union, was born in Germany, the son of a rabbi. When he was six, his father came to New York City to assume leadership of Temple Emmanuel, and Felix subsequently grew up in the United States. He graduated from Columbia College and returned to Germany for graduate work at the Universities of Berlin and Heidelberg. His father and the members of the Temple had hoped he would return home to assist him and eventually follow in his footsteps. In Germany, however, he encountered German philosophy and the higher criticism of the Bible. No longer a believer in God, supernaturalism, and religion, he returned to New York with a fervent belief in moral and ethical ideals.

He had only a brief opportunity to enunciate his new perspective before leaving for Cornell University to take a post teaching Hebrew and Oriental literature. However, his ideas had found an audience, and in 1876 he was called back to New York City to head a group that would put his philosophy into practice. He founded the Ethical Culture Society on May 15. He attempted to focus the society not upon the religions that had been rejected but rather upon the ethical ideals and moral concerns that had brought the group together.

As the leader of the Ethical Culture Society, Adler initiated many projects to embody his moral perspective. Education had become a major emphasis of his life, and so one of his first efforts became the founding of a kindergarten based upon the principles of the German educator Friedrich Froebel. The kindergarten emphasized education in working together harmoniously. The kindergarten grew into the Workingmen's school, which carried its influence into the grade school. The school, which continues to this day as the Ethical Culture School, included a program of art and nature study. It introduced the first "workshop" in an American grade school, which led to the introduction of that concept into the public school system. In 1881 he applied his concern for the poor to the development of a visiting nurse program that was later instituted throughout the city.

In 1894 he joined a campaign against child labor by becoming chairman of the National Child Labor Committee. During his seventeen years as head of the committee, he pressed for the prohibition of employing children and youth in hazardous jobs, the lengthening of the school year (which was less than six months long in some places), and the establishment of more protective child labor laws.

In 1902 he aided the cause of the garment workers by founding the Manhattan Trade School for Girls. Eight years later he played a crucial role in the settlement of a garment worker's strike that threatened to take the industry out of New York City.

Adler not only led the activist program of the society, he also disseminated his ideas through its growing organization. In 1882 he initiated the Chicago Ethical Society and three years later the Philadelphia Ethical Society. In 1886 he founded the society in St. Louis, and in 1891 he formed the American Ethical Union as a fellowship of all the societies.

Adler's ideas also spread internationally. Stanton Coit, a follower of Adler, lectured in England and helped found the society in London. Adler introduced the society to Berlin in 1891; in 1896 he brought the American and European work together in the International Union of Ethical Societies, which he chaired.

Some of Adler's admirers who wished to see his teaching spread endowed a chair at his alma mater, Columbia College, which had become Columbia University, where in 1903 he became a professor of political and social science. In 1908 he became the Theodore Roosevelt Exchange Professor at the University of Berlin and was honored in 1924 with an invitation to deliver the Hibbert Lectures at Oxford.

Adler was the author of many books, including *The Moral Instruction of Children* (1895), *The Reconstruction of the Spiritual Ideal* (his 1924 Hibbert lectures), and *An Ethical Philosophy of Life* (1918).

Felix Adler, *Creed and Deed: A Series of Discourses* (New York, 1877).

——— , *Life and Destiny* (New York, 1903).

——— , *The Religion of Duty* (New York, 1905).

——— , *An Ethical Philosophy of Life* (New York, 1918).

——— , *The Reconstruction of the Spiritual Ideal* (New York, 1924).

The Fiftieth Anniversary of the Ethical Movement, 1876–1926 (New York, 1926).

Leo Jacobs, *Three Types of Practical Ethical Movements of the Past Half Century* (New York, 1922).

Benny Kraut, *From Reform Judaism to Ethical Culture: The Religious Evolution of Felix Adler* (Cincinnati, Ohio, 1979).
Howard B. Radest, *Toward Common Ground* (New York, 1969).
DRB, 8–9.
WWW, I, 9.

AHMAD, Mirza Ghulam Hazrat (February 13, 1835, Qadian, Pakistan—May 26, 1908, Lahore, Pakistan); married Hurmat Bibi, 1852; divorced 1892; married Nusrat Jahan Begum, 1884.

Mirza Ghulam Hazrat Ahmad, founder of the Ahmadiyya Muslim Movement, was born of an old Punjabi family in a small Indian village in what is now Pakistan. Educated at home, he began his career as a minor government employee but resigned his job in 1868, after only three years, to become the supervisor of the family lands. In 1852 he married a cousin, who became the mother of his first two children. Increasingly Ahmad devoted his time to study of the Quran, the spiritual life, and religious writings.

From his study of both Muslim and non-Muslim religious books and from his observation of the condition of Islam in India, Ahmad concluded that Islam was in a declining state and under attack from other religions, especially Christianity. In 1879 he began writing a massive book, *Barahin-i-Ahmadiyah*, to defend the truth of Islam and to refute Christianity as well as other competing religions. At the time of its publication in 1880, Ahmad declared that God had appointed him to demonstrate the truth of Islam, the task he was fulfilling in writing the book.

In subsequent volumes, Ahmad took upon himself the title *mujaddid*, renewer of the faith, for the present age. Finally in 1891, Ahmad declared himself both the Promised Messiah—that is, the second coming of Jesus—and the Mahdi, the one who would come and reform Islam in a time of need. To substantiate his identification with Jesus, whom Muslims accept as a major prophet of Allah, Ahmad asserted that Jesus neither died in Palestine nor was he resurrected; rather, Jesus came to Kashmir, in northern India, where he died a normal death. As such, his second coming was not by way of a heavenly descent but in the person of one who bore the spirit and power of Jesus, namely Ahmad.

In 1901 Ahmad declared himself a prophet, thus asserting his equality with Mohammad. He also excommunicated all who rejected his prophethood. The belief that Ahmad was a prophet set the movement apart from Islam and resulted in the movement's rejection by Islam as a whole. Ahmad also dissented from other Muslims by declaring the end of *jihad*, the concept of a holy war. Ahmad's escalating claims, therefore, not only brought him support but made him many enemies. Among the first were some of his own cousins. They succeeded in alienating his wife, whom he divorced after many years of separation. Even before the divorce, he married the daughter of one of his followers, with whom he raised a second family.

Ahmad began to be surrounded by followers during the years of his writing the *Barahin-i-Ahmadiyah*. In 1889 he formally established his movement with headquarters at Qadain. The headquarters remained there until the center was destroyed in the riots occasioned by the creation of Pakistan. International headquarters were reestablished at Rabwah, Pakistan, where they remain. After Ahmad's death in 1908, Hazrat Maulawi Nuruddin, a close disciple, became head of the movement. He was succeeded in 1914 by Ahmad's son, Hazrat Mirza Bashiruddin Muhmud Ahmad (d. 1965).

The Ahmadiyya Movement came to the United States in 1921 and had its greatest success among American blacks. It is headquartered in Washington, D.C. A second branch of the movement was founded by Maulawi Muhammad Ali who considered Ahmad to be the greatest *mujaddid* and the Promised Messiah, but he denied that Ahmad ever claimed the same unique prophethood that Islam claims for Muhammad. Ali asserted that Ahmad's use of such terms was entirely allegorical and mystical. His branch of the movement came to America in the 1970s. Its international headquarters are in Lahore, Pakistan, and the American headquarters are in Walnut Creek, California.

Mirza Ghulam Hazrat Ahmad, *Our Teachings* (Rabwah, W. Pakistan, 1962).

——— , *The Teachings of Islam* (Rabwah, 1966).

——— , *How to Get Rid of the Bondage of Sin* (Rabwah, 1962).

——— , *Islamic Teachings on the Moral Conditions of Man* (Rabwah, n.d.).

A. R. Dard, *Life of Ahmad* (Lahore, 1948).

Muhammad Zafrulla Khan, *Ahmadiyyat, The Renaissance of Islam* (London, 1978).

Mirza Mubarak Ahmad, *The Promised Messiah* (England, 1968).

S. Abul Hasan Ali Nadwi, *Qadianism, A Critical Study* (Lucknow, 1974).

ALLEN, Asa Alonzo (March 27, 1911, Sulfur Rock, Arkansas—June 11, 1970, San Francisco, California); married Lexia circa 1934 (div. 1967).

Asa Alonzo Allen, the Pentecostal healing evangelist, was born into a poor Arkansas family. His father was an alcoholic, a condition he passed on to his son. Allen credited a three-month jail term for stealing with being the event that first began to settle him down. In 1934 he was converted during a revival meeting at a Methodist church under the leadership of evangelist Nina DePriestes. He also met and married his wife at about that same time.

As he found himself more at home among the Pentecostals, his life as a Methodist was very brief. In 1936 he was licensed to preach by the Assemblies of God and pastored a congregation briefly before embarking upon an evangelistic career. His years as an evangelist, traveling from town to town, were uneventful and financially unstable. In 1947 he tried the pastorate again and moved to Corpus Christi, Texas. While there he was given a copy of *The Voice of Healing*, the magazine of healing evangelist William Branham. In 1949 he attended an Oral Roberts revival meeting. After much thought, he came to the decision to reenter the evangelistic field with a healing message. His first set of meetings were in Oakland, California, where he experienced marked success. He sent an account of his work to *The Voice of Healing* and associated himself with the burgeoning deliverance movement of healing evangelists.

In 1951, at considerable financial risk, he bought a meeting tent and his career began to rise. He spoke primarily to the poor and those who identified with his unlearned and uncouth ways. He emphasized healing and miracles that were spectacular and even bizarre. He established his headquarters in Dallas and began the Allen Revival Hour, one of the early radio ministries.

A major setback occurred in 1955. Rumors had persisted that Allen was still addicted to alcohol though he had vigorously denied them. Then he was arrested for driving while intoxicated. The arrest led to his being dropped by *The Voice of Healing* and to his having to surrender his credentials to the Assemblies of God. Cut off from the mainstream of Pentecostalism, he moved quickly to consolidate his following and build an independent constituency. He began his own periodical, *Miracle Magazine*. In 1956 he announced the formation of the Miracle Revival Fellowship, an association of independent ministers and congregations, as an alternative to "denominational" churches. More than five hundred ministers were listed at the time of its first ordination. Over 200,000 people subscribed to *Miracle Magazine* in the first year.

In 1958 Allen was given land in Arizona where a community, Miracle Valley, was built. A large tabernacle was constructed, and the center became the home of Allen's training classes and publishing concern. He wrote many booklets that were distributed at his meetings around the country.

In the 1960s Allen placed an emphasis on prosperity in the healing services that had carried him for so long. He also became a vocal anti-segregationist and held integrated meetings throughout both the South and the North. His appeal to blacks increased, and he assigned blacks to his evangelistic team. His following was so loyal that they hardly noticed his 1967 divorce.

Allen died alone in a hotel room in San Francisco. The continued rumors of alcoholism persisted, and the press reported the cause of death as cirrhosis of the liver. He was succeeded by Don Stewart, who soon abandoned Miracle Valley and moved his headquarters to Phoenix. Miracle Valley remains the home of a small group of Allen's followers.

Asa Alonzo Allen, *Born to Lose, Bound to Win* (Garden City, N.Y., 1970).

———, *The Price of God's Miracle Working Power* (Lamar, Colo., 1950).

———, *My Cross* (Miracle Valley, Ariz., n.d.).

William Hedgepath, "He Feels, He Heals, and He Turns You On to God," *Look* 33, 20 (October 7, 1969), 23–31.

David Edwin Harrell, Jr., *All Things Are Possible* (Bloomington, Ind., 1975).

ALLRED, Rulon Clark (March 29, 1906, Chihuahua, Mexico—May 10, 1977, Murray, Utah); education: Los Angeles Naturopathic College, graduated 1930; married Katherine Lucy Haney, June 9, 1926.

Rulon Clark Allred, founder of the Apostolic United Brethren, a Fundamentalist Mormon (i.e., polygamy-practicing) group, was the son of Byron Harvey Allred, former Speaker of the House for the State of Idaho. Defying the ban on polygamy, the elder Allred had taken a second wife and in 1903 fled to the relative protection of Mexico, where Rulon, the second oldest of ten children, was born. Allred's father eventually affiliated with the Fundamentalist group formed in 1929 by Lorin Woolley, but Allred remained aloof and joined the Church of Jesus Christ of Latter-day Saints, which had abandoned the practice of polygamy. He married and attended a naturopathic medical college in Los Angeles.

In 1933 the elder Allred wrote a book, A Leaf in Review, which defended the practice of polygamy. The book prompted Allred to write a series of letters to his father attacking his beliefs; however, the result was that Allred was converted to his father's position. His conversion, in turn, led to the church's threatening him with excommunication, his medical practice dwindling and his wife leaving him. For a short period, he dropped medical work and sought employment in the oil fields of Southern California.

After the death of his father in 1937, Allred moved to Salt Lake City. Two years later, he received his license to practice. Meanwhile, he had affiliated with the Fundamentalists, then headed by John Barlow, who had succeeded to leadership in 1934. Barlow had been an early Fundamentalist leader, and had established the Fundamentalist settlement at Short Creek, Arizona. In suburban Salt Lake City Allred purchased a large home, which became the weekly gathering spot for Fundamentalists in the city. He remarried several times and began to raise a large family.

Allred rose to prominence in the Fundamentalist movement after he was arrested in the massive antipolygamy raid in Salt Lake City on March 7, 1944. Convicted, Allred went to prison in May 1945 for seven months. He was paroled with the promise to refrain from practicing or promoting polygamy. Allred kept his promise for a while, but in 1947 fled to Mexico where he lived for a few months on the ranch owned by the father of Joel and Ervil LeBaron. He returned to Utah in 1948 and only served a month in jail for violating parole.

In 1951 Barlow died and was succeeded by Joseph Musser, also one of the original leaders and prominent editor of the Fundamentalist periodical Truth. In 1949 Musser had suffered a paralytic stroke, and many Fundamentalists opposed his assuming control. Opposition increased when Musser named Allred, who had been Musser's physician, as a special counselor. Musser than disbanded the Council, named an entirely new one, and designated Allred as his successor. That action split the Fundamentalists. Musser died in 1954 and left Allred in charge of the dissident faction.

Following Musser's death Allred reorganized his following into the Apostolic United Order. In the spring of 1955 he traveled to Mexico to secure his following at Ozumba, a settlement southeast of Mexico City, where members of the Order were under the leadership of Margarito

Bautista. He also stopped at Colonia LeBaron and visited the LeBaron family, which had affiliated with Musser through Bautista. Within the year Joel LeBaron had formed his own church. During the 1960s, Joel's brother Ervil also formed a separate group, the Church of the Lamb of God. In 1972 Ervil killed Joel and began a heated campaign to subordinate all Fundamentalists under his control. He began to threaten Allred. On April 7, 1975, he sent a pamphlet, A Response to an Act of War, and a handwritten note demanding that Allred acknowledge Ervil LeBaron's authority.

On May 10, 1977, two female followers of Ervil walked into Allred's office in Murray, Utah, and shot him. Ervil was later convicted of the murder and has since died in prison. Allred was succeeded by Owen Allred, his brother.

Thirty-six of Allred's children sang at his funeral.

Rulon Clark Allred, Treasures of Knowledge, 2 volumes (Hamilton, Mont., 1981).

J. Max Anderson, The Polygamy Story: Fiction and Fact (Salt Lake City, 1979).

Ben Bradlee, Jr., and Dale Van Atta, Prophet of Blood (New York, 1981).

Verlan M. LeBaron, The LeBaron Story (Lubbock, Tex., 1981).

The Most Holy Principle, 4 volumes (Murray, Ut., 1970–1975).

AMMANN, Jakob (February 12, 1644?, Erlenbach, canton of Bern, Switzerland, Alsace).

Little is known of the early life of Jakob Ammann who caused the division of the seventeenth-century Swiss Brethren; even his birthdate is speculative. He is probably the Jakob Ammann born to Michael and Anna Rupp Ammann in 1644. Ammann emerges out of obscurity in 1693 as an elder among the Brethren of Erlenbach. He had introduced a number of beliefs and practices to his congregation. They met twice a year for communion (instead of the usual once) and practiced footwashing as part of the service. Ammann demanded a uniformity of dress, including hats, shoes, and stockings. He did not allow the men to trim their beards and excommunicated any who attended the state church.

His main concerns, however, were three: He introduced Meidung, shunning of excommunicated members, a practice manifested primarily in not eating with those who had been excommunicated; he advocated the excommunication of any who lied; and he condemned the Treuherzigen, the noble-hearted people who aided and protected the Brethren without joining them. Only the Brethren themselves were saved and destined for heaven.

In 1693, on his own initiative, he began a tour of Swiss congregations of whom he demanded conformity to his main concerns. A meeting of ministers was held at Eggiwill in an attempt to reach a unanimity of belief and practice. During the course of the meeting, Ammann excommunicated Hans Reist, pastor of the congregation at Emmental. Reist had not only disagreed with Ammann but also refused to attend the meeting. Ammann then excommunicated others and walked out angrily with his supporters. The action polarized the Swiss Brethren behind either Reist or Ammann. Ammann quickly issued an ultimatum that he circulated to all the Swiss ministers demanding the immediate acknowledgment of their adherence to Ammann's position and their acceptance of his "Biblical views."

Amman's message traveled to the Brethren in Alsace and the Palatine. In 1694 Ammann seems to have moved to Alsace where he received the largest support. He received almost total rejection in the Palatine. Of the sixty-nine ministers in Switzerland, Alsace, and the Palatine, a total of twenty-seven sided with Ammann. Attempts were made at reconciliation, and Ammann even admitted his role in bringing about the division because of his harsh personal manner. However, he and his followers, the Amish, would not yield on the issues that had led to the break in fellowship.

After the move to Alsace, Ammann faded back into obscurity. He appears on a census of family heads in 1704 and again in 1708 but is not heard of again until 1730, when his daughter joined the Reformed Church and reported her father dead.

The Amish movement continued through the centuries. With many of the Swiss Brethren, they left Switzerland in 1711 but traveled separately. The Amish began arriving in America as early as 1727, and a large migration occurred between 1815 and 40. By the 1880s several different groups had emerged as the Amish attempted to adapt to the changes and pressures of modern society.

John A. Hostetler, *Amish Society* (Baltimore, 1968).
John B. Mast, ed., *The Letters of the Amish Division* (Oregon City, Or., 1950); Me., 1, 98–9. ME, 1, 98–9.

ANDRAE, Johann Valentin (August 7, 1586, Herrenburg, Württemberg, Germany—January 27, 1654, Stuttgart, Germany); married Agnes Elizabeth Gruminger, August 2, 1614; education: University of Tübingen, B.A., 1603; M.A., 1604.

Johann Valentin Andrae, a German Lutheran pastor of the early seventeenth century, is best remembered as the originator of the Rosicrucian legend, which over the centuries has given inspiration to hundreds of occult organizations. Andrae came from a family of pastors. His grandfather was counted among the original Reformers. In 1591 he moved to Königsbronn where his father, a Lutheran minister, had become abbot. After his father's death in 1601, his mother moved the family to Tübingen, where Andrae entered the university. After graduation he became chaplain at Stuttgart but he was forced to resign in 1607 because of poor health. He moved back to Tübingen, where his mother had become court apothecary to Frederick I, the Duke of Württemberg.

During the period 1607–14, Andrae enjoyed the stimulus of the intellectual climate of Tübingen. He joined an informal circle around Christoph Besold, who introduced the introspective young pastor to mysticism, the occult, and the Kabbalah, the Jewish mystical occult system. His health improved during this time, and in 1614 he married and became the deacon at Vaihingen.

His interests in the occult grew, and before the end of 1614 he had published the *Fama Fraternitatis*, the first of several documents about a secret society founded by one Christian Rosen Cruez (or Rosenkreutz). The *Fama* was followed in 1615 by the *Confessio*. The two books described the career of Rosen Cruez, announced the existence of the secret fraternity, and invited inquiries from interested readers. The *Fama* and *Confessio* were followed by still a third book, the *Chemical Marriage*, supposedly written by Christian Rosen Cruez himself. Later Andrae confessed to having written an early version of the *Chemical Marriage* in 1605. There is little doubt that Andrae wrote the three books; however, his intentions and motivation remain a matter of intense controversy. Opinions range from those who believe that Andrae, in fact, exposed to the world an actually existing Rosicrucian Fraternity to those who believe Andrae attempted to create a hoax, purely and simply. Much opinion seems to favor the notion that Andrae wished to promote the idea of the formation of a secret society that would bring about needed social changes and that he derived the symbolism from his own coat of arms. This opinion is reinforced by his later writings and his membership in the Fruit-Bringing Society, one of several groups formed in the early seventeenth century to promote the German language.

Whatever his intent, the issuance of the three documents had already converted some to the Rosicrucian teachings and had elicited criticism from others. In 1619 Andrae published *The Tower of Babel* in which he confessed his authorship of the heretofore anonymous documents and the nonexistence of the Rosicrucian Fraternity. But it was too late; he no longer controlled what he had created.

Andrae moved from Vaihingen to become an overseer at Kalw. Shortly after the move he became a victim of the Thirty Years War. Soldiers passing through the town destroyed his home and all his possessions. Eighteen years later, the war again moved through the town. He fled to Stüttgart and became Court Prelate to the King of Württemberg. During his life, the prolific Andrae wrote more than one hundred books, the most notable of which, other than his Rosicrucian writings, was *Cynosure* (1640), a book on ecclesiastical discipline. In 1650 Andrae moved to Babenhausen, Bavaria, to become abbot, and there he died a few years later.

Johann Valentin Andrae: A reprint of the English translation of the three major works of Andrae and a selected bibliography of his writings may be found in Paul M. Allen, *A Christian Rosenkreutz Anthology* (Blauvelt, N.Y., 1968).

Christopher McIntosh, *The Rosy Cross Unveiled* (Wellingborough, 1980).

Frances A. Yates, *The Rosicrucian Enlightenment* (London, 1972).

A. E. Waite, *The Brotherhood of the Rosy Cross* (London, 1924).

ARNOLD, Eberhard (July 26, 1883, Königsberg, Germany—November 22, 1935, Darmstadt, Germany); married Emmy von Hollander, 1909; education: University of Breslau, University of Halle, University of Erlangen, Ph.D., 1909.

Eberhard Arnold, founder of the Bruderhof, a communal group that established itself in New York in the 1950s, was born of a scholarly family in Germany. When Eberhard was five, his father took a post as professor of Church History at the University of Breslau. The faith young Arnold received from his parents became focused even in childhood with concern for the inequalities of society and the lot of the poor. In 1899 he had a deep religious experience that produced a radical internal change. He became openly critical of the German middle class and spent his free time with groups like the Salvation Army who were concerned with the socially oppressed.

Under pressure from his parents, he completed his schooling. He associated with radical Christian student groups, among whom he met his future wife, Emmy. They married two years after he received his doctorate. For several years after their marriage, he lectured widely and came into open conflict with the church, which he criticized for what he considered its illegitimate connection with the state.

In 1913 he became ill, and he and Emmy moved to Bozen in the Tyrol. Shortly after the move they were joined by Emmy's sister, Else, who became Arnold's secretary. While relatively immobile, Arnold concentrated on developing the ideas that would later become dominant themes in his ministry and on writing his first book, *Innenland*, and several pamphlets. He also became absorbed with the history of the radical Reformation.

In 1914 Arnold was drafted into the Army, but discharged after only a short time because of ill health. His short stay merely served to confirm Arnold's abhorrence of war. In 1915 he moved to Berlin as the literary director of Furche-Verlag. He continued to lecture and became involved with the Socialist Christian and the German Student Christian Movements. In 1919 he led a Student Christian Movement conclave at Marburg. This event, in which the Sermon on the Mount was the topic of discussion, proved a turning point, as Arnold walked away with a new realization of the absolute ethical demands of Jesus. He began to hold openhouse discussions at his home about his ideas. He moved to a pacifist position and denounced private property as a root of war.

In 1920 he put his ideas into action. He rented a three-room apartment at Sannerz and, with a group of seven adults and three children, began a commune. It quickly grew to fifty people but was all but destroyed in 1922 when German financial crises drove most away. Arnold reorganized and began again. In 1926 he bought the Sparhof, a farm near Rhön. At the Rhonhof, as the community was called, Arnold emerged as the charismatic leader and theoretician. He still lectured widely and wrote his first important publication, *The Early Christians After the Death of the Apostles*. The community led a simple life. They ate plain, often poor, food but painted their cottages brightly as a reminder of God's work in creation.

In 1929 Arnold heard of the Hutterites and began correspondence. In 1930 he spent a year among the Hutterites, and, despite differences that could not be resolved, united the Bruderhof with them.

For the Bruderhof, 1931 was a year of great growth but the rise of National Socialism in Germany put pressure on Arnold and his following. The Nazis wished to put a teacher in the Bruderhof school. In response Arnold had the children moved to Switzerland and then to Lichtenstein, where a second *hof* was established. The second *hof* began to develop an international membership, especially after Arnold lectured in England in 1935. In the midst of the turmoil that led to World War II, Arnold took time off for a leg operation. A few days after the operation, he died suddenly. He was only fifty-two.

The Bruderhof was expelled from Germany in 1937. It settled in England, established a colony in Paraguay for a while, and eventually found a permanent home in the United States in 1954.

Eberhard Arnold, *The Early Christians* (Rifton, N.Y., 1970).

———, *Why We Live in Community* (Rifton, N.Y., 1967).

———, *Foundation and Orders, 1920–1929* (Rifton, N.Y., 1976).

———, *Love and Marriage in the Spirit* (Rifton, N.Y., 1965).

Benjamin Zablocki, *The Joyful Community* (Baltimore, Md., 1971).

Eberhard Arnold (Rifton, N.Y., 1964).

Emmy Arnold, *Torches Together* (Rifton, N.Y., 1971).

Hutlerian Society of Brothers and John Howard Yoder, eds., *God's Revolution, The Witness of Eberhard Arnold* (New York, 1984).

ATKINSON, William Walker (December 5, 1862, Baltimore, Maryland—November 22, 1932, Los Angeles, California); married Margaret Foster Black, October 31, 1889.

William Walker Atkinson, prominent New Thought metaphysical writer and, as Swami Ramacharaka, a major early exponent of Hinduism in America, began adult life as a businessman. He was admitted to the Pennsylvania bar in 1894 and launched a promising law career. After several successful years, however, the pressures of the profession led to a breakdown. Unable to receive help from the doctors, he discovered New Thought and was soon healed.

After his healing he moved to Chicago and led a second career as a New Thought writer and practitioner beside that of law. (He was admitted to the Illinois bar in 1903.) He wrote his first New Thought item, a pamphlet entitled "The Secret of the I AM," thousands of copies of which he distributed freely over the years.

In 1900 he became editor of *Suggestion*, a New Thought periodical. He also met Sydney Flowers, New Thought editor, publisher, and entrepreneur. He began to write for Flowers's monthly *New Thought*, which he edited from 1901 to 1905. He founded a Psychic Club, which combined interest in metaphysics with the occult, and the Atkinson School of Mental Science. Both were headquartered in the same building where Flowers's Psychic Research Company and New Thought Publishing Company were located. Through Flowers, Atkinson met Elizabeth Towne, the New Thought publisher who would later publish several of his books.

Atkinson joined forces with Flowers in 1901. During the next year he published his first three books: *The Law of New Thought; Thought Forces in*

Business and Everyday Life; and *Nuggets of New Thought*. These were followed by *Thought Vibrations* (1906); *Dynamic Thought* (1906); *The Secret of Success* (1908); *The Inner Consciousness* (1908); *The Will* (1909); *Your Mind and How to Use It* (1911); and *The Mastery of Being* (1911).

Although Atkinson was an extreme individualist and refused to form a New Thought church, his works were widely read and influenced many who did, such as Fenwicke Holmes, brother of Ernest Holmes of the Church of Religious Science. However, as influential as Atkinson's New Thought books may have been, they have been all but forgotten in contrast to the books for which he is most remembered. During the first decade of the twentieth century, he assumed the guise of a yogi and became the first successful popularizer of Hindu thought and practice in America. As Yogi Ramacharacka, he wrote approximately fifteen books, and so accurate a job of transmission did he do that Indian authors began to quote him as a genuine source.

His books as Yogi Ramacharacka were published by the Yogi Publication Society, a Chicago firm specializing in occult and Hindu literature, and included *Fourteen Lessons in Yoga Philosophy and Oriental Occultism* (1903); *Advanced Course in Yogi Philosophy* (1904); *Hindu Yogi Science of Breath* (1904); *Hatha Yoga* (1905); *A Series of Lessons on Raja Yoga* (1905); *Science of Psychic Healing* (1906); *Spirit of the Upanishads* (1907); *Mystic Christianity* (1907); *Reincarnation and the Law of Karma* (1908); *Hindu Yogi System of Practical Water Cure* (1909); and *The Life Beyond Death* (1912). The Yogi Publication Society has kept Atkinson's Hindu books in print to the present day.

During the last years of his life, Atkinson became closely associated with Elizabeth Towne, who published his books. He in turn wrote for her magazine, *The Nautilus*. From 1916 to 1919 he also edited the Chicago periodical *Advanced Thought*.

William Walker Atkinson (Swami Ramacharacka) *The Mastery of Being* (Holyoke, Mass., 1911).

——— , *Your Mind and How to Use It* (Holyoke, Mass., 1911).

——— , *Dynamic Thought* (Los Angeles, 1906).

——— (as Yogi Ramacharacka), *Raja Yoga* (Chicago, 1905).

——— , *Hatha Yoga* (Chicago, 1932).

The New Thought Annual (Chicago, 1902).

EOP, 763.

WWW, I, 35.

AUROBINDO, Sri (Arvinda Ackroyd Ghose) (August 15, 1872, Calcutta, Bengal, India—December 5, 1950, Pondicherry, India); married Mrinalini Bose, April 1901 (d. 1918); education: King's College, Cambridge, England, 1890–92.

The spiritual leader known to the world as Sri Aurobindo was born in Calcutta as Arvinda Ackroyd Ghose. His family, determined that he should be raised as a Westerner, sent him at the age of five to a school in Darjeeling run by a group of Irish nuns. Two years later they sent him to

England, where he stayed until he was twenty. His education culminated in two years at King's College, Cambridge. In spite of his forced Westernization, he developed an early attachment to India and a commitment to its independence. While still at Cambridge he headed a student group working for Indian self-rule.

In 1893 he returned to India in the service of the Maharaj of Baroda. He eventually became a professor of English and French and then Vice-Principal of Baroda University. During his thirteen years at Baroda, he was finally able to absorb the Indian culture he had been denied. He learned the Indian languages and he also launched the political phase of his career. Within a few months of his arrival in India, his first articles appeared in *Indu Prakash*, a nationalist newspaper in Bombay. He also joined a secret society pledged to work for India's independence.

In 1906 he moved to Calcutta to become principal of the Bengal National College. He continued his political activity as co-founder and eventually editor of *Bande Mataram*, the organ of the Bengal National Party, and he succeeded Bipan Chandra Pal as leader of the party. In 1908 he was arrested by the British for seditious activity and held in jail for more than a year before he was finally acquitted. The year turned out to be the turning point in Aurobindo's life.

As early as 1904, Aurobindo had for the first time discovered yoga and begun its practice. In January 1908, just four months prior to his imprisonment, he met Vishnu Bhasakr Lele, a yogi from Maharastra, under whose instruction Aurobindo experienced what he later described as the ability to silence the mind and encounter the spaceless and timeless Brahman. In jail, at times in solitary confinement, he continued to practice yoga and study the *Bhagavad Gita* and the *Upanishads*, the most sacred of the Hindu books. He also claimed that the voice of Vivekananda spoke to him and gave needed spiritual instruction. He came out of prison with a new direction to his life's work.

Upon his release from prison, he visited with the remnants of the Bengal Nationalist Party and started two new periodicals. Slowly he began to speak of his experiences in prison and to outline his new spiritual perspective and work. He remained under continual supervision by the British, who wished to deport him in their efforts to destroy the party completely. In 1910 he received a sudden call to leave British-controlled Bengal and go to Chandernagore in French India. Once there, he secreted himself and remained in solitary meditation. He then received guidance to go to Pondicherry, which he reached on April 4, 1910.

With a few followers, he set up what was to grow into his Ashram. He had come to believe that the forces that were to create an independent India had been set in place and that independence was only a matter of time. He now saw his task as entirely spiritual and began to concentrate on his call to revitalize and rebuild the national culture.

In 1914 he met Mira Richards (1878–1973), a young French woman who was to become his spiritual partner and who was to become known to Aurobindo's followers as the Mother. A student of the occult, she had had a vision of someone she had called Krishna. Her vision led her to

Pondicherry, where she discovered that it was Aurobindo, not the deity, Krishna, who was the person in her vision. Together they began the monthly periodical *Arya* as an organ to disseminate Aurobindo's teachings.

On November 24, 1926, Aurobindo experienced the descent of the divine consciousness into the physical. On this "The Day of Siddhi," Aurobindo retired from contact with the world and communicated to his disciples thereafter only through the Mother. He concentrated entirely on his spiritual task of meditation and writing and turned the work of the Ashram over to the Mother. He celebrated his seventy-fifth birthday as a triumph of his mission, for on that day, August 15, 1947, India's independence was declared. He died three years later at the age of seventy-eight.

Aurobindo practiced yoga in a search for the experience of a means of uniting the two polarities of existence, Spirit and Matter. Traditionally, yoga sought the Spirit as a means to transcend and ultimately escape life. The integral yoga of Aurobindo had as its object the movement into Spirit and the subsequent descent with its power and light back into life in order to transform it.

After Aurobindo's death the Mother carried on his work. In the years after World War II, a number of centers of his followers arose in the West. In the United States these include the Atmaniketan Ashram of Pomona, California, and Matagiri (the Divine Mother's Mountain) in Mt. Tremper, New York.

The Essential Aurobindo, ed. by Robert McDermott (New York, 1973).

Aurobindo, *Essays on the Gita* (New York, 1950).

———— , *The Future Evolution of Man* (Wheaton, Ill., 1974).

———— , *The Yoga and Its Objects* (Pondicherry, 1968).

K. R. Srinivasa Iyengar, *Sri Aurobindo. A Biography and a History* (Pondicherry, 1972).

Shuddhananda Bharati, *Sri Aurobindo, The Divine Master* (Pondicherry, 1948).

R. R. Diwakar, *Mahayogi* (Bombay, 1976).

Sisirkumar Mitra, *The Liberator* (Bombay, 1970).

M. P. Pandit, *Sri Aurobindo, a Survey* (Pondicherry, 1972).

Robert Neil Minor, *Sri Aurobindo, The Perfect and the Good* (Columbia, MO, 1978).

EOP 72.

BAAL SHEM TOV, Israel (Elul 18, 1698, Akop, Poland—Sivan 6, 1760, Mezshbozsh, Poland); married (second marriage) Leah Rachel.

Israel, the son of Eliezer, a rabbi in the small town of Akop in the Carpathian Mountains of southern Poland, was the founder of Hassidic Judaism and became the most famous bearer of the title *Baal Shem*. A *Baal Shem* is one who knows the secret mystical knowledge of the names of God and who works miracles by the power of the names. Little is known of Israel's early life and much is shrouded in legend. It is known that he was orphaned at the age of five and that he was raised and educated by the townspeople of Akop. An able student, he nevertheless frustrated his teachers by frequently disappearing into the mountains where he felt more at home.

One day in the woods, he met a member of the Tzadikim Nistarim, a secret order led by Rabbi Adam Baal Shem of Ropshitz. Members of the Nistarim wandered from town to town teaching and spreading encouragement to the persecuted. Israel went to live with Reb Meir, a member of the order, a *tzaddik* (a mystic teacher) and a tar maker by trade. He lived and worked with Reb Meir for several years before becoming a full member of the Nistarim in 1712.

In 1716 he became the *Bahelfer*, the assistant to the religious teacher, in the city of Brody. For the next three years, while still a member of the Nistarim, he daily taught the children under his care. Although still in his teens, he also became an influential leader in the Nistarim and persuaded them to expand their work by taking responsibility for religious education in areas where it was lacking. The Nistarim then began to organize schools and provide qualified teachers in many rural communities.

In 1719 Israel became the *shamash* (the equivalent of a church sexton) in his home town of Akop. The position provided time for heading of the Nistarim, to which he had succeeded as leader, and for studying the Torah for long hours. He also met and married his first wife.

During Israel's years at Akop, the son of Rabbi Adam Baal Shem came to stay in the town. Shortly before his death, Rabbi Adam had given his son a number of manuscripts on the kabbalah, the secret mystical doctrine that had arisen in medieval Judaism. The old rabbi's son gave the manuscripts to Israel and then became his pupil. During the next few years, both Rabbi Adam's son and Israel's wife died. With nothing to hold him in Akop, he moved to Tiosty, a small town in Galicia, where he opened a school for children. He married Leah Rachel, the daughter of Rabbi Ephraim Kutover and again settled in the town of Brody.

The year 1724 became the turning point in Israel's life. On his twenty-sixth birthday he had a visitation from Ahiya of Shilo, the prophet who had lived at the time of King David. For the next ten years, Israel lived in seclusion in the mountains, studied the Torah and kabbalah, and continued to commune with the spirit of Ahiya of Shilo. During this time he mastered the mystic arts and became known as the Baal Shem Tov, or BeShT for short. Ten years later, on his thirty-sixth birthday, the BeShT received the revelation of his mission in life. He was to leave the mountains and become a teacher of what was to become known as Hasidism.

In 1736 the Baal Shem Tov settled in the city of Mezshbozsh and began to teach the Hasidic doctrines. He appealed to the entire Jewish community and emphasized the accessibility of faith to each person. Crucial to the Hasidic way was *devekut*, the adhesion to, or cleaving to, God, not only in religious acts but in daily life. He emphasized the centrality of worship and the potential of prayer, but prayer not as request but as the experience of mystic oneness with God. The sense of oneness produces *simcha*, an intense joy, which is a necessary precondition of *simcha shel mitzvah*, joy in the performance of the commandments, the way of true worship. Joy, frequently expressed in ecstatic dance, has characterized Hasidism to the present day.

The BeShT's magnetic personality, his activity as a teacher and worker of miracles, and his approach to the common people soon brought him a following throughout southern Poland. He launched a movement that, at the beginning of the Nazi era, included almost half of European Jewry. Toward the end of his life, he faced charges of heresy from those who thought that the BeShT had assumed messianic pretentions.

After the Baal Shem Tov's death, his movement spread and prospered until the Holocaust all but destroyed it in Europe. Many Hasidic leaders did survive the Nazi onslaught and reestablished their movement in Israel and the United States, where it has experienced a rapid growth in the last half of the twentieth century.

Zalman Aryeh Hilsenrad, *The Baal Shem Tov* (Brooklyn, 1967).

——— , *Challenge* (London, 1970).

Ben Zion Bokser, *The Jewish Mystical Tradition* (New York, 1981).

Jacob S. Minkin, *The Romance of Hasidism* (New York, 1935).

EOP, 86.

BAHA'U'LLAH (November 12, 1817, Tehran, Persia (Iran)—May 29, 1892, Akka (Acre), Palestine (Israel); married Asiyih Khanum, October 1835 (d. 1886); married Fatimah Khanum, circa 1850; married Gohar Khanum, circa 1850.

The one known to the world as Baha'u'llah, the founder of the Baha'i faith, was born Mirza Husayn-Ali. His father, Mirza Buzurg, a wealthy and influential citizen of Tehran, held a number of government posts, including the governorship of some areas in northern Iran. Baha'u'llah received no formal education, that being reserved for the religious leaders. As was the custom and expectation of Persia at this time, Baha'u'llah married three times. Contemporary Baha'is point out that these marriages were contracted prior to his initial revelation in 1853. In his book of laws, the *Kitab-i-Aqdas*, he prescribes monogamy, the practice of his son and successor Abdu'l-Baha and his followers worldwide.

In May 1844 a new prophet arose in Persia. Siyyid Ali Muhammad of Shiraz, known as the Bab (Gate), claimed that he fulfilled the prophecies of Shi'ite Islam as the promised Qa'im, whose revelation would start a new era in religious history and whose own religion would find its ultimate fulfillment in "Him Whom God shall make manifest," one far greater than the Bab himself, whose advent would fulfill all religious prophecy about the "Promised One of All Ages." The Bab immediately attracted a following, among them Mirza Husayn-Ali, who in a short time was recognized as one of the Bab's chief spokespersons. The Bab was imprisoned, by order of the Shah, in northwest Persia (Adhirbayjan province) in 1847. He was executed there in 1850.

In 1848 Mirza Husayn-Ali traveled to Khurasan, where many of the Bab's prominent followers gathered to confer on the significance of the Bab's religion and his incarceration. During this conference Mirza Husayn-Ali assumed the title Baha and was known as Jinab-i-Baha (*Jinaj* being an honorific, meaning the honorable).

Prior to and following the Bab's execution, thousands of followers of the Bab were put to death in a country-wide effort to stamp out the new religion. In 1852 the failed attempt on the life of the Shah by two Babis (followers of the Bab) caused a renewal of the violence against the entire Babi community. Baha'u'llah was imprisoned in a Tehran dungeon, and it was during this imprisonment that he received the first intimations that he was the Promised One foretold by the Bab, intimations he did not reveal until a later time.

After several months, Baha'u'llah was released from prison and banished from Persia to Baghdad, Iraq, where he lived from 1853 to 1863. Leadership of the Babis had passed to Mirza Yahya, Baha'u'llah's half-brother, but during the years in Baghdad, due in large part to Mirza Yahya's inadequacies as a leader, most of the Babis increasingly looked to Baha'u'llah as the one capable of guiding the scattered and confused followers. On May 3, 1863, Baha'u'llah, with his family and a small group of followers, left Baghdad for Constantinople. Just prior to his departure from Baghdad, he announced to a very select group of family and followers that he was the Promised One foretold by the Bab.

After five months in Constantinople, Baha'u'llah was further exiled to Adrianople (now Edirne), where he remained until 1868. At Adrianople, through a series of tablets to the rulers of the world's nations and religions, he openly proclaimed himself to be the Promised One whom all religion prophesied and whose advent all awaited. These tablets were sent to, among others, the Shah of Persia, the Sultan of the Ottoman Empire, Napoleon III, Queen Victoria, Czar Alexander, Pope Pius IX, King Wilhelm, and the rulers of America.

In 1868 the Turkish authorities exiled Baha'u'llah and his followers to the penal colony at Akka, Palestine. For more than two years he was housed in a military barracks, but eventually restrictions were relaxed and he was permitted a move to a house within the colony's walls. Here Baha'u'llah revealed his most important volume, the *Kitab-i-Aqdas* (the Most Holy Book), the book of laws. Finally in 1879 he was permitted to live outside the city walls. He moved to a vacant mansion, Bahji, which was to remain his residence for the rest of his life. Bahji became his resting place and is now a shrine and place of pilgrimage for Baha'is.

Because of his confinement, Baha'u'llah's life in Akka was relatively secluded. Nevertheless he received a number of his followers. His writings are contained in more than one hundred volumes and tablets (short epistles), revealed from 1853 to 1892. While some of his writings have yet to be translated from the original Persian or Arabic, most of his important texts are available in English. They include *Gleanings from the Writings of Baha'u'llah*; *Prayers and Meditations*; the *Kitab-i-Aqdas*; *Epistle to the Son of the Wolf*; and *The Seven Valleys and the Four Valleys*.

A central teaching of Baha'u'llah is progressive revelation; that is, the belief that God had revealed himself through a series of Manifestations, who act as the divine representative of his will and who reveal his words and laws. The series of Manifestations includes Krishna, Buddha, Zoroaster, Moses, Jesus, Muhammad, and the Bab. Baha'is believe that

Baha'u'llah was the latest of these divine messengers. His teachings focus on the oneness of God and religion, the oneness of mankind, the elimination of all forms of prejudice, the equality of men and women, world peace and justice upheld and protected by a form of world government, the importance of monogamy, and universal education. His writings also contain the rules for the worship and conduct observed by Baha'is today.

Baha'u'llah's following did not spread to America during his lifetime. The first missionary, Ibrahim C. Kheiralla, who eventually left the faith and established a rival organization, arrived in December 1892, just months after Baha'u'llah's death. His first American follower was Thornton Chase, who became a Baha'i in 1894 after reading about the religion in material at a public library.

In his will and testament, Baha'u'llah appointed his son Abdu'l-Baha as the sole interpreter of his writings and as the "center of the Covenant."

Baha'u'llah, Gleanings from the Writings of Baha'u'llah (Wilmette, Ill., 1939).

——— , Prayers and Meditations (New York, 1938).

——— , Epistle to the Son of the Wolf (Wilmette, Ill., 1969).

——— , The Seven Valleys and the Four Valleys (Wilmette, Ill., 1945).

H. M. Balyuzi, Baha'u'llah (Oxford, 1980).

William McElwee Miller, The Baha'i Faith (South Pasadena, Calif., 1974).

William Sears, The Prisoner and the Kings (Toronto, 1971).

BAILEY, Alice LaTrobe Bateman (June 16, 1880, Manchester, England—December 15, 1949, New York, New York); married Walter Evans, 1907 (divorced 1919); married Foster Bailey, 1921.

Alice LaTrobe Bateman Bailey, founder of the Arcane School, was born into a wealthy family in England. She was, however, an unhappy child and tried on several occasions to commit suicide.

At the age of fifteen, an event occurred that was to later change her life. One Sunday, as she sat in her room reading, a tall stranger, dressed in European clothes and wearing a turban, suddenly walked in and sat down beside her. He told her that she had an important mission and must prepare herself. Young Alice thought he was Christ, and only in 1915, when she saw the stranger's picture on the wall of the Theosophical Society, did she recognize him as Koot Hoomi, one of the mahatmas who had worked with Helena Blavatsky.

Alice grew up in the Church of England and throughout her life lived in tension between a conservative evangelical Christianity and a natural bent toward mysticism. During her earlier years, the former dominated. At eighteen she attended finishing school in London, after which she worked for the YWCA for many years. While working for the YWCA at a soldier's home in India, she met Walter Evans, her future husband.

After their marriage in 1907, they moved to Cincinnati, Ohio, where Walter studied for the Episcopal priesthood at Lane Theological Seminary. After his graduation, they moved to California, but because of Walter's unstable temper, they separated in 1915 and were divorced soon after the War.

Alice was introduced to Theosophy in 1915 by two friends in Pacific Grove, California. Despite an initial negative response, she was impressed by three key Theosophical ideas: that there was a divine plan for the world, that a spiritual hierarchy existed, and that karma and reincarnation were truths. She became an active member and was soon teaching classes. In 1917 she moved to Krotona, the site of the American headquarters of the society. Her ability soon became evident, and she was made editor of *The Messenger*, the society's periodical. In 1919 she met Foster Bailey, the national secretary of the society.

In November 1919 she was contacted by another member of the spiritual hierarchy, Djwhal Khul, known popularly as the Tibetan. He invited Alice to be his amanuensis in the production of a set of books he wished released to the world. He would dictate via telepathy. The first volume, *Initiation: Human and Solar*, was begun in 1920. During the next thirty years, nineteen books were dictated.

In 1920 disagreements with the Theosophical Society arose, and both Foster and Alice were dismissed from their positions. They moved to New York, where Alice taught classes and Foster worked for an independent branch of the Theosophical movement. They were married in 1921.

By 1922 Alice had finished three books, two dictated by the Tibetan and one written by herself entirely. She and Foster formed the Lucis Trust to publish her works. They also began a magazine, *The Beacon*, and in 1923 founded the Arcane School, as a spiritual school for disciples.

The remainder of Alice Bailey's life was spent in continuing the writing with the Tibetan and building the work of the Arcane School, which rapidly grew into an international organization.

In 1932 the Tibetan prompted the organization of the New Group of World Servers to unite people of goodwill as harbingers of a coming world civilization. Closely related is the Triangles, an activity begun in 1937, to promote spiritual service through groups of three people working together.

The Arcane school also projected the ideal of a coming world religion that would unite East and West. The Tibetan dictated the first book directed toward this goal in 1927, *Light from the Soul*. Alice wrote *From Bethlehem to Calvary* in 1937. That same year she released possibly her most famous piece of writing, "The Great Invocation," a prayer for the restoration of God's plan on earth that is used with great frequency in many occult groups.

After her death, the Arcane School split into several groups. Foster headed the Arcane School and the Lucis Trust until his death in 1977.

Alice Ann Bailey, *The Unfinished Autobiography* (New York, 1951).

—————— , *Initiation: Human and Solar* (1922).

—————— , *Discipleship in the New Age*, Vol. I (1944), Vol. II (1955).

—————— , *A Treatise on White Magic* (1934).

J. Stillson Judah, *The History and Philosophy of the Metaphysical Movements in America* (Philadelphia, 1967).

EOP, 90.

BALLARD, Edna Anne Wheeler (June 25, 1886, Burlington, Iowa—
February 10, 1971, Chicago, Illinois); married Guy W. Ballard, 1916 (d.
December 29, 1939).

Edna Anne Wheeler Ballard, leader of the "I AM" Religious Activity
and co-founder of the Saint Germain Foundation, was raised in Iowa. An
early interest in music led to her becoming a concert harpist in 1912. She
taught harp during the 1920s and on one occasion gave a concert for the
Duke of Wales. She continued her interest in the harp all her life. Two
years after her marriage to Guy W. Ballard, she had her one child, a son,
Donald.

She shared an interest in occult metaphysics with her husband and,
during the 1920s in Chicago, worked in the Philosopher's Nook, a metaphysical bookstore, and edited a periodical, *The American Occultist*. She
remained in Chicago during the period that her husband had his initial
experiences with the Ascended Master Saint Germain at Mt. Shasta in
Northern California. However, soon after the encounters began, he wrote
her letters detailing the experiences and the teachings he was receiving.

Upon his return from California, she joined him in founding the Saint
Germain Foundation and the Saint Germain Press, and together they
taught as the Accredited Messengers of the Ascended Masters. Upon her
husband's death in 1939, she assumed total leadership of the movement.

At the time of her becoming head of the movement, the "I AM"
Activity began to face its most severe crisis. Several ex-members, including some previously on the national staff, made a number of accusations
against the Ballards. The charges led to an indictment of Edna, her son
Donald, and several other "I AM" leaders on nineteen counts of mail
fraud. In essence, they were charged with knowingly soliciting money to
support a religion which, the government contended, they knew to be
false. Though the initial charges were dropped, a new indictment was
issued in 1941 and in 1942, she was convicted, fined, put on probation and
the Foundation denied the use of the mails.

The conviction was appealed and reviewed by the Supreme Court. In
one of the most famous and important decisions on church and state,
Justice Douglas concluded that freedom of religion embraces ". . . the
right to maintain theories of life and of death and of the hereafter which
are rank heresy to followers of orthodox faiths. Heresy trials are foreign to
our Constitution. Men may believe what they cannot prove. They may
not be put to the proof of their religious doctrines and beliefs. Religious
experiences which are as real as life to some may be incomprehensible to
others." (*United States vs. Ballard*, April 24, 1944). The opinion, which
became one of the most quoted of Supreme Court decisions, essentially
assumed that the original conviction was based on a disapproval of the
Ballards' religious teachings.

The ruling did not end the legal troubles. The case was submitted to
the Supreme Court after a Court of Appeals reaffirmed the conviction,
and again it was overturned. The matter of mail service remained, and
separate court action was instituted for the return of their use. The order

revoking the ban was not issued until 1954. Then in 1957, the tax-exempt status was returned.

In 1941, as the court proceedings progressed, Edna moved to Santa Fe, New Mexico (though the official headquarters of the movement remained in Chicago) and established a second headquarters there. The "I AM" school, founded in Los Angeles, and the branch of the press opened in Denver were also relocated there. Though reduced in membership, the movement survived through the years of litigation.

After the final dismissal of the criminal charges, the rebuilding of the organization began in earnest, though with little fanfare. The national conclaves were moved to Mt. Shasta, site of Guy Ballard's original encounter with Saint Germain. In 1951 the Foundation purchased a former resort center near Mt. Shasta which became a site of pilgrimages and national gatherings.

Throughout the 1950s she expanded the Teachings. She added new volumes to the Saint Germain Series, the basic I AM textbooks. She made over two thousand recordings of dictations from the Masters and instituted a radio program which by the 1960s was heard over twenty-five stations.

After her death in 1971, leadership of the Foundation passed to the Board of Directors which had been created at the time of incorporation. Donald, also named an Accredited Messenger by the Ascended Master Saint Germain, died in 1973.

Charles S. Braden, *These Also Believe* (New York, 1949).

BALLARD, Guy Warren (July 28, 1878, Newton, Kansas—December 29, 1939, Los Angeles, California); married Edna Anne Wheeler, 1916 (d. February 10, 1971).

Guy Warren Ballard, leader of the "I AM" Ascended Master Religious Activity, and co-founder with his wife Edna W. Ballard of the Saint Germain Foundation and the Saint Germain Press, was born into a large family in rural Kansas. He attended business college and served in the army during World War I. He developed an early interest in mining, and after the War became superintendent of his uncle's lead and silver mine near Tucson, Arizona, a position he held until his uncle's death.

Along with mining, he developed an interest in the theosophy and the occult and was familiar with the literature which told of the masters, a group of ascended beings who secretly guided and helped the world from their cosmic perspective. In August 1930, business took Ballard to Northern California, where rumors that the mystic brotherhood of masters could be found at Mt. Shasta led him to spend his leisure hours on its slopes. Here in September 1930 the events which were to change his life and thrust him into the public spotlight occurred.

According to Ballard, while hiking around the mountain, he encountered another hiker, a mystic personage, who later revealed himself to be the legendary Comte de Saint Germain, the European nobleman known both for his diplomatic work and masonic activities in the eighteenth century. Having ascended, Saint Germain's task was to initiate the Seventh Golden Age, the permanent "I AM" Age of Eternal Perfection on earth. He had searched Europe for someone through whom he could release the Instruction on the Great Law of Life, but, failing to locate a suitable person, he turned to America and eventually found Ballard. Subsequently he designated Ballard and his wife, Edna, and their son, Donald, as the only Accredited Messengers of the Ascended Masters.

During the next months, Ballard had numerous extraordinary experiences with the masters, about which he wrote his wife, and began to receive messages, termed "discourses," from them. These were duly recorded in a series of books beginning with Unveiled Mysteries (1934). In 1931 he returned to Chicago and in 1932 founded the Saint Germain Press and Saint Germain Foundation. He began to hold gatherings in his home and at various locations around Chicago, which led in 1934 to the first ten-day class opened to the general public at the Civic Opera House in Chicago. The ten-day classes became the standard means of introducing the thought of the Ascended Masters to the public.

The teachings of the Ascended Masters centered upon the I AM Presence, the Primal Light which pours out of God, the Mighty Creative Fire or Great Central Sun. Individualized, the I AM Presence becomes the source of every life, the essence of each person. Individuals could call upon the I AM Presence and thus contact the Divine through the repetition of specific invocations, called "decrees."

Following the Chicago class, the Ballards began to travel across the United States beginning in the northeast. In 1935 they addressed over 7,000 at the Shrine Auditorium in Los Angeles. Through Ballard, Saint Germain also appointed other messengers to assist him and teach under his direction.

During the late 1930s, the movement led by Ballard became one of the most controversial in North America due in part to the large response and subsequent swift growth throughout the continent and in part due to the angry criticism of several former members and the sensationalized coverage of the classes by the press. Thus in November 1939, in order to maintain a serene atmosphere for sincere students, he closed the classes to the general public.

Ballard died in December 1939 and his wife assumed leadership of the Activity. Thus he did not live through the crisis of the 1940s in which the Press and Foundation leadership were indicted, convicted and only exonerated after taking the case to the Supreme Court twice, in 1944 and 1946. From the days of massive public interest during Ballard's lifetime, the movement adopted a very low profile, and many have thought it defunct. However, in the mid-1980s its headquarters in Schaumburg, Illinois, reported over 300 temples and sanctuaries in America and additional centers in Europe and Africa.

Guy W. Ballard, Unveiled Mysteries (written under the pseudonym Godfre Ray King) (Chicago, 1934).

———, The Magic Presence (Godfre Ray King) (Chicago, 1935).

———, The "I AM" Discourses by Saint Germain (Chicago, 1936).

———, Ascended Master Discourses by the Ascended Masters (Chicago, 1937).

Charles S. Braden, *These Also Believe* (New York, 1949).

Gerald B. Bryan, *Psychic Dictatorship in America* (Los Angeles, 1940).

David W. Stupple, *A Functional Approach to Social Movements with an Analysis of the I Am Sect and the Congress of Racial Equality* (Kansas City, Mo, M.A. Thesis 1965).

BALLOU, Adin Augustus (April 23, 1803, Cumberland, Rhode Island—August 5, 1890, Hopedale, Massachusetts); married Abigail Sayles, 1822 (d. February 20, 1829); married Lucy Hunt, March 3, 1830.

Adin A. Ballou, founder and leader of the Massachusetts Association of Independent Restorationists and the Hopedale Community, came from an old New England family. His father was a farmer and raised a large family to assist on the farm and a sawmill he owned. Ballou had to overcome a sickly childhood, but his early bodily infirmities gave him a love of intellectual pursuits. His family had been identified with Universalism, his relative, Hosea Ballou, being one of their outstanding preachers. Adin's parents, however, were converted in a revival and joined the Christian Connection, within which Adin's father became a deacon.

At the age of eighteen, Ballou had a visitation from a spirit who told him, "Adin, God commands you to preach the gospel of Christ to your fellow-men. Obey his voice or the blood of souls will be required at your hands." Reluctantly Ballou gave up more lucrative career options to enter the ministry. A few months later he preached his first sermon. The response was so great that, three months later, in September 1821, he was accepted as a minister in the Christian Connection.

Ballou did not take a parish immediately but traveled and preached regularly. He also began to study Universalism with the idea of refuting it. Instead, he was converted. As a result he was excommunicated from the Christian Connection, and on December 10, 1823, he was ordained as a Universalist minister. He became pastor at Milford, Connecticut, a post he served until 1827, when he moved to the Prince Street Church in New York City. In New York he established a periodical, *The Dialogical Instructor*, but his stay there lasted less than a year, and Ballou returned to Milford.

At Milford an issue that had been slowly dividing the Universalists came to a head. Ballou published an article claiming that the final reconciliation of men to God would come only after a period of reckoning in the afterlife. The majority party held that people were immediately reconciled to God at death. The issue led to a break, and Ballou and his supporters formed the Massachusetts Association of Independent Restorationists. He was forced out at Milford but was immediately offered the pastorate at nearby Menden, Connecticut. He became the editor of the association's periodical, *The Independent Messenger*.

During the years in the new association, Ballou took up the cause of social reform and became an outspoken advocate for the abolition of slavery, the rights of women, temperance, pacifism, and the abandonment of capital punishment. His social theorizing led to the idea of the Hopedale Community, formed in 1841 as an experiment in the reorganization of society under the laws of God. He established a stock company and bought a farm near Milford, where thirty people moved in the spring of 1842. True to form, he began a newspaper, *The Practical Christian*. The experiment began to grow and prosper, and within the decade there were more than 100 residents.

The downfall of the community grew out of the attempt to found a sister community at Union Grove, Minnesota. During the 1850s, two brothers, prosperous businessmen in their own right, had quietly bought up a majority of the stock. After the failure in Minnesota, they withdrew from the community and declared their ownership of the town. Hopedale dissolved. Ballou became pastor of a reorganized Hopedale Parish, affiliated with the Unitarians, and remained in that position until his retirement in 1880.

Ballou wrote a number of books, including *Spirit Manifestation*, which grew out of a brief period of experimentation with Spiritualism at Hopedale; an autobiography; a history of the Ballou family; and several religious tracts.

Adin Ballou, *Autobiography of Adin Ballou, 1803-1890* (Lowell, Mass., 1896).

————, *Christian Non-Resistance in All Its Important Bearings* (Philadelphia, 1910).

————, *An Exposition of Views Respecting the Principal Facts, Causes and Peculiarities Involved in Spirit Manifestations* (Boston, 1852).

————, *Primitive Christianity and Its Corruptions*, 3 volumes (Boston, 1870–1900).

Memorial of Adin Ballou (Cambridge, 1890).

Raymond Lee Muncy, *Sex and Marriage in Utopian Communities* (Bloomington, 1973).

John Humphrey Noyes, *History of American Socialisms* (reprinted as *Strange Cults and Utopias of 19th Century America*) (New York, 1966).

DAB, 1, 556–7.

EOP, 93.

WWWH, 38.

BEISSEL, Johann Conrad (March 1, 1690 (1691?), Eberbach, Palatinate, Germany—July 6, 1768, Ephrata, Pennsylvania).

Johann Conrad Beissel, early Seventh-Day Baptist leader and founder of the Ephrata Cloister, was the son of a baker. His drunken father died during his wife's pregnancy, and his mother died when Beissel was eight. He was finally apprenticed to a baker who possessed a jovial manner and was musically inclined. He taught Beissel both his trade and his music.

At the age of twenty-five, Beissel experienced a conversion and associated himself with the Pietists, the independent movement within Germany that emphasized personal religion as opposed to the formality of the state church. He moved to Heidelberg and hired himself to a baker. He was soon arrested, however, for his attendance at the Collegia Pietistica and was subsequently banished. He sought refuge at Schwarzenau, which had become a haven for various Pietist groups. He was attracted to the Community of True Inspiration (now popularly known as the Amana Community) but then became affiliated with Alexander Mack and (the Church of) the Brethren. He was not ready to settle yet and after a short stay he began to wander around Germany. He then heard of an American Pietist community that had been founded by Johannes Kelpius called the "Society of Woman in the Wilderness."

In 1720 Beissel traveled to Pennsylvania in an attempt to find the community, which had been located near Germantown. By this time the community had long since been disbanded and its remnants scattered. Beissel did find Peter Becker, leader at that time of the American contingent of the Church of the Brethren. He apprenticed himself to Becker to learn the weaver's trade, staying with Becker only a short while. In 1721, with three companions, he journeyed into the wilderness near Conestoga to establish a communal life. Along the way, he visited the remnants of a Dutch community in Maryland, the Labadists, and he absorbed Sabbatarian ideas from the Seventh-Day Baptists.

In 1724 a revival swept the Brethren, and the entire male membership of the Germantown congregation went into the countryside to contact the scattered flock. Beissel once again met with Peter Becker, allowed Becker to baptize him, and was voted leader of a congregation formed at Conestoga. Beissel soon ran into conflict with his congregation as he began to advocate what many saw as a Mosaic legalism. He emphasized the virtues of celibacy and Sabbatarianism. In 1728 a schism occurred. One of Beissel's followers rebaptized him, and he established a Sabbath-keeping congregation at Conestoga. He remained with his new congregation only four years, for in 1732 he called the elders together, gave them a Bible, instructed them to rule by it, and he disappeared into the wilderness again.

This time Beissel settled near Cocalico Creek. He was followed by a few of his congregation at Conestoga, and together they began what was to become the Ephrata Community. In 1735, the year of Alexander Mack's death, another revival swept the Church of the Brethren, and more people moved to join Beissel. Included were two important leaders, Peter Miller and Conrad Weiser.

As people joined him, Beissel organized his followers into three groups—householders (the married), solitary brethren, and spiritual virgins. The group erected the Kedar, a large community house. Under Beissel's chief assistant, Israel Eckerlin, community businesses were developed. An ordered life was adopted. A distinctive habit was worn, and new names given. Beissel became "Friedsam Gottrecht." He began a publishing enterprise that not only published the community's books and hymnals but, by the mid-1740s, became a major competitor of Benjamin Franklin's printing monopoly in Philadelphia.

For a short while, Beissel lost control of the community in a power struggle with Eckerlin, but after a period of illness, he recovered his health and expelled Eckerlin. His control of the community was unquestioned from that point. Upon his death, Miller succeeded him. Eventually the work of the community was absorbed by the Seventh-Day Baptists.

Johann Conrad Beissel, *Mysterion Anomias* (translated as *Book of the Sabbath*; Philadelphia, 1728).

Walter C. Klein, *Johann Conrad Beissel: Mystic and Martinet* (1690–1768) (Philadelphia, 1942).
James E. Ernst, *Ephrata: A History* (Allentown, Penn., 1963).

Corliss Fitz Randolph, "The German Seventh Day Baptists," in *Seventh Day Baptists in Europe and America* (Plainfield, N.J., 1910).

Floyd E. Mallet, *Studies in Brethren History* (Elgin, Ill., 1954).

Ira S. Franck, *The Ephrata Story* (1964).

DRB, 39–40.

DAB, 2, 142–3.

WWWH, 50.

BELL, Eudorus N. (June 27, 1866, Lake Butler, Florida—June 15, 1923, Springfield, Missouri); married Katie Kimbrough, July 13, 1909; education: John B. Stetson University, Deland, Florida; Southern Baptist Theological Seminary, Louisville, Kentucky, 1900–1902; University of Chicago, B.D., 1903.

Eudorus N. Bell, one of the founders of the Assemblies of God, was born in Florida on the heels of the Civil War. His father died when he was two, leaving Eudorus, his twin brother, Endorus, and the family in poverty. Very early in life he was converted and felt a call to the ministry. He was able to work his way through college, seminary, and graduate school and for seventeen years was a pastor in the Southern Baptist Convention. In 1907 while serving a church in Fort Worth, Texas, he traveled to Chicago and attended meetings at the North Avenue Mission conducted by William Durham. Durham had just returned from Los Angeles, where he had experienced the Baptism of the Holy Spirit evidenced by speaking in tongues. Durham passed the experience to Bell.

As a result of becoming a Pentecostal, Bell was forced to withdraw from the Baptist ministry. He aligned himself with a group of Pentecostals in the Southwest, became editor of a periodical, *Apostolic Faith*, and began pastoring a small congregation in Malvern, Arkansas. The group with which Bell associated was both theologically and organizationally opposed to the group headed by Charles Parham. They believed in the immediate possibility of any believer, not just those who had been sanctified, receiving the Baptism of the Spirit. They also saw the need for at least some minimal organization above the congregational level.

Having rejected the Apostolic group led by Parham, the group turned to C. H. Mason of the Church of God in Christ. Mason gave them credentials and allowed the largely white group to use the name of his predominantly black group. In 1912 Bell united this white Church of God in Christ with a Church of God group of like mind from the Southeast. They retained the name, Church of God in Christ. Bell became editor of the new group's periodical, *Word and Witness*.

Bell urged even greater organization within the Pentecostal Movement, and in 1913 he joined four colleagues in calling for a meeting of Pentecostals to build a national organization. Bell chaired this meeting, which led to the formation of the General Council of Assemblies of God, and he was named to the twelve-member Executive Presbytery. Shortly after the meeting, in the summer of 1914, Bell moved to Findlay, Ohio, took a position on the faculty of the Gospel School, and also worked with

J. Roswell Flower in publishing materials for the Assemblies. *Word and Witness* became an Assemblies publication.

In 1915 a group of Pentecostals in California began to articulate a theology that identified Jesus with God, the Father, and called for rebaptism of believers in the name of "Jesus Only." At first Bell editorialized against the new theology. Then, just before the Interstate Encampment in Jackson, Tennessee, he invited a Jesus Only evangelist, L. V. Roberts, to preach. He was the first to present himself for rebaptism, an event immediately heralded by the Jesus Only faction. Not wishing to become a divisive force, Bell resigned as editor of the *Word and Witness* and became pastor of a small church in Galena, Kansas.

The Assemblies of God was finally forced to deal with the non-Trinitarian issue. They appointed Bell to a committee to write a statement of fundamental truths to be considered at the 1916 meeting of the Assemblies. While working on the statement Bell completed his theological side-journey, and he soon rejoined the Trinitarians. The statement he wrote was adopted, and the non-Trinitarians left the Assemblies.

Bell slowly returned to a place of favor and power among his former colleagues. In 1917 he scouted the site in Springfield, Missouri, where the Gospel Publishing House moved. In 1918 he became the editor of the *Evangel*, the Church's periodical. In 1919 Bell became the General Secretary of the Church, and in 1920 he resumed the post of Chairman, which he held until his death in 1923.

Eudorus N. Bell, *Questions and Answers* (Springfield, Mo., 1923).

Carl Brumback, *Suddenly from Heaven* (Springfield, Mo., 1961).

Fred J. Foster, *Think It Not Strange* (St. Louis, Mo., 1965).

Vinson Synan, *Aspects of Pentecostal-Charismatic Origins* (Plainfield, N.J., 1975).

DRB, 41–2.

BENJAMINE, Elbert (C. C. Zain) December 12, 1882, Iowa—November 18, 1951); married Elizabeth Dorris, 1919 (d. 1942).

Elbert Benjamine, one of America's most famous astrologers and founder of the Church of Light, began to study the occult at the age of sixteen. Two years later, in 1900, he made his initial contact with the Brotherhood of Light, at that time a small occult order headquartered in Denver that circulated lessons written by Thomas H. Burgoyne. Over the next few years, while continuing his occult studies, he worked at a number of odd jobs. A crucial event occurred December 8, 1907, in Lake Charles, Louisiana. He offered a prayer that he be guided to the work on earth that would contribute the most to human welfare. He was assured by the members of the invisible spiritual hierarchy, which the members of the Brotherhood saw as heading their order, that he had an important lifelong task ahead of him.

Two years later, Minnie Higgins, one of the three leaders of the Hermetic Brotherhood of Luxor, the exoteric branch of the Brotherhood of Light, with whom Benjamine had been studying, died. He was called to Denver and elected to take her place as the order's astrologer (the Brotherhood was headed by an astrologer, a seer, and a scribe). The other two leaders also attempted to convince him to initiate a program of public education to spread the "religion of the stars" to the general public. They wanted him to write a complete course of occult study.

Benjamine declined the request, but a year later he relented and promised to write a twenty-one-part course of lessons on the twenty-one branches of occult science. He spent the next five years in study and began writing the lessons in March 1914. Meanwhile, the three leaders of the Hermetic Brotherhood of Luxor decided to close that branch of the Brotherhood of Light and thus left Benjamine to function as a Brotherhood of Light teacher and representative.

In May 1915 Benjamine moved to Los Angeles, wrote the *Outline of Initiation*, and began holding classes. A small membership began to gather around him. He waited until World War I ended to open membership in the Brotherhood to the public at large, but on Armistice Day, November 11, 1918, he began the first public class. Among the members of the class was Elizabeth Dorris, whom Benjamine married the following spring.

During the next two decades, Benjamine wrote the twenty-one courses, which were mimeographed and used in his classes. He issued them under the name C. C. Zain, a pen name he adopted to keep his official Brotherhood writings distinct from his personal statements. At the same time he was becoming a popular astrological writer and wrote numerous articles for various journals. He also wrote a set of ten astrological reference books, including the *Beginnner's Horoscope Reader*, *Astrological Lore of All Ages*, and *Chart Your Future*.

In 1932 Benjamine incorporated the Church of Light, and the Brotherhood of Light ceased to exist on the visible earth plane. Two years later he completed the twenty-one courses, which covered alchemy, tarot, astrology, and occult psychology and philosophy.

The Church of Light is an ancient wisdom school. It dates its beginning to 2440 B.C. and the establishment of the Brotherhood of Light by a group of dissenting Egyptians. It has, the church believes, always perpetuated itself from generation to generation until it reemerged in the nineteenth century as an organization and was incorporated in 1932. The church teaches members the occult techniques and knowledge necessary for their individual evolution.

After Benjamine's death, he was succeeded by Edward Doane as president of the church. By the time of his passing, the Church of Light had forty-one groups across the United States, and meetings in five countries—Canada, England, Mexico, Liberia, and Nigeria.

Elbert Benjamine, *The Influence of the Planet Pluto* (Chicago, 1939).

———, *Astrological Lore of All Ages* (Chicago, 1945).

———, *How to Use Modern Ephemerides* (Chicago, 1940).

———, *Beginner's Horoscope Maker* (Chicago, 1943).

———, *Stellar Dietetics* (Chicago, 1942).

——— (under pseudonym C. C. Zain), *Brotherhood of Light Lessons*, 210 lessons in 22 volumes (Los Angeles).

"A Great Soul Marches On," *The Church of Light Quarterly* 26, 1 (July 1951–January 1952), 1–2.

"The Founders of the Church of Light," *The Church of Light Quarterly* 45, 1 (February 1970), 1–2.

BERNARD, Pierre (1875, Leon, Iowa—September 28, 1955, Nyack, New York); married Blanche DeVries.

Pierre Bernard, founder of the Tantrik Order in America and known to many of his followers as Oom the Omnipotent, was born Peter Coons in a small town in Iowa. He was one of the most important persons in the spread of Eastern religion in the United States. His focus upon Tantric, and hence the sexual aspects of Hinduism, coupled with his own questionable past made him the continued target of sensational journalism, and rarely has he been treated seriously or objectively by those who wrote about him.

As a young man, Coons moved to California and worked at various jobs such as picking lemons and packing salmon. In 1905 he met Mortimer K. Hargis, and, together, they founded the Bacchante Academy to teach hypnotism and what they termed "soul charming," a practice that included the mysteries of sex. In 1906 the academy fell victim to the San Francisco earthquake.

Around 1909 Coons appeared in New York City. He took the title Oom the Omnipotent and founded the Tantrik Order in America. He taught yoga and Tantric Hinduism and quietly gathered disciples until 1910, when two followers left the order and complained to the District Attorney and the press that Oom was conducting weekly orgies and holding them prisoner. Oom was arrested, but the two women left town and the District Attorney dropped the case. Coons expanded his operation, always under the close scrutiny of the police who suspected him of merely trying to seduce young women and place them under his control.

He opened the New York Sanskrit College and later a physiological institute. At the time of the opening of the institute, he assumed the name Dr. Pierre Arnold Bernard, by which he was known for most of the rest of his life. Around the time of the end of the First World War, he met and married Blanche DeVries, an oriental belly dancer with high social connections. She introduced him to Ann, the wife of William K. Vanderbilt, and she became his disciple.

In 1924 the financially successful Bernard moved to Nyack, New York, and bought a seventy-eight-acre estate, which became his headquarters for the next thirty years. Adjacent to the mansion he built the Inner Circle Theatre, which housed his library of thousands of books on Eastern religion and the occult. The estate became the gathering place for the famous and a stopping point for visiting gurus.

Once settled in Nyack, Bernard became a community leader. He built a zoo and sponsored an annual town parade. He joined the volunteer fire department. He became a director and eventually treasurer of the local chamber of commerce. He bought up controlling stock in the bank in nearby Pearl River and named himself president of the establishment. By 1931 he owned twelve million dollars' worth of property in Rockland County.

During World War II, Bernard closed his yoga center and used his estate, which he turned over to the Wertheim family, to house refugees from Nazi Germany.

Among those who joined the colony that developed in Nyack, Bernard's nephew, Theos Bernard, wrote a thesis on yoga at Columbia University. Published in 1944 as *Hatha Yoga: The Report of a Personal Experience*, it has subsequently become a classic among American yoga texts.

Bernard died quietly after a brief illness in his eightieth year. He left a number of unanswered questions and unsubstantiated claims, such as his attainment of a teaching degree in Hinduism in India. No record of his having gone to India ever emerged. His obvious mastery of Hindu teachings (all of which he could have absorbed from his large library) and his obvious contribution to the growth of Hinduism in America seemed to be contradicted by his questionable credentials as a "doctor" and teacher, his obvious pandering to the wealthy, and his frequent changes of name and use of aliases.

Pierre Bernard, *In Re Fifth Veda*, International Journal of the Tantrik Order (New York, circa 1910).

Paul Sann, *Fads, Follies, and Delusions of the American People* (New York, 1967).

Charles Boswell, "The Great Fume and Fuss over the Omnipotent Oom," *True* (January 1965), 31–33, 86–91.

EOP, 104.

BESANT, Annie Wood (October 1, 1847, London, England—September 21, 1933, Adyar, India); married Frank Besant, December 1867.

Annie Wood Besant succeeded Madame H. P. Blavatsky and Henry S. Olcott as the leader of the Theosophical Society. During her years as, first, head of the Esoteric section (beginning in 1891) and then as president of the society (1907–1933), she oversaw the worldwide expansion of the society and its rebuilding in the United States (after the work was lost in 1895). From the age of five, Annie was raised by her widowed mother in a very religious environment. In her nineteenth year she met a minister-school master whom she eventually married. The marriage failed because of her increasing skepticism and an unwillingness to keep her opinions to herself. In 1893 she took her two children and left her husband. They were legally separated five years later.

During her years with Frank Besant, she had begun to write short stories. Once separated, she began to write essays on her skeptical views. In 1874 she met the atheist freethinker Charles Bradlaugh, with whom she developed an immediate friendship. She joined the National Secular Society, began to write for Bradlaugh's *National Reformer*, and gave her first public lecture, the "Political Rights of Women." Her relationship with Bradlaugh grew, and in 1876 they formed a partnership, the Freethought Publishing Company. Besant became coeditor of the *National Reformer*. Among their first publications, Knowlton's *The Fruits of Philosophy* advocated birth control, and in June 1877 the two were tried for publishing obscene literature with the intention of corrupting morals. Although they were found guilty and fined, the trial established Besant's reputation as an orator, skeptic, and advocate for women's rights.

During the 1880s she became a friend of George Bernard Shaw and developed an interest in socialism. She joined the Fabian Society. Her new interest led to a break with Bradlaugh, and in 1887 she resigned as coeditor of the *National Reformer*.

The following year Besant was given a copy of *The Secret Doctrine* by Helena P. Blavatsky, one of the founders of the Theosophical Society, for review. The event changed her life. In the book, its author, and the society, Besant found the answers that free thought and, before that, Christianity had failed to provide. She resigned from the National Secular Society (of which she was vice-president) and became an ardent spokesperson for Theosophy. She became coeditor of the society's magazine, *Lucifer*. In 1890 she made her first trip to the United States as Madame Blavatsky's representative.

Blavatsky died in 1891. Although a relatively new member, Besant became head of the Esoteric section and informally the second most powerful member, next to Olcott, the president. In 1892 she wrote her first two Theosophical books, the *Seven Principles of Man* and *Karma*. The following year she made her triumphal tour of the United States and spoke to overflow audiences at the World Parliament of Religions in Chicago.

Soon after her American tour, Besant moved to India, which became her home and headquarters for the rest of her life. In 1894 and 1895 she withstood a challenge to her power by W. Q. Judge. Though winning cost most of the American membership, she quickly reorganized the loyal following and rebuilt the society in America. By the time she succeeded Olcott as president in 1907, the society had stabilized and had begun a period of slow and steady growth.

In 1909 she organized the Order of the Star of the East to promote her belief that Jesus as Lord Maitreya had returned in the person of J. Krishnamurti. The Order flourished for twenty years but disbanded after Krishnamurti resigned in 1929.

Besant became very active in social reform, especially in the effort to spread education. She led the society in founding many schools, including some of the first in India for females. She believed strongly in Indian independence and was elected president of the Indian Nationalist Congress in 1917.

Her major occult work came in collaboration with an Anglican priest and later bishop of the Liberal Catholic Church, C. W. Leadbeater, with whom she wrote several books and whose causes she promoted through the society.

Besant wrote several hundred books on a variety of subjects from the occult to social reform to politics. She remained president of the society until her death in 1933.

Annie Wood Besant, *The Ancient Wisdom* (London, 1897).

———, *Esoteric Christianity* (London, 1901).

———, *Theosophical Lectures* (Chicago, 1907).

———, *Autobiography* (Adyar, India, 1939).

Theodore Besterman, *A Bibliography of Annie Besant* (London, 1924).

Arthur H. Nethercot, *The First Five Lives of Annie Besant* (Chicago, 1960).

———— , *The Last Four Lives of Annie Besant* (Chicago, 1963).
Esther Bright, *Old Memories and Letters of Annie Besant* (London, 1936).
DRB, 46–47.
EOP, 105.
DNB, 1931–1940, 72–4.

BLAVATSKY, Helena Petrovna Hahn (July 30, 1831, Ekaterinoslav (now Dnepropetrovsk), Ukraine—May 8, 1891, London, England); married Nikifor Vasilievich Blavatsky, July 7, 1848; married Michael C. Betanelly, April 3, 1875.

Madame Helena Petrovna Blavatsky, better known by her initials H.P.B., one of the co-founders of the Theosophical Society, grew up in an affluent Russian family in the mid-nineteenth century. The supernatural and the occult were part of her childhood, and Helena did automatic writing as a teenager. When she was twelve years old her mother died, and she went to live with her grandfather. A few days prior to her seventeenth birthday, she married General Blavatsky, but realizing that marriage did not suit her "free spirit," she left the general after three months and fled to Constantinople.

The flight to Turkey began a period of wandering that lasted almost two decades. In 1850 she was in Cairo exploring the occult and experiencing her first taste of hashish. She traveled to England in 1851 and circled the globe twice during the decade. In 1856 she was in India attempting to get into Tibet. (Followers and detractors still argue about her claimed success in that venture.) In 1858 she went to France and became associated with Daniel D. Home, the famous medium. Her period of attachment to Spiritualism began at this time. In 1871 she returned to Cairo. She organized a Spiritualist society that foundered within a few weeks because of inept fraudulent phenomena. While in Egypt, Blavatsky also met Emma Cutting, who would later so alter her life.

In 1873, H.P.B. landed in New York City and quickly became immersed in American Spiritualism. In 1874 she traveled to Chittenden, Vermont, where the Eddy brothers were conducting their materialization seances. Blavatsky joined the efforts and demonstrated her own abilities. While in Vermont she met Henry Steel Olcott. They teamed their efforts and upon their return to New York City, Olcott became the leader of a circle of people around H.P.B. Blavatsky, who in turn arranged Spiritualist phenomena especially for Olcott.

Joined by lawyer colleague William Q. Judge, Olcott and Blavatsky formed the Theosophical Society in 1875. The following year she moved into an apartment with Olcott and began the research and writing of her first book, *Isis Unveiled*, which appeared in 1877. The Theosophical Society did not prosper during the 1870s, and Blavatsky decided to join Olcott in a move to India in 1878. While their initial hopes for India were not realized, they began a magazine, *The Theosophist*, in 1879, and it soon provided them a living. The growth of the society allowed a move to Madras in 1882 onto a large tract of land donated to the work.

During the early years of the Theosophical Society, Blavatsky saw

Theosophy superseding the Spiritualism from which she had come. In place of the spirits of the dead, H.P.B. cultivated the contact with the Masters, or mahatmas, highly evolved beings who were teachers of occult wisdom. She regularly received messages from the mahatmas, which were precipitated on paper. Frequently such messages appeared as if from the sky or in the specially constructed cabinet at the headquarters in Madras.

During an 1884 visit to London, the favorable impression she gave a committee from the Society for Psychical Research was destroyed by charges of fraud made by her assistant in India, Emma Cutting Coulomb. The SPR sent Richard Hodgson to India to investigate. His report, published in 1885, concluded that Blavatsky was an accomplished fraud, an opinion confirmed later by more than one of her close associates. Neither Blavatsky nor the Theosophical Society has fully recovered from Hodgson's discoveries.

Advised against settling in India, Blavatsky moved to Germany and then settled in London in 1887. While living down the scandal that followed her, she did experience her most productive literary period. Her magnum opus, *The Secret Doctrine*, appeared in 1889, as did *The Voice of the Silence*, which became two of the most influential occult works ever written. She was able to attract a few new disciples; among them were the Countess Constance Wachtmeister, who defended Madame in *Reminiscences of H. P. Blavatsky and the Secret Doctrine*, and Annie Besant, who would succeed her as head of the Theosophists.

H. P. Blavatsky, *Isis Unveiled* (New York, 1877).

——— , *The Secret Doctrine* (Madras, 1889).

——— , *The Key to Theosophy* (London, 1889).

——— , *Collected Writings*, 11 volumes (Los Angeles and Wheaton, Ill., 1950–1973).

Marion Meade, *Madame Blavatsky* (New York, 1980).

Gertrude Marvin Williams, *Priestess of the Occult* (New York, 1946).

Howard Murphet, *When Daylight Comes* (Wheaton, Ill., 1975).

Iverson L. Harris, *Mme. Blavatsky Defended* (San Diego, 1971).

Charles J. Ryan, *H. P. Blavatsky and the Theosophical Movement* (San Diego, 1937).

DRB, 52–3.

DAB, 2, 361–3.

EOP, 114.

NAW, 1, 174–77.

WWW, H, 60.

BOOTH, William (April 10, 1829, Nottingham, England—August 20, 1912, London, England); married Catherine Mumford, June 16, 1855 (d. October 4, 1890).

William Booth, founder of the Salvation Army, was raised in the home of an unsuccessful business speculator. His formal education ended after several years at school, when his father's business efforts failed completely. William became an apprentice to a pawnbroker at the age of thirteen and remained in that position for the next six years. William's father died while he was in his midteens, and the event precipitated his first religious reflections. He joined the Methodist Church. He experienced a conversion and soon felt a call to preach. While still in his teens, he organized a small evangelistic band to preach to the poor.

After finishing his apprenticeship and after a year of unemployment, he moved to London and found work as a pawnbroker. He also became a local preacher for the Methodists, but he was expelled from membership when he became identified with the Reformers, a group in the process of splitting from the church. He was offered a position with the Reformers Church and began to preach to them on his twenty-third birthday. In the congregation was Catherine Mumford, who became his wife. After several months, he accepted a position as pastor of a Reformer's circuit at Spaulding. Though successful, he came to feel that the New Connection, another Methodist splinter group, would be a more congenial home. He moved back to London and began to study for the ministry with the New Connection. He was admitted on probation in 1854. He served as an assistant pastor in London but spent much of his time in evangelistic work. In 1855 he was appointed as a Connectional evangelist, and more than 3,000 people joined the Church under his ministry in the first year.

In 1857 Booth returned to the pastorate. In 1858 he was ordained and appointed to Gateshead, a dying church. He revived it during his three years there. After his years at Gateshead, Booth asked to be returned to full-time evangelism. When he was refused, Booth walked out of the Conference and turned down any appointment. He spent the next two years as an independent evangelist among any independent Methodists who would welcome him.

During the years at Gateshead, Catherine had begun to preach. In 1865 she began work in London. Booth joined her and began preaching in the slums in the East End. Strongly affected by his encounter with the poor, in 1865 he began the East London Christian Mission and began publishing a periodical, the *East London Evangelist* (later the *Christian Evangelist*). Within three years there were thirteen centers and the mission began to reach beyond London. The name was changed to the Christian Mission in 1868.

During the next decade, the work of the mission grew, and Booth emerged as the General Superintendent. He also began to see the need for a more disciplined core of workers. Around 1878 the idea of a "Salvation Army" emerged. Step by step the name was changed, a uniform adopted, the *Christian Evangelist* transformed into the *Salvationist*, and the General Superintendent became simply the General.

Another decade of growth followed, and then, in 1888, Booth awakened to the physical needs of the poor, to whom he had been preaching. He opened the first shelter to which the homeless could go for a night's sleep out of the cold. He began a broad investigation of the social conditions of the poor and penned his most famous book, *In Darkest England, and the Way Out.* He proposed a total program to aid the poor through rehabilitation and in some cases relocation to a more healthful environment.

After Catherine died in 1890, Booth began two decades of traveling during which time the Salvation Army spread to fifty-eight nations. Booth was honored worldwide for his accomplishments. He was received by both the King of England and President of the United States. He was awarded a doctorate by Oxford, and the city of London gave him the "Freedom of the City," its highest honor. He died in 1912.

William Booth, *In Darkest England, and the Way Out* (London, 1890).

——, *The Doctrines and Discipline of the Salvation Army* (London, 1881).

——, *Holy Living* (London, 1890).

——, *Purity of Heart* (London, 1902).

Harold Begbie, *The Life of General William Booth* (New York, 1920).

Richard Collier, *The General Next to God* (New York, 1965).

Minnie Lindsey Carpenter, *William Booth* (London, 1942).

William Hamilton Nelson, *Blood and Fire: General William Booth* (New York, circa 1929).

John Evan Smith, *Booth the Beloved* (London, 1949).

DNB, 1912–1921, 50–52.

BRANHAM, William Marrion (April 6, 1909, Burkesville, Kentucky—December 24, 1965, Amarillo, Texas); married Hope Brumbech, June 22, 1934 (d. August 22, 1937); married Meda Broy, October 23, 1941.

William Branham, the Pentecostal healer and prophet, was born in rural Kentucky and raised in poverty. His father, a logger, was frequently out of work and an alcoholic. The small amount of religion the young Branham received was in a Missionary Baptist Church. When William was very young, his family moved to Jeffersonville, Indiana, where he grew up.

Even as a toddler, Branham began to hear the voice of one he claimed to be an angel of the Lord. While he recalled visitations when he was only three years old, his first important visitation occurred when he was seven. The voice told him, "Never drink, smoke or defile your body in any way for I have a work for you to do when you get older." The mystical bent in his life led Branham to the Pentecostal Church where, on one of his first visits, he was healed after an anointing with oil. He felt the call to preach, and although uneducated and untrained, he formed an independent Baptist congregation and began holding tent meetings in Jeffersonville in 1933. His work was a success and his followers soon built a modest building, the Branham Tabernacle.

Branham's visionary experiences cut him off from the Baptists, and he was reluctant to associate with the Pentecostals because of their low social standing. He soon found his way to the meetings of the non-Trinitarian "Oneness" Pentecostals with whom he found fellowship. The next decade proved difficult. His wife and child were killed in the 1937 Ohio River flood. He was forced to work at a secular job while remaining a part-time pastor of the small independent tabernacle.

The turning point of his life came on May 7, 1946, when he had another angelic visitation. The angel announced the work ahead and gave to Branham the promise of healing power and the gift of knowledge (clairvoyance). Shortly thereafter, he received a call to come to St. Louis to pray for the healing of the daughter of a Oneness pastor of a United Pentecostal congregation. The child was healed and Branham was invited to preach at the Church. Out of his visit to St. Louis came an invitation to Shreveport, Louisiana, to preach at Jack Moore's church. Moore decided to join Branham as his manager, a crucial event, since Moore was both a capable manager and had many friends among the more numerous Trinitarian Pentecostals of the Assemblies of God. Through Moore, Branham was led to Gordon Lindsey, then pastor of an Assemblies of God congregation in Portland, Oregon. Lindsey, an expert organizer, also joined Branham.

In 1948 Branham started *The Voice of Healing* magazine and began in earnest the life of an itinerant healing evangelist. In 1950 during a meeting in Houston, a photograph showing a halo around Branham's head was taken. This photo was widely circulated and assisted in building Branham's reputation as a miracle worker. Branham's growing success led him to Europe (1950), Africa (1952), and back to Europe (1955).

His success was halted in 1955 by money problems. Mismanagement had crept into the organization. The Internal Revenue Service filed charges of tax evasion, and, even though the case was settled out of court, money problems hampered Branham the rest of his life. The late 1950s marked a low point in his ministry.

Around 1960, the crowds waning, Branham moved away from the wide range of miracles that had come to characterize his meetings and returned to a simple healing emphasis. He also began to introduce a set of doctrinal divergences that gradually alienated him from the growing number of healing evangelists that had appeared in Pentecostal circles. He declared that denominationalism was the mark of the beast. He asserted his preference for the Oneness position on God (i.e., against the Trinity). He focused on visions of the end of time and the coming destruction of the United States. Finally in 1963 he declared himself the messenger of the last days with the spirit of Elijah (as prophesied in Malachai 4 and the Book of Revelation 11:3). This last declaration most clearly separated Branham from the mainstream of Pentecostalism and from the healing movement his early ministry fostered. Until his death in an automobile accident, he continued to preach and call from Pentecostalism those who would follow his views.

Branham left behind two legacies. First, the Branham Tabernacle and the Tucson Tabernacle, in Arizona, remain as the center of those who still believe Branham was the Elijah messenger, and the associated Spoken Word Publishers continue to print his sermons. The larger legacy is the host of pastors and healing evangelists whom he brought into the healing ministry and/or inspired and who remain active in the 1980s.

William Marrion Branham, *Conduct, Order, Doctrine of the Church* (Jeffersonville, Ind., 1974).

——, *The Revelation of the Seven Seals* (Tucson, Ariz., 1967).

——, *An Exposition of the Seven Church Ages* (Jeffersonville, Ind., n.d.).

——, *Footprints on the Sands of Time* (Jeffersonville, Ind., n.d.).

Gordon Lindsey, *William Branham, A Man Sent from God* (Dallas, 1950).

In Memory of William Branham (privately printed, 1966).

Gordon Lindsey, "William Branham As I Knew Him," *The Voice of Healing*, February 1966.

Terry Sproule, *A Prophet to the Gentiles* (Blaine, Wash., n.d.).

BRESEE, Phineas (Franklin) (December 31, 1838, Franklin Township, Delaware County, New York—November 13, 1915, Los Angeles, California); married Maria E. Hibbard, 1860.

Phineas Bresee, founder of the Church of the Nazarene, was born to a farming family in New York. His parents neglected to give him a middle name, and so in later life he took Franklin, the name of the township in which he was born, as his own. He was seventeen when he was converted in a Methodist class meeting. Within a few months he was licensed to exhort and soon began holding prayer meetings. The following spring, just before the family moved to Iowa, he preached his first sermon.

Once the family settled in Iowa, young Phineas began to preach regularly and was licensed to preach. At the earliest opportunity, the Methodist Conference accepted him into membership, and in 1858 he was assigned his first pastoral charge at Holland, Iowa. In 1860 he returned to New York to marry a woman he had courted entirely by mail.

Over the next twenty-four years he served in a succession of appointments: Grinnell Circuit (1860), Galesburg (1861), Des Moines (1862), Winterset District as presiding elder (1864), Chariton (1866), Des Moines (1868), Council Bluffs (1870), Red Oak (1873), Clarinda (1879), and Council Bluffs (1881).

Bresee's final year in Iowa was spent trying to start a second Methodist Church in Council Bluffs. In 1883 he transferred to California and became pastor of First Methodist Church in Los Angeles. Once in California, Bresee openly aligned himself with the growing holiness movement. The holiness perspective was built upon the belief that Christians could by the action of the Holy Spirit become perfect in love. This perfection came as a second definite act of grace. Bresee had experienced this sanctification in 1866 while in Iowa.

In Los Angeles he began to emphasize holiness to his congregation and invited outstanding holiness preachers to speak at his church. After three successful years at Los Angeles, he moved to Pasadena. There, for the first time, he ran into opposition from some lay people over his holiness ideas. After four years at Pasadena, he moved to Asbury Church in Los Angeles for a year before becoming presiding elder of the Los Angeles district. During that year, he held a holiness campaign throughout the district. After his year on the district, he served Simpson Church in Los Angeles (1892) and Boyle Heights, also in Los Angeles, the next year.

In 1894 Bresee asked the Conference to allow him to take charge of the Peniel Mission, an interdenominational holiness center in Los Angeles. This request brought to a head the tension between Bresee's holiness emphases and the Conference leadership. They denied his request, and so he withdrew and went to the Peniel Mission. Unfortunately this relationship did not work out, and in 1895 he broke relations with the Mission. However, supporters from the Mission opened services a few blocks away, and on the third Sunday in October they organized the Church of the Nazarene with Bresee as pastor.

The new congregation grew steadily. A tabernacle was put up the next year, and in 1897 a branch was opened in Berkeley. The vision of spreading a holiness work on the West Coast emerged. Bresee began a church periodical, *The Nazarene* (later *The Nazarene Messenger*) and began organizing a movement. In 1898 the first delegated assembly from the several churches gathered and elected Bresee as superintendent. As the church grew, first two and then three districts were designated and churches were founded as far east as Chicago. Bresee was elected as the general superintendent of the work though he continued preaching duties in Los Angeles.

By 1905 the church had three districts. Bresee led the committee that formulated a plan of union with a similar body, the Association of Pentecostal Churches of America, with congregations primarily on the East Coast. With the merger in 1906, the new Pentecostal Church of the Nazarene became a national body. In 1908 the Holiness Church of Christ came into the church bringing its congregations, located primarily in the South.

The uneducated Bresee had thus built a successful thirty-year career in the Methodist Episcopal Church only to leave it and in twenty years build a national holiness body that has since become one of the largest holiness churches in the United States. Bresee preached his last sermons in August 1915 at the Los Angeles church he founded in 1895. He died a few months later on November 13, 1915.

Phineas Franklin Bresee, *The Certainties of Faith* (Kansas City, Mo., 1958).

———— , *Sayings of Our Founder* (Houston, Texas, 1948).

Donald Paul Brickley, *Man of the Morning* (Kansas City, Mo., 1960).

Harrison D. Brown, *Personal Memories of the Early Ministry of Dr. Phineas F. Bresee* (Seattle, Wash., 1930).

Ernest Alexander Girvin, *Phineas F. Bresee: A Prince in Israel* (Kansas City, Mo., 1916).

EWM, 1, 324-5.

BRITTEN, Emma Hardinge (1823, London, England—October 2, 1899, Manchester, England); married William Britten, October 11, 1870.

Emma Hardinge Britten, a leading figure in the occult revival of the late nineteenth century, was born Emma Floyd. Her father, a sea captain, died during her childhood, and Emma developed a devotion to her mother that remained strong throughout her life. Two early interests emerged in her youth—music and the occult. At the age of eleven, she was teaching piano and began to appear on stage as both a singer and pianist. She also became involved with a secret occult society through which her talents as a trance clairvoyant were developed. According to tradition, she was married to someone in the society by the name of Hardinge while in a trance state. Angered at what had occurred, she began to use the name as a means of revenge: the name Floyd disappeared.

After her experiences with the occult group, she further developed her musical abilities. In 1855 she was invited to New York City and made stage appearances at the Broadway Theater and Broadway Athenaeum. During her visit she encountered American Spiritualism. Her earlier interest in the occult was revived, and she became deeply involved in the Spiritualist movement. Continuing her music, she became the director of music at

Dodsworth House, while at the same time becoming famous in Spiritualist circles as both a speaker and a medium.

Emma stayed in America for a decade despite the protests of her mother, who wished her to return to England. She became involved in politics and campaigned for Lincoln's reelection in 1864. In 1865 she returned to England and immediately began to work with British Spiritualists. For the rest of the decade, she traveled back and forth across the Atlantic as a Spiritualist.

In 1869 she came to New York to arrange for the publication of her first major book. While in the United States, she met and married William Britten. They moved to Boston and began an occult magazine, *The Western Star*. It lasted only six issues because a fire destroyed their warehouse, offices, and all their supplies. The fire forced Emma to return to that for which she is best remembered—writing books. She published her first book, *Modern American Spiritualism*, a history of the youthful movement, in 1870. She moved to New York and began work on two books, *Ghostland* and *Art Magic*, both of which appeared in 1876. They received negative reviews from both Christian and Spiritualist periodicals because they put forth an occultism that was Theosophical in outlook. In fact, in 1875 she had become an intimate member of the circle that formed the Theosophical Society in America. She had attended and left the only written account of the meeting on September 7, 1875, at which the suggestion to form the Theosophical Society was made and many of the early meetings were held in her home. Both she and Colonel Olcott, president of the society, denied that her works were actually products of the society, as some reviewers had asserted.

A third book, *The Faith, Facts and Frauds of Religious History*, a book compiled from Britten's lectures on Christianity, also appeared in 1876. She attacked the uniqueness of Christianity and joined the process of education shared by Spiritualists, Theosophists, and freethinkers to inform the British and American publics of the beliefs and practices of other religions. A final major book, *Nineteenth Century Miracles* (1884), brought her history of Spiritualism up to date.

She and her husband lectured widely in the late 1870s. They took a tour of New Zealand and Australia, which brought them to California in 1879. Rejecting an offer to remain in California, they settled in England in 1881, where Emma continued to work until her death in 1899.

Although she left no organization behind, the Brotherhood of Light (now the Church of Light) count her as one of their founders in the United States, as do the Theosophists. By identifying herself as a Spiritualist and becoming the major chronicler of Spiritualism's first generation, she also moved beyond the central concerns of Spiritualism and spirit contact toward occult and magical philosophy. As occult organizations emerged in the early twentieth century, her books became a major source of information and inspiration.

Emma Hardinge Britten, *Modern American Spiritualism* (New York, 1870).

——— , *Nineteenth Century Miracles* (New York, 1884).

——— , *Ghostland* (Chicago, 1897).

——— with Alfred Kitson and H. A. Kersey, *The Lyceum Manual* (Rochdale, 1924).

The Church of Light Quarterly 50, 2 & 3 (Spring–Summer 1975), ii–vi.

EOP, 130.

BROOKS, Nona Lovell (March 22, 1861, Louisville, Kentucky—March 14, 1945, Denver, Colorado); education: Charleston Female College; Wellesley College.

Nona Lovell Brooks, founder of the Divine Science Church and a leading figure in the New Thought Movement, was born to a well-to-do family in Louisville, Kentucky, just as the Civil War broke out. Shortly after her birth, the family moved to a farmstead near Charleston, West Virginia, where Nona grew up. Her father had a prosperous salt-mining business. The family were Presbyterians, and Nona received a strong religious upbringing. The first religious experience she remembered occurred one Sunday morning after her family had left for church. Nona had a cold but decided to fight boredom with a walk in the garden. While there she experienced an engulfing by a supernatural light. Her response was a prayer, "Father, make me close to Thee."

During her teen years, the family fortunes failed when rock salt was discovered in New York. They moved to Colorado because of her mother's health and, when she was nineteen, Nona's father died. The misfortunes culminated when she received a letter from her boyfriend, away at seminary preparing for the ministry, saying that he was to marry another.

At this crucial point in her life, she met a Mrs. Bingham, a friend of her sister Alethea. Mrs. Bingham had been very ill and had traveled to Chicago to see a specialist. There she had encountered Emma Curtis Hopkins, the teacher of Christian Science. Through Hopkins's work she was healed. She then returned to Pueblo and began holding classes, which she encouraged Alethea to attend.

In the months after her arrival in Colorado, Nona had suffered from a throat infection that would not clear up; it was only at her sister's insistence that she also attended the classes. During the third class, Mrs. Bingham's message of the Omnipresence of God was received by Nona, and she was healed. The family did not believe her until, at the dinner table, she ate normally for the first time in months. Using the techniques taught by Mrs. Bingham, both Nona and Alethea began to heal others.

The sisters were so impressed with what had occurred that they told their minister, who then invited them to speak at the church. The elders, however, did not agree. They not only refused to allow Nona to speak but dropped her from teaching Sunday school.

Meanwhile the problem of building a career, since she had not married, presented itself to Nona. She attended Pueblo Normal School and at the age of twenty-nine began a year at Wellesley College to prepare herself as a teacher. After a year at Wellesley, she returned to Pueblo for two years before moving to Denver. Another sister, Fannie James, had been living in Denver for several years and had begun teaching metaphysical classes in her home. She had also been corresponding with Melinda Cramer in San Francisco, a New Thought teacher who had been teaching "Divine Science." Nona began to assist her sister and to call her work by Cramer's name.

In 1898 they founded the Divine Science College in downtown Denver. Soon after the college opened, the students asked for Sunday services. Nona traveled to San Francisco where Cramer ordained her. She returned to hold her first Sunday worship on January 1, 1899.

Once established at the college and ordained, Nona became the leader of a growing movement. In 1902 she began *Fulfillment*, a monthly magazine. In 1915 she added *Daily Studies in Divine Science*, the first of the daily devotional magazines (now *Aspire*). In 1922 she led the Divine Science movement into the International New Thought Alliance, in which she became a prominent leader.

From the base in Denver, Divine Science gradually spread as students from her college opened centers around the country. Slowly a loose association of churches and practitioners emerged. Although a member of an unorthodox metaphysical healing church, Nona became a leading citizen in Denver and served on many boards and agencies, including the State Prison Board. In 1926 she was finally invited to join the Ministerial Alliance.

In the late 1920s and early 1930s, she spent a decade in travel, having relinquished her pastorate and presidency of the college. She took Divine Science to Australia and opened two centers there. In 1938 she returned to Denver and spent her last years serving again as president of the college. She retired in 1943, just two years before her death.

Nona L. Brooks, *Mysteries* (Denver, 1924).

——— , *The Prayer That Never Fails* (Denver, 1935).

——— , *Short Lessons in Divine Science* (Denver, 1928).

Hazel Neale, *Powerful Is the Light* (Denver, 1945).

Charles S. Braden, *Spirits in Rebellion* (Dallas, 1963).

Tom Beebe, *Who's Who in New Thought* (Lakemont, Ga., 1977), 32–33.

Louise McNamara Brooks, *Early History of Divine Science* (Denver, 1963).

BROTHERS, William Henry Francis (April 7, 1887, near Nottingham, England—July 21, 1979, Woodstock, New York); education: Lake Forest College.

William Henry Francis Brothers, founding bishop of the Old Catholic Church in America, began life as William H. Francis. He added the name Brothers, his mother's maiden name, at some point later in life. After a childhood in England, he moved to Waukegan, Illinois, in 1901, where his father established the first mechanized lace-making factory in the country. As a young man, he decided to become a monk, and in 1908 joined a monastic community in Waukegan founded by Dom Augustine de Angelis Harding. In 1909 the small community moved to Fond du Lac, Wisconsin, where it came under the patronage of Protestant Episcopal Bishop C. C. Grafton. Grafton gave the community a building, renamed St.

Dunstan's Abbey, assumed the role of nonresident abbot, and appointed Brothers as prior. The community incorporated as the American Congregation of the Order of St. Benedict.

For many years Grafton had been seeking closer relations with independent Old Catholic groups and in that endeavor had supported, for a time, the work of J. R. Vilatte, a Belgian priest, consecrated in 1891 by the Independent Catholic Church of Ceylon. Grafton had also courted Bishop A. S. Kowlowski, head of a small group of Polish Old Catholics in Chicago. After the move to Fond du Lac, Brothers began to move in Old Catholic circles. In 1910 Vilatte ordained him to the priesthood. Then in 1911, the congregation, with Grafton's full support, was received by the Polish Old Catholic Church, then headed by Bishop J. F. Tichy, who had succeeded Kowlowski in 1907.

Soon after moving the congregation under Tichy's care, Grafton, in 1912, died. Then, within months, Tichy had a paralyzing stroke. In 1914 Tichy resigned in favor of Brothers, who became bishop-elect of the church, which had in the meantime lost most of its members to the Polish National Catholic Church. Pushed back on his own resources, Brothers moved St. Dunstan's back to Waukegan.

A new possibility for affiliation came in 1916, when the Duc de Landas Berghes, who had been consecrated by A. H. Mathew, Old Catholic bishop in London, came to the United States and took up residence at St. Dunstan's. In his effort to extend the jurisdiction of Bishop Mathew, the Duc de Landas Berghes consecrated Brothers on October 3, 1916, and the following day Brothers assisted him in the consecration of Carmel Henry Carfora.

As with Bishop Vilatte earlier, Brothers soon broke relations with both Landas Berghes and Carfora. On January 8, 1917, he assumed the titles of Archbishop and Metropolitan of the Old Catholic Church in America, the renamed remnant of Kowlowski's jurisdiction. He moved to Chicago, pastored a single congregation, and began the task of building his jurisdiction. In 1918 he consecrated Antonio Rodriguez to work among Portuguese-Americans in New England. He received Stanislaus Mickiewicz, bishop of the Lithuanian National Catholic Church, into his jurisdiction.

In 1924 Brothers moved to New York City and continued to expand his jurisdiction. He consecrated Albertus Jehan to continue the work in Chicago. He received Joseph Zielonko, an independent bishop, to head a Polish mission. Most importantly, he attracted the former Episcopal bishop of Arkansas, William Montgomery Brown. After a year in Chicago, Brothers could report congregations throughout the East and Midwest, a seminary, and a weekly periodical, *The Messenger*.

The bright future for Archbishop Brothers seemed even brighter in 1927, when the Episcopal Synod of the Polish Mariavite Church gave the Old Catholic Church in America oversight of the Mariavites outside of Poland. Brothers also aligned the Old Catholic Church with the so-called Soviet Living Church, a shortlived faction of the Russian Orthodox Church under Bishop John Kedrovsky. From 1926 to 1936, the Old Catholic Church in America grew from nine to twenty-four parishes and from 1,888 members to 5,470 members. He also reestablished St. Dunstan's Abbey in the early 1930s, first at Cos Cob, Connecticut, then at New Bedford, New York, and finally at Woodstock, New York. In 1948 the community was dispersed when its facilities were burned. By that time Brothers had moved to Woodstock, where he continued to reside for the rest of his life.

Brothers, in spite of many defections, held his jurisdiction together into the 1950s. It slowly began to disintegrate, and in 1962 he took the church into the Russian Orthodox Catholic Church. He accepted reordination as a Mitred-Archpriest. Five years later, Brothers withdrew from the Russian jurisdiction and reconstituted the Old Catholic Church in America. He consecrated Joseph MacCormack as his successor. Brothers died in 1979, and as of 1984, his Old Catholic Church continues with three parishes and four monastic communities within its jurisdiction.

William Henry Francis Brothers, *Concerning the Old Catholic Church in America* (New York, 1925).

———— , *The Old Catholic Church in America and Anglican Orders* (New York, 1925).

John LoBue, "An Appreciation, Archbishop William Henry Francis Brothers, 1887–1979," *The Good Shepherd* 12 (1980).

Peter F. Anson, *Bishops at Large* (London, 1964).

J. Febronius, *What Is Old Catholicism?* (New York, 1939).

Arthur C. Piepkorn, *Profiles in Belief*, Vol. 1 (New York, 1977).

BROUGHTON, Luke Dennis (April 20, 1828, Leeds, Yorkshire, England—1898, New York, New York); education: Eclectic Medical College, Philadelphia.

Luke Dennis Broughton, the single-most important person in the revival of astrology in the nineteenth century, was born into an astrological family. His grandfather, a physician, had come to astrology through reading Nicolas Culpepper's *Complete Herbal* (first published in 1652) and had used astrology in his medical practice. Broughton's father, also a physician, was brought up with astrology, a practice he passed on to his six children. Luke's older brother, Mark, had headed an astrological society in England and had published both an almanac and an ephemeris, the book of tables of planetary positions, while in England. Mark moved to the United States and in 1849 began publishing *Broughton's Monthly Horoscope*.

Luke's attraction to astrology stemmed from a prediction his father had made after looking at his horoscope. He told Luke's mother that the young child would not talk until he was six and would have a speech impediment until he was eighteen or nineteen. With this accurate prediction to think about, Luke began to study astrology at age eighteen. He married when he was twenty-four and came to the United States two years later.

He moved to Philadelphia and took up his occupation as a weaver. While attending the Eclectic Medical College, he worked in a chemical laboratory. He also took up the work his brother had let lapse, and in 1860 began *Broughton's Monthly Planet Reader and Astrological Journal* (1860–69).

In 1863 Dr. Broughton moved to New York City and opened his medical office. Like his father and grandfather before him, he emphasized herbs and astrology and eventually wrote a book on *Astro-Medical Botany*. In 1866 he rented a hall on Broadway and began to hold lectures on astrology. His lectures attracted immediate attention and no little controversy. His work now grew into an astrology center, and Broughton divided his time between his medical practice and astrology work. He soon became the country's largest distributor of astrological literature and the major teacher of the next generation of astrologers. He wrote several books, including *Planetary Influence* (1893) and *The Elements of Astrology* (1898).

The growth of astrology in the 1880s and 1890s did not go unnoticed, and attacks occurred with growing frequency. Broughton took every opportunity to defend the fledgling field. He decried laws against astrology. In 1886 he championed the cause of a Mr. Romaine, who had been sentenced to eighteen months in prison for practicing astrology. He regularly wrote against the popular debunkers of astrology such as Charles Dana, editor of the *New York Sun*, astronomer Richard A. Proctor, and encyclopedists Thomas Dick and William and Robert Chambers.

Broughton was quick to attack practitioners of astrology he believed to be unqualified. He denounced C. W. Roback, who wrote the first book on astrology published in America, as a fraud. He attacked also Hiram Butler, author of a massive volume entitled *Cosmic Biology*, and New York astrologer Eleanor Kirk, as authors of pseudo-astrology books to be strictly avoided by serious students.

The four decades of Broughton's career saw astrology move from an almost nonexistent state to the point where astrologers—many of whom were his students and clients—could be found in most major cities. When he died, his daughter continued his astrology practice in New York City, and several of his sons also carried on the family tradition.

Luke Dennis Broughton, *Planetary Influence* (New York, 1893).

———, *The Elements of Astrology* (New York, 1898).

BUCHMAN, Frank Nathan Daniel (June 4, 1878, Pennsburg, Pennsylvania—August 7, 1961, Freudenstadt, Germany); education: Muhlenburg College, 1897–99, B.A.; Lutheran Theological Seminary at Philadelphia, 1899–1902; Westminster College, Cambridge, England, 1921–22.

Frank Buchman, founder of Moral Re-Armament, came from a German Lutheran family in eastern Pennsylvania. He decided to go into the ministry, and after graduating from the seminary, he became the pastor of the Church at Overbrook, Pennsylvania. While there he started a hospice for young men for which he became the full time-head in 1905. In 1908 after a period of intense conflict with the Lutherans' Board of the Inner Mission, which had ultimate oversight of the hospice, he resigned. The break with the hospice left Buchman embittered and with a heavy sense of failure. It also precipitated a spiritual crisis.

According to Buchman, the crisis was resolved on a trip to England later that year. In a meeting at Keswick, he had a religious experience that changed his life and allowed him to appropriate personally what he knew the church had been teaching him all his life. He returned to the United States and took a position as the YMCA secretary at Pennsylvania State College, a job he held until 1916 when he became an extension lecturer at Hartford Theological Seminary in Connecticut. Both positions allowed him to travel, and annually he took international trips holding evangelistic meetings, during which he perfected the personal approach to converting people that was to characterize his mature work.

In 1918 in Kulang, central China, he held the first of what came to be known as "house parties." With the help of a Christian layman of considerable political influence, Buchman brought a group of people together during which time they were encouraged to tell their personal stories, confess their sins, and allow Christ to have first place in their lives. Buchman believed that by confessing and forsaking sin a cleansing and change of life were possible. Buchman began to hold "house parties" in various locations around the world. After one in England in 1921, the First Century Christian Fellowship was organized by people who had been changed through Buchman's ministry.

While on a visit to South Africa in 1929, a porter scribbled "Oxford Group" on the reserved train compartments for a group of his followers, many of whom just happened to be from Oxford University. The press picked up the name, and in the 1930s the fellowship became popularly known as the Oxford Group Movement.

During the 1930s the movement spread internationally, and Buchman became an object of controversy because of his ability to travel in the company of the rich and famous, many of whom professed to having had their lives changed by him. He was also condemned for his seeming support of Hitler, whom he lauded as an anticommunist.

In 1938 the fellowship grew into Moral Re-Armament, through which Buchman offered a program for all the people who had been changed in the group movement to now change the world. The early slogan for MRA, coined on the brink of World War II, became "guidance or guns." Buchman was offering the Oxford Group's method of sitting in the silence and waiting for God to speak and guide as an alternative for settling disputes by war.

Buchman saw MRA as a multinational movement and thought its ideology capable of support by people of any faith. Its focuses were the four moral absolutes of honesty, purity, unselfishness, and love, the following of which Buchman saw as the means to overcome conflict on both a personal and international level.

The remaining years of his life were spent in international travel, preaching to large crowds of MRA supporters and consolidating the gains around the world. He died at the age of eighty-two. Although still active in many countries, MRA has not been able to perpetuate the enthusiasm and impact of the years of Buchman's active life. The international headquarters of the movement is in Switzerland, and the headquarters for the United States is in Washington, D. C.

Frank Buchman, *Remaking the World* (London, 1961).

Eighty, by His Friends (London, 1958).

Tom Driberg, *The Mystery of Moral Re-Armament* (New York, 1965).

A. J. Russell, *For Sinners Only* (New York, 1932).

DRB, 76–8.

WWW, 4, 131.

BURGOYNE, Thomas H. (April 14, 1855, Scotland—March 1894, Humbolt County, California).

Thomas H. Burgoyne, one of the founders of the Hermetic Brotherhood of Luxor, a branch of the Brotherhood of Light, was born in Scotland. In early life he became an amateur naturalist and is said to have spent many hours roaming the moors near his home. He was also a natural seer and as a child contacted the Brotherhood of Light, a spiritual hierarchy claimed by occultists to be in ultimate control of the world. He later met M. Theon, designated earthly head of the Brotherhood.

Around 1880 Burgoyne came to America. His articles on occult subjects began to appear around 1885. Several articles he wrote on the tarot appeared in *The Platonist* in 1887–88. Burgoyne moved to California where he contacted Captain Norman Astley, a retired British officer and member of the Brotherhood. Astley suggested that Burgoyne write a basic set of Brotherhood of Light lessons. Burgoyne agreed on the condition that Astley supply him with a living while he worked. Astley organized a class to which Burgoyne presented the lessons. While teaching and writing, he lived with the Astleys at Carmel.

In 1889 these lessons were published as *The Light of Egypt*. About this same time, the group that had gathered around Burgoyne formed the Hermetic Brotherhood of Luxor as an exoteric branch of the Brotherhood of Light. The Hermetic Brotherhood of Luxor was headed by three leaders—a scribe or secretary, an astrologer, and a seer. Burgoyne was the original secretary.

The Brotherhood of Luxor saw itself in continuity with an original Brotherhood of Light formed in 2440 B.C. This group had separated itself from the theocracy that ran Egypt and had functioned as a secret occult order. It continued to exist on both the exoteric and esoteric levels throughout the centuries.

Burgoyne continued to write for the Brotherhood but saw only one of his books, *The Language of the Stars* (1892), in print before his death. *Celestial Dynamics* appeared in 1896, and volume two of *The Light of Egypt* in 1900. They were all published by Henry Wagner's Astro-Philosophical Publishing House.

Burgoyne tried to present a Western occult teaching that centered upon the science of correspondences, which deals with the spiritual and physical influences of the planets and stars upon the human organism. He related the religion of the stars to the total occult philosophy called

Hermeticism, which built upon the correspondence between the whole of creation (the macrocosm) and the human individual (the microcosm). His teachings formed an occult option to the Eastern Theosophy of Helena P. Blavatsky and opposed the ideas of reincarnation and karma.

Upon Burgoyne's death, he was succeeded as secretary by Wagner's wife, Belle M. Wagner. The Hermetic Brotherhood continued until 1913, when the three leaders decided to close it and accept no more members. One of the three, Elbert Benjamine, began to teach under the authority of the Brotherhood of Light after World War I, and his work now continues as the international Church of Light.

Burgoyne, almost forgotten even within the occult community, was a major force in the occult revival of the late nineteenth century in America. According to occult scholar A. E. Waite, Burgoyne was, in fact, Thomas Henry Dalton who had been imprisoned in 1883 in Leeds, England on charges of fraud. After his release, he met a Peter Davidson (M. Theon ?, Norman Astley ?), the founder of the Hermetic Brotherhood of Luxor. After a scandal, he and Davidson fled to the United States and continued to manage the Order.

Thomas H. Burgoyne, *The Light of Egypt*, Vol. I (San Francisco, 1889), Vol. II (Denver, 1900).

——— , *The Language of the Stars* (Denver, 1892).

——— , *Celestial Dynamics* (Denver, 1896).

"Founders of the Church of Light," *The Church of Light Quarterly* 45, 1 (February 1970), 1–3.

Ellie Howe, ed. *The Alchemist of the Golden Dawn* (Wellingborough, 1985).

A. E. Waite, *A New and Revised History of Freemasonry* (1923).

CARFORA, Carmel Henry (August 27, 1878, Naples, Italy—January 11, 1958, Chicago, Illinois); education: Ph.D., University of Naples, 1903; DSTh, Theological Institute of Naples, 1904.

Carmel Henry Carfora, founder and archbishop of the North American Old Roman Catholic Church, was raised in a Roman Catholic family in Naples, Italy. In 1895 he entered the Order of Friars Minor and was ordained to the priesthood six years later. After finishing his education, he was sent to the United States as a missionary to work among Italian-speaking immigrants, first in New York and then in West Virginia (1906–08).

In 1908 Carfora ran into trouble with the newly appointed Apostolic Delegate to the United States and, after some harsh words, left the Roman Church. He proceeded to form an independent mission among people loyal to him. He subsequently formed three others, including one in Youngstown, Ohio, which he began serving as pastor in 1910. He also began to cooperate with Bishop Paolo Miraglia-Gulotti, an independent Catholic bishop who had formed the Italian National Episcopal Church. Gulotti had brought his church to the United States because he had little success in gaining members in Italy. It is believed that in 1912 Gulotti consecrated Carfora to the episcopacy, though no records of the consecration have survived. However, on June 14, 1912, Carfora incorporated his parishes as the National Catholic Diocese in North America.

In 1914 Bishop and Prince de Landas Berghes came to the United States. He brought with him the Old Catholic orders of Arnold Harris Mathew. Carfora came into communion with Landas Berghes and his Old Roman Catholic Church. On October 3, 1916, Landas Berghes consecrated his first bishop, William Henry Francis Brothers, and, the following day, Carfora.

Brothers left Carfora and Landas Berghes after a few months, and in 1917 the two bishops united their two jurisdictions as the North American Old Roman Catholic Diocese. In 1919 Landas Berghes gave up his role in the diocese and submitted to Rome. Carfora, now in total charge of the diocese, changed its name to the North American Old Roman Catholic Church, established his see in Chicago, and began the task of building the church into a national and even international body.

At the time of his consecration, Carfora was named Archbishop of Canada. After Landas Berghes withdrew, he assumed control of all of North America. Then, in 1922, he was elected Supreme Head of the Church, and the following year, he declared himself the "Most Illustrious Lord, the Supreme Primate," with the understanding that his judgments on doctrine and matters of faith were to be considered final when he spoke *ex cathedra*. Thus, Carfora took upon himself the powers of a pope.

During the remaining years of his life, Carfora attempted to build a coalition of congregations each consisting of first-generation immigrants. Besides the Italian parishes he had personally formed, he initiated work and consecrated bishops for Polish, Lithuanian, Portuguese, Ukrainian, and Mexican parishes. His strongest support came from West Indian blacks, among whom he supervised work led by H. A. Rogers. The work that Carfora built proved most unstable. The black parishes were the largest group to remain with him until his death.

In the years after World War II, Carfora began talks with several different Orthodox churches on the possibility of uniting his church with an Orthodox body as a Western rite diocese. The most promising offer came from the Ukrainians, but Carfora turned them down when they refused to guarantee his role as bishop. Thirty-two parishes, however, left Carfora's jurisdiction and joined the Ukrainian Orthodox Church.

During the last years of his life, Carfora suffered from both asthma and heart-trouble. In 1953, on a visit to parishes in Texas, he developed pneumonia and was taken to a Roman Catholic hospital in Galveston. While there, pressure for him to renounce his work was applied, and his episcopal ring, the sign of his office, was stolen and destroyed. Although he recovered enough to return to Chicago, he retired and turned over the governance of the church to Bishop Rogers. He remained archbishop in name only for the remaining five years of his life.

Carfora's main legacy to American religion was in creating (partially unwittingly) many independent Catholic jurisdictions. Records indicate that he consecrated more than fifty men to the episcopacy, only a few of whom remained in communion with him, much less under his jurisdiction, at the time of his death. Most left to form rival jurisdictions to the North American Old Roman Catholic Church, which is today a small body made up primarily of the remnants of the West Indian parishes.

Carmel Henry Carfora, *Historical and Doctrinal Sketch of the Old Roman Catholic Church* (Chicago, 1950).

Jonathan Trela, *A History of the North American Old Roman Catholic Church* (Scranton, Pa., 1979).

Peter Anson, *Bishops at Large* (London, 1964).

Karl Pruter and J. Gordon Melton, *The Old Catholic Sourcebook* (New York, 1983).

CARUS, Paul (July 18, 1852, Ilsenburg, Germany—February 11, 1919, La Salle, Illinois); married Mary Hegler, March 29, 1888; education: University of Greifswald, University of Strassburg; University of Tübingen, Ph.D., 1876.

Although German-born philosopher Paul Carus never became a Buddhist, he initiated and supported many early efforts to spread Buddhism in America and became a major force in its development. Carus came from a family of distinguished scholars. His father was the First Superintendent of the Church of Eastern and Western Prussia. Carus was given the best education possible, and after receiving his doctorate, he accepted a position at the military academy of Dresden. His views were too liberal, however, and the school forced his resignation. He journeyed to America and eventually settled in Illinois.

In 1887 Edward G. Hegler, a Chicago zinc manufacturer began a journal, *Open Court*, and selected Carus, who had contributed several philosophical articles, to edit the magazine. The following year Carus married Hegler's daughter. The success of the magazine led to the founding of a second periodical, *The Monist*, which handled the more technical philosophical works, and the publication of books, many written by Carus.

The work at Open Court Publishing Company allowed an outlet for Carus's developing philosophical position. He had discarded the Christian orthodoxy of his youth and had become a monist. He believed that the laws of nature and the laws of the mind were identical and that philosophy could become the same objective discipline as science. He saw God as the impersonal world order and believed individuals survived death only through the influence of their lives.

His philosophical position also gave Carus an openness to Buddhism. He appreciated Buddhism as a nonsupernatural religion, not based on miracles or a personal deity. He thought that on a practical level it could be the best tool for healing the split between science and religion and for uniting all the major world religions. Carus saw in Buddhism the essence of what was best in Christianity.

Buddhism made its first major appearance in America at the 1893 World Parliament of Religions in Chicago. Carus attended and met the two Buddhist delegates, Anagarika Dharmapala, founder of the Maha Bodhi Society, and Soyen Shaku, a Zen monk. Though he did not believe that raising money for the restoration of a Buddhist shrine, the goal of the Maha Bodhi Society, was the best way to approach Americans with Buddhism, he agreed to start and head the American section of the society. He also planned an 1896 national tour for Dharmapala, whose work was well publicized in the *Open Court*.

Soyen Shaku had stayed with Carus at his home in LaSalle, Illinois. Through correspondence with Carus, Shaku kept alive his vision of America as a mission field and arranged the move of D. T. Suzuki to LaSalle. Suzuki lived with Carus from 1897 to 1909, during which time he wrote his first books and worked with Carus on the translation of several oriental classics, beginning with *Tao Te Ching*.

After the World Parliament, Carus emerged as the first major sympathetic American voice for Buddhism. His *The Gospel of Buddha* (1894) was hailed by Buddhists as a true presentation of their religion in English. It was translated into many languages, including Japanese and Chinese.

The Gospel of Buddha became Carus's most widely read and remembered work. He wrote several other Buddhist books, such as *Karma, A Story of Buddhist Ethics* (1894), *Buddhism and Its Christian Critics* (1899), and *The Dharma* (1906), and assisted in the translation of many Chinese and Japanese texts. Some of his poems were set to music and included in the English-language hymnal of the Buddhist Churches of America. All the while he continued to edit two magazines, manage a publishing company, and write a variety of books on various religious and philosophical topics. *A Study of Fallacies of Agnosticism* (1899), *The History of the Devil* (1900), *Chinese Thought* (1907), and *The Foundation of Mathematics* (1908) are but a few of the more than fifty books he wrote that illustrate his broad interests and accomplishments.

Paul Carus, *The Gospel of Buddha* (Chicago, 1894).

———, *The Dharma* (Chicago, 1906).

———, *Karma, A Story of Buddhist Ethics* (Chicago, 1894).

———, *The Canon of Reason and Virtue* (Chicago, 1913).

———, *The Dawn of a New Religious Era* (Chicago, 1916).

William Peiris, *The Western Contribution to Buddhism* (Delhi, 1973), 251–55.

Rick Fields, *How the Swans Came to the Lake* (Boulder, Colo., 1981).

DRB, 93.

WWW, I, 201.

CAYCE, Edgar (March 18, 1877, near Hopkinsville, Kentucky—January 3, 1945, Virginia Beach, Virginia); married Gertrude Evans, June 17, 1903 (d. April 1, 1945).

Edgar Cayce, clairvoyant diagnostician and founder of the Association for Research and Enlightenment, was born in rural Kentucky, the son of a small-town businessman. The family were members of the Christian Church (Disciples of Christ). Cayce had only a grammar school education and seemed destined for an unspectacular life in photography, his chosen profession. A series of events beginning in 1900, however, changed the course of his life.

Cayce caught a cold and developed laryngitis. The loss of voice remained, and a year later Cayce had accepted the possibility that he would never speak above a raspy whisper. Then an acquaintance tried hypnosis. He went into a trance and, under the guidance of the hypnotist's questions, diagnosed his own condition and prescribed a cure. Gradually he was healed. As news of the occurrence spread, neighbors asked Cayce to read for them.

In 1903 he moved to Bowling Green, Kentucky. The six years there were marred by a fire that left him in debt. His last three years were spent in paying off his losses. In 1909, just prior to a move to Alabama, he met Dr. Wesley Ketchum, a homeopathic physician in his hometown. He accurately diagnosed Ketchum's physical condition. Healed of his problem, Ketchum, during the time Cayce was in Alabama, publicized his experience to both his medical colleagues and the press. After a year in Alabama, Cayce was induced by Ketchum to return to Hopkinsville and begin daily readings for the sick. The partnership did not last long, however, and Cayce returned to his photography business in Alabama. He still gave occasional readings and even attempted to use his ability to find oil in Texas (without success).

In 1923 Arthur Lammers, a Theosophist and student of the occult and Eastern religion, persuaded Cayce to come to Ohio to do readings on metaphysical issues. These readings first opened the issue of reincarnation, and Cayce began to explore the previous reincarnations of individuals. After these initial sessions, Cayce gave not only health readings but life readings in which he discussed the prior earth incarnations of individual clients. He closed his Alabama studio and moved to Dayton.

In 1925 Cayce made a final move, to Virginia Beach. Backed by a wealthy businessman, Morton Blumenthal, Cayce formed an association and formulated plans for a Cayce Hospital, which opened in 1928. Two years later Atlantic University was added to the expanded complex. Unfortunately, Blumenthal's business failed in 1931, and without his support both hospital and university were lost. In response, the family and a few supporters formed the Association for Research and Enlightenment. Its main activities were the facilitating of Cayce's daily readings and the issuance of a newsletter to members. In 1932 the first gathering of the association was held, and the organization grew slowly but steadily. In 1940 a wing was added to the Cayce home to serve as an office. Cayce continued to give readings until he collapsed from exhaustion in August 1944. He died the following year.

Cayce's ability to put himself into a trance state and give psychic readings was by no means unique. Known as traveling clairvoyance, it was widely and successfully practiced by a number of psychics in the nineteenth century, for example, Sleeping Lucy Cook of Montpelier, Vermont, who claimed to have read for over two hundred thousand people and opened a store to sell the medicines she prescribed. Cayce's uniqueness came from the stenographic records kept of his readings for over two decades. These extensive records became a vast library for research after Cayce's death.

In succeeding years the A.R.E. was reorganized. A private Edgar Cayce Foundation was formed to take ownership of and preserve the Cayce papers. The A.R.E. is an open-membership organization of people interested in the teachings derived from Cayce's work. The A.R.E. Press is the publishing arm.

Cayce's teaching closely resembles Theosophy, which Cayce slowly absorbed from the people around him, and emphasizes karma and reincarnation. The A.R.E. also places much emphasis on preventive medicine and the use of specific remedies prescribed in the readings.

Edgar Cayce, *The Edgar Cayce Reader*, Vol. I (1969), Vol. II (1969).

Thomas Sugrue, *There Is a River* (New York, 1942).

Hugh Lynn Cayce, *Venture Inward* (New York, 1966).

Joseph Millard, *Edgar Cayce* (Greenwich, Conn., 1967).

Anne E. Neimark, *With This Gift* (New York, 1978).

EOP, 152.

WWW, 4, 163.

COLLIN, Michel (1905, Beachy, France—June 23, 1974, Nancy, France); education: University of Metz, University of Lille.

Michel Collin, the self-proclaimed Pope Clement XV and founder of the Apostles of Infinite Love, grew up in a small town in France. At the age of seven, he had a revelation from God in which he was told that he would be first a priest, then a bishop, and eventually the pope. During his childhood and youth, he became a visionary and had frequent conversations with Jesus and the Virgin Mary.

After finishing his education, he was ordained a Roman Catholic priest in 1933. He proceeded to create two missionary orders, the Apostles of Infinite Love and the White Phalanx. Beginning in 1942, he sent more than 300 typewritten pages recounting his visions to Pope Pius XII. In these he claimed that he had been mystically consecrated a bishop by Jesus on April 28, 1935, at Vaux-le-Metz.

The Holy Office took guarded notice of this radical visionary for a decade. Then on October 7, 1950, he claimed to have been mystically elevated to the papacy by God at Sorrento. He further claimed that his becoming pope was part of the third secret revealed to the children in 1917 at Fatima, Portugal, by the Virgin Mary. The church moved swiftly and on January 7, 1951, condemned Collin for false mysticism and the propagation of a false and superstitious cult. It laicized him.

Collin did not stop functioning, and claimed that on March 25, 1961, at Aix-la-Chapelle, Jesus had revealed to him the secret of Fatima and had ordered him to begin functioning as Pope Clement XV concurrently with Pope John XXIII. The papal name was descriptive of Collin, a mild, clement person with a devotion to the fifteen mysteries of the rosary.

Clement moved to Clemery in Lorraine and converted a farmhouse into Le Petit Vatican de Marie Coredemptrice. He began a monthly newsletter, *La Verité*. He opened a hotel in Pont-a-Mousson, a nearby village, to accommodate pilgrims. By the time of his death he had found some 8,000 followers primarily in France, Switzerland, and Germany, including the faithful from Belgium, Luxembourg, and Holland.

He built a hierarchy headed by twelve male cardinals. Bishops included both men and women. Priests included children, but only in cases where both parents were also priests. Priests could, obviously, marry.

Collin's movement crossed the Atlantic in the 1960s when Father Jean, a French Canadian who had built an independent monastic movement headquartered at St. Jovite, Quebec, heard of Collin. He sent a priest to investigate. After a favorable report, Father Jean allowed Clement to ordain and then consecrate him a bishop. Meanwhile, in 1965, Clement had been consecrated by Archbishop Cyprian Camge, leader of one of several Old Catholic bodies that trace their orders to Archbishop Joseph René Vilatte. The Canadians did not stay under Clement's control for long, however, for in 1968 they broke out from his authority, and Father Jean declared himself Pope Gregory XVII.

While stormy relations with the Canadians proceeded, an American priest in Rome, Father John Higgins, heard of Clement, became his follower, and eventually was consecrated by Clement in 1969. The next year he was invited to head the Parish of St. Joseph in Cicero, Illinois. After Clement's death, Higgins broke relations with his French followers, and since that time his parish has been Clement's only outpost in North America.

Clement departed from Catholic doctrine on several major points. He believed that the Virgin Mary was a part of the Trinity and a co-redeemer with Christ. He also taught that the secret of Fatima prophesied that from 1960 "There shall be no more conclaves for the election of the Pope," and in the future each Pope shall select his own successor. Clement believed that John XXIII had secretly selected Clement to succeed him to the papal office. (Higgins has recognized no successor to Clement, although there are several claimants in France.)

Michel Collin, "Self-Styled 'Pope' Dies in France," *Chicago Tribune*, June 24, 1974.

Denis Hart, "Revelations in a French Farmhouse," *The Critic*, XXXII, 6 (July–September 1974), 26–33.

COOPER, Irving Steiger (March 16, 1882, Santa Barbara, California— January 17, 1935, Hollywood, California); married Susan L. Warfield, April 8, 1927; education: University of California.

Irving Steiger Cooper, the first Regionary Bishop of the Liberal Catholic Church in the United States, was born and raised in California and graduated from the University of California. Soon after graduation he was introduced to Theosophy. He became an avid student and within a few years was a national lecturer for the society. In 1911 he attended the annual meeting of the society and remained in India, where he became the secretary of Charles W. Leadbeater, an Anglican priest and leader of the Theosophical Society at its international headquarters in Adyar.

In 1915 several priests and one bishop had left the jurisdiction of British Old Catholic Bishop Arnold H. Mathew, who had demanded all priests within his jurisdiction to withdraw from the Theosophical Society. The bishop, F. S. Willoughby, consecrated two of the priests, Robert King and Rupert Gauntlett. The new bishops and their supporters reorganized as the Old Catholic Church on February 13, 1916, and elected James Ingall Wedgwood their first Presiding Bishop. After his consecration, Wedgwood traveled to Australia and consecrated Leadbeater (who had moved to Sydney in 1914), who in turn established the Australian branch of the Liberal Catholic Church, as the new church was renamed.

Meanwhile in India, Cooper wrote his first books on Theosophy: *Methods of Psychic Development* (1912); *Theosophy Simplified* (1915); and *Reincarnation* (1917). After the formation of the Liberal Catholic Church in Australia, he moved to Sydney as a lecturer for the Theosophical Society. Through his admiration for Leadbeater, he became quickly involved in the Liberal Catholic Church and was consecrated a priest in 1918. He assisted Wedgwood and Leadbeater in the editing of *The Liturgy of the Mass* (1917), the church's first liturgical work, and its revision, which appeared the next year as *The Liturgy of the Holy Eucharist.*

Wedgwood traveled to the United States in 1917 and ordained the first three priests of the Liberal Catholic Church, one each in Chicago, Los Angeles, and New York. He added a fourth the next year. Wedgwood then selected Cooper to head the church in the United States and on July 13, 1919, at St. Alban's in Sydney, assisted by Leadbeater, consecrated Cooper and named him Regionary Bishop for the United States.

Cooper began his duties in 1920. He established himself at Krotona, the Theosophical community that had been formed in Hollywood. His first project was the erection of a Pro-Cathedral. He raised the money, and St. Alban's was built adjacent to Krotona. For many years it was the headquarters of Liberal Catholicism in the United States.

During the 1920s Cooper traveled the country on behalf of the small church. He also continued his strong support of the Theosophical Society. In 1926 he toured with Annie Besant and Krishnamurti in their efforts to promote Krishnamurti as the Coming World Teacher. In 1928 the church had grown to the point that a first Provincial Convocation could be called. At that gathering held at St. Alban's, a constitution was adopted and the American corporation created.

Cooper continued as Regionary Bishop until his death in 1935, though he was forced into a semiretirement from 1930 to 1933 as a result of a prolonged illness. In 1934 he published his major work, *Ceremonies of the Liberal Catholic Rite*, a thorough revision of the church's liturgy, on which he had worked for many years. It remains the standard liturgy for the church.

Irving S. Cooper, *Ceremonies of the Liberal Catholic Rite* (Los Angeles, 1934).

———— , *Methods of Psychic Development* (Adyar, India, 1912).

———— , *The Secret of Happiness* (Chicago, 1925).

———— , *Theosophy Simplified* (Wheaton, Ill., 1928).

Ubique, 4, 3 (March 1935), a memorial issue to Bishop Cooper.

WWW, 1, 259.

CRAWFORD, Florence Louise (September 1, 1872, Coos County, Oregon—June 20, 1936, Portland, Oregon); married Frank M. Crawford.

Florence Louise Crawford, founder of the Apostolic Faith Church of Portland, Oregon, was born to a family of freethinkers. Her parents often entertained prominent atheists passing through Oregon on lecture tours. She often sang at free-thought meetings during her early years. Her first contact with Christianity came when she and a friend slipped away from home and attended a camp meeting. Before she was converted, however, she married and bore a son, Raymond Robert (1900).

She dated her conversion from one evening while attending a ball. While on the dance floor, she heard a voice speak to her, which said, "Daughter give me thine heart." She realized that it was the voice of God. She left the dance and began a period of spiritual struggle that culminated in her visiting a friend some days later where she accepted God into her heart.

After her conversion she threw herself into a life of active Christian service. She became president of the California Women's Christian Temperance Union, visited in the jails, aided reform movements, and preached in the slums. She also developed a hunger for a deeper Christian experience. She had read of John Wesley and had come to believe in the experience of sanctification in which a person is made holy by the Spirit of God.

Eventually, in 1906 a Christian friend directed Mrs. Crawford to the group who were meeting at Azuza Street in Los Angeles. The small mission had become the scene of an interdenominational gathering at which the baptism of the Holy Spirit, as evidenced by the speaking in tongues, was being preached. Mrs. Crawford attended the meeting. One evening she experienced sanctification, and three days later received the baptism of the Holy Spirit.

Mrs. Crawford had been a sickly person. She had had three attacks of spinal meningitis, which had affected her eyes. She also had lung trouble and wore a harness from a childhood fall. Shortly after receiving the baptism of the Holy Spirit, she was completely healed of all her bodily defects.

Mrs. Crawford began to work at the mission on Azuza Street and was appointed State Director by William J. Seymour, the pastor. In that capacity she traveled to Oakland and San Francisco to spread the word of the Pentecostal revival. Then, in the fall of 1906, she received a call to broaden the scope of her work. In December she traveled to Salem, Oregon, to speak at a meeting. From there she was invited to come to Portland, Oregon, and take charge of a small mission that had been set up in a refurbished blacksmith shop. She moved to Portland in 1907 and began holding meetings each evening. The response was immediate, and by the following fall the group had outgrown their facilities and was forced to move.

While centering her work in Portland, Mrs. Crawford traveled widely and held meetings as far away as Minneapolis and St. Paul, Minnesota, and Winnipeg, Canada. She established the Apostolic Faith Church (a name first used by Charles Parham, who began the modern Pentecostal movement) to administer her work. In 1908 the headquarters of the church were moved into the building at Front and Burnside streets in downtown Portland; for the rest of her life, the story is one of the building of a growing international Pentecostal church.

In 1908 Mrs. Crawford's son was converted and two years later was ordained to the ministry. He became her major assistant and, at the time of her death, moved from his position of assistant overseer to general overseer.

The same call that brought Mrs. Crawford to Oregon had convinced her that she had a worldwide ministry. In the summer of 1908, during the annual camp meeting, she issued the first copies of *The Apostolic Faith*, the church's newspaper. She had brought the mailing list of the California mission with her when she moved to Portland. Before the year was out both Norwegian and German editions were being produced. In 1911 the first missionary established a church in Sweden, and work began in Norway the following year.

In 1913 work began among sailors on the waterfront of Portland. The converted seamen soon were taking the Apostolic Faith around the world. In 1919 Mrs. Crawford's son began a ministry with an airplane purchased by the church. It was used to spread the Gospel in the Northwest through the distribution of literature and helped unite the church's congregations.

By the time of her death in 1936, Mrs. Crawford headed a strong Pentecostal body with congregations in the northwestern United States and Canada and mission work in each of the Scandinavian countries.

The Life That Brought Triumph (Portland, Ore., 1955).

The Apostolic Faith (Portland, Ore., 1965).

Saved to Serve (Portland, Ore., 1967).

CROWLEY, Aleister (October 12, 1875, Leamington, Warwickshire, England—December 1, 1947, Hastings, England); married Rose Edith Kelly, August 12, 1903 (div. 1909); married Maria Theresa Ferrari de Miramar, August 16, 1929; education: King's College, London, 1894–95; Trinity College, Cambridge, 1894–97.

Aleister Crowley, the most renowned magical practitioner and theoretician of the twentieth century, was born Edward Alexander Crowley. His parents were members of the Exclusive Plymouth Brethren, the separatist fundamentalist Christian body founded by John Nelson Darby, and his father was a preacher for the group. Crowley rebelled against his strict upbringing and earned the label "The Beast 666" (from Revelation 13:18) given by his mother. In 1887 his father died, and young Crowley spent the next seven years in a series of public schools. In 1894 he entered King's College and the following year attended Trinity College, Cambridge, but failed to finish his degree.

Crowley's college days were dominated by poetry, at which he showed some real talent; sex; and the growing pursuit of magic and the occult. Having been introduced to magic through his books, he eagerly took the opportunity to join the Hermetic Order of the Golden Dawn after meeting a member, George Cecil Jones. He was initiated in 1898. In magic, Crowley found his true calling, and he progressed within the order quickly. His progress was blunted, however, by his involvement in the battles between S. L. MacGregor Mathers, the Outer Head of the Order who resided in Paris, and the British members. As the warfare heated, Crowley abruptly left England and began a period of traveling. He made his first visit to the United States at this time.

With his new bride, Crowley traveled to Cairo, Egypt, for his first major magical accomplishment. At his wife's insistence, he sat for three days (April 9–11, 1904) to receive material from a spirit entity, Aiwass. *The Book of the Law*, as Aiwass's dictation was called, became the basis of Crowley's new system of magic, "Thelema" (from the Greek word for *will*). Its basic tenet was "Do what thou will shall be the whole of the law." Crowley taught that the magician's goal was to discern his true will (or destiny); once discerned, he could do ought but follow it.

In 1907 Crowley founded his own magical order, the Argenteum Astrum (Silver Star) and, two years later, began issuing his first major magical work, the *Equinox*, a semiannual periodical. It included not only the teachings of his order but revealed much of the secret material of the Golden Dawn.

The progress of the A.A. was halted in 1912 when Crowley met Theodore Ruess, head of a German magical order, the Ordo Templi Orientis (O.T.O). Crowley was accepted into the highest levels of the O.T.O. and organized a British branch called the Mysteria Mystica Maxima. The O.T.O. taught a form of sex magic derived in part from the teachings of American Rosicrucian Pascal Beverly Randolph. Crowley accepted Ruess's invitation to rewrite the order's rituals. The O.T.O. had previously created ten degrees, including ones for the practice of autoerotic (VIII°) and heterosexual (IX°) sex magic. Crowley's new rituals added an experimental degree for homosexual (anal intercourse) magic (XI°) which he initiated in 1913.

In 1914 Crowley journeyed to America where he spent the war years. During his five-year stay, he carried out his first set of IX^0 workings. As a result of his magical accomplishment during this period he declared himself a magus, the second highest grade of magical attainment. He also established in Vancouver, British Columbia, under Frater Achad (Charles Stansfeld Jones), the most stable lodge the O.T.O. possessed during his lifetime. After Achad left the O.T.O., his successor Wilfred Smith moved the Vancouver Lodge to Pasadena, California, and continued the work as the Agape Lodge, which lasted into the 1950s.

Crowley left America for Sicily in 1919 and established the Abbey of Thelema at Cefalu. During workings there, he attained the highest magical grade, ipsissimus. Kicked out of Italy by Mussolini in 1923, he resided first in Tunis and then France, before returning to England for the last fifteen years of his life. By this time he had become a heroin addict, a condition he unsuccessfully fought for many years.

Crowley was succeeded by Karl Germer, under whom the O.T.O. languished. It all but died during the 1960s. However, during the 1970s the

O.T.O. experienced a remarkable revival and by the 1980s three rival branches, the largest of which is headed by Grady McMurtry in Berkeley, California, were functioning in the United States. The O.T.O.'s reemergence coincided with a revival of interest in Crowley's writings, most of which were reprinted in new editions.

Aleister Edward Crowley, *Confessions* (New York, 1969).

——— , *Magick in Theory and Practice* (New York, 1965).

——— , *Magick without Tears* (St. Paul, Minn., 1973).

——— , *The Holy Books of Thelema* (York Beach, Me., 1983).

Will Parfitt and A. Drylie, *A Crowley Cross-Index* (New York, 1976).

C. R. Cammell, *Aleister Crowley* (London, 1969).

Francis King, *The Magical World of Aleister Crowley* (New York, 1978).

Susan Roberts, *The Magician of the Golden Dawn* (Chicago, 1978).

EOP, 204.

CUMMINS, George David (December 11, 1822, Smyrna, Delaware— June 25, 1876, Lutherville, Maryland); married Alexandrine McComb, June 24, 1847 (d. April 1900); education: Dickinson College, 1836–41, B.A.

George David Cummins, founder and first bishop of the Reformed Episcopal church, had a diverse religious background. His father died when he was four, and seven years later he was sent to a boarding school in Newark, New Jersey, managed by a Presbyterian clergyman. At the age of fourteen he entered Dickinson College with the intention of pursuing a law career. His law education ended in his seventeenth year during a revival at the college. He had a conversion experience and decided to enter the ministry. From the Methodist school, he joined the Baltimore Conference of the Methodist Episcopal Church. In 1842 he was appointed to the Bladensburg circuit and in 1843 to Charleston, West Virginia.

In July 1845 he left the Methodists and joined the Protestant Episcopal Church. He was confirmed and ordained to the diaconate in October. In the spring of 1846 he became assistant minister of Christ Church in Baltimore, the beginning of an outstanding career in the church. In 1847 he began a six-year stay as rector of Christ Church, Norfolk, Virginia. He was married and ordained as a priest the same year.

During the next two decades, Cummins served St. James, Richmond, Virginia; Trinity Church, Washington, D.C.; St. Peter's Church, Baltimore, Maryland; and Trinity Church, Chicago. Then in June 1866, while he was on a trip to Europe recovering from a period of illness, he was elected Assistant Bishop for Kentucky. He was consecrated bishop in November in ceremonies at Louisville.

Although Cummins had left the Methodist Episcopal Church, he brought much of Methodism with him and had become identified with the evangelical, or Low Church, party within the Episcopal Church. At the general convention in 1868, he spoke strongly for keeping the Episcopal Church aligned to the Reformation and opposed the growing emphasis upon liturgy and attention to Roman Catholicism.

For Cummins, the issue of High Church versus Low Church came to a focus in October 1873. He addressed the Evangelical Alliance meeting in

New York City and on Sunday, October 12, took part in a joint communion service in one of the Presbyterian churches. His participation led to a strong reaction and protest. In face of the protest, he decided that attempts to stop the growing "errors" he saw creeping into the Episcopal Church were useless and he withdrew. With his small band of supporters, he organized the Reformed Episcopal Church in New York City on December 2, 1873.

The new church continued Low Church Episcopalianism but altered the church government at several key points. It declared the bishopric a part of the order of presbyter and not a separate order of ministry. It did away with the House of Bishops and placed ultimate authority in the general council, over which the bishop presided.

During the three remaining years of his brief life, Cummins dealt with all the problems faced by the new communion, including a series of lawsuits over use of parish property. Several days after the founding, he consecrated Charles Edward Chaney as a bishop of the church. As a mere formality, in June 1874, Cummins was formally deposed from the ministry of the Protestant Episcopal Church.

Cummins lived to see the Reformed Episcopal Church become a national body (though it has never grown to a point to rival its parent body). He died at his home after a brief illness.

Anne Darling Price, A History of the Formation and Growth of the Reformed Episcopal Church, 1873–1902 (Philadelphia, 1902).

Paul A. Carter, "The Reformed Episcopal Schism of 1873: An Ecumenical Perspective," Historical Magazine of the Protestant Episcopal Church, XXXIII, 3 (September 1964), 225–38.

WWWH, 130.

CUTLER, Alpheus (February 29, 1784, Plainfield, New Hampshire—August 10, 1864, Manti, Iowa); married Lois Lantrop, 1808.

Alpheus Cutler, founder of one of the "reorganized" branches of the Church of Jesus Christ of Latter-day Saints (Mormon), was raised on a farm but became a stone mason and architect. Shortly after his marriage he moved to Upper Lisle, New York. He fought in the War of 1812 as a captain under General Winfield Scott. In the 1820s he moved to Chautauqua County, New York, where he was to eventually meet with members of the Church of Jesus Christ of Latter-day Saints.

In 1832 some Mormons came through Chautauqua County, and Cutler allowed them to hold a meeting in his house. During the course of this meeting, his seriously ill daughter, Lois, was healed and professed belief in the Mormon message. Her healing led to Alpheus's joining the church also. He was baptized January 20, 1833, and soon moved to Kirkland, Ohio, to assist in the building of the temple. While there he was ordained an elder. After the dedication of the temple, Cutler was licensed to preach and was sent on a preaching mission to Iowa.

In 1839 Cutler moved his family to Ray County, Missouri, adjacent to the Mormon settlement at Far West, where he operated a grist mill. While there, he barely escaped the mob violence that followed the Mormons wherever they tried to settle. He was to be the chief architect of the temple at Far West, but the project was only begun before the group moved to Nauvoo, Illinois.

After Cutler moved to Nauvoo in 1839, he became a member of the High Council and the next year was appointed by Joseph Smith to serve on the committee to build the temple. He worked in the tithing office and collected the materials donated by the members for the project. He had final approval on the plans as they developed.

During his years at Nauvoo, his key role in the church is shown by his various appointments. In 1843 he was ordained to the prophetic office by Smith as one of a Quorum of Seven who would carry on should anything happen to their Prophet. He headed Smith's personal bodyguard and after Smith's murder in the jail at Carthage, he helped bury him. He was also put in charge of one of the emigration companies when the church was forced out of Nauvoo.

In 1846 he left with the main body of the church in the move to Council Bluffs, Iowa. While there he joined with those who opposed the doctrinal innovations of Brigham Young. In 1847 he went on a mission to the Indians in Kansas and stayed for five years, and so he did not take part in the migration of the main body of the church to Utah. He returned to Iowa in 1852 and contacted a small group of Mormons who had settled at Big Grove, Iowa. Within a few weeks the group established a settlement at Manti, Iowa.

In the 1850s members of the church who had not moved to Utah were still engaged in discussions of the future course they should take or which claimants to leadership they should follow. In 1853 Cutler had a vision of two crescent moons with their backs together. He shared his vision with the others at Manti and claimed that it was a sign told him by Joseph Smith that he should reorganize the church. He based his authority on the 1843 ordination to the Quorum of Seven. He noted that each of the others ordained with him was dead and not one had exercised his authority.

He reorganized the church on September 19, 1853, and rebaptized those present. His movement grew slowly and peaked in membership in 1859 with 183 members. About half of these were lost the next year to the reorganized church headed by Joseph Smith, III. By this time Cutler's health had failed, and he soon died. In 1865 the entire group moved to Minnesota and finally settled in the small community of Clitherall. In the 1920s a second branch of the church was founded in Independence, Missouri. It survives as one of the smaller of the Mormon bodies.

Daisy Whiting Fletcher, *Alpheus Cutler and the Church of Jesus Christ* (Independence, Mo., 1970).

Russell Rich, *Those Who Would Be Leaders* (Provo, Utah, 1967), 49–51.

DARBY, John Nelson (November 18, 1800, Westminster, Ireland—April 29, 1883, Bournemouth, England); education: Trinity College, Dublin, graduated 1819.

John Nelson Darby, the most influential of the several men who could be considered founders of what has come to be called the Plymouth

Brethren, was the son of a well-to-do Irish landowner from King's County (now Offaly County). He graduated from college at the age of nineteen as the Classical Gold Medallist and seemed destined for a law career. He was called to the bar in 1822, but, in the meantime, he had experienced a religious conversion and had decided to become an Anglican priest. He was ordained deacon in 1825 and priest in 1826. He was appointed priest of the curacy in the county of Wicklow, a rural parish in mountainous country.

In 1827 he was thrown from a horse and required a long period of convalescence, some of which he spent at his brother-in-law's home in Dublin. During his stay at Wicklow, Archbishop McGee of Dublin issued a demand that all converts from Roman Catholicism also take an oath of allegiance to the British crown. In response, Darby penned his first writing, an open letter criticizing the archbishop and the church for being subservient to the state. This letter was the first manifestation of Darby's concerns for the issues of ecclesiology. During his period of convalescence, however, these issues came to the fore. While in Dublin he became aware of several loosely connected groups of individuals who had separated from both the Church of England and other dissenting groups. He resigned his curacy (though not his relation to the Church of England) and began to meet with a small group to study the Bible and break bread.

Darby's relationship to these brethren led to his first publication, a pamphlet, *On the Nature and Unity of the Church*, in which he stressed the need for an expression of the unity of the church. He found the proposals of interdenominational cooperation or the union of existing church bodies inadequate. The church must be one in mind, united in Christ, and open to all true believers. Its symbol of unity would be the Lord's Supper. Although he remained a priest in the Church of England for many years to come, Darby had essentially set a direction that would lead to the formation of a body that would seek unity outside of denominational Christianity.

In 1830 Darby traveled to England at the invitation of Francis Newman, brother of Cardinal-to-be J. H. Newman, where he met B. W. Newton and George V. Wigram. In 1832 the three formed a congregation centered upon the chapel at Plymouth, England, which Wigram had previously opened as a preaching center. From this congregation the movement would receive its popular though unofficial designation as the Plymouth Brethren. Wigram soon moved to London, and Darby began a career of traveling on behalf of the Brethren and writing. Thus Newton was left in charge.

Darby traveled widely through Britain and Ireland holding Bible study groups and forming and nurturing Brethren congregations. In 1839 he traveled to Switzerland and spent five years initiating the movement there. Returning to England in 1944, Darby went to Plymouth, where trouble was reported. During his stay there he came into open conflict with Newton whom he accused of clericalism—that is, the attempt to have himself and a few others vested with the role as leaders apart from the members of the congregation. He also accused Newton of departing from orthodox Christology. The conflict led to a break in fellowship, and Darby's supporters withdrew from Newton, as did the remainder of the Brethren. The schism at Plymouth, minor in itself, led to a major split within the Brethren movement. The congregation at Bethesda admitted members of Newton's congregation to the Lord's Supper on the grounds that the members were personally free from Newton's alleged doctrinal errors. The issue divided the movement into the Open Brethren, who agreed with Bethesda's action, and the Exclusive Brethren. The latter "excluded" those who took an "open" position from fellowshiping with them in the Lord's Supper. Darby was the dominant figure in the Exclusive Brethren, though the group functioned without designated officials.

Darby's travels brought him to North America six times, in 1862, 1864, 1866, 1872, 1874, and 1876. He also traveled extensively in Europe and made one trip to the Caribbean (1868) and to New Zealand (1875–76). He wrote voluminously on theological and biblical subjects and helped develop the dispensational approach to biblical interpretation.

Shortly before Darby's death, the Exclusive Brethren began splitting into a number of factions.

John Nelson Darby, *The Collected Works*, 34 volumes (Oak Park, Ill., 1971).

W. G. Turner, *John Nelson Darby* (London, 1944).

Hy. Pickering, *Chief Men Among the Brethren* (London, 1918).

F. Roy Coad, *A History of the Brethren Movement* (Exeter, 1968).

Napoleon Noel, *The History of the Brethren* (Denver, Colo., 1936).

DAVIS, Andrew Jackson (August 11, 1826, Blooming Grove, New York—January 13, 1910, Watertown, Massachusetts); married Della E. ("Katie"), July 1, 1848 (d. November 2, 1853); married Mary Robinson Love, 1855.

Andrew Jackson Davis, one of the founders of Spiritualism, was born into a poor farming family. His father supplemented his income with weaving and shoemaking and moved frequently during Davis's early life to find employment. Davis had little religious training and education. As a child he moved to Staatsburg (1828), Hyde Park (1832), and Poughkeepsie (1838), where he was apprenticed to a shoemaker in 1841.

In 1843 a phrenologist and mesmerist by the name of Grimes came to Poughkeepsie. Though he had little success with Davis, William Levingston, a local tailor who picked up the practice of mesmerism from Grimes, began to experiment with the teenage Davis. Davis not only moved into a deep hypnotic trance but proved to be clairvoyant. The experiments, which began on December 1, 1843, led to a life-changing vision by Davis on March 6, 1844.

Following a hypnotic session out of which Davis did not completely come, he wandered into the countryside. He communicated with two spirit entities identified as Emmanuel Swedenborg, the Swedish seer, and Galen, the ancient Greek physician. They instructed him in the art of healing and told him that he would become a light to the world.

After this visionary experience, Davis devoted all his magnetic trances to healing and diagnosis in a manner much like that later identified with Edgar Cayce. He and Levingston opened a clairvoyant clinic.

In 1845 Davis broke his relationship with Levingston and teamed with Dr. S. S. Lyon of Bridgeport, Connecticut. They moved to New York City, and with the help of Rev. William Fishbough of New Haven, they began to receive information from the spirit world. The three met regularly from November 28, 1845, to January 25, 1847. The information that Davis dictated became his first book, *The Principles of Nature* (1847). Davis and Lyon also opened a clinic.

During 1847 Davis began to gather a group of followers around him. He began a periodical, *The Univercoelum* (1847–49). He also discovered he did not need the assistance of a magnetizer to move into a trance. He could do it at will and remember what occurred for later recording. He thus began writing his most significant work, *The Great Harmonia*, which was to be published in five volumes from 1850 to 1855, and to go through forty editions and/or printings.

At the very beginning of his movement, he underwent a major loss of support because of a scandal. He had come to believe in the doctrine of spiritual affinity, namely, that men and women should seek a mate who was their spiritual counterpart. That mate was rarely the one to whom they were married. Davis found his to be a married woman. His relationship to her caused many, including Rev. Thomas Lake Harris, then pastor of a Swedenborgian church in New York City, and S. B. Brittan, the editor of *The Univercoelum*, to withdraw their support. The woman, who eventually became Davis's wife, had underwritten the publication of *The Principles of Nature*.

After Brittan's departure, Davis lent his support to the *Spirit Messenger*, being published in Springfield, Massachusetts, and in 1860 the *Herald of Progress*. He continued to lecture and write and in 1886 earned a medical degree from the United States Medical College in New York. He settled in Boston where he practiced medicine and herbology and ran a bookstore. He retired on August 11, 1909, his eighty-third birthday, and died a few months later.

Davis's philosophy dominated Spiritualism in the nineteenth century. He spread a belief in God as the active moving principle in nature and originated the popular idea of Summer Land, the heaven where springtime and harvest-abundance are perpetual and to which the soul of the dead go at death.

Andrew Jackson Davis, *The Harmonial Philosophy* (Chicago, 1920).

———, *The Penetralia* (Boston, 1858).

———, *Events in the Life of a Seer* (Boston, 1873).

———, *A Stellar Key to the Summer Land* (Boston, 1867).

———, *The Magic Staff* (Rochester, 1910).

Slater Brown, *The Heyday of Spiritualism* (New York, 1970).

Frank Podmore, *Mediums of the 19th Century* (New Hyde Park, N.Y., 1963).

DRB, 124–5.

EOP, 213–15.

DAB III, 105.

DHARMAPALA, Anagarika (David Hewivitarne) (September 17, 1864, Columbo, Ceylon (now Sri Lanka)—April 29, 1933, Sarnath, India).

Anagarika Dharmapala, one of the founders of Buddhism in the United States and Europe, was born David Hewivitarne, to a middle-class Singalese family. His grandfather had donated the land for the first Buddhist monastic college in Ceylon. David inherited the strong devotion to Buddhism within his family and as a child regularly attended the Kotahena Temple near his home. He also listened to the anti-British polemics of Buddhists angered at attempts to Christianize Ceylon, then a British colony.

To give David the proper education, his Buddhist parents enrolled him in St. Benedict's Anglican School. Thus, at the age of ten, David began to attend church daily and, as part of his studies, memorized large portions of the Bible. After finishing at St. Benedict's, he proceeded to St. Thomas's Collegiate School. His years of schooling did nothing to convert him to Christianity; instead they served only to build his resentment to Christians, whom he saw as hypocrites, and the British. In 1883 he witnessed a riot caused by Christians attacking a Buddhist procession, and as a result he withdrew from St. Thomas's and continued his education in the library.

During this period he encountered the Theosophical Society, which had entered Ceylon and strongly identified itself with Buddhism. Dharmapala joined. He visited Madame Blavatsky, the founder of the society, in India and began a study of Pali, the tongue in which the original Buddhist books were written. In 1884 Colonel Olcott, the president of the Theosophical Society, persuaded the British Secretary of the Colonies to remove rules allowing marriages in Ceylon only in Christian churches and to designate Wesak (Buddha's birthday) as a holiday. He became an overnight hero in Ceylon, and during the next decade David vigorously assisted Olcott's efforts to raise money for Buddhist schools (an alternative to British Christian education) and to unite Buddhism. At this time he took the name by which he is generally known, meaning "homeless protector of the Dharma."

In 1888 he began the life of travel that made him known worldwide. He joined Olcott in a visit to Japan, though he reacted so badly to the winter that he spent much of the trip in bed. In 1891 he made a trip to Sarnath and Bodh-Gaya, where the Buddha received Enlightenment. He was horrified at the condition of the Buddhist sites, then under Hindu ownership. He dedicated himself to their restoration; upon his return to Columbo, on September 30, 1891, he organized the Bodh-Gaya Maha Bodhi Society and began to raise funds. In 1892 he began the *Maha Bodhi Journal*.

In 1893 Dharmapala spoke at the World Parliament of Religions in Chicago. He met Paul Carus of Open Court Publishing Company, who founded the American chapter of the Maha Bodhi Society. After the sessions of the World Parliament, at a meeting of the Theosophical Society in Chicago, he formally administered the Buddhist vows to C. T. Strauss, a Swiss visitor, who became the first Westerner to be formally accepted as a Buddhist. Upon his return trip to Ceylon he met

Mary E. Foster, a wealthy Hawaiian, who became his patron and contributed over one million ruples to his work over the next four decades. He returned to the United States in 1896–97. In the midst of his national lecture tour, in May 1897, he celebrated the first Wesak festival in the United States.

The remainder of his life was spent in traveling and writing on behalf of the Maha Bodhi Society. He made trips to America again in 1902–03 and 1925–26. On the later trip he also established the Maha Bodhi Society in England and began the *British Buddhist*. He made a separate trip to England in 1927 and celebrated the first Wesak there.

Dharmapala lived his life as a Buddhist layman, but on January 13, 1933, a group of Singalese monks ordained him as a *bhikkhu* (monk) at Sarnath, the first such ordination on Indian soil in over seven centuries. He took the name Sri Devamitta Dharmapala. He died a few months later. He left behind an international Buddhist organization and gave to the Buddhists of Ceylon a vision of Buddhist growth in the West that has made them among the most vigorous publishers of English-language Buddhist literature.

Anagarika Dharmapala, "The World's Debt to Buddha" and "Buddhism and Christianity" in J. W. Hanson, ed., *The World's Congress of Religions* (Chicago, 1894), 377–87, 413–16.

Rick Fields, *How the Swans Came to the Lake* (Boulder, Colo., 1981).

DINGLE, Edwin John (Ding Le Mei) (April 6, 1881, Paignton, Devonshire, England—January 27, 1972, Yucca Valley, California); married Marijane Dingle.

Edwin John Dingle, founder of the First Church of Mystic Christianity and the Institute of Mentalphysics, was raised in Cornwall. His father, a journalist, had died when Dingle was quite young, and he and his brother lived with his grandparents. As a youth, he was apprenticed to the owner of the newspaper and printshop in the town of Launceston and learned the newsman's trade. He became a journalist and in 1900 went to Singapore to cover the Orient.

While in Singapore he met a teacher, a guru, with whom he studied meditation and yoga. He then reached a point as a student when a pilgrimage was required before further teaching would be given. At about this same time he acquired an assignment to report on and assemble information about the geography of the interior of China. Thus, on February 22, 1909, he left Singapore for a year's expedition and pilgrimage across China. While in China he lived through the Chao-t'ong Rebellion, one of a series of anti-Western disturbances that shook China in the early twentieth century. He arrived in Burma in February 1910.

The trek across China had taken its toll on Dingle's health. He had caught malaria, and his first weeks in Burma were spent recovering his health. One day, while he was sick with fever, the guru appeared to him and told him to proceed to Tibet where teachers were waiting for him. As soon as he was able, he made an expedition to Tibet and for nine months lived in a monastery.

After the trip to Tibet, Dingle returned to England. He wrote two books on his experiences, *Across China on Foot* (1911) and *China's Revolution, 1911–12*. After several years he again went to China and established a publishing firm in Shanghai, the Far East Geographical Establishment. In 1914 he published the bilingual "New Map of China," the standard map of the area for many years. Four years later he published *Dingle's New Atlas and Commercial Gazetteer of China*. He began a weekly periodical, *China and the Far East Finance and Commerce*. In recognition of his accomplishments, the Royal Geographical Society made him a fellow.

In 1921 Dingle retired to Oakland, California. In 1927 he was asked to lecture in New York. After the lectures, seven people requested that he begin a class on what he had learned from his Eastern teachers. That class, which began November 7, 1927, is seen as the beginning of the Institute of Mentalphysics, though the incorporation did not occur until 1934.

"Mentalphysics," as Dingle termed his system, was the synthesis of all he had learned in the Orient. He saw it as a nondogmatic system that concentrated on meditation, *pranayana* (breathing), yoga, and other techniques for personal development. He also believed in vegetarianism. He emphasized truths he saw as basic to all religions: God's Universal Law, the universality and oneness of Life, and belief in the Omnipotent Creator of the Universe. In Los Angeles he established the International Church of the Holy Trinity (referring to the trinity of the Body, Mind, and Spirit of Man) to spread the inner teachings of the church, that is, the Science of Mentalphysics. Dingle taught group classes and gave private instruction. He developed a correspondence course, which was offered both nationally and internationally to those who could not attend classes at the center in Los Angeles.

The institute experienced considerable growth in the 1940s. A retreat center, now known as the Teaching and Spiritual Center, was purchased in 1941. In 1948 Dingle initiated the Preceptor Course to train leaders and instructors to assist him and carry on the work after his death. Dingle moved into semiretirement in 1968 and died in 1972. He was succeeded by Donald L. Waldrop, the present chancellor of the Institute of Mentalphysics.

Edwin J. Dingle, *Borderlands of Eternity* (Los Angeles, 1939).
——— , *The Art of True Living* (Los Angeles, 1937).
Key to the Mysteries of Life (Yucca Valley, Calif., n.d.).
——— , *The Voice of the Logos* (Los Angeles, 1950).
"Ding Le Mei Memorial Issue," *The Mansion Builder* (September 1972).
EOP, 240.

DIVINE, Father Major Jealous (circa 1889—September 10, 1965, Philadelphia, Pennsylvania); married Peninah (Sister Penny) (d. circa 1940); married Edna Rose Ritchings, April 29, 1946.

Prior to 1914 there is no verified record of the life of the person known as Father Major Jealous Divine. According to one story, he was born George Baker around 1880 on a rice plantation on Hutchinson Island in the Savannah River in Georgia. He was the son of sharecroppers. In 1899 he appeared in Baltimore as a gardener. He met Samuel Morris, an itinerant preacher who called himself Father Jehovia, and became his assistant. They split in 1912, and Baker, then known simply as the Messenger, developed his own following. In 1914 he was arrested in Valdosta, Georgia, as a public menace and ordered to leave the state.

According to another source he was born in Providence, Rhode Island, in 1880. Followers generally accept June 6, 1882, as the date of the marriage to his first wife.

All accounts agree, however, that he emerged in Brooklyn in 1914 as the head of a small group of followers. In 1919 he moved to Sayville, New York, on Long Island, and lived a quiet life with his followers. The home in which he lived was bought by his wife, known as Peninah or Sister Penny. He ran ads in the local papers offering to supply workers for various odd jobs around the home. By 1924 he had between thirty and forty followers, all black. By 1926 whites had joined the movement from the holiness churches and the New Thought and Christian Science movement.

Through the 1920s he began to be accepted by his followers as God. Many were impressed by the miraculous healings that were reported to have occurred. Others were drawn to him because of his seeming ability as a black man to withstand the forces of an oppressive society and even turn them to his own ends. Through 1931 his following grew steadily, a fact that led to the single most famous incident in his life.

On Sunday, November 15, 1931, police, in response to complaints about traffic congestion, arrested Father Divine for disturbing the peace. He pleaded not guilty and accused the police of racial discrimination. He was tried and convicted. In spite of the jury's asking leniency, the judge sentenced him to a year in jail. Two days later, the judge, without warning, died of a heart attack. Divine was reported to have remarked, "I hated to do it!" In any case, the incident made him a nationally known figure, and his followers regularly celebrate June 7, the day of the judge's death, by publishing accounts of death and suffering striking down people whose activities do not harmonize with Father Divine.

After Father Divine's conviction was reversed a few weeks later, he moved with his followers to Harlem, where the services he had offered members in Sayville were expanded, and in the midst of the Depression a national movement began to emerge. He offered members inexpensive food and shelter, opened an employment service, and daily demonstrated God's abundance with lavish banquets. He also taught his followers to work hard and expect a fair wage. When a person joined the movement he was told to pay off his debts, cancel insurance, return any stolen funds, and pay his own way.

As the movement grew, a number of hotels were purchased and transformed into "heavens." At these locations, anyone could get inexpensive lodging and food. His followers also organized a number of businesses that employed members.

In 1946 Father Divine married Edna Rose Ritchings, a Canadian, and their wedding day is a major holiday for the movement. In the 1940s Father Divine moved his headquarters to Philadelphia, and then in 1954 the Woodmont Estate in suburban Philadelphia was given to him. Termed the Mount of the House of the Lord, the estate became his home, and he was enshrined there after his death in 1965.

For the members of the International Peace Movement, which he founded, Father Divine is God. He considered the Peace Movement to be *the* Christian movement and all others but man-made organizations. The Peace Movement claims its role as the one family of God on earth because of its life of brotherhood, racial equality, liberty, and justice. Divine believed that each individual had a right to independence, a job, self-respect, and the recognition of Father Divine.

After his death, his wife, Mother Divine, became head of the Peace Mission.

Kenneth E. Burnham, *God Comes to America* (Boston, 1979).

Mother Divine, *The Peace Mission Movement* (Philadelphia, 1982).

Sara Harris, *Father Divine* (New York, 1971).

John Hoshor, *God in a Rolls Royce* (New York, 1936).

Robert Weisbrot, *Father Divine and the Struggle for Racial Equality* (Urbana, Ill., 1983).

DRB, 128–9.

DOW, Lorenzo (October 15, 1777, Coventry, Connecticut—February 2, 1834, Washington, D.C.); married Peggy Holcombe, September 3, 1804 (d. January 6, 1820); married Lucy Dolbeare, April 1, 1820.

Lorenzo Dow, the fiercely independent Methodist preacher, founded no church himself; however, his activity became the direct inspiration for the founding of a new form of Methodism in England. Primitive Methodism would eventually come to the United States to take its place among the many radical revivalist sects of the last century.

Dow was raised in New England. As a child he was a visionary and reported many dreams of a prophetic nature from which he received guidance. At the age of fourteen, he had a dream in which he visited heaven and from which he received his call to preach. He was also visited by an old man whom he later claimed was John Wesley.

When he was seventeen, Dow met the Methodists and was converted. He felt a call to preach but resisted. In 1793 he had two spells during which he lost both his strength and sight. He tried to preach. His parents did not approve, and the Methodists advised him to wait. Then he had a vision of the old man of his childhood, whom he now identified as John Wesley (the founder of Methodism). Wesley reiterated Dow's call to preach.

In 1796 Dow began to travel with an itinerant preacher. After several rebuffs by the Conference, he was finally licensed to preach. Appointed to a circuit in Canada, in 1799 he left his charge, without notice or permission, and traveled to Ireland. Dow spent a year trying to preach as he toured the land, but he met with little success. He almost died from smallpox, which left him badly scarred. His main accomplishment seemed to have been the absorption of a massive dislike for Roman Catholicism, of which he became a lifelong foe.

He returned to the United States in 1801, and, despite his having left his work, was accepted back into the connection on trial. His formal relationship to the church was short-lived, for he soon left again to begin a life as an itinerant preacher. His first tour was of the South. In 1802 he was in New York where he met Peggy Holcombe to whom his first words were a proposal of marriage, and hers, an acceptance. They married two years later. That same year he published the first edition of his *Journal*, which not only gave him a chance to answer his critics but brought him much fame. Soon after, he published *The Chains of Lorenzo*, in which he attacked Calvinism as leading naturally to atheism. Traveling without any denominational support, he was able to support himself through land speculation, a side business he carried on all his life. Also, as an able orator, he could always draw a crowd, and was content to leave his many converts for others to organize.

In November 1806 Dow crossed the Atlantic for a second time to visit England and Ireland. His former presiding elder, Nicholas Snethen, wrote letters to his British Methodist acquaintances and denounced Lorenzo. In spite of a cold reception in many quarters, Dow enjoyed a pronounced success with his preaching and the distribution of his *Journal*. His greatest success came as he aligned himself with a group promoting camp meetings. Shortly before leaving for America, he spoke on the efficacy of camp meetings to a group at Harriseahead in April 1807. As a result, Hugh Bourne led a camp meeting at Mow Cop beginning May 31. These seeming excesses led the Methodist Conference at Liverpool to condemn camp meetings and eventually led Bourne and his supporters to leave and found the Primitive Methodists.

Meanwhile, Dow returned to America and a heated confrontation with Snethen. As a result, Bishop Francis Asbury excluded Dow from all Methodist meetings. Dow moved to Mississippi but continued traveling about and preaching wherever audiences would listen. In 1816 he bought a vast tract of land in Wisconsin, where he planned to found a City of Peace modeled on Philadelphia, which was to include a refuge for blacks. The plan was never realized, however, as the deed of cession for the Indians was ruled invalid. In 1818 Dow made his last trip to England where he found the Primitive Methodists a going concern, though it would be another decade before they would attempt to plant work in America.

Shortly after his return to America, his wife died. Three months later he remarried. He continued his itinerant work until his death in 1834.

Lorenzo Dow, *The Chain of Lorenzo* (Augusta, Ga., 1804).

———, *The Eccentric Preacher* (Lowell, Mass., 1841).

———, *Life and Travels of Lorenzo Dow* (Hartford, Conn., 1804).

———, *History of Cosmopolite* (New York, 1814).

———, *Reflections* (Dublin, 1806).

Peggy Dow, *Vicissitudes in the Wilderness* (Liverpool, 1818).

Charles Coleman Sellers, *Lorenzo Dow, the Bearer of the Word* (New York, 1928).

EWM, 1, 711–2.

WWWH, 155.

DOWIE, John Alexander (May 25, 1847, Edinburgh, Scotland—March 9, 1907, Zion, Illinois); married Jeanne Dowie, May 26, 1876; education: Edinburgh University.

John Alexander Dowie, the flamboyant founder of the Christian Catholic church, grew up in a Scottish family in extreme poverty. He learned early in life to abhor the evils that so beset the poor—alcohol, in particular. A sickly child, he attended school only sporadically. He was both a precocious and religious child, however, and he educated himself in large part. He read the Bible through when only six years old and signed a temperance pledge the next year.

When he was thirteen, his family moved to Australia. There, during his teen years, he decided to go into the ministry and at age twenty-two returned to Edinburgh to pursue his ministerial education. This education was cut short, however, by a cablegram requesting him to return to Australia; his father had run into financial trouble. After clearing up his father's affairs, he entered the ministry in the Congregational Church and served parishes at Alma, South Australia, and at Manly Beach and Newton, New South Wales. While at Newton, he married his cousin Jeanne Dowie. In 1878 he resigned from the Congregational church and formed an independent congregation in Sydney. He immediately entered into warfare with the main sources of sin—liquor, newspapers, theaters, physicians, and other churches. So hostile did his relation with his designated enemies become, that his office was bombed.

During the 1870s, however, he discovered the new factor that changed the course of his life—divine healing. He came to a belief in healing over a number of years, but once convinced of it, began practicing it. He found that the response was immediate and positive. He also began to see that his mission was international in scope. He organized the International Divine Healing Association, and chapters soon sprang up in Australia and New Zealand.

In 1888 he resigned his pulpit and set out on a world tour to spread the message that God heals. He arrived in San Francisco on June 7 and spent the next two years conducting healing missions on the West Coast and in making his way to Chicago for a healing convention in 1890. Along the way he visited Salt Lake City and was impressed with the "Zion" being built by the Latter-day Saints. He decided to make Chicago his headquarters. In May 1893 he opened a tabernacle near the entrance to the World's Fair, a major step in building a successful healing ministry in the city.

While some flocked to his work, for others Dowie soon became an object of scorn and even hatred. His low opinion of doctors and ministers in more established churches did not help his progress. He opened a "healing home" near his tabernacle to accommodate people from out of town who wished to come to his meetings. He was arrested on many occasions for practicing medicine without a license. The Post Office attempted to revoke his mailing permit soon after he began his weekly periodical, *The Leaves of Healing*, in 1894. None of the charges proved substantial, and all were eventually dropped.

In 1896 he organized the Christian Catholic Church and was appointed general overseer. Four years later, on New Year's Eve, as the new century began, he announced to his members that land had been purchased in Lake County, Illinois, forty miles north of Chicago. The church would move to Zion, the name of the site, and build a city. It would be a Christian city where children could be raised without the sinful influences of Chicago. He would allow no liquor, pork, tobacco, or drugstores. Lots were made available for immediate purchase, and some small factories moved in to provide jobs.

As Zion progressed, Dowie experienced a further expansion of the image of his mission. In 1901 he proclaimed himself the embodiment of three Old Testament prophecies: The Messenger of the Covenant (Malachi 3:1–3), Elijah the Restorer (Malachi 4), and the Prophet promised by Moses (Deuteronomy 18: 15–18). He also moved to restore the "apostolic" offices to the church and proclaimed himself First Apostle. His vision was universal, and he saw cities like Zion being built around the world.

Unfortunately, as Dowie looked upon the world, Zion was facing a severe financial crisis. Oblivious to the threat, in 1906 Dowie traveled to Mexico to start a new city and placed Wilbur Glenn Voliva, the head of the Australian branch, in charge. Voliva, after learning of the financial situation, asked the church members to suspend Dowie as general overseer. The court moved the city into receivership, had the citizens withdraw their support of Dowie, and held an election. Voliva was elected in Dowie's place.

Dowie died just months after the election, and as general overseer, Voliva led the church for thirty-six years.

John Alexander Dowie, *The Sermons of John Alexander Dowie* (Dallas, Texas, 1979).

Gordon Lindsey, *John Alexander Dowie* (Dallas, Texas, 1980).

Arthur Newcomb, *Dowie, Anointed of the Lord* (New York, 1930).

Philip L. Cook, *Zion City, Illinois, John Alexander Dowie's Theocracy* (Zion, Ill., 1970).

DREW, Timothy (Noble Drew Ali) (January 8, 1886, North Carolina—July 20, 1929, Chicago, Illinois).

Timothy Drew, known by the members of the Moorish Science Temple of America which he founded by the name of Noble Drew Ali, was born in rural North Carolina. Like many black children of his time, he received little formal education; however, prior to World War I, he traveled around the world and encountered the cultures and religions of the East and Middle East with their relative lack of racial discrimination. He was most impressed with Islam and claimed that he had received his title "Ali" from Sultan Abdul Asis Abn Saud during a visit to Mecca.

From his reading and travel, he concluded that the black people in America were Asiatics, specifically, Moors. Their homeland was not Ethiopia but Morocco, and they were descendents of the Moabites of Canaan. Religiously they were Islamic. In 1912 Drew requested President

Woodrow Wilson to turn over the Moorish flag, which he believed had been placed in a safe in Independence Hall in 1776. Ali asserted that the cherry tree supposedly cut down by George Washington was, in fact, the bright red Moorish flag, which black people flew freely prior to the American Revolution in recognition of their true nationality.

Drew posed an entirely alternative view of black history in the United States. He believed that the Continental Congress had stripped black people of their Moorish nationality and relegated them to a status of Negro, Colored, and Ethiopian, which rendered them fit only for slavery. In 1779 the government had assigned them to perpetual slavery. As slaves the Moorish-Americans abandoned Islam for the "strange Gods of Europe" and thus became willing victims in the conspiracy to hide their origins. Drew felt that Allah had commissioned him to set his people free, and he began to preach the message of Moorish identity. To join his movement one had only to accept this identity and pay Drew one dollar. In turn Drew gave each an identification and membership card.

Drew opened his first Moorish Temple in Newark, New Jersey, in 1913, and over the next decade extended his movement to Pittsburgh, Detroit, and several southern cities. In 1925 he moved to Chicago and established a headquarters temple. In 1926 he incorporated his growing organization as the Moorish Temple of Science (changed to the Moorish Science Temple of America in 1928).

In 1927 Drew published *The Holy Koran* (not to be confused with the orthodox Islamic *Koran* or *Qu'ran*), a sixty-page compilation of Moorish beliefs. While affirming some central Islamic beliefs, *The Holy Koran* drew from a variety of non-Islamic sources, most prominently *The Aquarian Gospel of Jesus Christ* by Spiritualist Levi Dowling. Drew saw himself as the prophet of Allah and, as such, a thought of Allah manifested in the flesh. Allah is the Father God. He is the author of love, peace, freedom, and justice.

In the wake of his success in Chicago came trouble. Some of the temple's leaders were growing wealthy exploiting temple members by selling products such as Old Moorish Healing Oil and Moorish Purifier Bath Compound. Drew moved to oust the leaders, and during the period of strife, his business manager was killed. Drew was not in Chicago when the death occurred, but nevertheless, upon his return, he was arrested. He was released on bail and died before the trial. The cause of death was never determined.

Drew was succeeded by R. German Ali, who headed the movement for many years. One of his members, Wallace Fard, left the temple, claiming to be a reincarnation of Drew, and began what became known as the Nation of Islam (now the American Muslim Mission) in Detroit in 1930.

Arthur Huff Fauset, *Black Gods of the Metropolis* (Philadelphia, 1944).

Frank T. Simpson, "The Moorish Science Temple and Its 'Koran,'" *Moslem World* 37 (January 1947), 56–61.

Edwin E. Calverley, "Negro Muslims in Hartford," *Moslem World* 55 (October 1965), 340–345.

DRUMMOND, Sir Henry (December 5, 1786, the Grange, Hampshire, England—February 20, 1860, Albury, Surrey, England); married Henrietta Hay, circa 1808; education: Oxford University, 1802–4.

Sir Henry Drummond, one of the founders of the Catholic Apostolic Church, was the son of a wealthy banker. When he was eight, he inherited a large fortune upon his father's death. His mother remarried and moved to India when he was sixteen, and he went to live with his grandfather. He attended Harrow and then Oxford, though he did not finish his degree. After leaving college, he married and went into the banking business. In 1824 he was elected to the House of Commons but withdrew for reasons of health.

In 1819 Drummond purchased Albury Park, a vast estate where in 1826 he convened the first of several conferences of ministers and lay people to discuss the "signs of the times," that is, questions of prophecy, the second coming of Christ, the return of the Jews to the Holy Land, and the apocalyptic passages of Scripture. Approximately thirty men, mostly Anglican, attended each of the annual gatherings. Scottish Presbyterian minister Edward Irving, pastor of the Caledonian Church in London, was also among the prominent people who attended.

Drummond acted as scribe for the sessions. His report appeared in 1833 as the three-volume *Dialogues in Prophecy*. The group concluded by the end of its 1829 meeting that the present era of the church would end abruptly in judgment; the Jews would return to the Holy Land; the millennium would follow; and the Second Coming, which would initiate this string of events, was imminent. They began to look for an outpouring of the charismatic gifts of the Holy Spirit (healing, prophecy, speaking in tongues, etc.) and felt it was their duty to pray for the revival of the gifts.

By 1830 word reached the group that the gifts had reappeared in Scotland and subsequently among members of Irving's congregation in London. Prayer groups were formed to investigate, explore, and experience the gifts. At first, Drummond stayed aloof from the London meetings but organized a prayer group at Albury Park. By 1832, however, he had become convinced that the gifts were genuine. As they began to appear in Albury, he broke with the local parish minister.

On October 10, 1832, Drummond was attending a prayer meeting in London when a member of the group, exercising a prophetic gift, announced that Drummond was a pastor and should feed the sheep. A few weeks later, Drummond, exercising the same gift, named another member of the group, John Bate Cardale, as an "Apostle." Then in December 1832 still another prophet named Drummond an angel (i.e., a bishop, from Revelation 2), and Cardale, assuming his apostolic authority for the first time, immediately ordained Drummond. Drummond assumed the role of an ordained minister over the group in Albury.

On September 25, 1833, Drummond was called to the office of Apostle also, and, after the group of twelve was completed, participated in the ceremony of the "Separation of the Apostles," by which they gave up all ministerial functions related to a local congregation and assumed leadership of the whole church.

After the separation, the Apostles lived at Albury for a year and regularly met to consider questions of doctrine and church order. At their last gathering in June 1836, Drummond announced a plan by which the world would be divided into twelve areas likened unto the twelve tribes of Israel. Drummond was assigned Scotland and Switzerland, representative of the Tribe of Benjamin. At about this same time Drummond was also assigned the task of editing the Testimonies, two documents embodying the Apostles' message to Christendom. The first, called the lesser Testimonies, was addressed to the church in England and the later or greater Testimonies to the church outside of England. Drummond was active in the delivery of both documents, which were presented to the representatives of both church leaders and secular rulers.

Drummond spent the remaining years of his life in philanthropic activity for the Catholic Apostolic Church (as the group became known). Along the way, he wrote a theological text, *Abstract Principles of Revealed Religion* (1845) and was reelected to Parliament in 1847.

Drummond was also the source of one other innovation in the church. In the mid–1840s a number of the leaders had noticed a growing apathy in the church. Drummond, speaking prophetically, announced a new activity—sealing—the laying-on-of-hands for the gift of the Holy Spirit to the church's laity.

The Catholic Apostolic Church grew throughout the nineteenth century but declined after the death of the last Apostle. A group in Germany split from the church and created a perpetuating Apostleship. The New Apostolic Church has continued to grow worldwide and in 1980 reported almost four hundred congregations and 28,000 members in the United States alone.

Henry Drummond, *Abstract Principles of Revealed Religion* (London, 1845).

——— , *A Narrative of the Circumstances Which Led to the Setting-up of the Church of Christ at Albury* (1833).

Rowland A. Davenport, *Albury Apostles* (Great Britain, 1970).

DNB, 6, 28–9.

DURHAM, William H. (1873, Kentucky—July 7, 1912, Los Angeles, California).

William H. Durham, the exponent of the so-called "Finished Work of Calvary" perspective on Pentecostalism and pastor of the North Avenue Mission, the first Pentecostal congregation in Chicago, left only scant records of his early life. Raised in rural Kentucky, he joined the Baptist Church when he was eighteen years old. By his own account, he was sincere but unconverted at that time. Only in 1898, some seven years later, while living in Minnesota did he have the conversion experience that he sought. He continued his search, and two years later had a sanctification experience and affiliated with the Holiness movement. The Holiness movement believed that subsequent to salvation the believer is sanctified, that is, cleansed of the inherited sinful nature by a second work of grace. Durham became pastor of a small Holiness mission on the northside of Chicago.

In the spring of 1906, Durham heard of the revival that was taking place at the Holiness mission on Azusa Street in Los Angeles. William J. Seymour, the pastor, was preaching a new doctrine, that subsequent to sanctification the believer could receive the baptism of the Holy Spirit and that such a baptism was evidenced by the believer speaking in unknown tongues (*glossolalia*). Durham preached against the doctrine, but he began to change his mind when he became impressed by the demeanor of those visitors to his mission in Chicago who had experienced the baptism. Then in the fall of 1906, when some of his own members began to speak in tongues, Durham became convinced of the validity of the baptism.

In early 1907 he took a leave of absence from the mission and traveled to Los Angeles. He wanted to wait, not distracted by his pastoral duties, for the baptism, which he received on March 2, 1907. Durham returned to Chicago and preached the Pentecostal message with great success. Within a year he established ten missions as satellites of the North Avenue Mission. In 1908 he began the *Pentecostal Testimony*, a periodical.

In the wake of his success, Durham struggled with the theology of Seymour's Pentecostal Holiness perspective. He concluded that he had been in error; Christ had finished the work of both salvation and sanctification on the cross. The sinner could appropriate both by faith; hence there was no need for a second sanctifying work of grace. Durham articulated his new theology at a Pentecostal convention in 1910 in Chicago and through the pages of his magazine.

In February 1911 Durham returned to Los Angeles ready to share his new insight. He first approached Elmer Fisher, pastor of the Upper Room Mission where many of the white Pentecostals had assembled. Fisher, however, quickly rejected his new ideas. He then turned to the Azusa Street Mission, by then consisting mostly of black members. Seymour, the pastor, was in the East, and Durham assumed the pulpit. Hundreds flocked to hear him. Seymour heard of Durham's doctrinal deviation and returned to stop him. On March 2, 1911, he locked the doors of the Azusa Mission against Durham.

Durham, having built a sizable following in the few weeks he had been in Los Angeles, moved his meetings to a building at Seventh and Los Angeles streets. Although opposed by most Pentecostal leaders, he persevered in his preaching, and more than a thousand people attended Sunday services. In February 1912 he traveled to Chicago for what he intended to be a two-week set of meetings to bolster his midwestern work. During this visit, however, he caught a cold and died a few months later of complications.

Durham died while still in his thirties and at the height of his success. His "Finished Work" message created the first major theological division in Pentecostalism. It was eventually accepted by most Pentecostals from non-Holiness backgrounds, and in 1914 it was accepted by the General Council of the Assemblies of God, the largest of the white Pentecostal bodies.

Memorial issue of the *Pentecostal Testimony* 2, 3 (July 1912).

Frank Bartleman, *Another Wave Rolls In!* (Northridge, Calif., 1962).

Edith Blumhofer, "The Finished Work of Calvary." *Assemblies of God Heritage* 3, 3 (Fall, 1983).

Carl Brumback, *Suddenly From Heaven* (Springfield, Mo., 1962).

DYLKS, Joseph C.

Nothing is known about Joseph C. Dylks prior to his sudden appearance in August 1828 in the small community of Salesville, in Guernsey County, Ohio. Dylks gathered a following who believed him to be the Messiah and whom he called the "little flock."

Dylks appeared during a Sunday afternoon camp meeting service near Salesville. During the sermon he interrupted the service with a "shout and a snort." The noise caught everyone's attention, and they soon realized that he had slipped into their midst without anyone noticing his arrival. He wore a black broadcloth suit, unusual attire for the community.

During the first weeks of his residency in the town, Dylks attended the religious services of the different church groups and frequently disturbed the services with his shout and snort. He also visited from home to home and made friends among the people who offered him their hospitality. On several occasions he spoke and expounded the Bible at worship gatherings. Meanwhile, he confided to various individuals that he was a celestial being on a heavenly mission. He made several significant converts including Michael Brill, the first settler in Salesville, and Robert McCormick, a United Brethren preacher and the town schoolteacher.

Dylks claimed that he had come into the camp meeting in his spiritual body and then took on a corporal body, clothed as they first saw him. He could, he asserted, appear and disappear at will and perform miracles. Eventually, he claimed that he was the true Messiah who had arrived to establish the millennium. Dylks would never die, and all who believed in him would live forever in their natural bodies and inherit the earth. Other prominent claims included the assertions that the kingdom would spread over the whole earth, that Dylks's body could only be touched with his permission, that not one hair of his head could be taken from him, and that with a shout he could destroy the universe.

Three weeks after his appearance, he accompanied McCormick on a preaching tour in the Leatherwood, as the area around Salesville was called. During this trip, McCormick later testified, Dylks bestowed upon him the title of St. Paul, fought and defeated the Devil, and cured the son of a minister in a neighboring community. Upon their return from the trip, Dylks made the first public declaration of his mission and informed the community of the conversion of its leading citizens. A majority of the community became converts, and the single church building shared by all the different groups in the community was taken over and rededicated to the new order.

The spread of Dylks's following led to organized opposition by others in the community. One evening they stormed into a meeting of the little flock. One man took a lock of hair as a trophy, and the group carried Dylks into court. The judge could find Dylks guilty of no crime and freed him. A mob then drove him into hiding in the woods.

On October 28, 1828, a mere three months after he came to Salesville, Dylks felt safe enough to meet and organize his following. Because of the violent opposition, he told them that he would bring down the New Jerusalem in Philadelphia. He appointed apostles to head the work. With McCormick and two of the new apostles, he left for Pennsylvania. As the four approached Philadelphia, he sent McCormick and one apostle into the city. After Dylks failed to meet them, McCormick returned to Salesville and recounted his discouraging story.

Dylks was never seen again by anyone in Salesville, but the "little flock" continued for many years in hope of his soon manifestation. Seven years after Dylks's disappearance, the other apostle who had remained with Dylks when McCormick went into the city suddenly appeared in Salesville. He delivered one lecture in which he testified that he had seen Dylks ascend into heaven and that he would shortly return to set up his Kingdom. The next day the apostle left and was never seen again.

Dylks attained some fame as the leading character in a novel by William Dean Howells, *The Leatherwood God*.

R. H. Taneyhill, *The Leatherwood God* (Cincinnati, 1870).

George Kummer, "Introduction" to *The Leatherwood God* by Richard H. Taneyhill (Gainesville, Fla., 1966), vii–xv.

EDDY, Mary Baker Glover (July 16, 1821, Bow, New Hampshire—December 3, 1910, Brookline, Massachusetts); married George W. Glover, December 10, 1843 (d. June 27, 1844); married Daniel Patterson, June 21, 1853 (div. 1873, d. 1896); married Asa Gilbert Eddy, January 1, 1877 (d. June 2, 1882).

Mary Baker Eddy, the founder of the Church of Christ, Scientist, was raised by devout Congregationalist (i.e., Calvinist) parents. Health problems in her youth limited her formal education. She did write poems, forerunners of the hymns she would later pen for her church. When she was fifteen she moved to Sanbornton Bridge, New Hampshire, and two years later joined the Congregational Church at Tilton. For a short time she attended Holmes Academy.

In 1843 she married for the first time and moved to South Carolina. The marriage ended with her husband's premature death, and she returned to New Hampshire where she bore her first child, an event followed by a period of sickness and unhappy incidents. She was engaged for a short time, but her fiancé died before the wedding. Her mother died in 1849, and she went to live with her sister Abigail. In 1853 she married again, but for the next decade her health did not improve and her husband was frequently away. When war broke out, he joined the Union Army. In March 1862 he was captured, but during the autumn, he escaped and returned to the north.

A few months after her husband's capture, she entered a water-cure sanatorium. While there she heard of Dr. Phineas Parkhurst Quimby, a mental healer in Portland, Maine. In October she traveled to meet him. Soon after her arrival, she experienced a relief from her symptoms and was open in her praise of him. She became his student and spent many hours trying to understand his teachings, especially in light of the Bible, and share them with others. Over the several years she worked with him, however, she found that her illness would periodically return and that Quimby's teachings did not conform to her understanding of Scripture.

On February 1, 1866, two weeks after Quimby's death, she fell on icy pavement and was injured. Three days later, according to her own account, while reading the Bible, the healing truth dawned upon her. She recovered her health immediately, to the amazement of doctors and friends. This event marks the beginning of Christian Science. From that time she abandoned Quimby's system and spent the rest of her life exploring and developing the implications of her discovery. Along the way she obtained a divorce from her husband.

In 1867 she began to actively use the new truth she had found. She healed her niece, Ellen Pilsbury. She took her first student and began writing what would be her first major publication, *The Science of Man*, which she began using as a textbook in 1870.

In 1872, she began writing *Science and Health* (later retitled *Science and Health with Key to the Scriptures*), the first edition of which was published in 1875. A few months before it appeared, she obtained a letter of dismissal from the Congregational Church and turned her attention to the movement she would come to lead, the development of which proceeded in several stages. In 1976 the Christian Science Association, a fellowship of students in Massachusetts was organized. Three years later the Church of Christ, Scientist was formed. The Massachusetts Metaphysical College was chartered in 1881, the same year Eddy was ordained as pastor of the church. The first issue of the *Journal of Christian Science* appeared in 1883. Student teachers outside of Massachusetts formed the National Christian Scientists Association in 1886.

Eddy went through a period of doubt about the developing movement in the late 1880s and reorganized it. In 1889 the Christian Science Association, the college and the church were all dissolved. In 1892, the church was reorganized, and the *Journal*, which had been given to the National Christian Scientist Association, returned to church control. The Association met for the last time in 1893 at the World Parliament of Religions in Chicago. During the 1890s, Eddy worked on the Church Manual, a codification of the by-laws by which the Church is still governed.

During the 1890s, Julius and Annetta Dresser accused Eddy of taking Quimby's teachings, distorting them, and presenting them as her own. They began a controversy which has continued to the present. There is little doubt that Eddy began an important phase of her search for healing and a religious perspective upon life and health with Quimby and that she appreciated his help. She also shared several ideas with him, such as an emphasis upon the impersonal attributes of God, in distinction with their common orthodox opponents. There is also no doubt that she never shared his basic hostility to the Christian Church, that she abandoned Quimby's basic philosophical notions and healing practices, especially the surviving Mesmeric techniques, and that she developed Christian Science quite independently of his teachings.

It is also true that the Church of Christ, Scientists which she founded did not arise as one extreme of the New Thought Metaphysical movement. Rather, the opposite is true. Several of Eddy's students, most prominently Emma Curtis Hopkins, who saw her teachings more as a point of departure from which they could develop their own teachings, rather than a complete system to be closely followed, joined efforts with the Dressers and others in the 1890s to found the New Thought movement, of which Eddy and the Church of Christ, Scientist inadvertently became a major source.

Mary Baker Eddy, *Science and Health* (Boston, 1875).

———— , *The Science of Man* (Lynn, Mass., 1876).

———— , *Science and Health with Key to the Scriptures, Authorized Edition* (Boston, 1906).

———— , *Poetical Works* (Boston, 1936).

———— , *Prose Works* (Boston, 1925).

Charles S. Braden, *Christian Science Today* (Dallas, Texas, 1958).

Stephen Gottschalk, *The Emergence of Christian Science in American Religious Life* (Berkeley, Calif., 1973).

Robert Peel, *Mary Baker Eddy* (New York, 1966, 1971).

Sibyl Wilbur, *The Life of Mary Baker Eddy* (Boston, 1913).

Hugh A. Studdert Kennedy, *Mrs. Eddy* (San Francisco, 1947).

NAW, 1, 551–61.

DRB, 139–41.

DAB 6, 7–15.

EOP, 279.

WWW, 1, 357.

EIELSEN, Elling (September 19, 1804, Voss, Norway—January 10, 1883, Chicago, Illinois); married Sigrid Nilson Tufte, July 3, 1843.

Elling Eielsen, founder of the first synod among Norwegian-American Lutherans, was raised by devout parents who followed the Norwegian lay preacher Hans Nielsen Hauge (1771–1824). Hauge, responding to both the rationalistic tendencies in Norwegian Lutheranism as well as to a deep personal religious experience traveled around Norway in 1796 speaking and writing of the need for repentance and a godly life. While critical of the clergy, he advocated loyalty to the state church. He was frequently arrested under the Conventicle Act that forbade itinerant lay preachers. Arrested in 1804, he remained in prison for seven years. When released his health was broken.

Eielsen, according to convention, was confirmed in 1820, but experienced a deep renewal some years later. Like Hauge, who had frequently visited his home, he became a lay itinerant and traveled throughout Norway, Sweden, and Denmark. His arrest in Denmark in 1837 perhaps spurred his consideration of the possibility of migrating to America. He arrived in America in 1839, and on September 22 preached his first sermon to a group of Norwegian immigrants in Chicago. He settled among the

Norwegians in the Fox River Valley of Illinois. Within a year he had visited all the Norwegian settlements in Illinois and Wisconsin, where he found the freedom to preach that had been denied him in Scandinavia.

During the first years of his itinerancy, no ordained Norwegian clergy were present in America. Possibly the threat of their imminent arrival led Eielsen to seek ordination. Pastor Francis Alex Hoffman of the Ministerium of Northern Illinois ordained Eielsen in October 1843. In the mid-1840s Eielsen's work was strengthened by two colleagues, Paul Anderson and Ole Andrewson. They encouraged him to organize his followers, who had no church to tend to their needs. On April 13–14, 1846, at a meeting at Jefferson Prairie, Wisconsin, where Eielsen had moved, the first synod was organized. The new church was called the Evangelical Lutheran Synod in America. Eielsen, who was elected president, wrote the constitution. It assumed a loose organization in which lay leadership and preaching would predominate and tendencies to popish clericalism would be prevented. The constitution also demanded that members have experienced conversion.

Two years later Eielsen experienced the first of three defections when Anderson and Andrewson took over the synod and separated from Eielsen. In 1850 Eielsen reorganized his followers and reaffirmed the 1846 constitution. Six years later A. Rasmussen disagreed with Eielsen over the idea of the purity of the church implied in a totally converted membership. He withdrew and took half the membership with him. As before, Eielsen continued his evangelistic labors and rebuilt the membership. In 1859 he made a tour in Texas and spent much of 1860–61 in Norway.

In the 1870s Eielsen found another group within the church that advocated a revision of the constitution. At the synod meeting of 1875 this group led in the adoption of some changes to the constitution and renamed the church as Hauge's Norwegian Evangelical Lutheran Synod in America. In February 1876 a minority met at Jackson, Minnesota, and reaffirmed their loyalty to the 1846 constitution and to Eielsen as president. At the next meeting of the Hauge synod, Eielsen was removed from membership. The minority continued with the original name.

Eielsen died in 1883. Subsequently all of the synods that broke from his merged into what are today the major Lutheran bodies (the American Lutheran Church and the Lutheran Church in America). The Evangelical Lutheran Church in America (Eielsen Synod) has become the smallest Lutheran body in America. It reported in 1971, the time of its 125th anniversary, five congregations being served by one pastor and fewer than two hundred members.

E. Clifford Nelson and Eugene L. Fevold, *The Lutheran Church Among Norwegian-Americans* (Minneapolis, Minn., 1960).

C. J. Carlsen, *Elling Eielsen, Pioneer Lay Preacher and First Norwegian Pastor in America* (Master's thesis, University of Minnesota, 1932).

Chr. O. Brohaugh and I. Eisteinsen, *Kortfattet Beretning om Elling Eielsens Liv og Virksomhed* (Chicago, 1883).

DAB, 6, 61–2.

WWWH, 167.

EVANS, Warren Felt (December 23, 1817, Rockingham, Vermont—September 4, 1889, Salisbury, Massachusetts); married Charlotte Tinker, June 21, 1840; education: Middlebury College 1837–38; Dartmouth College 1838–40.

Warren Felt Evans, the pioneer New Thought theoretician and writer, was the son of a farmer. He left college in his junior year to become a Methodist minister, and between 1844 and 1864 he served eleven charges in that capacity. During his years as a Methodist, he began reading the works of Emmanuel Swedenborg. He was converted by his reading, and he joined the Church of the New Jerusalem in 1863. His changing of denominations coincided with a period of illness described as "a nervous affection, complicated by a chronic disorder." Having heard of Phineas P. Quimby, he traveled to Portland, Maine. He was not only healed under Quimby's care but became converted to Quimby's ideas. Evans became convinced that he, like Quimby, could also practice mental healing, and, encouraged by his mentor, he set up practice in Claremont, New Hampshire. In 1867 he moved to Boston and opened an office. He bought a home in Salisbury, Massachusetts, two years later, and for the next twenty years he received patients in his home.

Evans never attempted to gather a following. He is best remembered as the first writer on Quimby's ideas, and, because Quimby never wrote a book and his papers were not published until the twentieth century, Evans's books were the first to introduce the public to New Thought. His first book on mental healing, *The Mental Cure*, which appeared in 1869, six years before Mary Baker Eddy's *Science and Health with Key to the Scriptures*, holds the distinction of being the very first volume on New Thought. It was followed by *Mental Medicine* (1872); *Soul and Body* (1875); *The Divine Law of Cure* (1881); his most popular book: *Primitive Mind Cure* (1885); and *Esoteric Christianity and Mental Therapeutics* (1886).

Evans created a synthesis of Quimby and Swedenborg. With Quimby he agreed that physical pathology was basically a pathology of the mind. If one can change the belief, one can cure the disease. Quimby gave up magnetic healing, but Evans continued to practice it through the laying on of hands during most of his life. With Swedenborg, Evans believed in the correspondence of the material and spiritual worlds and the life lived in communion with angels. Unlike Quimby, Evans placed great importance upon the diagnosis of disease. In practice he arrived at a system that closely resembles twentieth-century psychosomatic medicine.

In the end, Evans arrived at a Christian pantheism (his term). He taught of a God that was both personal, as love and wisdom (two of Swedenborg's prime concepts), and impersonal. The universe is continually created out of a God who is omnipresent. Christ, as principle, was distinct from but fully accepted by Jesus who became the Anointed One. The Christ Principle is the Word, or *Logos*, that lights everyone in the world. In spreading the teachings of Quimby, Evans was recovering the primitive teachings of Christianity.

Warren Felt Evans, *The Mental Cure* (Boston, 1869).

———, *The Divine Law of Cure* (Boston, 1881).

——— , *Mental Medicine* (Boston, 1872).

——— , *Esoteric Christianity* (Boston, 1886).

——— , *Primitive Mind Care* (Boston, 1885).

Charles S. Braden, *Spirits in Rebellion* (Dallas, Texas, 1963).

J. Stillson Judah, *History and Philosophy of the Metaphysical Movements in America* (Philadelphia, 1967).

Tom Beebe, *Who's Who in New Thought* (Lakemont, Ga., 1977), 69.

DRB, 153–4.

DAB, 6, 213–14.

FETTING, Otto (November 20, 1871, St. Clair, Michigan—January 30, 1930, Port Huron, Michigan).

Otto Fetting, whose revelations led to a new branch of the Mormon family of Churches called the Church of Christ (and also called Fettingite to distinguish it from other groups with a similar name), was born and raised in the Reorganized Church of Jesus Christ of Latter-day Saints. He was baptized in 1891 and ordained to the priesthood eight years later. During the second and third decade of this century, many members of the Reorganized church left and joined the Church of Christ (Temple Lot), a small body that owned the plot of ground in Independence, Missouri, Joseph Smith had designated as the site upon which to build the temple. Fetting joined the Church of Christ (Temple Lot) in 1925. Fetting was immediately accepted into a leadership role and, in the fall of 1925, was appointed to serve on the finance committee for the group. In 1926 he was called and ordained an apostle.

In February 1927, Fetting received a visitation from a heavenly being whom he later identified as John the Baptist. The messenger announced that the time was at hand to rebuild the temple. In the second message, 1929 was set as the date to start, and in the fifth message, the church was given seven years to complete the building. The messages also ordered that the priesthood be given to black men. Fetting presented the messages to the church, and they were tentatively accepted. Plans were finalized for the building, and on April 6, 1929, Fetting broke the sod for the excavation of the site. During the excavation the original foundation markers placed by Joseph Smith, Jr., were discovered.

On July 18, 1929, Fetting received the twelfth message. It called for a rebaptism of the entire church (many of whom had been received from the Reorganized church without rebaptism). Fetting's advocacy of rebaptism caused considerable controversy, and a special conference was called in October 1929 to consider the "new doctrine." Fetting's teachings were rejected, but Fetting and another apostle, Walter F. Gates, continued to teach them. As a result the two were disfellowshipped. In April 1929 Fetting organized a new body, which he called the Church of Christ. About 1,400 of the members of the Church of Christ (Temple Lot) followed Fetting (approximately one-third of the membership).

Fetting continued to receive messages sporadically; the last was received just two days before he died. In April 1936 the Temple Lot Church officially rejected all of Fetting's messages, the first eleven of which they had still tentatively accepted. In 1937 a member of the Fetting church, W. A. Draves of Nucla, Colorado, began to receive messages from, he claimed, the same messenger as Fetting. His messages split the Fetting church into two almost equal factions, though most of the leadership rejected Draves's messages.

Otto Fetting, *The Word of the Lord* (Independence, Mo., 1971).

——, *The Midnight Message* (Independence, Mo., 1927).

George Bartholomew Arbaugh, *Revelation in Mormonism* (Chicago, 1932).

Willard J. Smith, *Fetting and His Messenger's Messages* (Port Huron, Mich., n.d.).

B. C. Flint, *An Outline History of the Church of Christ (Temple Lot)* (Independence, 1953).

Denominations That Base Their Beliefs on the Teachings of Joseph Smith (Salt Lake City, Utah, 1969).

Russell R. Rich, *Little Known Schisms of the Restoration* (Provo, Utah, 1967).

FILLMORE, Charles Sherlock (August 22, 1854, St. Cloud, Minnesota—July 5, 1948, Kansas City, Missouri); married Mary Caroline "Myrtle" Page, March 29, 1881 (d. October 6, 1931); married Cora G. Dedrick, December 31, 1933.

Charles Sherlock Fillmore, co-founder of the Unity School of Christianity, the largest of the New Thought metaphysical groups, was the son of an Indian trader living in the wilds of pioneer Minnesota. He was raised by his Episcopalian mother, a seamstress. He had little formal education and had to go to work early to support his mother. He was able to supplement his education with a wide variety of reading, which included material on occultism, Eastern religions, metaphysics, and Spiritualism.

In 1874 he left home and moved to Caddo, Oklahoma, and then to Denison, Texas, where he became a railroad clerk. It was at Denison that he met Myrtle Page, a schoolteacher, who was to become his first wife. In 1879 he was fired from the railroad for sticking up for a friend. He moved to Gunnison, Colorado, and went into the mining and real estate businesses. In 1881 he went east, married Myrtle, and returned with her to Colorado. They settled in Pueblo, where Charles was in business with the brother-in-law of Nona Brooks, who would later found the Divine Science Church.

In 1884 the couple moved to Kansas City. Two years later E. B. Weeks, a student of Emma Curtis Hopkins, lectured in Kansas City on Christian Science. The Fillmores attended the lectures; Myrtle, much impressed, began to practice the teachings and over the next year was completely healed of the tuberculosis that was threatening her life. Only over a period of time, after he had had a chance to study metaphysics and travel to Chicago for one of Hopkins's classes, did Charles become convinced of the truth of the teachings.

Having become convinced, Charles threw himself into spreading the message. He did so at a time when his personal finances were at a low point as a result of a severe depression in the Kansas City real estate market. In 1889 he launched a magazine, *Modern Thought*, which followed the Christian Science principles as taught by Hopkins but also reflected

the wide interest of the Fillmores in the occult, Eastern religions, and
Spiritualism. Within a few years, they had to renounce both Spiritualism
and the occult publicly. They also began to hold classes, build a circulating
library of metaphysical books, and conduct Sunday services in the afternoon.

Once begun, the work grew slowly but steadily. In 1890 the Society of
Silent Help was begun as a healing prayer group for subscribers to *Modern
Thought* who could not attend the classes and worship services. In 1891
Unity was begun as a magazine for the society.

During the early years there had been a search for a name to tie the
work together. In 1890, following Hopkins's lead, the magazine had been
renamed *Christian Science Thought*. When Mary Baker Eddy objected, they
changed the name to *Thought*. Finally, in 1891, Charles decided upon the
name *Unity*, and gradually that name and the winged-sphere symbol began
to dominate all the Fillmores' efforts.

From the original publishing and prayer efforts, a movement began to
take shape, and in 1903 the Unity School of Practical Christianity (since
1914 the Unity School of Christianity) was incorporated. In 1909 another
magazine, *Weekly Unity*, was added, and Charles published his first book,
Christian Healing, which had grown out of his class lessons.

During the 1920s, the work expanded greatly. A vegetarian restaurant,
Unity Inn, was opened in Kansas City. In 1922, Fillmore initiated radio
broadcasts on WOQ, the oldest licensed station in the Midwest, and two
years later Unity purchased the station outright. In 1924 *Unity Daily Word*
(now *Daily Word*), a monthly magazine of daily meditations destined to
become their largest circulating periodical, was begun.

Over the years many groups had begun meeting, using the Unity
literature as teaching and discussion aids, and people who had attended
classes at Kansas City established themselves as teachers. The Fillmores,
however, saw a growing problem in that some of the groups and leaders
were delving into many areas that they did not wish associated with Unity.
Thus in 1925 they formed the Unity Annual Conference, an organization of
recognized ministers and teachers who oversee Unity centers.

In 1933, two years after his wife died, Fillmore remarried. He also
finished and published his second major book, the *Metaphysical Bible
Dictionary*, a guide to the New Thought interpretation of the Bible by the
use of allegory. In 1933 he retired from the Unity pulpit and began a period
of travel, teaching, and lecturing that lasted for the rest of his life. He
remained active until a few weeks before his death at ninety-three.

Charles Sherlock Fillmore, *Christian Healing* (Kansas City, Mo., 1909).

———— , *The Twelve Powers of Man* (Lee's Summit, Mo., 1930).

———— , *Metaphysical Bible Dictionary* (Kansas City, Mo., 1931).

———— , *Jesus Christ Heals* (Kansas City, Mo., 1939).

Hugh D'Andrade, *Charles Fillmore* (New York, 1974).

Charles S. Braden, *Spirits in Rebellion* (Dallas, Texas, 1963).

James Dillet Freeman, *The Story of Unity* (Unity Village, Mo., 1978).

DRB, 156–7.

WWW, 3, 280–81.

FILLMORE, Mary Caroline "Myrtle" Page (August 6, 1845, Page-town, Ohio—October 6, 1931, Kansas City, Missouri); married Charles Sherlock Fillmore, March 29, 1881 (d. July 5, 1948); education: Oberlin College, 1868–69.

Mary Caroline Page, always called "Myrtle," the nickname she picked up in childhood, was the co-founder with her husband, Charles Fillmore, of the Unity School of Christianity, the largest of the New Thought bodies. She was born to an influential, well-to-do family and was raised as a strict Methodist. She had the benefits of a fine education (for the time), and at age twenty-two she entered Oberlin College and took the "Literary Course for Ladies." Upon graduation she moved to Clinton, Missouri, where her brother David lived and taught school.

She was about thirty years old when she moved to Denison, Texas, where she met Charles Fillmore, her future husband. They became close friends and continued to correspond after she moved back to Clinton and he went to Colorado. In 1881 they were married, and she went first to Colorado and then to Kansas City (in 1884) with him.

In Kansas City, life did not go well for Myrtle. Always active in teaching and in church activities, she became ill with tuberculosis and the doctors could not help her. Then in 1886 E. B. Weeks, a representative of the Hopkins Metaphysical Institute, founded by Emma Curtis Hopkins, came to town and lectured on Christian Science. She shared an interest in unorthodox teachings, including Spiritualism and the occult, with her husband, and together they attended the lectures—an event that changed Myrtle's life.

While Charles remained unimpressed with the lectures, Myrtle came away repeating what she had learned, "I am a child of God and therefore I do not inherit sickness." She rid herself of the idea, which had been impressed upon her from childhood, that she was destined to become an invalid and that she possessed a tendency toward tuberculosis. She felt she was healed and began what would be a year of complete recovery from her sickness. Myrtle's recovery became the first event upon which Unity would be built. She began to tell people about her healing, while Charles began to study metaphysics to discover the truth for himself. Seeing other healings helped convince him.

In 1889 the couple began *Modern Thought*, a periodical to spread the teachings of metaphysics. Besides sharing the work with Charles in each of the ventures they launched, Myrtle bore three children, Lowell (1882), Rickert (1884), and Royal (1889), and assumed responsibilities as a mother and housewife. As a result of her double careers, she had had a vision of a large body of people, including many children, who, however, were completely undisciplined. The thought came to her, "Who will take care of the children?" The answer came, ". . . this is your work."

Soon after the Unity Society began meeting, she founded a Sunday school and in 1893 started *Wee Wisdom*, the oldest children's magazine in America. Out of her work with the magazine, which she edited for over thirty years, came her only book, *Wee Wisdom's Way*.

Myrtle also took the lead in the formation of the Society of Silent Help (now known as Silent Unity), the prayer circle for absent healing, and she announced its formation in 1890. During the remaining years of her life she shared in the growth of the Unity School of Christianity, which she helped co-found in 1903. Besides the Sunday school at the Kansas City center, she had charge of the Wednesday classes and wrote voluminously for several periodicals.

She passed away only a few months after celebrating her fiftieth wedding anniversary.

Myrtle Page Fillmore, *The Letters of Myrtle Fillmore* (Kansas City, Mo., 1936).

——— , *Wee Wisdom's Way* (Kansas City, 1920).

Thomas E. Witherspoon, *Myrtle Fillmore, Mother of Unity* (Unity Village, Mo., 1977).

Charles S. Braden, *Spirits in Rebellion* (Dallas, Texas, 1963).

Hugh D'Andrade, *Charles Fillmore* (New York, 1974).

James Dillet Freeman, *The Story of Unity* (Unity Village, Mo., 1978).

DRB, 157–8.

FLOWER, Joseph James Roswell (June 17, 1888, Belleville, Ontario—July 23, 1970, Springfield, Missouri); married Alice Marie Reynolds, June 1, 1911.

Joseph James Roswell Flowers, one of the founders of the Assemblies of God, was born in Canada. His mother was the daughter of a Methodist presiding elder. When he was a child, his family moved to Toronto, where his parents encountered some members of John Alexander Dowie's Christian Catholic Church. Impressed by a healing of a crippled man, the family moved to Dowie's community at Zion, Illinois, in 1902. Once at Zion, however, the family was disappointed by the conditions they found, particularly the internal discord. They soon settled in Indianapolis, where the elder Flower worked for the Indiana Seed Company. The family joined the Christian and Missionary Alliance, the church founded by Albert B. Simpson.

In 1907 Glenn A. Cook, a minister who had attended the services at Azusa Street in Los Angeles and who had received the baptism of the Holy Spirit under the ministry of William J. Seymour, came to Indianapolis. He held services at the Alliance church and expounded the experience of speaking in tongues as evidence of receiving the Holy Spirit. After his parents received the baptism, Flower attended the services and was converted. A year later he received the baptism of the Holy Spirit. He had been studying for a legal career, but gave up law for the ministry.

Flower began to assist in meetings in Indianapolis and travel with gospel bands around the Midwest. He also founded a Pentecostal periodical, *The Pentecost* (later *Grace and Glory*), and worked as its foreign editor and associate editor. Flower married Alice Marie Reynolds, and they spent a year in evangelistic work in northern Indiana before joining with D. Wesley Myland, a former Alliance minister, in founding Gileah Bible School in Plainfield, Indiana. Myland had founded the World's Faith

Missionary Association after leaving the Alliance, and he ordained Flower and gave him ministerial credentials from his association.

Flower lived in a cottage next to the school and there located the press upon which he printed the first issues of *The Christian Evangel* (later renamed *Pentecostal Evangel*), which became the official periodical of the Assemblies of God.

Being among those who saw the need for more stable structures within the burgeoning Pentecostal movement, Flower joined colleague E. N. Bell, editor of *Word and Witness*, for a general convention of Pentecostal ministers and lay people in Hot Springs, Arkansas. That meeting, which opened April 2, 1914, resulted in the formation of the General Council of the Assemblies of God. Flower was elected secretary. After the meeting, he moved his family and printing equipment to Findley, Ohio. Then in 1915 he moved again to St. Louis. *The Christian Evangel* and *Word and Witness* were merged, and a new periodical, *The Weekly Evangel*, continued to serve the Assemblies.

Soon after the move to St. Louis, the Assemblies were disturbed by the "Jesus Only" controversy. E. N. Bell and other prominent leaders denied the Trinity and were rebaptized in the Name of Jesus. Flower emerged as the defender of orthodox faith.

During his long life, Flower served numerous posts with the organization he helped to create. He was secretary of the General Council (1914–1917) and foreign missions secretary (1919–1925). In 1917 he moved to Springfield, Missouri, to oversee the publishing house.

Possibly the low point in a distinguished career came in 1925 when, along with John W. Welch, chairman of the General Council, Flower presented the General Council with a proposal for a constitution. The plan was rejected, and Flower was not reelected to his post. He moved to Scranton, Pennsylvania, as pastor of an Assemblies congregation. He was elected eastern district secretary and in 1929 superintendent of the eastern district. Then in 1931 he again became a national officer when he was elected assistant general secretary. In 1935 he was elected general secretary and treasurer, a post he retained until the two positions were separated in 1947. He retired from office in 1959.

Mark T. Boucher, *J. Roswell Flower* (Springfield, Mo., unpublished paper, 1983).

William W. Menzies, *Anointed to Serve* (Springfield, Mo., 1971).

Carl Brumback, *Suddenly from Heaven* (Springfield, Mo., 1961).

WWW, 5, 239.

FORD, Arnold Josiah (1890s (?), Barbados—circa 1935, Addis Ababa, Ethiopia); married Mignon Ford.

Arnold Josiah Ford, early black Jew and founder of the Beth B'nai Abraham congregation in New York City, was born in Barbados, the son of an evangelist. He taught music in the British navy and was a clerk in Bermuda before settling in the United States around 1912. From 1912 to 1920 he served as bandmaster for the New Amsterdam Musical Association in New York. In 1917 he encountered Marcus Garvey, the fiery black nationalist leader who came to America in 1917 and founded the Universal

Negro Improvement Association. Garvey, like Ford, was a West Indian and drew Ford into the leadership ranks of the U.N.I.A. in New York City. Ford became the choirmaster and bandmaster for the association. He co-authored "Ethiopia, Land of Our Fathers," the U.N.I.A.'s anthem, and compiled *The Universal Ethiopian Hymnal*, to which he contributed many original works.

During his first decade in America, Ford repudiated the Christian faith in which he was raised and began to identify himself as a Jew. He identified black people with the Jews in bondage in the Old Testament and Jehovah as the God who would lead them to their homeland, Ethiopia. He tried to persuade Garvey to adopt Judaism as the faith of the U.N.I.A. Although Garvey did not accept the suggestion, Ford continued to be active in the association through the 1920s.

In 1924 Ford founded Beth B'nai Abraham, a black Jewish synagogue. He learned Hebrew and introduced orthodox Jewish practices. He is also credited with introducing both to other black Jewish groups already operating in New York. The membership grew steadily during the next six years, but in 1930 the congregation collapsed financially and lost its property. At this point Ford turned over the remnant of this organization to Wentworth A. Matthew, head of another black Jewish group, the Commandment Keepers, and authorized Matthew to continue his work.

During the 1920s news of the Falashas, the Jewish Ethiopian tribe discovered in the nineteenth century, became common knowledge, primarily through the efforts of Jacques Faitlovitch who had organized a committee to "rehabilitate" the Falashas. In New York Faitlovitch heard of the black Jews and contacted them, including Ford, to see if there was any connection. Where none existed, Faitlovitch's efforts created one.

In 1930 Ford left the United States and settled in Addis Ababa. He did not reside among the Falashas, but he did become well known for his musical ability within the small community of American blacks living in Ethiopia. He lived long enough to see Haile Selassie's coronation in 1935. His common-law wife survived him, and in the early 1940s she founded the Princess Zannaba Warq School. She was still alive in 1966 for the Silver Jubilee.

Because of the lack of material on Ford (and the lack of effort to assemble the small amount available) a number of errors crept into accounts of his life. One scholar speculated that Ford could be the same person who appeared in 1930 in Detroit as Wallace Fard Muhammad, the founder of the Nation of Islam. The speculation was based upon the similarity of the names and the references to Allah in some of his Ethiopian hymns. The discovery of Ford and his family in Ethiopia disproved that hypothesis. It has also been stated that Ford's attachment to Judaism led to a split with Garvey. However, that does not seem to be the case, since he remained active in the U.N.I.A. through the 1920s. Finally, one writer has claimed that Ford merely served as the temporary leader for the Commandment Keepers while Matthew was away at school. Again, it seems that Matthew never attended school and he was active in Harlem during the years Ford was head of Beth B'nai Abraham.

Arnold Josiah Ford, *The Universal Ethiopian Hymnal* (New York, 1920s).

Randall K. Burkett, *Garveyism as a Religious Movement* (Metuchen, N.J., 1978).

Kenneth J. King, "Some Notes on Arnold J. Ford and New World Black Attitudes to Ethiopia," in Randall K. Burkett and Richard Newman, *Black Apostles* (Boston, 1978).

Albert Ehrman, "Black Judaism in New York," *Journal of Ecumenical Studies* 8, 1 (Winter 1971), 103–13.

FORD, Arthur Augustus (January 8, 1897, Titusville, Florida—January 2, 1971, Miami, Florida); married Sallie Stewart, 1922 (divorced, 1927); married Valerie McKeown, 1937 (divorced); education: Transylvania College 1917–18, 1919–20.

Arthur Augustus Ford, the most famous Spiritualist medium of the twentieth century and founder of the International General Assembly of Spiritualists, was baptized an Episcopalian according to his father's wishes but was raised in the Baptist church of his mother. Early in his teen years, he experienced a conversion and was rebaptized a Baptist. About the same time he and his father began reading Unitarian tracts, and at age sixteen he was excommunicated from the Baptist Church because of his acceptance of the Unitarian views. The next year he joined the Disciples of Christ. In 1917 he moved to Lexington, Kentucky, to attend Transylvania College and to prepare for the ministry.

He stayed two years at Transylvania in the middle of which he spent a year in the army. At the end of his second year, he was ordained and became pastor of the Christian Church in Barbourville, Kentucky. His oratorical abilities came to the fore while he was a young pastor, and in 1922 he was invited to join the Swarthmore Chautauqua Association of Pennsylvania as a lecturer.

As Ford was pursuing his more orthodox career, another world began to impinge upon him. Prior to his nineteenth year, he had noticed nothing psychic in his life. Then, a few minor events occurred during his year in the army. He began to hear voices that spoke names. After the names were heard, they would appear on the casualty list within a few days. During his years as a pastor, Ford traveled to New York to investigate first hand the American Society for Psychical Research and Spiritualism. During his years on the lecture circuit, he became deeply involved with Spiritualism. He discovered his ability to go into a trance, an ability he partially ascribed to his friendship with Swami Yogananda, who had just begun his American teaching career. He was twenty-four when Fletcher, his lifelong spirit guide, emerged and took control of his trance sessions.

His increasing involvement in Spiritualism, his speaking ability, and his development as a trance medium brought him a following, and with the encouragement, he founded the First Spiritualist Church of New York City. He immediately ran into conflict with institutionalized Spiritualism. In the mid–1920s the National Spiritualist Association was the only Spiritualist association; it was a staunch enemy of reincarnation, a belief Ford inherited from Yogananda. In the late twenties he was almost expelled from the association.

In 1936 Ford formed his own International General Association of

Spiritualists, breaking with both the National Association and the General Association of Spiritualists, which had been formed in 1930 as a rival organization. He remained president of the IGAS for two years and was its leading member for many years thereafter. In 1937 he married for the second time and moved to Hollywood. He also left his pastorate to assume a role as public spokesperson for Spiritualism, a role broken only for a few years after World War II when he founded and pastored the Church of Metaphysical Science in Miami.

During his early years as a medium, Ford became nationally famous for breaking the code that Harry Houdini had established with his wife prior to his death. Houdini's widow verified Ford's message (though she later disavowed it). He also became an alcoholic while ending his addiction to morphine, which had been prescribed for him by a doctor after an auto accident.

After World War II, Ford became increasingly associated with mainstream religious leaders. A number of the people affected by Ford gathered in 1956 to form the Spiritual Frontiers Fellowship, a national church-related organization for the exploration of the psychic and religious. Ford devoted much of the last years of his life to the SFF.

Two incidents stand out from Ford's last years. In 1965 he gave sittings for Sun Myung Moon, the founder of the Unification Church. His kind words about Moon and his prophetic role were publicized by Unification Church members and became a source of embarrassment to Spiritual Frontiers Fellowship members.

In 1967 Ford conducted a televised séance with Episcopal Bishop James A. Pike. The séance had a marked affect upon the bishop, whose excursions into the psychic somewhat dominated the rest of his life. After Ford's death, evidence was discovered that Ford had faked the séance. Other charges of his cheating made by associates also emerged, as did speculation that many of the papers his secretary burned were "research" notes. While most of his associates remained convinced of his genuine and remarkable mediumistic ability, the evidence of fakery cast a permanent shadow across his career.

Arthur Ford, *Why We Survive* (Cooksburg, N.Y., 1952).

———, *Nothing So Strange* (New York, 1958).

———, *Unknown But Known* (New York, 1968).

———, *The Life Beyond Death* (New York, 1971).

Allen Spraggett with William V. Rauscher, *Arthur Ford: The Man Who Talked with the Dead* (New York, 1973).

EOP, 340.

FOX, Ann Leah (1814?, Rockland County, New York—November 1, 1890, New York, New York); married? Fish, 1828 (divorced?); married Calvin Brown, 1851 (d. 1853); married Daniel Underhill, 1858.

FOX, Catherine (1839?, near Bath, Consccon, Ontario, Canada—July 2, 1892, New York, New York); married Henry D. Jencken, December 14, 1872 (d. 1881).

FOX, Margaret (1833?, near Bath, Consccon, Ontario, Canada—March 8, 1893, Brooklyn, New York); married Elisha Kent Kane, 1856 (d. February 16, 1857).

Modern Spiritualism traces its origins to 1848 and the events that occurred involving the three daughters of John and Margaret Fox—Leah, Catherine (usually called Kate), and Margaret. Despite their being thrust into the public spotlight for several decades, little is known of their life prior to 1848. John and Margaret Fox began married life in Rockland County, New York, where Leah was born. They moved to Canada, just north of Rochester, New York, and Margaret and Catherine were born there. In the 1840s they moved to Wayne County, New York, and in 1847, John Fox became the blacksmith in the small community of Hydesville. They attended the Methodist church. Many years previous to this move, Leah had married. Her husband had deserted her, and she lived in Rochester with her daughter, making her living as a music teacher.

On December 11, 1847, the Fox family moved into a vacant cottage in Hydesville. In March 1848 the family began to hear strange rappings in the house. The young girls found that the noises responded intelligently to their questions, and they concluded that they were produced by the spirit of a departed former resident of the house. They created a simple code to facilitate communication. Word of this extraordinary phenomenon spread through the community, and curious neighbors flocked to the Fox home to ask questions of this supposed spirit entity. Amid the confusion, Kate went to live with her brother David in Auburn and Margaret went to Rochester. However, the rappings continued, and in Rochester, a group who believed that the sisters were communicating with the dead emerged.

The phenomenon may have soon ended had it not been for one of the believers, Eliab W. Capron, who became the girls' promoter. In 1849 he organized a public meeting in Rochester at which a committee of prominent local citizens was appointed to investigate the rappings. Not only did it report its inability to explain the noises by any normal means, but a second investigating committee reported the same results. During the summer of 1850, Capron took the sisters to New York, where they gave demonstrations and met Horace Greeley, editor of the *New York Tribune*, who became their supporter and publicized their activities.

The rappings, whose promoters believed originated from the spirits of the dead, elicited an immediate response from the public. Groups attempting similar spirit contact were organized across the United States. The Fox sisters periodically toured the country, lecturing and giving demonstrations, but others, many more capable and articulate than the sisters, also claimed an ability to contact the spirit world. Some of these, such as Andrew Jackson Davis and Thomas Lake Harris, became the leaders of a growing international Spiritualist movement.

While Spiritualism took on a life of its own, at a lecture/demonstration in Philadelphia, Margaret Fox met the famous arctic explorer, Elisha Kent Kane. Following his death in 1857, she claimed that in 1856, just before he left for England, the two had exchanged vows before her family and thus she was his common-law wife. Her claims led to controversy when the Kane family refused to pay an annuity he had left her. Eventually she published her story of the relationship along with his letters.

While Margaret developed her relationship with Kane, Leah married again, became a widow, and married again during the decade, and by the end of the 1850s had retired into a domestic life. Both she and Margaret took second place to Kate, who for the next two decades was the most active medium of the three. A patron, Horace H. Day, formed the Society for the Diffusion of Spiritual Knowledge and hired Kate to give Spiritualist meetings. She attracted many of the famous, including Robert Dale Owen, to her sittings.

Their success as mediums in a growing Spiritualist movement was blunted for both Margaret and Kate as alcoholism, which was to plague them for the rest of their lives, developed. In 1865 Kate entered a sanitorium for a protracted period of treatment, with only temporary results. In 1871 she left the United States for England, where she promoted the new movement. She married and had two children, and with her husband's assistance, she was able to control her drinking. After his death in 1881, her alcoholism again came to the fore. She was arrested on several occasions, and in 1888 she lost custody of her children. Kate's problems brought Margaret to her defense and prompted the most important series of events in the sisters' life since the initial rappings.

Margaret blamed Kate's problems on Spiritualism. Then she confessed that the rappings had been a hoax that she and Kate had accomplished by throwing their toes out of joint. She denounced Leah as the person who forced them to continue the hoax after the first few weeks. Spiritualism, which had suffered from other revelations of hoaxes by fake mediums, was stung by Margaret's accusations, but the force of her confession was blunted by her retraction the next year. In 1889, complaining that she had been tricked into making the initial confession, Margaret launched a national tour to reaffirm her belief in the genuineness of her mediumship and the world of spirits. The tour, not a financial success, virtually ended the sisters' public career.

The last years of Leah, Kate, and Margaret were spent quietly in New York City. Leah had settled into a domestic existence and demonstrated her mediumship only to small groups on a nonprofessional basis. Kate and Margaret ended their years overcome by poverty and alcohol.

Despite the ambiguity of their lives, Spiritualists eulogized each of the sisters at the time of their deaths. In spite of mediums and theoreticians who arose at the beginning of the movement to organize and lead it, Spiritualists still recognize the Fox sisters as the first of the modern mediums.

Ann Leah Underhill, *The Missing Link in Modern Spiritualism* (New York, 1885).

Margaretta Fox Kane, *The Love-Life of Dr. Kane* (New York, 1865).

Mariam Buckner Pond, *Time Is Kind* (New York, 1947).

Slater Brown, *The Heyday of Spiritualism* (New York, 1970).

William G. L. Taylor, *Katie Fox* (New York, 1933).

Earl L. Fornell, *The Unhappy Medium: Spiritualism and the Life of Margaret Fox* (Austin, TX, 1964).

GARDNER, Gerald Brousseau (June 13, 1884, Blundellsands, England—February 12, 1964, at sea); married Donna, 1927 (d. 1960).

The founder of the modern religion of Wicca or Witchcraft, Gerald Brousseau Gardner came from an old Scottish family. An asthmatic child, he was raised by his nurse and received only minimal formal education. He made up for his educational lack through reading and through his travels, which were partly spurred by the search for a more healthful climate. In 1900 he moved to Ceylon (now Sri Lanka) and began a career as a plantation worker and later (1923) as a civil servant. During the next four decades, he traveled throughout southern Asia, Indonesia, and Palestine, where he absorbed the local cultures and religions.

His lack of formal training did not prevent him from becoming an accomplished amateur archeologist and anthropologist. He participated in the excavation of Lachish in Palestine, where a statue of the mother goddess, Ashtaroth, was found prominently in place beside the statue of Yahweh, the Hebrew deity. He developed a fascination with the Kris, the Malaysian ceremonial weapon, and his book *Kris and Other Malay Weapons* (1936) became the standard reference work on the subject.

During his years in Asia, he spent much of his free time with the local religious leaders from whom he absorbed the knowledge of magical practice and teachings. He briefly joined a Masonic lodge in Ceylon. While recovering from a leg injury, he was introduced to sunbathing and nudity. Each element became important to the religion he later developed.

Gardner retired and returned to England shortly before World War II. He settled in the New Forest area, where he began constructing modern Witchcraft. According to his followers, he joined an occult group, the Corona Fellowship of Rosicrucians, which had been founded by Mabel Besant-Scott, the daughter of Theosophist Annie Besant. Through the group he reportedly met some witches and eventually their priestess, Dorothy Clutterbuch, affectionately known as "Old Dorothy." Dorothy initiated Gardner, and he, in his delight with what he had found, wished to tell everyone about it. The group prevented him from revealing anything until the priestess's death. Then, in 1949, under his witch name "Scire," he published a novel, *High Magic's Aid*, in which much of the life and ritual of the witches was revealed. Finally, after the repeal of the last of England's Witchcraft laws in 1951, Gardner was allowed to go public. He claimed in his book *Witchcraft Today* (1954) that Wicca was a dying religion, and he merely wanted some record of it to survive.

Recent studies of Gardner's papers have questioned this popular account of Gardner's discovery of Witchcraft and suggest that Gardner did not discover Wicca. Rather, he along with his associates created it as a new eclectic occult religion that incorporated the various religious and magical resources available to them. Using some well-known magical texts, especially the writings of Aleister Crowley, Gardner fashioned a magical religion centered upon the worship of the Mother Goddess. His new faith was neither as exacting nor as demanding as Crowley's ritual magick. He designed Witchcraft for popular use. He took much of the initiation ritual from Masonic sources. He adopted the old pagan agricultural festivals as major holidays (termed sabbats) and added biweekly "esbats" (lesser rituals, at the new and full moons), the regular times when witches gather in their small groups, called covens.

Wicca is built upon the Mother Goddess, about whom Gardner had written a novel, *A Goddess Arrives*, in the 1930s. The coven conducted its worship and practice of magic in the nude within a circle. It was led by the priestess and the priest who embodied the Goddess (Arada) and the God (Cernunnos) respectively.

After the publication of *Witchcraft Today* and subsequently *The Meaning of Witchcraft* (1959), Gardner's fame as a witch drew increasing numbers who sought him for initiation. To those he initiated he gave a set of rituals; they, in turn, went forth to found their own covens.

Raymond and Rosemary Buckland, initiated by Gardner in 1963, brought Witchcraft to the United States. Alexander Sanders, a British witch, created his own variation on Gardnerian Wicca, which spread throughout England and came to the United States in the late 1960s. During the 1970s Witchcraft grew rapidly, and many variations of Goddess worship were developed that accommodated ethnic traditions and individual tastes.

Gardner died of heart failure while on an ocean voyage. He had lived the last years of his life on the Isle of Man, where he ran a Witchcraft museum. After his death, the museum collection was sold to Ripley's Believe It or Not.

Gerald B. Gardner, *Kris and Other Malay Weapons* (Singapore, 1936).
———— (under pseudonym, Scire), *High Magic's Aid* (London, 1949).
————, *Witchcraft Today* (London, 1954).
————, *The Meaning of Witchcraft* (London, 1959).
————, *A Goddess Arrives* (Stockwell, 1948).
J. L. Bracelin, *Gerald Gardner: Witch* (London, 1960).
Doreen Valiente, *An ABC of Witchcraft, Past and Present* (New York, 1973).
EOP, 365.

GESTEFELD, Ursula Newell (April 22, 1845, Augusta, Maine—October 22, 1921, Chicago, Illinois); married Theodore Gestefeld.

Ursula Newell Gestefeld, Christian Science and New Thought leader, was such a sickly child that those who knew the family doubted that she would survive childhood. She overcame her childhood frailties, however, married newspaperman Theodore Gestefeld, and raised a family of four children. A housewife, she moved with her family to Chicago in the 1870s, where her husband edited the German-language newspaper *Staats-Zeitung* and served as a reporter for the *Chicago Tribune*.

In 1884 she was given a copy of *Science and Health with Key to the Scriptures* by Mary Baker Eddy. She had an immediate response and joined Eddy's first Chicago class in May 1884. Eddy recognized her capabilities, and Gestefeld quickly became a prominent teacher with a large following. In 1887 she published her first book, *What Is Mental Medicine?* Two more books, *Ursula N. Gestefeld's Statement of Christian Science* (1888) and *The Science of the Christ* (1889), quickly followed. These books, particularly the second one, brought her into conflict with Eddy. While writing as a Christian Scientist, she gave no credit to Eddy and mentioned her only in passing. Instead of referring students to *Science and Health* as an authoritative textbook, she held up her own work as a simple statement of *Science and Health*, a book, she complained, that was difficult to comprehend.

Eddy, who was already experiencing the rivalry of a group of metaphysical mental-cure practitioners and teachers in Boston, viewed Gestefeld's activity with alarm. She saw her Chicago disciple as deviating from Christian Science teachings and distorting Eddy's own understanding of Truth. She had her dismissed from the Chicago church without a hearing. Gestefeld responded with an attack upon Mrs. Eddy in her book *Jesuitism in Christian Science* (1888).

Except for a few years (1892–95) following her husband's death when she lived in New York City, Gestefeld made her headquarters in Chicago. Not allowing her ouster from Christian Science to stop her, she spent the early 1890s developing her own variation of Christian Science, which she termed the "Science of Being," and published numerous books on the subject: *A Chicago Bible Class* (1891); *A Modern Catechism* (1892); *And God Said* (1895); and *How We Master Our Fate* (1897).

In 1897, in Chicago, she founded the Exodus Club, a metaphysical organization that became the Church of New Thought in 1904. During this period she also edited a monthly magazine, *The Exodus* (1896–1904), and became a prominent leader in the New Thought movement. She addressed the first convention of the International New Thought League (later Federation) in Boston in 1899, and in 1903 she became its vice-president. She traveled to London for the 1914 Convention, at which time its present name, the International New Thought Alliance, was adopted. In the 1890s she had already established a Science of Being Center in England.

The last twenty years of Gestefeld's life were spent teaching and writing. Her son, Harry Gestefeld, ran the Gestefeld Publishing Company in Pelham, New York, from which most of her books were issued. In 1910 she published her most important work, *The Builder and the Plan*, which presented her mature Science of Being system. Although it drew heavily on Christian Science, it differed at many points, including the dropping of many of Christian Science's specifically Christian emphases. She wrote several other books including a feminist novel, *The Woman Who Dares* (1892), which protested the unreasonable sexual demands of husbands upon their wives.

Although her books were popular with New Thought leaders for many years, her church did not long survive her death and her following was absorbed into the larger New Thought movement. Her cremated remains were buried in Chicago.

Ursula N. Gestefeld, *Jesuitism in Christian Science* (Chicago, 1888).

———, *A Statement of Christian Science* (Chicago, 1888).

———, *The Science of the Christ* (Chicago, 1889).

———, *The Builder and the Plan* (Chicago, 1910).

Charles S. Braden, *Christian Science Today* (Dallas, 1958).

WWW, 1, 449.

GODDARD, Dwight (July 5, 1861, Worcester, Massachusetts—July 5, 1939, Randolph, Vermont); married; education: Worcester Polytechnical Institute; Hartford Theological Seminary, graduated 1894.

Dwight Goddard, founder of the Fellowship Following Buddha and one of the pioneer non-Oriental Buddhists in the United States, began his adult life as a mechanical engineer. After ten years in engineering, however, he turned his back on the business world and entered Hartford Theological Seminary to prepare himself as a Christian missionary. Following graduation, he was sent to China by the Baptist church. While there, he met and married his first wife, who was serving as a medical missionary.

After almost two decades in the mission field, he became discouraged with the progress of the church as a religious force and developed an interest in Buddhism. At first he believed that the two faiths had much in common and sought ways to reconcile them. In San Diego in 1924, he proposed the formation of a Christian and Buddhist Fellowship. In further pursuit of his goal, he entered Shokoku (Zen) monastery in Japan to study with Roshi Taiko Tamazaki. Then, in 1927, he published his first major book, *Was Jesus Influenced by Buddhism?*

Gradually, he became convinced that the goal of mixing or reconciling Buddhism and Christianity was futile, and he slowly lost his interest in Christianity. He then conceived of a Buddhist missionary effort within the United States. During this period of growing interest in Buddhism, he divorced his first wife and remarried. That second marriage also ended in divorce.

After his second divorce, having become convinced that Zen was the form of Buddhism closest to the teachings of the Buddha, Goddard built a home and temple near Union Village, Vermont, from which he could both live the secluded ascetic life his faith demanded and launch his Buddhist mission program. He began a magazine, *Zen*, and published his most important book, *A Buddhist Bible*. This volume brought together in a popular edition essential Buddhist writings, many translated for the first time into English from Indian, Chinese, Japanese, and Tibetan schools.

In 1934 Goddard proposed the organization of a Fellowship Following Buddha as a means of spreading Buddhism among non-Oriental Americans. He suggested the establishment of two cooperative homes, one in Vermont and one in California, where a small group of brothers could live the quiet Buddhist life and where those wishing to learn about and practice the faith could reside for brief periods. In good weather, the brothers could travel between the two locations teaching classes and distributing literature. This semimobile life would, Goddard believed, be the most efficacious in spreading interest in Buddha.

Goddard's plan was not implemented beyond the establishment of his own personal temple in Vermont. He died in 1939 and his idea along with him. However, his writings, which were circulated widely and reprinted in the 1970s, laid the foundation upon which a popular Buddhism began to grow in the 1960s.

Dwight Goddard, *A Buddhist Bible* (Thetford, Vt., 1938).

———, *Was Jesus Influenced by Buddhism?* (Thetford, Vt., 1927).

———, *Buddha, Truth and Brotherhood* (Santa Barbara, Calif., 1934).

———, *Buddhist Practice of Concentration* (Santa Barbara, Calif., 1934).

David Starry, "Dwight Goddard—the Yankee Buddhist," *Zen Notes* XXVII, 7 (July 1980), 1–3.

Rick Fields, *How the Swans Came to the Lake* (Boulder, Colo., 1981).

GOLDSMITH, Joel Sol (March 10, 1892, New York, New York—June 17, 1964, London, England); married Rose Robb, 1930's (d. 1943); married Nadea Allen, 1945 (div. January 10, 1956); married Emma Lindsey, March 10, 1957.

Joel Goldsmith, spiritual healer and mystical teacher and founder of the Infinite Way, was born in New York City. Although his parents were Jewish, they did not practice their faith and Joel attended a Reform temple for only a few weeks in preparation for his bar mitzvah. His education ended after one month of high school, and he joined his father's importing business to begin a career in merchandising and sales.

His interest in spiritual healing began while his father was on a business trip to Europe. In England his father became ill, and the doctors did not think he would live. Coincidentally the father of the girl that Joel was dating was a Christian Science practitioner. He offered to treat Joel's father, who completely recovered. As a consequence Joel began to study Christian Science.

After World War I, in which he served as a marine, he returned to his father's business. The business failed, however, and he had to go on the road as a salesman. He also developed tuberculosis, and after being given three months to live by the doctors, he turned to a Christian Science practitioner and was healed. He also sought help for his business career, which was steadily disintegrating.

A crucial series of events occurred in November 1928. As a result of being cured by a Christian Science practitioner, Joel discovered that he no longer had a desire to smoke, drink, play cards, or bet on horse races. The "businessman" in him had died. People then began to turn to him for healing prayer, and to his amazement, they were healed. He took a class in Christian Science, joined the church, and finally opened an office as a practitioner. At about this same time he married. In 1933 he moved to Boston. After a slow beginning, he had a successful career as a practitioner, eventually locating his office across the street from the Mother Church. He also became the First Reader at Third Church in Boston.

In 1943 he moved to Florida. After a few months there, his wife died; he returned to Boston briefly before moving to California. In Santa Monica he renewed his acquaintance with Nadea Allen, and in 1945 they were married. Shortly after the wedding, his life changed dramatically. He also decided to sever his ties with any organization, and in 1946 he withdrew from the Church of Christ, Scientist. He began writing a book and contemplated a quiet life in semiretirement working as a healer with the few who would come to him. He also went through a series of mystical experiences, which he described as an initiation into spiritual truth. After the initiation, he quickly finished his first book, called *The Infinite Way*.

He was asked to teach a Bible class, which reluctantly he began. As the class grew, he received invitations to speak and to teach at different locations. In 1950 he was called to Hawaii. He liked it so much that he decided to move there, and he made Honolulu the center from which he taught and traveled to meet with the ever-increasing number of students worldwide. It was at about the time that he moved to Hawaii that his marriage failed. He was divorced in 1956, and the following year he married one of his students, Emma Lindsey.

The last fourteen years of Goldsmith's life were his most productive. His classes provided materials for a continuing series of books, and among his pupils were capable editors to transcribe and prepare them for publication. During the last decade of his life, Lorraine Sinkler did most of the editing of his material. His books include *Practicing the Presence* (1961); *The Thunder of Silence* (1961); *Our Spiritual Resources* (1962); *The Contemplative Life* (1963); and *Man Was Not Born to Cry* (1964).

When Goldsmith left the Christian Science organization, he did not wish merely to replace it with one of his own. He rejected organizing the Infinite Way into anything more than an informal circle of his pupils. Groups of students who meet together to listen to his tapes and study his writings have arisen, and centers for the distribution of his materials have grown up around the country and world. His pupils carry on his work in much the same informal way as they had during his life.

Joel S. Goldsmith, *The Infinite Way* (San Gabriel, Calif., 1947, 1961).

————, *The Heart of Spiritual Healing* (New York, 1959).

————, *The Contemplative Life* (New York, 1963).

————, *Living the Infinite Way* (New York, 1961).

Lorraine Sinkler, *The Spiritual Journey of Joel S. Goldsmith* (New York, 1973).

————, *The Alchemy of Awareness* (New York, 1977).

GRANT, Frederick William (July 25, 1834, London, England—July 25, 1902, Plainfield, New Jersey).

Frederick William Grant, founder of one of the larger of the American branches of the Plymouth Brethren, was raised in England and attended King's College School. Disappointed at not being able to secure a position in the War Office, he migrated to Canada in 1855. Though he did not have seminary training, the Church of England in Canada ordained him. As an Anglican priest, he encountered and read literature from the Plymouth Brethren, which caused him to leave the Anglican Church. He moved first to Toronto, then to Brooklyn, New York, and eventually settled in Plainfield, New Jersey.

Grant became well known among the Exclusive Brethren—those who did not fellowship with non-Brethren groups—through his speaking and books, including *Life and Immortality* (1871); *Numerical Structure of Scripture* (1877); and *Facts and Theories as to a Future State* (1879).

Toward the end of the life of John Nelson Darby (d. 1883), founder of the Plymouth Brethren, Grant became aware that his study of the Bible had led him to opinions that diverged from Darby's. Waiting until after Darby's death, Grant published *Life and the Spirit* (later expanded and reissued as *Life in Christ and Sealing with the Spirit*). He taught that the Old Testament saints had received eternal life in Christ; that a new believer at once received eternal life in Christ; that faith in Christ is faith in the risen and glorified Christ rather than in his work—that is, the atonement; and that a Christian may be justified and have peace and not know it.

The circulation of the booklet led to a controversy among the Brethren, who objected as much to the manner in which Grant spread his new ideas as to the ideas themselves. Many complained that Grant was intentionally trying to cause a division. The division actually began in Canada where leaders began to denounce Grant's work as heresy. On November 27, 1884, the Brethren in Montreal issued a protest asking Grant to withdraw the booklet. He refused. On December 7 the assembly declared him a heretic and admonished him to reject his false teachings. When he further refused, they disfellowshiped him.

On December 21, 1884, Grant met with his supporters at "a separate table" set up on Craig Street, where his home assembly in Plainfield, New Jersey, supported him. The schism widened to include assemblies throughout North America. Grant had developed an important ally in his home assembly, Timothe Ophir Loizeaux, who with his brother Paul Loizeaux of New York City had founded a major Brethren publishing concern. During the next two decades, the Loizeaux brothers published Grant's many titles.

Grant's split with the Exclusive Brethren did not lead him toward the Open Brethren. Thus in the 1890s when a group of the Grant Brethren had begun to advocate and practice a limited communion with the Open Brethren (those Plymouth Brethren most inclusive in their approach to non-Brethren), Grant steadfastly refused to consider rapprochement with the Open Brethren until they renounced their errors. "Truth," he wrote in 1894, "cannot live without warfare in a world away from God." Grant's hard line led to a split in his following.

Grant's leadership and continued reputation among the Brethren are based on his work as a Bible student. He was originally converted to Christianity by reading the Bible and studied it all his life. He became impressed with the numerical relations implicit in the form and groupings of Biblical writings. His single most famous book is a multivolume commentary, *The Numerical Bible*. He wrote many books, most published in undated editions by the Loizeaux Brothers Bible Truth Depot, including *Atonement in Type, Prophecy and Accomplishment*; *The Crowned Christ*; *A Divine Movement*; *Genesis in the Light of the New Testament*; *God's Evangel*; *The Hope of the Morning Star*; *The Prophetic History of the Church*; and *Reasons for My Faith As to Baptism*.

Frederick William Grant, *The Numerical Bible* (New York, 1892–1903).

——— , *Atonement in Type, Prophecy and Accomplishment* (New York, n.d.).

——— , *The Prophetic History of the Church* (New York, 1902).

——— , *A Divine Movement* (New York, n.d.).

——— , *Genesis in the Light of the New Testament* (New York, 1945).

Napoleon Noel, *The History of the Brethren* (Denver, Colo., 1936).

Hy. Pickering, *Chief Men Among the Brethren* (London, 1918).

GURDJIEFF, Georgei Ivanovitch (January 13, 1872 (?)/November 28, 1877 (?), Alexandropol, Armenia—October 29, 1949, Paris, France); married Countess Ostrowsky.

The origins of Georgei Ivanovitch Gurdjieff, one of the most influential of the modern spiritual teachers, are shrouded in mystery. His passport gave November 28, 1877, as his birthdate, whereas his followers celebrate the anniversary of his birth on January 13, 1872. Biographers suggest other dates. He is believed to have been born in a small town on the Turkish-Armenian border, which was renamed Leninkan after the Russian Revolution. As a boy, Gurdjieff moved with his Greek family to nearby Kars, where he studied with the dean of the Orthodox cathedral. He learned about the mysticism of the Russian Orthodox Church and some of its esoteric practices such as the techniques of prayer. Possessing a searching and curious mind, he developed an early interest in both Western science and the desire to explain the inexplicable phenomena of miracles and the occult.

In 1896 he left home and began a long period of wandering, which is partially chronicled in his semiautobiographical *Meetings with Remarkable Men*. In his almost three decades of travel, he claimed to have been one of the Seekers of the Truth, a small group committed to the search for the ancient wisdom. Gurdjieff claimed to have journeyed from Ethiopia to Tibet. Undoubtedly he met many holy men and studied with a number of esoteric orders. The most significant training may have come from various Sufi orders in Turkey. As he traveled, he made his living following different trades, from selling carpets to demonstrating hypnotism. It is rumored that he was also a Russian spy for several years, although no conclusive evidence of this allegation has appeared.

In 1912 he appeared in Moscow, and at sometime during the next three years he married the Countess Ostrowsky, a lady of the Russian court. By 1915 he moved between St. Petersburg and Moscow teaching groups, which included such members as the composer Thomas de Hartmann and his wife. In Moscow he also met his most prominent disciple, Pyotr Demianovitch Ouspensky, who had just returned to Moscow after a period of travel in search of the truth he finally found in Gurdjieff. Threatened by the Revolution, Gurdjieff and his students fled Russia in 1917. They arrived in Tiflis, Armenia, where they were joined by Alexander and Jeanne de Salzmann, but continued to move from place to place until they finally settled in Paris. Gurdjieff bought a chateau near Fontainebleau and founded his famous Institute for the Harmonious Development of Man in 1922. For the rest of his life, Gurdjieff taught his small but highly motivated and influential groups of students and perfected his system of thought and practice. Students included novelist Katherine Mansfield (who died at the institute), A. R. Orage, and Maurice Nicoll.

Gurdjieff taught that humans are "asleep," operated like puppets by forces unknown to them. Individuals are needed who have learned to master their lives by "awakening" their lost contact with a Higher force and through this to direct awareness of other forces and energies that move within them and around them on this planet. To assist this process,

Gurdjieff developed a series of dancelike exercises, called the Gurdjieff movements. He also placed students in situations of personal conflict and intense interaction with others and assigned them tasks designed to force self-consciousness. His system has been termed the Fourth Way, the way of the person encountering ordinary life as opposed to the first three ways of the yogi, monk, or fakir. His system of knowledge is symbolized in the Enneagram, a nine-pointed symbol in a circle.

Gurdjieff made his first visit to America in 1924, where he found students prepared by the English translation of Ouspensky's book, *Tertium Organum* (1920), and the recruiting activities of Orage. Soon after his return from the United States, he was injured in an automobile accident. After his hospital stay he continued to work with his students but shifted much of his energy to the writing of his several books—*All and Everything: Beelzebub's Tales to His Grandson*; *Meetings with Remarkable Men*; *Life Is Real Only Then, When "I Am"*; and *The Herald of Coming Good*. He circulated these among his students, and only the last one was published before his death.

In 1933 Gurdjieff closed the institute. He traveled widely and worked with his students in Paris and New York. At the time of his death he was almost unknown and had only a few hundred students. Popular acclaim came only after the publication of his books and the establishment of teaching centers by his pupils to work together and promote the ongoing study of his teaching and ideas by establishing Gurdjieff societies and foundations in major centers around the world. The most prominent of these is the Gurdjieff Foundation in Paris, directed by Jeanne de Salzmann, who studied with Gurdjieff from 1919 and was his secretary at the time of his death. In the United States, a similar Gurdjieff Foundation, now located in San Francisco, was founded in 1953. Other students, such as John G. Bennett, Robert De Ropp, and William Nyland, founded their own groups for the study of Gurdjieff's teaching and ideas. Although they did not study with Gurdjieff or his senior pupils, others who consider Gurdjieff's ideas of vital interest have developed their own interpretation of his ideas and now lead study groups and issue writings related to Gurdjieff's ideas. There are also individuals who offer their own unique adaptations of Gurdjieff's ideas and/or who attempt to blend his approach with various other systems and ideas. Best known among these are E. J. Gold, Oscar Ichazo, René Lefort, Jan Cox, Rajneesh, and Thane Walker.

Interest in Gurdjieff has generated extensive literature on him in English and French, and his writings have been or are being translated into most major languages.

George I. Gurdjieff, *The Herald of Coming Good* (Paris, 1933).

——, *All and Everything* (New York, 1950).

——, *Meetings With Remarkable Men* (New York, 1963).

——, *Life Is Real Only Then, When "I Am"* (New York, 1975).

James Webb, *The Harmonious Circle* (New York, 1980).

J. Walter Driscoll and the Gurdjieff Foundation of California, *Gurdjieff: An Annotated Bibliography* (New York, 1984).

Kathleen Riordan Speeth, *The Gurdjieff Work* (Berkeley, 1976).
Kathleen Riordan Speeth and Ira Friedlander, *Gurdjieff, Seeker of Truth* (New York, 1980).
EOP, 396.

HARRIS, Thomas Lake (May 15, 1823, Fenny Stratford, Buckingham-shire—March 23, 1906, New York, New York); married Mary Van Arnum, 1845 (d. 1850); married Emily Isabella Waters, 1855 (d. 1885); married Jane Lee Waring, 1891.

Thomas Lake Harris, founder of the Brotherhood of the New Life, was born into a strict Calvinist family in England. He migrated to the United States at the age of five and settled in Utica, New York. His mother died soon after the move and, rejecting his stepmother, he left home at the age of nine and found work. Eventually he became a Universalist minister and served churches in the Mohawk Valley and New York City. In 1846 he married for the first time.

During his years as a Universalist he began to read the writings of Emmanuel Swedenborg and slowly converted to his ideas. In 1847 he became pastor of the First Independent Church Society of New York. He had a brief association with Spiritualist Andrew Jackson Davis but broke off the relationship because of a scandal in Davis's private life. In 1851 he became involved with the Apostolic movement headed by a Seventh-Day Baptist preacher, J. D. Scott, who had become a trance medium. Scott formed the Mountain Cove Community in Fayette County, Virginia. When a split developed in the community, Harris was called in to settle the dispute. He ruled the community for a year, but eventually the group rejected his authority.

Harris returned to New York and spent the next years as a teacher and trance lecturer. A poet, he could move into trance and dictate long poems containing the ideas of what would become his own form of Spiritualism. He also pastored the Swedenborgian church on Washington Square, in New York.

In May 1859 he traveled to Scotland and England to gather converts. They were few in number but included the wealthy Laurence Oliphant. He returned to the United States as the Civil War began, and in 1861 he founded his Brotherhood of the New Life in a community near Wassaic, New York. Two years later, using money from Jane Waring, a convert, he bought land near Amenia, New York, and expanded the community. Finally, in 1867, he moved the community onto land at Brocton, New York, with money donated by Oliphant, who had come to the United States after the war.

The community thrived, but in 1875 Harris moved with a few followers to Santa Rosa, California, and established the Fountain Grove community. He moved to escape the New York winters and commune yearround with fairies, spiritual beings who prefer lush gardens and warm weather. In 1881 he closed the Brocton community entirely, and all the members moved to California. In 1885 his second wife died, and in 1891 he married his long-time follower Jane Waring. He departed from the community in

1892, soon after the marriage, and resettled in New York, where he lived out his remaining years.

After Harris left, the community dwindled. In 1900 Harris sold his interest to the five remaining members. Kanaye Nagasawa, the survivor of the five, inherited the total property in the 1920s and continued to work the land until his death in 1934.

Harris developed a complicated and sophisticated form of Spiritualism, and it was one of the most misunderstood and misrepresented aspects of his life. He attempted to distinguish himself from both the Spiritualists and the communalists, with whom he had a strong connection. Beginning with the Swedenborgian idea of conjugal love and the spiritualist notion of spiritual affinities, Harris told his followers to develop a relationship with their heavenly counterpart. This heavenly counterpart was to be sought in the physical bodies of the opposite sex. The person who embodied the counterpart was rarely one's natural spouse. Community members thus discontinued relations with their husbands and wives and sought the person who embodied their counterpart. Harris's belief system also included a bipolar deity (male-female) and fairies.

Harris's doctrine could easily have degenerated into community sex, and his very sensual poetry gave room for outsiders to believe such. Harris was a celibate, however, and taught his members that only in the celibate state could the true relationship be developed.

Thomas Lake Harris, *An Epic of the Starry Heaven* (New York, 1854).

——— , *A Lyric of the Golden Age* (New York, 1856).

——— , *The Wisdom of Angels* (New York, 1957).

——— , *Brotherhood of the New Life: Its Fact, Law, Method and Purpose* (Fountain Grove, Calif., 1891).

——— , *The New Republic* (Santa Rosa, Calif., 1891).

Herbert W. Schneider and George Lawton, *A Prophet and a Pilgrim* (New York, 1942).

Arthur A. Cuthbert, *The Life Worldwork of Thomas Lake Harris, Written from Direct Personal Knowledge* (Glasgow, 1909).

William P. Swainson, *Thomas Lake Harris and His Occult Teaching* (London, 1922).

Robert V. Hine, *California's Utopian Colonies* (New Haven, Conn., 1966).

DAB, 8, 322–23.

EOP, 407–8.

HAYWOOD, Garfield Thomas (July 15, 1880, Greencastle, Indiana— April 12, 1931, Indianapolis, Indiana); married Ida Howard, February 11, 1902.

Garfield Thomas Haywood, the first presiding bishop of the Pentecostal Assemblies of the World, was born in rural Indiana but moved to Indianapolis at the age of three. His father became a foundry worker. Young Thomas attended both the Methodist Episcopal Church and the Baptist Church for a period and served as a Sunday school superintendent in each. Although he was able to complete only two years of high school, the influence of his mother, a school teacher, led him to continue his education informally. He was later known as a widely read pastor. He also had a love of the fine arts, and after leaving school he found employment as a cartoonist on two weeklies serving the black community.

In 1907 two women who had been at the Apostolic Mission on Azuza Street in Los Angeles and who had received the Pentecostal baptism of the Holy Spirit as evidenced by the speaking in tongues came to Indianapolis and shared their experience with several acquaintances. Out of their work a small interracial Pentecostal assembly emerged. Elder Henry Prentiss, who had been at Azuza Street, became the pastor. Haywood joined the group in 1908 and quickly rose to a position of leadership. In 1909, when Prentiss moved on, Haywood succeeded him as pastor.

Under his pastorate, the Apostolic Faith Assembly, as the group became known, grew steadily and had to move frequently into ever larger quarters. In 1910 Haywood began *The Voice in the Wilderness*, a periodical, from the print shop he had established in his home. He also printed numerous tracts and booklets and eventually published his own hymn-book, *The Bridegroom Cometh*.

About this time, Haywood led the Apostolic Faith Assembly to affiliate with the Pentecostal Assemblies of the World, a loose fellowship of Pentecostal assemblies that had been founded in 1906 (the first year of the Pentecostal revival) by J. J. Frazee (often mistakenly cited as Frazier) in Los Angeles. In 1912 the Assemblies had their annual convention in Indianapolis, for the first time, in the new church building of the Apostolic Faith Assembly.

In 1914 the Pentecostal movement was divided by a new teaching that denied the doctrine of the Trinity and called upon Christians to be baptized (or rebaptized) in the name of "Jesus Only." The newly formed Assemblies of God rejected the new teaching. As it spread, J. Roswell Flower began to issue warnings against it. He wrote Haywood, who replied in an oft-quoted letter, "Your warning came too late. I have already accepted the message and have been baptized."

Haywood's acceptance of the "Jesus Only" doctrine made him a major focus of the new movement, and the Pentecostal Assemblies of the World grew rapidly as those who had accepted the new doctrine affiliated with it. Then in 1918 the P.A. of W. merged with the other major Jesus Only group, the General Assembly of the Apostolic Assemblies. Although a black man, Haywood was one of the leaders of the new organization, which kept the name Pentecostal Assemblies of the World. He pastored one of the largest Pentecostal congregations in the world, edited a major periodical, and was a poet-hymn writer and author of note. He was elected Secretary-Treasurer of the new body.

The Apostolic Faith Assembly continued to grow and moved into a new permanent building in 1924. Renamed Christ Temple, the twelve-hundred-seat church was served by Haywood as pastor for the remainder of his life.

The same year Christ Temple opened, the Pentecostal Assemblies was rent with a racial schism. Many of the white members withdrew and formed what was to become the United Pentecostal Church. The withdrawal of most of the white leadership left Haywood the dominant personality in the Pentecostal Assemblies of the World. In 1925 the P.A. of W. completely reorganized. The board of presbyters was abolished and a council of bishops created. Haywood was elected as the Presiding Bishop, a position he retained for the rest of his life. He also served as editor of the Assemblies' magazine, the *Christian Outlook.*

Garfield Thomas Haywood, *The Birth of the Spirit in the Days of the Aposltes* (Indianapolis, Ind., n.d.).

——— , *Feed My Sheep* (Indianapolis, Ind., n.d.).

——— , *The Finest of the Wheat* (Indianapolis, Ind., n.d.).

——— , *The Victim of the Flaming Sword* (Indianapolis, Ind., n.d.).

——— , *The Bridegroom Songs* (Indianapolis, Ind., n.d.).

Morris E. Golder, *The Life and Works of Bishop Garfield Thomas Haywood* (Indianapolis, Ind., 1977).

——— , *History of the Pentecostal Assemblies of the World* (Indianapolis, Ind., 1973).

——— , *The Bishops of the Pentecostal Assemblies of the World* (Indianapolis, Ind., 1980).

Fred J. Foster, *Think It Not Strange* (St. Louis, Mo., 1965).

Paul D. Dugas, comp., *The Life and Writings of Elder G. T. Haywood* (Portland, Ore., 1968).

James L. Tyson, *Before I Sleep* (Indianapolis, Ind., 1976).

HEINDEL, Max (Carl Louis Von Grasshoff) (July 23, 1865, Denmark?—January 6, 1919, Oceanside, California); married ? (d. 1905); married Augusta Foss, August 10, 1910 (d. May 9, 1938).

The occult teacher known to the world as Max Heindel was born of an aristocratic German family as Carl Louis Von Grasshoff, the eldest son of François L. Von Grasshoff. When he was sixteen, he traveled to Glasgow, Scotland, where he trained as a maritime engineer and eventually rose to become chief engineer on one of the Cunard liners. In 1895 he settled in New York City as a consulting engineer, and while there he met and married his first wife.

He moved to Los Angeles in 1903 where he became interested in the occult. He joined the Theosophical Society in America and served as the vice-president of the Los Angeles branch during 1904–5. Through Theosophy, he was introduced to astrology, which became a lifelong interest. In 1905 he began lecturing on the West Coast, but his activities were continually interrupted by recurrent heart trouble.

In 1907 he traveled to Germany. While there, a Being, whom he later described as an Elder Brother of the Rosicrucian Order, appeared to him several times. The Being told Heindel he had been under observation and had passed a test. He was given instructions on how to reach the Temple of the Rose Cross located near the border of Germany and Bohemia. Heindel went to the temple where he remained for a month. During this period he was taught the knowledge for his first book, *The Rosicrucian Cosmo-Conception.* (Some have suggested, based upon the similarity of Heindel's and Rudolf Steiner's ideas, that Heindel, in fact, studied with Steiner while in Germany.)

Upon his return to the United States, he edited and rewrote the material he had received and finished it in September 1908. He moved to Columbus, Ohio, began teaching, and formed the first Rosicrucian center. After leaving Ohio, he moved to Seattle, Washington, where he met William M. Patterson, who financed the publication of *The Rosicrucian Cosmo-Conception*, which appeared in November 1909.

Having created centers in Columbus, Seattle, North Yakima, Washington, and Portland, Oregon, he moved to Los Angeles the same month his book was published. He taught until March 1910, when his heart trouble put him back into the hospital. He claimed that while in the hospital he journeyed to Germany in his etheric body accompanied by his teacher. There he was told of the future Rosicrucian work planned for him, including the erection of a temple on Mt. Ecclesia near Oceanside, California. In 1909 he also renewed his acquaintance with Augusta Foss whom he had met prior to his first wife's death. She assisted him in his work, and they were eventually married.

The remaining years of Heindel's life were quite productive. He wrote a number of books including *The Rosicrucian Mysteries* (1911); *Freemasonry and Catholicism* (1919); and *Mysteries of the Great Operas* (1921). His interest in astrology made the Rosicrucian Fellowship one of the major factors in the twentieth-century revival of astrological interest. Besides his major books, *The Message of the Stars* and *Simplified Scientific Astrology* (both of which were published posthumously), he featured a regular astrological column in his monthly magazine, *Rays from the Rosy Cross*, and the fellowship published an annual *Ephemeris*, the daily chart of planetary positions needed for the erection of a birth chart.

On December 25, 1920, the year after his death, the temple on Mt. Ecclesia was dedicated, and his wife carried on his work until her death in 1938.

Max Heindel, *The Rosicrucian Cosmo-Conception* (Oceanside, Calif., 1909).

———, *The Rosicrucian Mysteries* (Oceanside, Calif., 1911).

———, *The Rosicrucian Philosophy, Questions and Answers* (Oceanside, Calif., 1922).

———, *Simplified Scientific Astrology* (Oceanside, Calif., 1928).

Mrs. Max Heindel, *The Birth of the Rosicrucian Fellowship* (Oceanside, Calif., n.d.).

Christopher McIntosh, *The Rosy Cross Unveiled* (Wellingborough, 1980).

EOP, 421.

HENSLEY, George Went (187–?—July 25, 1955, Lester's Shed, Florida); married Sally.

George Went Hensley, a minister of the Church of God (Cleveland, Tennessee), introduced the practice of handling snakes into Pentecostalism and later became the acknowledged leader of the independent snakehandling churches across the Appalachian region of the southern United States. He had been converted and joined the small Holiness church in 1908, just at the time that Pentecostal practices (speaking in tongues and the gifts of the spirit) as a sign of the baptism of the Holy Spirit were being introduced into the church.

Fired with a convert's zeal, Hensley set up a brush arbor at Owl Holler (about twelve miles from Cleveland, Tennessee) and began to preach on Mark 16: 17–18 and the signs that would follow those who believe. Some men in the neighborhood who had known Hensley prior to his conversion turned a box of poisonous snakes loose in front of Hensley while he was preaching. Surprising everyone, Hensley reached down and gathered the serpents in his arms and continued his preaching.

Among the leaders of the Church of God, including A. J. Tomlinson, the events of Hensley's ministry were received as further proof of the outpouring of Pentecostal power within the church. Tomlinson invited him to Cleveland and publicized his ministry in the church's periodical. By 1914 Hensley had introduced the practice throughout the church, and Tomlinson reported, "Many of our people have been handling poison serpents at the Tabernacle. The power of God was demonstrated marvelously."

Hensley founded a church near Sale Creek in Grasshopper Valley and built a small congregation. After almost a decade of snake handling without incident, a member of the group, Garland Defries, was bitten and remained in serious condition for several weeks. Although he did not die, the incident quelled the enthusiasm for snake handling around Sale Creek. Hensley soon moved his ministry to Pine Mountain, Kentucky (near Harlan), and became pastor of the East Pineville Church of God. Meanwhile, continued practices of snake handling within the Church of God created an issue for the growing denomination, which had been continually facing charges of fanaticism simply because of tongues-speaking. In 1928 the Assembly of the Church denounced the practice of handling snakes. Gradually the practice became confined to a small group of independent churches scattered from West Virginia to Florida.

In 1943 Raymond Hays, a follower of Hensley's, came to Grasshopper Valley and founded the Dolly Pond Church of God with Signs Following. This church became the focus of a major controversy two years later when a preacher, Lewis Ford, died after being bitten by a snake at the church. Twelve church members were arrested. Hensley and Tom Harden, the Dolly Creek pastor, were subsequently arrested for "disturbing the peace" when they handled snakes in front of a member's home in Chattanooga. The trial proceedings of the members were not decided until February 11, 1948 when the judge fined each man $50.00. Several months previously, their lawyer announced that a new church would be opened, the South Chattanooga Church of God. Hensley, then pastor of a congregation in Brightsville, Tennessee, became the assistant pastor of the new church.

Hensley continued to move about and visit the various snake-handling groups. He claimed to have been bitten several hundred times. The last time was on July 24, 1955, during a service at an arbor at Lester's Shed, near Altha, Florida. He was bitten while returning a diamond-back rattlesnake to a box and died the next day.

Weston La Barre, *They Shall Take Up Serpents* (New York, 1969).

Diary of A. J. Tomlinson, I (Queens Village, N.Y., 1949).

J. B. Collins, *Tennessee Snake Handlers* (Chattanooga, Tenn., circa 1946).

HERR, John (September 18, 1782, Lancaster, Pennsylvania—May 3, 1850, Humberstone Township, Welland County, Ontario, Canada); married Betsy Graff, April 7, 1807.

John Herr, the founder of the Reformed Mennonite Church, was raised in the Mennonite community in Lancaster County, Pennsylvania. Around 1800 his father, Francis Herr, separated from the Mennonite Church. According to Mennonite Church records, he was expelled for dishonesty in the sale of a horse, but according to the Reformed Mennonite Church he had withdrawn after the church conference had rebuffed his call for reforms. In either case, he began to hold informal meetings in his home, attended by his large family and others who had separated from the Mennonite church. Herr emphasized his lay status, and always spoke, for example, from a sitting position when delivering his exhortations.

In 1810 Francis Herr died, and John Herr was selected to continue the work of his father. He decided to organize the group on a more formal basis. On May 30, 1812, at his home in Strasburg, the group elected him pastor and bishop and selected Abraham Landis, a member of the group, to baptize him. (None of Francis Herr's children had been baptized.) Herr then baptized Landis and Abraham Groff. Groff had been elected deacon and Landis was elected a preacher. Herr baptized forty-one lay members and in November led in the dedication of their first meeting house, called Longenecker's.

Herr became an energetic and gifted leader. He traveled extensively to the Mennonite communities in Ontario and western New York where he founded congregations. He began to write and produced six small books: *The True and Blessed Way* (German edition, 1815; English edition, 1816); *A Brief and Apostolic Answer to a Letter Written by a Minister of the Mennonite Church* (1819, 1842); *The Illustrating Mirror* (1827, 1834); *Letter from John Herr to a Number of Converts in Erie Co. N.Y.* (1833); and *A Remarkable Vision* (1835). Herr published the first edition of *Foundations* by Menno Simons and seems to have been partially responsible for the first English edition of the *Martyr's Mirror* (1836), the classic work on religious suffering during the Reformation.

Herr and his group had no doctrinal difficulties with the Mennonite church. Herr taught that Menno Simons had taught the sound and orthodox truth and that the church that formed around him was the true and Holy Spirit-possessed church of Christ. But, Herr claimed, by the nineteenth century, the Mennonite Church had become an apostate and spiritless and dead body. Its members were carnal and unconverted. Herr's message primarily reached members of the Mennonite Church who shared his assessment.

Herr led a strict group that believed itself the true Church. He condemned participation in worldly practices such as county fairs, drunkenness, and frivolity. He emphasized foot washing, the use of the holy kiss, and the disciplining of lax members through excommunication and shunning. Herr rejected fellowship with members of churches other than his own and admitted only Reformed Mennonites to communion.

At the time of his death, Herr had organized more than two thousand members. During the period since his death, there was a steady decrease in members, and less than a thousand remained by the 1960s. The most famous member of the church was Milton Snavely Hershey, founder of the Hershey Chocolate Corporation, whose grandfather had been a Reformed Mennonite bishop.

John Herr, *Complete Works* (Buffalo, N.Y., 1890).

John F. Funk, *The Mennonite Church and Her Accusers* (Elkhart, Ind., 1878).

Christianity Defined (Lancaster, Pa., 1958).

ME, 2, 712.

WWWH, 248.

HICKS, Elias (March 19, 1748, Hempstead Township, New York—February 27, 1830, Jericho, New York); married Jemima Seaman, January 2, 1771 (d. March 17, 1829).

Elias Hicks, to whom the Religious Society of Friends (General Conference) looks as its founder, was born to an old Colonial family. Shortly before Elias's birth, his parents had joined the Society of Friends (the Quakers). With little formal education, Elias was forced to educate himself. His mother died when he was eleven, and two years later he went to live with his married brother. In 1765 he apprenticed himself to a carpenter. He married the daughter of Jonathan Seaman, a well-to-do farmer in Jericho, Long Island, and the couple moved to the farm. Elias managed the farm for the rest of his life.

At the age of twenty-six, the mildly religious Hicks experienced a period of intense spiritual struggle followed by what he described as an opening of the light upon his soul. It led to a rededication of himself as a Quaker. The following year he spoke for the first time before his meeting (congregation) and soon became very active in its affairs. His first task was an appointment to a committee to combat slavery within the Quaker movement. He also became a leading opponent of Quaker involvement in the American Revolution. In 1778 the meeting appointed him a minister. He began to speak regularly at Jericho, and the following year began the first of his many travels to visit Quaker meetings around the country.

Hicks was a gifted orator, and meetings welcomed his visits. He was devoted to the Quaker doctrine of the Inner Light. He called upon his audiences to yield to the Christ within the human heart, to crucify the sins of the flesh, and to do the will of God. He emphasized the mystical aspects of Christianity and the universal timeless message of the possibility of salvation by turning to that light that abides within every soul as a Divine Spark. His message came as an attack upon Deism and the coldness of rationalism, which during the last decades of the eighteenth century invaded the Friends fellowship.

Early in the nineteenth century, Hicks faced what was to become a more formidable opponent in the growth of Evangelicalism. In England, Quakers had absorbed much from the Wesleyan Evangelical revival, and ministers came to America to spread their message. They emphasized the authority of the Bible, the atoning work of Jesus, and the necessity of adherence to a traditional Protestant doctrinal stance.

By the second decade of the new century, Hicks had emerged as the leading spokesperson opposing the demands of the new Evangelicals. As early as 1783, before Evangelicalism had become a factor, he had opposed the requests for a uniform book of "Discipline" for American Friends. He continued that stance in the face of Evangelicalism. He believed strongly that religion was first and foremost a matter of a personal relationship and not of opinion or doctrinal formulation. He challenged the authority of the Bible by arguing that its message must be tested and judged in the light of inner experience.

In the early 1820s the growing division of perspective among Quakers became visible to all, and after the publication of a polemical work, the *Letters and Observations Relating to the Controversy Respecting the Doctrines of Elias Hicks* (1824), Hicks's name was inseparably attached to the anti-Evangelical faction.

The Hicksite Separation began in Philadelphia, the center of the Quaker movement, in 1827. Hicks was not present and his following was in the minority. It spread to New York in 1828, where Hicks was present and his following in the majority. Eventually the schism traveled throughout the meetings within America. Hicks, already an old man when the schism began, died soon afterward, but not before preparing much of his *Journal* (1832), which appeared posthumously for publication. Those meetings that stood with Hicks in the 1820s eventually organized into a separate national body known today as the Religious Society of Friends (General Conference).

Elias Hicks, *Observations on the Slavery of the Africans and Their Descendents* (New York, 1811).

―――, *A Series of Extemporaneous Discourses* (Philadelphia, Penn., 1825).

―――, *Journal of the Life and Religious Labours of Elias Hicks, written by himself* (New York, 1832).

Henry W. Wilbur, *The Life and Labours of Elias Hicks* (Philadelphia, Penn., 1910).

Bliss Forbush, *Elias Hicks: Quaker Liberal* (New York, 1956).

Robert Doherty, *The Hicksite Separation* (New Brunswick, N.J., 1967).

DRB, 203–4.

DAB, 9, 6–7.

WWWH, 250.

HOLDEMAN, John (January 31, 1832, New Pittsburg, Wayne County, Ohio—March 10, 1900, near Galva, Kansas); married Elizabeth Ritter, November 18, 1852 (d. 1932).

John Holdeman, the founder of the Church of God in Christ, Mennonite, was born among devout Mennonites in rural Ohio. His father was a schoolteacher. Holdeman was converted at the age of twelve, but his youth was a period he described as a time of "wicked sinfulness." He married in 1852, and five months after the ceremony his first child was born. The local scandal surrounding his marriage seems to have precipitated a reexamination and reconsecration of his life. In 1853 he experienced a new sense of forgiveness and a call to the ministry and was baptized. For the next six years he studied the Scriptures, the writings of Mennonite history, and languages.

During this period he became deeply concerned about the state of the church, which he felt included too many unconverted members. He condemned the worldly conversation that dominated church life and the laxity in avoiding the excommunicated. Slowly he began to separate from the Mennonites among whom he lived. In 1859 he began to travel and preach. He organized a small congregation near his home, although most of his converts were his own family. A church building was finally erected in 1878.

Soon after he began his travels, Holdeman issued his first books: *The Old Ground and Foundation* (German edition, 1862; and English edition, 1863); *A Reply to the Criticisms of John Roseborough* (1864); and *Eine Vertheidigung gegen die Verfaelscher unserer Schriften* (1865). His message of the necessity of the new birth and separation from the world met its greatest success in Manitoba, where he converted the bishop of the Kleine Gemeinde, a Russian Mennonite group, and about half the membership. He also had some success among the Russian Mennonites in Kansas, where he converted members of the General Conference Mennonites.

In 1882 Holdeman's mother died. He sold the family farm and moved to Jasper County, Missouri, with as many members of the Ohio congregation as would follow. For the next fifteen years he served as pastor, itinerant evangelist, and moderator for the Church of God in Christ, Mennonite. He continued to write and publish. Included among his works were *A Treatise on Redemption, Baptism, and the Passover and the Lord's Supper* (1890) and *A Treatise on Magistracy and War, Millennium, Holiness and the Manifestation of Spirits* (1891).

In 1897 Holdeman moved to McPherson County, Kansas, and began *Botschafter der Wahrheit*, which he edited from June 1897 to his death in 1900.

John Holdeman, *A History of the Church of God as It Existed from the Beginning Whereby It May Be Known, and How It Was Propagated until the Present Time* (Lancaster, Penn., 1876).

———, *A Mirror of Truth* (Hesston, Kans., 1956).

———, *The Old Ground and Foundation, Taken from the Word of God* (Lancaster, Penn., 1863).

———, *A Treatise on Magistracy and War* (Carthage, Mo., 1891).

Clarence Hiebert, *The Holdeman People* (South Pasadena, Calif., 1973).

Inez Unruh, "Portrait of a Prophet," *Mennonite Life* (July 1959), 123-4.

ME, 2, 789.

HOLMES, Ernest Shurtleff (January 21, 1887, Lincoln, Maine—April 7, 1960, Los Angeles, California); married Hazel Durkee Foster, October 23, 1927 (d. May 21, 1957).

Ernest Shurtleff Holmes, New Thought leader and founder of Religious Science, was born to a poor family in rural Maine. He received little education, and after leaving school at the age of fifteen, he moved to Boston and worked at several odd jobs. From 1908 to 1910, he returned to school to pursue a course in public speaking at the Leland Powers School of Expression. Possibly as important as the speech training he received, he met an instructor and several fellow pupils who were Christian Scientists. They introduced him to the movement and to *Science and Health with Key to the Scriptures.* This book, combined with his other reading, which included the New England Transcendentalists, most notably Ralph Waldo Emerson, helped shape Holmes's fertile mind.

In 1912 he moved to California. His brother, Fenwicke, a Congregational minister, had preceded him and become pastor of the church in Venice, California. Both brothers developed an interest in New Thought and read the works of Judge Thomas Troward and W. W. Atkinson. Ernest took the correspondence course from Christian Larsen.

Ernest found a job with the city. An engineer he had met through his work took an interest in the metaphysical books Ernest always seemed to be reading and invited him to speak to an informal gathering at his house. A woman in attendance invited him to speak at the Metaphysical Library, where, in 1916, he gave his first public lecture on Troward.

In 1917 he teamed with his brother, Fenwicke, to found the Metaphysical Institute and the magazine *Uplift.* They lectured at the Grand Theatre in Los Angeles and at Long Beach, where they opened a Metaphysical Sanitarium. They traveled nationally, lecturing and giving classes. In 1919 they published their first books, *Creative Mind* by Ernest and *The Law of Mind in Action* by Fenwicke. Their partnership came to an end in 1925 when Ernest decided to settle in Los Angeles and his brother wished to continue to travel and lecture.

In 1926 Ernest published his major work, *The Science of Mind.* He saw the "Science of Mind" as the study of Spirit, the ultimate Intelligence underlying the cosmos. Spirit was beyond understanding fully but found its individual expression in each person. Mind, or Spirit, works through individuals through Law. Love was the essence of Law.

In 1927 Holmes founded the Institute of Religious Science and School of Philosophy and began the *Science of Mind* magazine. He also married. Around him a movement began to grow. Students of the Institute began to found centers of their own, and the increasing size of his audience required several moves to larger locations. In 1935 the organization was reincorporated and moved into permanent headquarters on Wilshire Boulevard in Los Angeles. In 1949 he began a radio show, "This Thing Called Life," heard weekly over the Mutual network, and in 1956 he did a twenty-six-week series for television.

Holmes had resisted turning his work into a church, but the spread of his movement finally convinced him that it was the right direction, and in 1954 the institute became the Church of Religious Science. In 1960 he presided at the dedication of the Founder's Church of Religious Science in Los Angeles.

Two Churches have grown out of the work of Ernest Holmes. In 1949 ministers who had trained with Holmes and had formed centers to teach Religious Science came together to form the International Association of Religious Science Churches. Although this body was separate from the institute, Holmes became a charter member and honorary president. The IARSC chartered churches and licensed ministers, and the institute trained them. In 1954 a reorganization took place aimed at bringing the churches and the institute together. The institute reincorporated as the

Church of Religious Science and took as many of the congregations of the IARSC under its umbrella as wished to join. Most did. Those that refused to join remained as the IARSC.

Ernest Shurtleff Holmes, *The Science of Mind* (New York, 1944).

————, *How to Use the Science of Mind* (New York, 1948).

————, *This Thing Called Life* (Los Angeles, Calif., 1943).

————, *What Religious Science Teaches* (Los Angeles, Calif., 1944).

————, with Maude Allison Lathem, *Mind Remakes Your World* (New York, 1941).

Reginald C. Armor, *Ernest Holmes, The Man* (Los Angeles, Calif., 1977).

Charles S. Braden, *Spirits in Rebellion* (Dallas, Texas, 1963).

Tom Beebe, *Who's Who in New Thought* (Lakemont, Ga., 1977), 101-3.

Fenwicke L. Holmes, *Ernest Holmes, His Life and Times* (New York, 1970).

DRB, 211-2.

HOPKINS, Emma Curtis (September 2, 1853, Killingly, Connecticut— April 25, 1925, New York, New York); married George Irving Hopkins, July 19, 1874) (div.); education: Woodstock Academy, Connecticut.

Emma Curtis Hopkins, teacher of New Thought, was born of a well-to-do old New England family. She received an excellent education and upon graduation from Woodstock Academy joined the faculty for a short period. She became one of Mary Baker Eddy's early pupils and enrolled in her class in Boston in December 1883. Mrs. Eddy recognized her pupil's ability and made her assistant editor, and then editor, of the *Christian Science Journal*, a post she held from September 1884 to October 1885. Why she was abruptly dismissed from her job as editor remains a matter of conjecture, but it is known that she was both an intelligent and independent thinker. She freely compared Mrs. Eddy's teachings to those of the mystics of the ages. Although she saw Mrs. Eddy in the lineage of great mystic teachers, others viewed Hopkins as undermining the unique authority of Mrs. Eddy and being eclectic in her teaching.

After she broke with Mrs. Eddy, she moved to Chicago and opened the Christian Science Theological Seminary. She held public lectures each Sunday and began a magazine, *Christian Metaphysician* (1887-97). She also traveled around the country giving classes. She quickly became the most popular teacher of New Thought and most of the people who were to become the founders of the International New Thought Alliance and the leaders of the New Thought churches and organizations in the early twentieth century sought her out and studied under her. Her pupils included Malinda Cramer and Nona Brooks (Divine Science); Charles and Myrtle Fillmore, and Harriet Emilie Cady (Unity School of Christianity); Ernest Holmes (Religious Science); Annie Rix Militz (Home of Truth); and Elizabeth Towne, president of the International New Thought Alliance and prominent editor, writer, and publisher.

Hopkins was a mystic and she saw Christian Science as a mystical system in tune with the work of the great mystics and sages of all centuries. She saw a unified teaching running through the sacred books of the world. This mystical thread was the subject of her most important book, *High Mysticism* (originally published as a series of twelve booklets), written in 1920–22.

During the last years of her life, Mrs. Hopkins closed the seminary in Chicago and moved to New York City. She continued to teach and write and included metaphysical writer Ella Wheeler Wilcox among her pupils. She died of a heart attack.

After her death, her sister Estelle Carpenter and several of her pupils decided to establish an organization to publish and perpetuate her teachings. They moved to a farm in Connecticut (called Joy Farm) and set up the Ministry of the High Watch. Their efforts kept Mrs. Hopkins's books in print. They also gathered her articles from the *Chicago Inter-Ocean* and published them as the *Bible Interpretation Series*. The farm was eventually sold and the work passed to a couple named Bogart, who carried on the publishing and distribution as the High Watch Fellowship.

Mrs. Hopkins's ministry was also carried on by H. B. Jeffery, an associate whose *Mysticism* draws heavily on Mrs. Hopkins's thought. His work survives as the Christ Truth League in Fort Worth, Texas.

Emma Curtis Hopkins, *High Mysticism* (Philadelphia, Penn., 1920–22).

———, *Christian Science Lessons* (Chicago, 1894).

———, *Class Lessons, 1888* (Marina del Rey, Calif., 1977).

———, *Esoteric Philosophy in Spiritual Science* (Cornwall Bridge, Conn., n.d.).

———, *Judgment Series in Spiritual Science* (Cornwall Bridge, Conn., n.d.).

Tom Beebe, *Who's Who in New Thought* (Lakemont, Ga., 1977).

Charles S. Braden, *Spirits in Rebellion* (Dallas, Texas, 1963).

DRB, 215–16.

HUNT, Ernest (August 16, 1878, Hoddesdon, Hertfordshire, England— February 7, 1967, Honolulu, Hawaii); married Dorothy Poulton; education: Eastbourne College.

Ernest Hunt, founder of the Western Buddhist Order and leader of the Hawaiian branch of the International Buddhist Institute, was born in England and as a young man became a seafarer. In India he had been introduced to Buddhism. Upon his return to England, he studied for the Anglican priesthood, but on the eve of his ordination he converted to Buddhism.

In 1915, with his wife, Dorothy, he migrated to Hawaii and worked on a plantation. In the early 1920s he moved to the big island and opened Sunday schools for the English-speaking children of Japanese plantation workers. In 1924 Bishop Yemyo Imamura of the Honpa Hongwanji Buddhists ordained both Hunt and his wife. Hunt took the name Shinkaku (meaning "true light-bearer"), by which he was most commonly known.

In 1926 the Hunts moved to Honolulu, and Shinkaku became head of the Hongwanji English Department, which Bishop Imamura had created to reach the many non-Japanese-speaking youth of the Hawaiian Buddhist families. Hunt became an active teacher to the children and youth. He composed the *Vade Mecum*, a book of Buddhist ceremonies in English, while Dorothy, a poet, wrote many hymns for use in the English services.

Hunt's irenic spirit and his nonsectarian approach to Buddhism attracted non-Japanese Hawaiians to Buddhism. In 1928 about sixty people who had been studying with him were formally initiated into the Buddhist religion and formed the Western Buddhist Order as a nonsectarian branch of the Honpa Hongwanji Mission with the purpose of spreading Buddhism among Occidentals.

In 1929 Abbot Tai Hsu of the Lin Yin Temple in Hangchow, China, stopped in Honolulu on his return from the West Coast of the United States. During his brief stay, he presented Imamura and Hunt with the idea of beginning a Hawaiian branch of the International Buddhist Institute. With the goal of breaking down sectarian barriers among Buddhists, branches had already been formed in London, New York, and Chicago. Such a proposal was in line with Hunt's whole approach to Buddhism, and he supported the idea enthusiastically. Hunt became the first vice-president, and Bishop Imamura was elected president for life.

Through the institute, Hunt was able to put into practice his belief that the surest way to Nirvana was through the practice of *metta*, active goodwill. Hunt organized the institute members, who visited prisons and the sick (including lepers), taught children, built a library, and started a Sunday school for the deaf and blind. The efforts of the IBI revitalized the Hongwanji Sunday school program throughout the islands. He and his wife collaborated in the writing and production of Sunday school lessons.

During the years of the institute, Hunt was at the height of his literary production. He edited four volumes of the *Hawaiian Buddhist Annual*. He wrote a small pamphlet, *An Outline of Buddhism: The Religion of Wisdom and Compassion*, for which the Burmese Theravada Buddhists granted him ordination and the honorary degree of Doctor of the Dharma. His wife also received ordination. He also edited the magazine of the institute, *Navayana*.

Hunt's career was abruptly interrupted by the death of Bishop Imamura on December 22, 1932. Imamura was succeeded by Bishop Zuigi Ashikaga, who, after a very brief stay in Hawaii, was succeeded by Gikyo Kuchiba. Kuchiba turned out to be a fierce Japanese nationalist and dedicated Shin Buddhist. He opposed Hunt's nonsectarian approach to Buddhism, and soon after his arrival in 1935 he fired Hunt and disbanded the English Department.

Forced out, Hunt moved his membership to the Soto Temple and placed himself under the bishop, Zenkyo Komagata. In 1953 he was ordained a Soto-Zen priest and ten years later became the only Caucasian priest in the Western world to receive the rank of Osho for the Soto sect. As a Soto priest he continued to write and produced such works as *Gleanings from Soto-Zen* and *Essentials and Symbols of the Buddhist Faith*. He also spent many hours at the temple conversing with the increasing numbers of tourists who stopped to talk about Buddhism.

He died at the age of almost ninety in his home in Honolulu.

Ernest Hunt, *An Outline of Buddhism* (Honolulu, 1929).

———, *Gleanings from Soto-Zen* (Honolulu, 1953).

———— , *Essentials and Symbols of the Buddhist Faith* (Honolulu, 1955).

Louise H. Hunter, *Buddhism in Hawaii* (Honolulu, 1971).

William Peiris, *The Western Contribution to Buddhism* (Delhi, India, 1973), 68–69.

HURLEY, George Willie (February 17, 1884, Reynolds, Georgia— June 23, 1943, Detroit, Michigan); married Cassie Bell Martin (d. June 28, 1960); education: Tuskegee Institute, Tuskegee, Alabama.

George Willie Hurley, founder of the Universal Hagar's Spiritual Church, rose from his rural Georgia home to become a divine personage to the many members of the congregations he founded in the American Midwest and East. Raised a Baptist, he became a minister. Eventually he found his way into the Methodist church. He met his future wife in 1908, and they and their family moved to Detroit in 1919. Hurley joined the Triumph Church and Kingdom of God in Christ, a holiness church that taught sanctification (i.e., that believers could be sanctified by a second instantaneous work of grace) and fire baptism (an experience of the power of the Holy Spirit). Hurley became a minister in the church and within a short time was appointed its Presiding Prince of Michigan.

While a minister in the holiness group, Hurley was invited to a service at a spiritualist church (within the black community, spiritualist churches are usually termed Spiritual churches). He left the holiness group, joined the International Spiritual Church, and soon was ministering as a spiritualist preacher.

Soon after becoming a spiritualist, he had the vision that set the course of his future life. Around 1923 he saw a "brown-skinned damsel" who, in the vision, was transformed into an eagle. He interpreted the eagle to be the church that he was to establish. Thus on September 23, 1923, he began the first congregation of the Universal Hagar's Spiritual Church. The following year he organized the School of Mediumship and Psychology to train the members of the congregation in the psychic arts.

As head of his own independent church, Hurley developed his spiritualism in a quite eclectic fashion. He drew heavily upon the *Aquarian Gospel of Jesus Christ*, a spiritualist classic authored by Levi Dowling, and named his church periodical *Aquarian Age*. He also drew from his own religious background, Catholicism and the Ethiopianism that had become popular in the black community after World War II. He taught that black people (Ethiopians) were the first people in the world, the original Hebrew nation, and as such were God's chosen people. White people were the children of the biblical Cain, cursed with a pale, leprous skin.

During the first decade of leadership of Universal Hagar's Spiritual Church, Hurley assumed a divine role. He claimed that at the age of thirteen the Holy Spirit had led him to fast for forty days, at the end of which God told him that none of the religions of the world conformed to God's will, and from that point on, the Spirit of God dwelt within his body. Hurley, a black man of humble birth, was born to the God of the Aquarian Age, just as Jesus was the God of the prior Piscean Age and, before that, Moses (Arian) and Adam (Taurian) were for their respective ages. (According to many astrologers, earth history is told through a series of successive periods, or Ages, each approximately two thousand years in length and named for a particular sign of the zodiac.) Hurley taught that the Aquarian age began after the signing of the Armistice following World War I and would last seven thousand years. It would be a period of peace and social harmony and would lead to the end of Protestantism, segregation, and the rule of the powerful over the powerless.

At the time of his death, the Universal Hagar's Spiritual Church had almost forty congregations. He passed the succession of leadership to Rev. Thomas Surbadger, who had managed the church's business for many years. However, he resigned in favor of Hurley's widow, who led the church until her death in 1960.

Hans A. Baer, *The Black Spiritual Movement: A Religious Response to Racism* (Knoxville, Tenn., 1984).

HUTTER, Jacob (?, Moos, South Tyrol, Italy—February 26, 1536, Innsbruck, Austria); married ? (d. 1538).

Almost nothing is known of Jacob Hutter prior to 1529, when he appeared among the Swiss Brethren in Austerlitz, Moravia. He was born and raised in the hamlet of Moos. According to tradition, he was a hatmaker (hence his name), but most now doubt that supposition. He was a leader of the Brethren in the Tyrol and had succeeded George Blaurock, the pastor in the Puster Valley, after the latter's execution.

In 1529 Hutter's followers were suffering persecution. He had heard that a safe haven was available in Moravia. Hutter traveled to Austerlitz and found the group led by Jacob Wiedemann. He was so impressed that he joined the group in the name of his congregation. He then returned to the Tyrol to organize the movement of his people. Their arrival in large numbers placed strains upon the Austerlitz group. A faction emerged that protested Wiedemann's authoritarian leadership. Eventually 350 of the 600 members departed Austerlitz in the dead of winter of 1530 and established themselves at Auspitz.

Both groups appealed to Hutter to arbitrate. He worked out an agreement. Then the group at Auspitz split. Again Hutter came to Moravia and reorganized the two groups under the leadership of a third group located at Rossitz.

On August 11, 1533, Hutter arrived in Auspitz to assume leadership of the groups. At first they did not accept his exercising authority. The group had in 1528, under Wiedemann, accepted the community of goods. Hutter told them that their misfortunes were due to their insufficient attachment to worldly goods and their families and their holding on to jealous feelings toward one another. Then Hutter seized the moment and accused the wife of one of the leaders, Simon Schuetzinger, of hoarding money. Upon searching her bedroom, it was discovered that Schuetzinger was hoarding various items as well as money. In the midst of the controversy Hutter was elected chief elder, or *Vorsteher*.

Hutter moved immediately to reorganize and strengthen the group both communally and economically. He impressed upon them their elect status and the disciplines of a shared life.

The role of Moravia as a haven for Hutter's group came to an end quickly. In 1535, reacting to events in Germany, King Ferdinand of Austria made a personal trip to Moravia and demanded the expulsion of the Brethren. Reluctantly the nobles assented. The group at Auspitz scattered, and Hutter returned to the Tyrol. He wrote a remonstrance to the government in Moravia in which he cited the peaceful nature of the Brethren and pleaded for a place for them to live.

Ferdinand placed a price on Hutter's head and on November 29, 1535, both he and his wife were arrested in St. Andrew's, Austria. He was sent to Innsbruck, where he was tortured but refused to give away the names or hiding places of his followers. He was burned alive. His wife escaped from prison but was recaptured and executed two years later.

Hutter neither founded the group that bears his name nor did he introduce their most distinctive practices, in particular, communal living. He is credited, however, with having taken the loosely organized band and within a few short years molding it into a strong group that survived the persecution and hardship that recurred over many years. They recognized his crucial role by calling themselves by the name of their martyred leader.

Eventually they were forced to migrate several times to locations in Europe and Russia. They finally came to North America in the 1870s. Today their colonies are spread across the prairies in Canada and the United States (Montana, North and South Dakota), and they have emerged as the most successful communal group in terms of both size and existence in modern history.

John A. Hostetler, *Hutterite Society* (Baltimore, Md., 1974).

Victor Peters, *All Things Common* (Minneapolis, Minn., 1965).

John Horsch, *Hutterian Brethren, 1528-1931* (Cayley, Alberta, 1977).

IRVING, Edward (August 4, 1792, Annan, Scotland—December 7, 1834, Glasgow, Scotland); married Isabella Martin, October 13, 1823; education: Edinburgh University, 1805-09; Divinity Hall, 1809-15.

Edward Irving, one of the founders of the Catholic Apostolic Church, was born to a Church of Scotland family. He showed an early desire to enter the ministry and, at the age of thirteen, entered Edinburgh University with that goal in mind. He graduated in 1805 and began work at the Divinity Hall. He spent only one full session at his divinity studies and did not complete his work until 1815. He was not able to find a parish until 1819 and, in the meantime, supported himself teaching school and as a private tutor.

In October 1819 he became assistant pastor at St. John's Parish in Glasgow, which was headed by Dr. Thomas Chambers, one of the outstanding Church of Scotland ministers of the nineteenth century. The post proved a stepping-stone to his own parish, the Caledonian Chapel at Hatton Garden in London. This small congregation was a suitable first parish for a young minister. It was also a parish with much potential for

growth. That growth began the following year as a result of a chance
remark by a member of the House of Commons commending him to his
colleagues. Once the public became aware of Irving, his congregation grew
steadily. In need of expansion, the Caledonian Chapel picked up a proposal for a National Scots Church for London, and in May 1823, began an
appeal for funds. The foundation stone was laid in 1824 and the church
opened in May 1827.

During the period that the new church was being planned and built,
Irving married, published his first book, *For the Oracles of God: Four
Orations, For Judgment to Come: An Argument In Nine Parts* (1823), and
began his association with Henry Drummond, an association that would
change his life.

Irving met Drummond in 1825. The following year Drummond began
to hold meetings at his estate at Albury to discuss the issues of unfulfilled
prophecy. In 1829 the group, of which Irving was an integral part, had
reached a number of conclusions: that the end of the Christian dispensa-
tion was near at hand, that it would include the destruction of the visible
Church, and that the 1,260-day prophecy of Daniel ended in 1783. They
also turned their attention to a search for the manifestation of the gifts of
the Spirit in the Church as a sign of the second coming.

In 1830 members of the Albury circle received word that some of the
gifts, preeminently, speaking in tongues, had appeared among some people in Scotland. They sent a committee to investigate. The committee
reported that they felt the Spirit of God at work, and members of the
circle began to hold prayer meetings seeking an outpouring of the Spirit.
In April one member spoke in tongues.

By 1831 Irving had problems from other sources and did not participate
in the prayer meetings. In 1828 Irving had been attacked for an unorthodox
Christology. In response he published a book, the *Orthodox and Catholic
Doctrine of Christ's Human Nature* (1830). The Presbytery of London decided to examine the book in light of orthodoxy. Irving reacted by
withdrawing from the presbytery, which, in November, reached a negative
decision. That decision led to a review of Irving's orthodoxy by the
general assembly of the Church in Scotland, which, in 1831, condemned
Irving's views.

In the weeks prior to the assembly meeting, a group at Irving's church
had been praying about the assembly. After the assembly had met, they
began to pray for a bestowal of the gifts of the Spirit. In July two members
spoke in tongues. Irving investigated and became convinced of their
miraculous nature. The manifestation of tongues was confined to the
small group until October, when one member spoke in tongues at the
Sunday-morning worship service. At first Irving stopped the members,
but in November he changed his position and allowed them.

Irving's condoning of the public display of the gifts led the trustees of
the Church to ask for a trial before the London presbytery. After a trial in
April 1832, the presbytery reached a decision and declared him unfit to be
a minister. He was not allowed to preach again at his church. He preached
the next service in the open air, and about six hundred people indicated

their allegiance to him. They met on Newman Street, the first congregation of what was to become the Catholic Apostolic Church.

The group moved quickly to reestablish an apostolic order. Irving was summoned to a trial at his home presbytery of Annan. On March 13, 1833, they declared him no longer a Presbyterian minister. He returned to London and was received by the congregation as a deacon, but on April 5, he was reordained to the office of angel, or chief pastor. He preached at the church until September 1834 when he felt a call to go to work as a prophet in Scotland, where he died after a brief illness.

Drummond emerged as the leader of the group, which grew and spread throughout the British Isles and Europe. It spread to the United States in the 1840s but was never large. It did give rise to a schismatic group in Germany, however, the New Apostolic Church, which in the 1970s reported more than three hundred congregations in the United States alone.

Edward Irving, *The Collected Works of Edward Irving*, 5 volumes (London, 1864-65).

Jean Christie Root, *Edward Irving, Man, Preacher, Poet* (Boston, 1912).

H. C. Whitley, *Blinded Eagle* (London, 1958).

A. L. Drummond, *Edward Irving and His Circle* (London, n.d.).

Rowland A. Davenport, *Albury Apostles* (Great Britain, 1970).

Gordon Strachan, *The Pentecostal Theology of Edward Irving* (London, 1973).

DNB, 10, 489-93.

JANSSON, Eric (December 19, 1808, Bishopskulla, Sweden—May 13, 1850, Cambridge, Illinois); married Maria Kristina Larsdotter, 1835 (d. 1849); married Anna Sophia Gabrielson, September 16, 1849.

Eric Jansson (or Janson), the founder of the Bishop Hill (Illinois) religious community, was raised a Lutheran in a small town in rural Sweden. His uneventful youth, which included only a minimal education, was broken in 1830 by a severe attack of rheumatism. The attack became a moment of religious awakening in which Jansson realized that he was a sinner and that he lacked the power of true faith. He saw the educated Lutheran clergy as blind teachers of the blind and that the source of all healing, both spiritual and physical, was Jesus. Jansson was healed of his affliction at this moment and began preaching the possibility of a sinless perfection. He came to believe that individuals were justified (saved) and sanctified (made holy) all at once and that the world was divided between the sinners and the holy believers.

After his experience he began to participate in the *lasare*, informal lay gatherings that met for prayer and mutual exhortation. He began to share his ideas and gathered a few followers during the decade of the 1830s. In 1841 clergy and community hostility to his preaching led to his moving north to Halsingland to preach. There he met Jonas Olsson, who assisted in his initial efforts and became a lifelong follower. His success as an itinerant in the north and the growing hostility in his hometown led to a permanent change of residence in 1844. He made the town of Stenbo his new center of operations.

In the summer of 1844 Jansson decided to go on the offensive against the Lutheran clergy who had caused him so much trouble. On June 11,

1844, he sponsored a massive book burning in Alfta. He was arrested and banished from the province. On October 28 he held a second book burning. He was arrested and given tests for sanity.

The growth of his following, his heightened profile as a result of arrests and book burnings, and his continued hostility to the Lutheran Church caused a rising tide of violent activity to be directed against the Janssonists. During 1845 migration to the United States became the most attractive option; in the fall of 1845 Jonas and his brother, Olaf Olsson, went to America to explore the prospects of moving.

Shortly after the Olssons left, Jansson was arrrested again. He was rescued by followers and escaped to Norway. In 1846 he joined many of his followers in a migration to the New World. In all, about 1,200 immigrated. Land was purchased near present-day Galva, Illinois, and the Janssonists established a community, which they named Bishop Hill after their leader's birthplace. They practiced a community of goods, but out of economic necessity rather than idealogy or religious teaching, and this practice was abandoned in a few years. Also, for several years, the group abandoned marriage and sex but resumed normal family life as soon as expediency allowed.

For several years the community prospered, although only 750 of the 1,200 who immigrated survived the trek across the continent. Then in 1849 cholera struck the group. Over 200 died, including Jansson's wife. The event shook the faith of many, since Jansson had taught them that the holy life would also lead to a long life free from illness.

The cholera epidemic was followed by trouble from an ex-member, John Root. Root had joined the movement in America and married one of the members. However, when he decided to leave, Jansson refused to return the property Root had donated to the community, and his wife refused to go with him. The tension, which lasted for many months and included Root's kidnapping his wife and the Jansonnists' rescuing her, climaxed in May 1850, when Root murdered Jansson.

Jansson's untimely death further speeded the demise of the community. He was succeeded by Jonas Olsson, who kept the group together until the national financial crisis of 1857, after which the group divided and finally abandoned the communal life in 1863.

Eric Jansson, *Ett ord i sinom tid, eller en kort wederlaeggning af "Erik Jansisnen i Helsingland"* (Soederhamn, 1846).

———, *Foerklaring oefver den Helige Skrift, eller cateches Foerfattad i fragor och svar* (Soederhamn, 1846).

———, *Nagra ord till Guds foersamling* (Soederhamn, 1846).

———, *Nagra sanger samt boener* (Galva, Ill., 1857).

Paul Elmen, *Wheat Flour Messiah* (Carbondale, Ill., 1976).

George Swank, *Bishop Hill, Showcase of Swedish History* (Galva, Ill., 1965).

JONES, Charles Price (December 9, 1865, Texas Valley, near Rome, Georgia—January 19, 1949, Los Angeles, California); married Fannie Brown, 1891 (d. 1916); married Pearl E. Reed, January 1918.

Charles Price Jones, founder of the Church of Christ (Holiness) U.S.A., was raised a Baptist in rural Georgia. After his mother's death, he left home and eventually settled in Crittenden County, Arkansas, at Cat Island. There he was converted and joined the Locust Grove Baptist Church. Within a few months he began to preach, and two years later, in 1887, he was licensed to preach. He entered Arkansas Baptist College and while pursuing his studies taught school. In July 1888 he became pastor of Pope Creek Baptist Church. In October he was ordained and became pastor of St. Paul Baptist Church in Little Rock in November 1888. After graduation from Arkansas Baptist College in 1891, he pastored Bethlehem Baptist Church in Searcy, Arkansas. He stayed in Searcy a year and then moved to Selma, Alabama, to become pastor of Tabernacle Baptist Church.

During his years in Selma, Jones encountered the holiness movement. The movement taught that Christians could experience a second definite work of grace subsequent to a salvation-conversion experience in which the Holy Spirit sanctified the person—that is, made one holy. Jones experienced sanctification in 1894. In 1895 Jones became pastor of Mt. Helm Baptist Church in Jackson, Mississippi. He also began to preach holiness to his Baptist audiences—at Mt. Helm, at revival services, and to fellow ministers at association meetings.

Jones encountered considerable opposition from colleagues and parishioners because holiness was foreign to Baptist doctrine. The beginning in 1896 of a holiness periodical, *Truth*, and the publishing of his booklet, *The Work of the Holy Spirit in the Churches*, did little to ease the tension. Having found other black ministers who had accepted holiness, he called a convention to meet in June 1897. A consensus was reached among Baptist ministers at the convention that a split was developing and that independent congregations had to be created. The first was pastored by C. H. Mason, who would later found the Church of God in Christ.

In 1898 Jones became pastor of Sweet Rest Church in Jackson, while continuing at Mt. Helm. In 1900 he withdrew from the Jackson Missionary Baptist Association, the association of ministers and churches connected with the National Baptist Convention, and attempted to remove the word *Baptist* from the name of the Mt. Helm Church. The association moved against him, and in 1902 he was forced out. With his supporters from Mt. Helm, he formed Christ Temple Church.

Jones's church had become the center of the loose confederation of Baptist holiness ministers that began to call itself the Church of God, and Jones served as president of the annual convention. The Church of God grew steadily until 1907 when a split developed between Jones and C. H. Mason. Mason had traveled to Los Angeles and had encountered the Pentecostal movement. He returned and tried to lead the church into the practice of speaking in tongues as a sign of the baptism of the Holy Spirit. The split led to a period of court litigation, which ended in 1909. The remaining Church of God reorganized and the Church of Christ (Holiness) U.S.A. emerged.

In 1915 William Washington organized an independent Church of Christ (Holiness) in Los Angeles. At Washington's invitation, Jones visited California and held a series of revival services. From this visit, Jones organized the Christ Temple Church of Los Angeles in 1917 and became its pastor, a post he held for the remainder of his life. Until 1927 Jones had solely headed the growing Church as president and overseer. In 1927 he became Senior Bishop, and a group of four bishops were elected to assist him.

Jones died in 1949. Besides the leadership he gave the church, he became known for his poetry, having written more than a thousand songs. Many of these were published in the *Jesus Only Standard Hymnal*, the hymn book of the Church of Christ (Holiness).

C. P. Jones, *His Fulness* (Jackson, Miss., 1913).

——— , *Jesus Only, Songs and Hymns* (Jackson, Miss., 1901).

——— , *The History of My Songs* (Los Angeles, Calif., n.d.).

Otho B. Cobbins, *History of Church of Christ (Holiness) U.S.A., 1895–1965* (New York, 1966).

JONES, James Warren (May 13, 1931, near Lynn, Indiana—November 18, 1978, Jonestown, Guyana); married Marceline Baldwin, June 12, 1949 (d. November 18, 1978); education: Indiana University, Bloomington, 1950; Butler University, Indianapolis, B.S., 1961.

James Warren Jones, known as the founder of the Peoples Temple, was not so much the founder of a new religious group as the founder of a congregation in the Christian Church (Disciples of Christ). In 1960 the Peoples Temple joined the Disciples and Jones was ordained by them in 1964. Both remained in good standing with the church, and during the 1970s Timothy Stoen, an associate pastor at the temple, served on the regional board of the Disciples in Northern California.

Both Jones and his congregation were accepted and recognized as part of mainstream Christianity. He was given several humanitarian awards and during the mid-1970s the Peoples Temple was extolled in periodicals and church school material in several major denominations as a model of Christian social concern. Although some people had called for an investigation of the beliefs and practices of the temple, Jones retained the full support of his denomination up to the moment of his death.

Jones was the son of a semiinvalid, alcoholic road-construction worker. His early religious training was diverse; he attended a variety of different churches in his community. He also developed an early social vision centered upon the possibility of interracial harmony. In 1952 he became pastor of Somerset Methodist Church in Indianapolis. Two years later he left Methodism to found an independent congregation, which he called Community Unity, that combined his social vision with Pentecostalism. In 1956 he moved into a larger building and renamed his church Wings of Deliverance. Wings of Deliverance soon became the Peoples Temple. During these years Jones met Father Divine. His own authoritarian personality was drawn to Father Divine's messianic pretensions, and Jones began to model the Peoples Temple and his position within the congregation on Father Divine's Peace Mission.

Jones's outspoken views on race, his activism, and the resulting negative community reaction began to produce a level of paranoia. In 1961 he left for two years, traveling to Hawaii, Texas, and Brazil. Shortly after his return he had a vision of a nuclear holocaust and, in 1965, moved the congregation to Ukiah, California, which he believed would be one of the safest havens from radioactive fallout.

In California Jones began both to build the Peoples Temple and to involve himself in local politics. During his first months in California he became head of the Mendocino County grand jury. He was later appointed to the board of the San Francisco Housing Authority and became the acquaintance and political ally of mayors and governors.

Within the temple, Jones's leadership became increasingly autocratic. In 1971 buildings were purchased in Los Angeles and San Francisco, and congregations were begun among poor blacks. A small group of whites joined the temple and a high proportion moved into leadership positions. As the membership grew, along with Jones's power, he took control of individuals' lives. He often rearranged marriages, enforced corporal punishment among the children, and engaged in illicit sexual encounters with many members, both male and female. He became increasingly vocal as a socialist but continued the lively worship services that combined elements of Pentecostalism, Spiritualism, and miracle healings.

In 1973 he founded an agricultural colony in rural Guyana, South America. In 1977, under the threat of an exposé article by *New West* magazine and the resulting attention and investigations it might bring, Jones and many of his followers moved to Jonestown, Guyana. During the next year the population of Jonestown grew to more than nine hundred. Meanwhile, because of defections and threatened court actions, Jones's situation deteriorated. Jones became more paranoid and offered the option of revolutionary suicide to his people. Suicide drills were organized and carried out at irregular intervals.

In November 1978, U.S. Congressman Leo Ryan traveled to Guyana to investigate the Peoples Temple. On November 18, he and many of his party were shot and killed, and almost all of the residents of Jonestown died, either by suicide (taking poison), by injections of poison, or by gunshots. Jones died of a gunshot wound, although it is unknown whether it was self-administered.

In the wake of the tragedy in Guyana and the numerous court actions, the Peoples Temple was dissolved.

Tim Reiterman, *Raven* (New York, 1982).

Bonnie Thielman, *The Broken God* (Elgin, Ill., 1979).

Jeannie Mills, *Six Years with God* (New York, 1979).

Charles Krause, *Guyana Massacre* (New York, 1978).

George Klineman and Sherman Butler, *The Cult That Failed* (New York, 1980).

JORDAN, Clarence (July 29, 1912, Talbotton, Georgia—October 29, 1969, Americus, Georgia); married Florence Kroeger, July 1936; education: Georgia State College of Agriculture, University of Georgia, 1929–33, B.S.,

1933; Southern Baptist Theological Seminary, 1933–39, Th.M., 1936, Ph.D., 1939.

Clarence Jordan, the founder of Koinonia, a radical Christian communal experiment in rural Georgia, came from a well-to-do Baptist family in Georgia. He entered college in 1929 to study agriculture. He also took R.O.T.C. and was offered a commission after graduation. However, during his college years he had become increasingly aware of a conflict between his own religious convictions and participation in military service. He resigned the commission and accepted a license to preach in the Baptist church. In the fall of 1933 he entered the Southern Baptist Theological Seminary in Louisville, Kentucky. During his seminary days he pastored several local churches on a part-time basis.

After receiving his Th.M. degree in 1936, he decided to continue at Louisville and entered the doctoral program. He also accepted an offer to teach a course at Simmons University, a black school. Even before his years at seminary, he had become convinced of the conflict between the New Testament and the patterns of racial segregation and inequality in the South and in the Southern Baptist Convention.

In 1939, as his education was near completion, he accepted the position of director of the Sunshine Center in the black section of Louisville. He concentrated on communication and interaction between the races. He was soon promoted by the local association (the Long Run Baptist Association) to the position of superintendent of missions. He spread his ideas to other missions and recruited seminarians who shared a similar perspective. One of the seminarians evolved a campus fellowship that met for Bible study and worship; this was given the name Koinonia. (*Koinonia* is a Greek word used to describe the close communion among Christians in the New Testament.) Speaking before Koinonia, Jordan increasingly shared his ideas about pacifism, racial equality, and communal sharing of property. He also joined the pacifist Fellowship of Reconciliation (FOR).

In 1941, at an FOR meeting, he met Martin English, a missionary caught in the United States by the war. Jordan and English developed the idea of a farming community that would put their ideas into practice. They formed Koinonia Farm and in the fall of 1942 settled on four hundred acres near Americus, Georgia. They established a commune, originally of their two families. They began with chickens and worked cooperatively with other farmers in egg production. Slowly they initiated agricultural improvements, which they hoped could be easily assimilated by other farmers. Jordan also became a popular speaker nationally.

In 1948 a long period of conflict with the community began when Jordan and the residents at Koinonia openly opposed the new postwar draft. Two years later continuing friction led the Rehobeth Baptist Church, which Jordan attended, to withdraw membership from all the residents of Koinonia. After the trouble at Rehobeth, Jordan was no longer congregationally attached.

In 1956 Jordan's attempt to assist two black students to enter college led to a community boycott of Koinonia and to a number of years of violence, blamed primarily on individual night riders and the White Citizens Council. As a result, Koinonia lost its economic base in local agriculture but continued by processing and selling shelled pecans across the United States. The pressure of the violence led Jordan to begin formal work on a new translation of the Scriptures, which would highlight its contemporary message to the segregated South. The result, which appeared in segments throughout his life, came to be known as the Cotton-Patch Version, characterized by its southern vernacular and substitution of biblical locations with southern ones.

Koinonia survived the tensions of the decade of violence, but Jordan professed a certain loss of direction. In 1968 he reorganized Koinonia as Koinonia Partners. He proposed a program that focused on the communication of the radical Gospel developed in the Cotton-Patch Bible, intense encounters with seekers, and a Fund for Humanity to capitalize industry, farms, and homes for the poor. His last years were spent in promoting the idea of reorganizing one's life as a partner with God.

Clarence Jordan, *To God's People in Washington or Romans* (Americus, Ga., 1968).

———, *A Letter to the Christians in Atlanta or First Corinthians* (Americus, Ga., 1968).

———, *A Second Letter to the Christians in Atlanta or Second Corinthians* (Americus, Ga., 1968).

———, *The Substance of Faith and Other Cotton Patch Sermons* (New York, 1972).

———, with Bill Lane Doulos, *Cotton Patch Parables of Liberation* (Scottdale, Penn., 1976).

Dallas Lee, *The Cotton Patch Evidence* (New York, 1971).

ESB, 3, 1786-7.

JUDGE, William Quan (April 13, 1851, Dublin, Ireland—March 21, 1896, New York, New York); married Ella M. Smith, 1874 (d. April 17, 1931).

William Quan Judge, one of the co-founders of the Theosophical Society, was born into a Methodist family in Ireland. His first interest in things mystical seems to have begun in childhood, when a serious illness kept him bedridden for a year. That illness also became the start of a sickliness that plagued Judge all his adult life.

In 1964 Judge's family moved to the United States, and Judge began the struggle to build a career. In 1872 he received his citizenship and was admitted to the New York State Bar. He specialized in commercial law. Two years later he married.

His life was changed in 1874 after he read a series of newspaper articles by Henry Steel Olcott concerning his adventures with Helena Petrovna Blavatsky at a Spiritualist gathering in Vermont. He sought out Olcott, who introduced him to Blavatsky. The following year the three formed the Theosophical Society, one of the first occult organizations in the United States. Three years later Blavatsky and Olcott, the two most accomplished occultists of the group, moved to India. They left Abner Doubleday (of baseball fame) and Judge in charge.

With no one having the occult knowledge of his two mentors, Judge, the neophyte, felt cut off and alone. Between his periodic illnesses and his travels to see to business interests in Venezuela and Mexico, he could give very little time to the society, which languished.

Then in 1884 Judge traveled to India. The trip seemed to have invigorated him, and he returned to begin the most productive segment of his career, despite the fact that he arrived in India just as the storm of charges of Blavatsky's fakery reached significant levels. Upon his return from India, he surveyed the state of the society in America and saw the need of reorganization. He requested a change and it was granted. In 1886 the American section was formed and Judge was elected general secretary. Under his leadership it became a prosperous body.

The formation of the American section also marked the beginning of a seven-year period of literary productiveness for Judge. He began two periodicals, The Path (1886) and The Theosophical Forum (1889). He produced two classics of Theosophical literature, An Epitome of Theosophy (1888) and The Ocean of Theosophy (1893). His interest in Hinduism led him to publish two translations of major Indian scriptures, the Yoga Aphorisms of Patanjali (1889) and the Bhagavad Gita (1890), both with extensive commentaries.

In 1888 Judge traveled to London to participate in the formation of the Esoteric section, an organization for the most dedicated Theosophists. He wrote The Book of Rules for the Esoteric section. When Blavatsky died in 1891, Judge became joint outer head of the Esoteric section along with Annie Besant.

Even as his health began to fail, Judge was called upon to face the most arduous tasks of his life. In 1893 he organized and managed the appearances of Theosophists Annie Besant, Hevavitarne Dharmapala, and G. N. Chakravarti at the Parliament of Religions in Chicago.

Immediately after the parliament, he had to face the new forces within the Theosophical Society that had arisen in India and England since the death of Blavatsky. In 1893 he was accused of falsely claiming uninterrupted contact with the "Masters" believed to secretly run the society. The charges were dismissed at a trial in the summer of 1894 in London but were revived in December at a meeting in India after a public airing of the accusations in the press.

Despairing of healing the rift that had developed, at the American section meeting in April 1895, Judge called for it to become independent. He was elected president, but he did not get to enjoy his new status for long because his health continued to disintegrate and, before another convention could be held, he died.

William Q. Judge, Echoes from the Orient (New York, 1890).

———, Letters That Have Helped Me (New York, 1891).

———, The Ocean of Theosophy (New York, 1893).

———, Isis and the Mahatmas (London, 1895).

———, Echoes of the Orient (San Diego, Calif., 1975).

Sven Eek and Boris de Zirkoff, "William Quan Judge, His Life and Work," in Echoes of the Orient (San Diego, Calif., 1975), xix–lxviii.

EOP, 486.

WWWH, 286–87.

KAWATE, Bunjiro (Konko Daijin) (September 29, 1814, Kandori, Urami Village, Bitchu Province, Japan—October 10, 1883, Otani, Japan); married Tose Furukawa, December 13, 1836 (d. February 1885).

Bunjiro Kawate, founder of Konkokyo (literally, the Religion of Golden Light), one of the so-called new religions from Japan, was born Genshichi Kandori in a small village in rural Japan. He was the second son in a family of farmers. As was frequently the practice, since the first son received the family inheritance, Genshichi was given for adoption to a family without a male child. Thus, at the age of eleven, Genshichi was adopted by the Kawate family of the nearby village of Otani and renamed Bunjiro Kawate. He received a year of education, during which time he learned to read and write. He was in poor health as a youth but worked hard and earned the respect of his new neighbors.

In 1831 his stepfather died, leaving Bunji head of the household. Not only did he have to run the farm, but he had to assume numerous official government duties for the village. He prospered in his new responsibilities however, and in a few years had doubled the family inheritance. He married and began to raise a family.

Although Bunji had been raised a nominally religious person who made occasional visits to the local Shinto temple, a pilgrimage to Shikoki Island, site of a large Shingon Buddhist shrine, led to the awakening of his religious consciousness. Then in the mid–1850s, a series of misfortunes led to the suggestion that he had offended Koijin, a Shinto deity believed to have a malevolent nature and to be easily offended. In the midst of his attempts to placate Koijin, he received an initial revelation that Koijin was, in fact, a benevolent deity. In 1858 Bunji began to speak the words of another Shinto deity, Kane no Kami, and as a result he directed his devotion to this deity. On September 23, 1858, Amaterasu, traditionally the Supreme Deity of Shinto, told Bunji that he was to become the "first disciple" of Kane no Kami. In his devotion, he learned that Kane no Kami was identical to Koijin. In the past Koijin had been misunderstood as evil, and Bunji came to understand that the traditional practices followed to ward off his evil influence were actually counterproductive superstitions that insulted the deities.

In 1859 Bunji retired from both public life and farming. He was told to rise above personal desires and henceforth serve Tenchi-Kane no Kami, the Principal Parent of the Universe. He was directed to initiate the practice of *toritsugi* (mediation) in which people invoked Bunji and he in turn bore their problems and sins to the Deity. On May 1, 1860 he began to keep a toritsugi record book. Konkokyo can be said to have begun at that time.

From his initial followers in Otani, the faith spread to neighboring towns. In 1861 Bunji had a *hiromae* (worship center) constructed, to which people could come for toritsugi day or night. In 1864 he received official permission to conduct religious services and three years later was appointed as a Shinto priest by the government. Shortly after his appointment he was given a new title by Tenchi-Kane no Kami, Ikigami Konko Daijin (Living God of Golden Light), by which he is commonly known by his followers to this day. The name *Ikigami* implied that God is born in each person.

Konkokyo survived the initial years of unrest that followed the Meiji Restoration in 1868 but was temporarily suppressed in 1872. In February 1873 Konko Daijin was forced to stop giving toritsugi. On March 13 he was ordered to consider himself reborn and to take a bath as a physical cleansing accompanying his rebirth. Several days later he was allowed to resume his religious functions. Then on April 11 he received the *Tenchi Katasuke*, the Reminder of Heaven and Earth, a basic teaching that was reproduced and given to all of his followers. It stated, "Through Ikigami Konko Daijin, To Tenchi Kane no Kami, With Heart and soul pray, The Divine favor depends on your own heart, On this very day pray."

The remainder of Konko Daijin's life was spent in giving toritsugi to followers who came to his center in Otani and directing the spread of his movement. His form of Shinto, centered upon a single benevolent deity, the practice of toritsugi, and the recognition of individuals' mutual dependence upon each other found support throughout Japan.

Upon Konko Daijin's death, his son Konko Ieyoshi became the patriarch. Leadership has been passed through the family in each generation.

Konkokyo came to America in 1919 and spread throughout the Japanese-American communities. Although concentrated in Hawaii and along the West Coast, centers can be found throughout the United States.

Bunjiro Kawate, *The Sacred Scriptures of Konkokyo* (Konko-cho, Japan, 1933).

Konko Daijin, A Biography (San Francisco, Calif., 1981).

Harry Thomsen, *The New Religions of Japan* (Rutland, Vt., 1963).

KEIL, William (March 6, 1812, Prussia—December 30, 1877, Aurora, Oregon); married Louise.

William Keil, the founder of two of the most successful communes in nineteenth-century America, Aurora and Bethel, grew up in Germany and became a tailor. In 1838 he settled in New York City, where he opened a successful tailoring shop. He also left the Lutheran church for the Methodist. Increasingly, however, he had become dissatisfied with "sectarian" religion and he left the Methodists also.

Then in 1843 he sold his business and moved westward with the idea of founding a free nonsectarian church in the relative freedom of western Pennsylvania. He moved among the German-speaking immigrants and was finally welcomed as a guest in the home of Andrew Giesy, which became his headquarters. Almost the entire family joined the congregation he was gathering. He also encountered the remnants of a group that had left the community of George Rapp at Economy and had settled at Phillipsburg.

Keil, without formal college or seminary training, preached a simple nondoctrinaire message built around the value of unselfishness, the very essence of love. Slowly he began to see the fundamental truth "Love one another" as implying a community of goods. While some became close disciples, many misunderstood and persecuted him. Meetings were disrupted and mobs threatened him. He told his followers to love those who placed themselves in the position of enemies. It is possibly during this time that rumors arose of Keil's assuming the role of one to be worshipped and being one of the two witnesses of the last days (Revelation 11:3), a rumor vigorously denied by followers who knew him.

As the communal implications of his message came to the fore, Keil decided to move his followers further west and build a communal colony. In 1844, with a few followers, Keil moved to Shelby County, Missouri, and bought fifty-three hundred acres, and began to build the town of Bethel. The followers in Pennsylvania joined him as they were able to divest themselves of their property and move.

On August 30, 1844, a very simple set of rules was adopted that declared that the society "must not rest on anything else than the love of God." No doctrinal requirements were set, and it is known that at least one Jewish family were active members. Keil was the acknowledged leader and acted informally as a benevolent autocrat, although a formal organization of twelve advisers was elected. By 1855 approximately a thousand persons lived at Bethel.

During the 1850s Keil decided to found a second colony in the Far West and in 1853 he sent a small group to Oregon to locate a site. They purchased land near Wallapa, Washington. Keil joined them in November 1855 and immediately decided that the site was unsuitable. He moved to Portland while his followers began to search for a more adequate location. They finally purchased land in the Willamette Valley and built the town called Aurora (after one of Keil's children).

Keil lived in Portland for two years. Having acquired some medical knowledge, he practiced magnetic healing and made his living in Portland as a physician. He moved to Aurora in the Spring of 1857 after a home had been built for him.

The community at Aurora swelled to approximately a thousand members during the 1860s. Three wagon trains brought some of the Bethel members.

Keil died in 1877, and a collective leadership succeeded him. Both Bethel and Aurora soon dissolved, the former in 1880 and the latter in 1881. Keil had been unable to groom a successor.

Bethel and Aurora became an enigma to communal observers because the communities had a very loose religious bond, few rules, and allowed some people who owned their own property to be members. The simple but definitive philosophy and Keil's personality, however, seem to have been all that was necessary.

Robert J. Hendricks, *Bethel and Aurora* (New York, 1933).

William Alfred Hines, *American Communities* (New York, 1909).

Charles Nordhoff, *The Communistic Societies of the United States* (London, 1875).

KELPIUS, Johannes (1673, Halwegen, Transylvania—February (?) 1708, Germantown, Pennsylvania); education: University of Tübingen; University of Altdorf, Ph.D., 1689.

Johannes Kelpius was the leader of the Chapter of Perfection (aka, the Society of Woman in the Wilderness), the first occult body in what is now the United States. Although orphaned in childhood, he received a fine education. His dissertation, written at the age of sixteen, was a treatise on natural theology, which was published and went through several editions. Shortly after graduation he coauthored a treatise on theology with his former instructor, Johannes Fabricius, and then wrote a volume on the ethics of Aristotle. His books attracted the attention of mathematician and astronomer Johann Jacob Zimmerman, who combined an interest in science, astrology, theology, and alchemy—all at a time in which the exploration of the occult arts and orthodox theology could co-exist. Zimmerman joined several mystical fraternities and led Kelpius into an association with the mystical pietist movement, which had attracted some disfavor because pietists tended to remain aloof from the formal activities of the state church.

Zimmerman had also absorbed some apocalyptic ideas and expected the return of Christ in the 1690s. He drew a small group of dedicated followers around him, including Kelpius, and proposed that they migrate to the American colonies and establish a small, disciplined commune to await the return of Christ. Zimmerman, with the aid of William Penn, readied the group to move to Pennsylvania, but he died on the eve of the voyage. Kelpius became the group's leader.

Departing from Germany in the summer of 1693, the group arrived in Pennsylvania on June 23, 1694, after stops in Holland and England. The day after their arrival, Kelpius led the group in the celebration of St. John's Eve, the surviving Sonnenweld-feuer of Norse Paganism, marking the beginning of the waning of the sun's power after midsummer.

Kelpius saw to two immediate needs. First, he secured land in Wissahickon Creek in Germantown to settle his small band, and, second, he initiated a program for the education of the local children who were without a school. Locally referred to as the Woman in the Wilderness (a reference to Revelation 12:14–17), the chapter constructed a cubic building forty (a perfect number) feet on each side, with an astronomical observatory on the roof.

Kelpius, in accordance with the chapter ideals, practiced celibacy and thus never married. He was of frail constitution and in the rugged environment developed tuberculosis. He had little concern for death, however, because he believed that he would live to see the Second Coming of Christ, at which time he would be translated into a new body.

Kelpius kept the small group unattached from other groups in the Colonies, though he showed a broad ecumenical spirit. He participated in the dedication of the Swedish Lutheran Church at Wicacoa. He was called upon to settle some differences between groups of Seventh-Day Baptists. He offered the entire community the services of the chapter, which provided horoscopes, amulets, and medical assistance.

Kelpius's tuberculosis kept him in bed an increasing amount of time during his last years. In the winter of 1706–07, while convalescing, he composed possibly his last literary work, a twenty-five-stanza hymn, "A Loving Moan of the Disconsolate Soul in the Morning Dawn." He died at the age of thirty-five early in 1708. He was succeeded by Conrad Matthai, a Swiss convert, but the group was already disintegrating and soon fell apart completely. Its only remnants are the hexmeisters, who still live in eastern Pennsylvania and practice a folk-magic system passed on by individuals who at one time lived in the chapter.

Johannes Kelpius, *The Diarium of Magister Johannes Kelpius* (1917).

Julius F. Sachse, *The German Pietists of Provincial Pennsylvania* (Philadelphia, Penn., 1895).

Corliss Fitz Randolph, "The German Seventh-Day Baptists" in *Seventh-Day Baptists in Europe and America* (Plainfield, N.J., 1910), 935–1257.

WWWH, 290.

KENT, Grady R. (April 26, 1909, Rosebud, Georgia—March 31, 1964).
Grady R. Kent, founder of the Church of God (Jerusalem Acres), was born in rural Georgia. Little is known of his parents and early life. He was poor and had only a third-grade education. As a young man he found his way into the Congregational Holiness Church, a congregation of the small holiness denomination, and there in 1930 was converted. He soon found that Pentecostalism offered him more, and he joined the Church of God (Cleveland, Tennessee). Kent experienced a baptism of the Holy Spirit as evidenced by speaking in unknown tongues, the distinctive feature of Pentecostalism, and felt a call to the ministry. The Church of God refused to license him unless he first attended Bible school. Instead Kent began to travel in the mountains preaching at Church of God congregations. He was welcomed by many ministers who appreciated his abilities and were under the impression that he had the proper credentials. When the church officials discovered what Kent was doing, they excommunicated him.

Kent turned to the Church of God of Prophecy, the denomination formed by the followers of A. J. Tomlinson, the former general overseer of the Church of God (Cleveland, Tennessee). He was ordained in 1932 and appointed evangelist for Georgia. His success led to his appointment in 1935 as state overseer in Minnesota. He held that post for two years before moving to Nebraska for two more. In 1938 he moved back to Georgia as pastor of the Church of God of Prophecy congregation. While there his preaching aroused the ire of the Ku Klux Klan. He later recounted this period, including one incident in which he barely escaped with his life, in a book entitled *Sixty Lashes at Midnight*.

He was next called to Cleveland, Tennessee, to pastor the Wildwood Avenue Church of God of Prophecy. He was also appointed head of the Church of God Marker Association, a church department whose task was to mark significant locations in the life and history of the church. Kent claimed to have originated the idea of Field of the Woods, the 160-acre memorial site, near the place where A. J. Tomlinson joined the Church of God in 1903.

According to Kent, while pastoring the Wildwood Avenue Church, he began to prophesy about the restoration of the church, which had arisen anew in 1903 (when Tomlinson found the church in North Carolina). The true church had been lost in the Middle Ages and begun anew in 1903.

Trouble for Kent in the Church of God of Prophecy began in 1948. A. J. Tomlinson had died in 1944 and had been succeeded by his son Milton. Four years later Milton led in the introduction of a more democratic church government to replace the theocratic form that had existed under his father. Kent opposed the move. He also began to argue for a return of church structures as described in the Bible—the twelve, the seventy, and so on. Finally he began to preach and prophesy about the last days, emphasizing that one who had the spirit of John the Revelator would appear to proclaim the program of the church for the endtime. His ideas were rejected, and so on February 13, 1957, he resigned from the Church of God of Prophecy.

Kent met with his followers four days after his resignation to begin the reformation of the Church of God. In gradual steps the new organization restored the biblical offices, purchased a tract of land in Cleveland, Tennessee, called Jerusalem Acres (from which the church takes its popular designation), and incorporated as The Church of God. During the reformation period, officially February 13, 1957, through June 13, 1960 (the three and a half years symbolizing the time of Jesus' earthly ministry), Kent restructured and stabilized the church.

In the four remaining years of his life, as chief bishop of the church, he added many of its distinctives. He banned many traditional holidays such as Christmas and Easter as "pagan" and reinstituted the Old Testament feasts. The birth of Christ is celebrated in October. He inaugurated the Church Air Force, Navy, Army, and Motorcycle Corps to spread the gospel "to the Highways and hedges." Kent died in 1964 and was succeeded by Marion W. Hall, who was replaced by Robert S. Somerville in 1972 after being charged with immoral conduct. Kent is remembered today by his followers as the person bearing the spirit of John during the endtime.

Grady R. Kent, *Treatise of the 1957 Reformation Stand* (Cleveland, Tenn., 1964).

———, *Sixty Lashes at Midnight* (Cleveland, Tenn., 1963).

———, *The Church of God Manual of Apostle Doctrine and Business Procedure* (Cleveland, Tenn., 1972).

Lynn Murphy, "Grady R. Kent: St. John II" (unpublished paper in the files of Lee College, Cleveland, Tenn.).

KETCHAM, Robert Thomas (July 22, 1889, Nelson, Pennsylvania— August 21, 1978, Chicago, Illinois); married Clara (d. 1920); married Mary Smart, June 1922.

Robert Thomas Ketcham, leading voice of fundamentalism and one of the founders of the General Association of Regular Baptist Churches, was born of Methodist parents in rural Pennsylvania. His father was a farmer. His mother died when he was seven, and his father remarried four years later. His stepmother was a Baptist, and thus young Bob was led to change his church membership. About this same time his father relocated the family to Galeton, Pennsylvania. When Bob was sixteen, he declared his independence and left home, an action that put an end to his formal education. He never finished high school.

Although raised in the church, Ketcham was twenty years old before he experienced a conversion. That experience was followed by a call to preach, and in 1912 he accepted the call to become pastor of First Baptist

Church in Roulette, Pennsylvania. During his three years at Roulette, he first experienced two problems that were to confront him for the rest of his life. First, in an attempt to improve himself educationally, he enrolled in the correspondence course offered by Crozer Theological Seminary. In his readings, however, he discovered material that deviated from the orthodox Christian faith in which he had been raised. He dropped the course and continued his study on his own.

Secondly, a serious eye problem, keratocoma, a condition that distorts the cornea, emerged. His vision was severely impaired all of his life.

He entered into his pastoral work with great enthusiasm, and his native ability compensated for his lack of formal education. He had great success at the small church, and finally, in 1915, he was ordained. That same year he became pastor of the First Baptist Church at Brookville, Pennsylvania, and four years later moved on to Butler.

Since the time he dropped his work from Crozer, Ketcham had become aware of a liberal element in the Northern Baptist Convention and had become strongly identified with the fundamentalists, those who held strictly to orthodox Christian beliefs, particularly the deity of Christ, His virgin birth, substitutionary atonement, and literal second coming. A decade of concern became focused in 1919 when the convention launched the New World movement, which Ketcham saw as a liberal program that denied fundamental faith and, in addition, that by the manner in which it was promoted attacked the local autonomy of the congregations. The program led to his concentrated study of liberal influence in the Convention and to his first publication, A *Statement of the First Baptist Church Butler, Pennsylvania, with Reference to The New World Movement and the $100,000,000 Drive* (1919). The pamphlet, which was reprinted and widely distributed, made Ketcham a leading figure when the fundamentalists met prior to the 1920 convention.

Ketcham joined heartily in the formation in 1923 of the Bible Baptist Union, which sought to unify fundamentalist Baptists across the nation. Meanwhile, he moved to Ohio and accepted calls to pastor first at Niles and then Elyria (1926). In his parsonage at Elyria in 1928, Ketcham met with the group of pastors who moved to form the Ohio Association of Independent Baptist Churches. Like Ketcham, each felt that the Bible Baptist Union had become ineffective and that there was no possibility of returning the convention to fundamentalism. Two years later the Union came to the same conclusion and began the process that led to its replacement by the independent General Association of Regular Baptist Churches. Ketcham did not attend its initial meeting in 1932 but attended the two crucial sessions in 1933 (at which he was elected vice-president) and 1934 (at which he was elected president). At these sessions he led the fights to separate the association completely from the convention as a fellowship of congregations.

For the next three decades he remained the dominant voice in the association. In 1938 he moved to abolish the president's office in favor of a collective leadership by a Council of 14, to which he was elected and on which he served as secretary-treasurer and editor of *The Baptist Bulletin*. In

1939 he became pastor of the largest Baptist church in Iowa, the Walnut Street Church in Waterloo. Problems with his eyes and duties at his pastorate forced him to resign the editorship in 1945. However, the next year he was named the national representative of the association. He resigned his pastorate and worked for the association for the next ten years. His duties included the editorship of the *Bulletin*. He gave up the editorship again in 1955 and resigned his executive position in 1960 (following a major heart attack). He was named national consultant to the association, a position he resigned in 1966. His health deteriorated during the last decade of his life, but he continued to preach whenever possible, his last sermons being delivered from a stool.

He is remembered for molding the life of the General Association of Regular Baptist Churches for its first generation and becoming one of fundamentalism's leading spokespersons in the era after World War II.

Robert Thomas Ketcham, *A Statement of the First Baptist Church Butler, Pennsylvania, with Reference to The New World Movement* (Butler, Penn., 1919).

———, *I Shall Not Want* (Chicago, 1953).

———, *The Answer* (Chicago, 1956).

J. Murray Murdoch, *Portrait of Obedience* (Schaumburg, Ill., 1979).

George W. Dollar, *A History of Fundamentalism in America* (Greenville, S.C., 1963).

KHAN, Hazrat Inayat (July 5, 1882, Baroda, Gujerat, India—February 2, 1927, Delhi, India); married Ora Ray Baker, March 20, 1913 (d. 1949).

Hazrat Inayat Khan, founder of the Sufi Order, the first Sufi organization in the West, was born into a family of musicians. His grandfather had founded two music schools in Baroda, one of which focused upon Western music. As a youth, Khan became an accomplished musician and also developed a contemplative nature. At the age of twelve he left home to pursue his life of contemplation and music. He eventually became a court musician for the Nizam of Hyderabad. He developed an early yearning to go to the West but was prevented by family responsibilities.

During his years at Hyderabad, he began a spiritual search among the Sufis. He made a pilgrimage to Ajmer, the headquarters of the Chishti Order of Sufis. At the age of twenty-four, he met Murshid Khwaja Abu Hashim Madani, a sheikh of the Nizami branch of the Chishti Order who lived in Hyderabad. He took initiation from the sheikh. Eventually, Kahn received the succession from his murshid and a mission to take Sufism to the West. Prior to his leaving, however, he made a pilgrimage of India and settled in Calcutta where he founded a music school.

Khan left India on September 13, 1910. He settled in New York where he lectured on music at Columbia University. He also began to lecture on Sufism and for several years toured the United States. In Berkeley, California, he met his first initiate, Mrs. Ada Martin, to whom he gave the name Rabia. In Nyack, New York, he met Ora Ray Baker (b. May 8, 1890), his future wife. She was the cousin of Mary Baker Eddy, the founder of Christian Science, and was at the time of their meeting living under the guardianship of her half-brother, Pierre Bernard, the founder of the Tantrik Order in America. Bernard disapproved of their relationship, and she lost contact with Khan when he left for Europe in 1912. She rejoined him in England, however, and they were married.

Khan founded the Sufi Order in 1916 in London, which became his headquarters during the war. After the war he moved to Suresnes, a Paris suburb, where he established an international movement headquarters to administer the growing organization. He conducted an annual summer school at Suresnes and spent the remainder of the year on tours to lecture and build the order.

Khan made lecture tours to the United States in 1923 and 1925. Rabia Martin was made a murshid, the Sufi equivalent of minister, and a Sufi temple was opened in San Francisco. In England a strong Sufi society had been built during the war years, and it began to issue a quarterly magazine, *Sufism*, and published Khan's lectures and poetry.

On September 13, 1926, Khan called his students to gather at Suresnes, on the slopes of Mt. Valerien, to lay the foundation stone for the Universal, a temple of all religions, a visible manifestation of Khan's belief in the essential unity of all religions. Khan left immediately for India, where he died the following year. He was only forty-four years old.

Khan's early death caught the order unprepared. In the United States Murshid Martin claimed that Khan had passed the succession to her and most of the American movement followed her. She led the order until her death in 1947 and passed her succession to Murshid Ivy O. Duce. Duce became a disciple of Meher Baba and reorganized the order under his guidance. It has since been known as Sufism Reoriented.

The European branches of the order did not accept Martin, and control of the order was assumed by surviving members of the family. In more recent years, it accepted Khan's son, Pir Vilayat Inayat Khan, who was only eleven when his father died, as Khan's successor. Pir Vilayat has revived the order in the United States and during the 1970s began issuing a multivolume edition of Hazrat Inayat Khan's complete writings and lectures.

Hazrat Inayat Khan, *The Mind-World* (London, 1935).

————, *The Way of Illumination* (Southampton, 1922).

————, *The Sufi Message of Hazrat Inayat Khan*, 12 volumes (London, 1960–69).

Elisabeth deJong-Keesing, *Inayat Khan*, (The Hague, 1974).

Jean Overton Fuller, *Noor-un-nisa Inayat Khan* (Rotterdam, 1971).

Musharaff Moulamia Khan, *Pages in the Life of a Sufi* (London, 1971).

Pir Vilayat Inayat Khan, *The Message in Our Time* (New York, 1978).

KING, Joseph Hillery (August 11, 1869, Anderson County, South Carolina—April 23, 1946, Anderson, South Carolina); married Willie Irene King, August 10, 1890 (div.); married Blanche Leon Moore, June 1, 1920; education: School of Theology, U.S. Grant University, Chattanooga, Tennessee, 1895–97.

Joseph Hillery King, one of the leaders in the development of what is today known as the Pentecostal Holiness Church, was one of eleven children born to a tenant farmer in South Carolina. The family was poor and constantly on the move. As a result, King received very little education.

On his sixteenth birthday, he was converted in a Methodist-led holiness camp meeting. A week later he felt a call to preach and within a few months, on October 23, 1885, he experienced sanctification, which holiness doctrine defines as the second work of grace by which the soul is cleansed and made perfect in love. King began to work in revival meetings assisting the preachers. He applied for a license to exhort, and although denied the first time, he received it in 1887.

After a short time in the army, he married. Unfortunately he found his wife to be so completely unaccepting of his commitment to become a minister that they soon parted. In 1891 he received his license to preach, and the next year was assigned to his first pastoral charge as the assistant pastor for the Rock Spring–Walton circuit in the Georgia Conference of the Methodist Episcopal Church. He served several circuits until 1895 when he was appointed to the Lookout Mountain circuit, an appointment that allowed him to attend college.

During the years in Chattanooga, he felt increasing tension with the Methodists over the issue of holiness. He also became associated with the radical holiness group, the Fire-Baptized Holiness Association. The FBHA not only believed in sanctification but looked for an additional, "third work of grace," an experience that they called "fire-baptism." The leader of the group, B. H. Irwin, had developed this doctrine from his reading of the early Methodist writer John Fletcher. In 1897, shortly after graduation, King decided to become a full-time evangelist for the association and he left the Methodist Episcopal Church.

In 1898 he went to Canada for two years to help spread the work in and around Toronto. Then in 1900 Irwin called King to his Iowa headquarters to assist him in editing the periodical *Live Coals of Fire* and in running the association. Shortly after arriving in Iowa, Irwin was involved in a public scandal that led to his withdrawing from the work he had founded. King was left in charge and, at a call meeting of the leadership, was elected general superintendent and appointed editor of the periodical. King then began a general itinerancy throughout the association. He held revival meetings and built the organization, which in 1902 took the name Fire-Baptized Holiness Church. He moved the headquarters to Georgia.

In 1907 G. B. Cashwell, a holiness preacher who had received the Pentecostal baptism of the Holy Spirit with the evidence of speaking in tongues, held a revival in Taccoa Falls, Georgia, and spread the new message. King attended and after much struggle became a Pentecostal. He helped spread the message throughout the church and, within a short time, all the ministers accepted it as the truth they had been seeking with the "fire-baptism."

With the added impetus of the Pentecostal message, King continued his work for the church. In 1909 he led in the founding of the Falcon Publishing House (to publish the church's periodical, now called the *Apostolic Evangel*) and an orphanage, both located at Falcon, North Carolina.

In 1911 he began a world tour on behalf of foreign missions. While he was away on what became a two-year venture, the church merged with the

Pentecostal Holiness Church, whose name they took, and King was elected the assistant general superintendent and president of the General Mission Board. Upon his return to the United States, he assumed his church duties. In 1914 he also became pastor of the congregation in Memphis.

In 1917 King was elected general superintendent for the Pentecostal Holiness Church, a position he held for the rest of his life. Three years later he remarried. When he died in 1946, the minuscule holiness group he inherited in 1900 had grown into a national Pentecostal body with missions around the world.

Joseph H. King, *Yet Speaketh* (Franklin Springs, Ga., 1940).

Joseph E. Campbell, *The Pentecostal Holiness Church, 1898–1948* (Franklin Springs, Ga., 1951).

A. D. Beacham, Jr., *A Brief History of the Pentecostal Holiness Church* (Franklin Springs, Ga., 1983).

KNAPP, Martin Wells (March 27, 1853, Clarendon, Calhoun County, Michigan—December 7, 1901, Cincinnati, Ohio); married Lucy J. Glenn, 1877 (d. September 5, 1890); married Minnie C. Ferle, September 14, 1892; education: Albion College, 1870–76.

Martin Wells Knapp, holiness leader and founder of the International Holiness Union and Prayer League (currently a constituent part of the Wesleyan Church), was born in rural Michigan. His father, a farmer, although a class leader in the Methodist Episcopal church, was unable to pass along his religion to the young Martin. Martin did have a desire for education, however, and in his seventeenth year enrolled in Albion College. Unfortunately, because of his father's bad health, he had to work the farm most of the time and never finished his degree. During his college days he met his future wife. As a result of her prayers and encouragement, Knapp experienced a conversion and received a call to preach.

He joined the Michigan Conference of the Methodist Episcopal Church and successively served pastoral charges at Pottersville (1877); Duplain circuit (1880); Lions (1883); and Montague (1884). While serving the Duplain circuit under the ministry of bishop-to-be William Taylor, Knapp experienced sanctification. Holiness theology taught the possibility of a second act of grace above that of salvation in which a believer is cleansed completely of inbred sin and filled with perfect love. After he experienced sanctification, Knapp became increasingly involved in the larger holiness movement, which had arisen after the Civil War. In 1886 he wrote the first of many books, *Christ Crowned Within*.

In 1887, at Knapp's request, the Michigan conference "located" him, thus freeing him from having to hold a pastoral appointment. He began full-time evangelistic work. In 1888 he began *The Revivalist*, a periodical promoting the holiness movement.

His first years as an evangelist were plagued with personal problems in both health and finances and culminated in the death of his first wife.

In 1892 he remarried and moved to Cincinnati. There he began to build the work for which he is remembered. He began a publishing concern. In 1894 he purchased land near Flat Rock, Kentucky, and established Beulah Heights School. He built a tabernacle adjacent to the school and held a camp meeting there each summer. In 1897 he opened a mission in Cincinnati. That same year he helped form the International Holiness Union and Prayer League. He was elected vice-president at the organization meeting, which was held in his home. In 1900, on a two-acre plot in the western part of Cincinnati, he opened God's Bible School.

Knapp's leadership in the holiness cause led to increased friction with the Methodist Episcopal church, which was moving away from the holiness position. In 1898 he was censured by the Michigan Conference for holding an unauthorized revival meeting in Maryland. When he retired in 1899, the censure was removed; however, Knapp felt increasingly alienated from Methodism, which he believed was becoming too worldly. Thus he withdrew completely from the church in 1900. He died of typhoid the next year.

Although he lived less than half a century, Knapp left an extensive legacy. *The Revivalist* and God's Bible School, placed in the hands of an independent board prior to his death, continue to serve the more conservative wing of the contemporary holiness movement. Charles and Lettie Cowman, who attended God's Bible School soon after it opened, changed their missionary plans and committed themselves to evangelizing Japan. From their work grew the Oriental Missionary Society and the American-based Oriental Missionary Society Holiness Conference. The International Holiness Union and Prayer League, originally conceived as an interdenominational society to promote holiness, began to form independent holiness congregations. It went through a series of mergers that led to the formation of the Pilgrim Holiness Church in 1922. That body united with the Wesleyan Methodist Church in 1968 to form the Wesleyan church.

Martin Wells Knapp, *Christ Crowned Within* (Cincinnati, Ohio, 1886).

———, *Out of Egypt into Canaan* (Albion, Mich., 1887).

———, *Impressions* (Cincinnati, Ohio, 1892).

———, *Holiness Triumphant* (Cincinnati, Ohio, 1900).

A. M. Hills, *A Hero of Faith and Prayer* (Cincinnati, Ohio, 1902).

KNEELAND, Abner (April 7, 1774, Gardner, Massachusetts—August 27, 1844, Salubria, Iowa Territory); married Waitstill Ormsbee, April 9, 1797 (d. 1806); married Lucinda Mason, circa 1807; married Eliza Osborn, August 11, 1813; married Dolly Rice, 1834.

Abner Kneeland, outstanding free-thought leader and founder of the Salubria free-thought community, was a self-educated man. He began his adult life as a carpenter, became a teacher in Vermont, and eventually accepted a call to the ministry, first as a Baptist and then a Universalist. His first full-time pastorate was in Langdon, New Hampshire, in 1804. He was the clerk of the Universalist General Convention from 1807 to 1815. In 1825 Kneeland became the minister of the Prince Street Universalist Church in New York City. By 1829 his heretical views had split even the liberal Universalist parish, and he was dismissed. The Universalists accepted his voluntary self-suspension later that year. In the latter half of 1829, he renounced Christianity in a series of public lectures in New York

City (later published in a book entitled A *Review of the Evidences of Christianity*). He then proceeded to reorganize his followers and the free-thinkers of New York into a group, the Moral Philanthropists, which continued to meet for ten years.

Kneeland moved from New York to Boston in 1830 and accepted a position as lecturer at the newly formed First Society of Free Enquirers. He founded the magazine *The Boston Investigator* in 1831. His lectures and magazine proved surprisingly popular, much to the alarm of orthodox religious leaders. Kneeland spoke freely throughout New England and New York State. Besides his lectures on religion, he distributed birth control information and was probably the anonymous publisher of the first birth control book in the United States, Knowlton's *Fruits of Philosophy*.

In 1834 the authorities in Boston indicted Kneeland for blasphemy. He was convicted on the second trial, after the first ended in a hung jury, and he appealed his conviction twice. In 1836 the Supreme Judicial Court of Massachusetts upheld his conviction and sentenced him to sixty days in jail. Despite appeals signed by many of the notables of the day, Kneeland had to serve out his sentence. The basic statement Kneeland made that had been found to be blasphemous was a line from his philosophical creed, "Universalists believe in a God, which I do not."

His conviction and jail sentence aroused freethinkers around the United States, many of whom had formed local free-thought groups not unlike the one Kneeland lectured before in Boston. In August 1836 Kneeland used his popularity at the convention of freethinkers held at Saratoga, New York, to urge the formation of the United Moral and Philosophical Society for the Diffusion of Useful Knowledge—the first truly national free-thought association in the United States.

However much success and fame his Boston work provided, Kneeland grew tired of his responsibilities. He and a group of friends decided to form a utopian colony in the Iowa Territory. They set out for Iowa in 1839. Kneeland stopped frequently along the route to lecture before finally arriving at the chosen site in Van Buren County. The group formed the community of Salubria, located on the banks of the Mississippi River. During the several years remaining in his life, Kneeland became politically active. He was the Van Buren County Democratic chairman but was defeated in his bid for a seat in the Iowa legislature. Kneeland died suddenly in 1844, and his community did not long survive him. He is buried at the cemetery at Farmington, Iowa.

While the several organizations which Kneeland was associated with and/or founded did not survive for many years, his weekly periodical, *The Boston Investigator*, continued until 1904 and tied together several generations of freethinkers in America. His blasphemy prosecution is the most famous in American history.

Abner Kneeland, A *Review of the Evidences of Christianity* (New York, 1829).

——— , *National Hymns, Original and Selected, for the Use of Those Who Are "Slaves to No Sect"* (Boston, 1836).

DeRobigne Mortimer Bennett, *The World's Sages, Infidels and Thinkers* (New York, 1876).

Samuel Porter Putnam, *Four Hundred Years of Freethought* (New York, 1894).
Robert Clifton Whittemore, *Makers of the American Mind* (New York, 1964).
DAB, 10, 457–8.
WWWH, 298.

Gordon Stein

KNOCH, Adolph Ernst (December 12, 1874, St. Louis, Missouri— March 28, 1965, Los Angeles, California); married Olive Elizabeth Hyde (d. September 7, 1926); married Sigrid von Kanitz, 1932.

Adolph Ernst Knoch, the translator of the Concordant version of the Scriptures and founder of the periodical *Unsearchable Riches*, was born to German-American parents in St. Louis. At age ten he moved to Los Angeles. Converted while reading the Bible, he joined the Plymouth (Open) Brethren and became active in teaching. He married and began a career as a printer. In 1906 their son Ernest was born.

Knoch was an intense amateur Bible student. His study led him to points of disagreement with the Brethren, and around the turn of the century he was excommunicated. Prior to his leaving the Brethren, he became acquainted with the magazine *Things to Come*, published in England by Anglican Bible student E. A. Bullinger. In 1906 Knoch sent Bullinger an article spelling out his discoveries concerning baptism, namely, that water baptism had been superseded by the one spirit baptism of Ephesians 4:5. To Knoch's surprise, Bullinger published the article and accepted the view in his later writings. Also as a result of the article, another reader of the magazine, Vladimir Galesnoff, began to correspond with Knoch.

In the correspondence, Knoch began to explain his desire to make a new translation of the Scriptures, a literal translation in which each Greek word would be assigned a standard English word equivalent. The two agreed to begin a magazine as a ministry to Bible students. In October 1909 the first issue of *Unsearchable Riches* appeared.

The first part of what was to become the Concordant version of the Bible appeared in 1919, *The Unveiling of Jesus Christ* (i.e., the Book of Revelation). Other books followed until the complete New Testament was issued in 1926. A second printing was made in 1930. During this period Knoch was assisted in his work by his wife and partner. After Galesnoff died in 1921 and Knoch's wife in 1926, his son Ernest and his son's wife, Alberta Marie Lundquist (whom Ernest had married in 1930) became his prime assistants.

With the New Testament complete, Knoch began the work on the Old Testament with a trip to the Holy Land. He stopped in Germany on the way and returned to Germany after his visit. There he met and wed Countess Sigrid von Kanitz, who had been publishing a periodical, *The Overcomer*, in which she had been placing material from *Unsearchable Riches*. He also decided to stay in Germany and produce a German version of the Concordant New Testament. Knoch remained in Germany until 1939. With war approaching, he returned to Los Angeles with his wife.

Knoch next set himself the task of producing an international edition of the Concordant New Testament, using the format of the German edition (which appeared in 1944) and the keyword concordance (which appeared in 1946). He also worked on the Old Testament translation, a work that consumed the rest of his active life. He lived to see only a portion of Genesis and Isaiah (published in 1957 and 1962 respectively), though he finished the entire work.

The ministry he initiated with the publication of *Unsearchable Riches* led to the formation of numerous groups of Bible students who gathered regularly to read Knoch's material and who accepted his unique theological perspectives. Knoch followed the pattern of the Plymouth Brethren of dividing history into segments called dispensations, which Knoch termed *eons*. He disagreed with the Plymouth Brethren in teaching universal reconciliation, the impersonality of the Holy Spirit, and sabbath (Saturday) worship. Knoch's Concordant version has never received widespread use outside of the Bible students associated with *Unsearchable Riches*. Most Biblical scholars rejected the methodology of translating the Greek and Hebrew literally, word for word.

Adolph Ernst Knoch, *The Unveiling of Jesus Christ* (Los Angeles, Calif., 1932).

——— , *Concordant Literal New Testament* (Saugus, Mass., 1966).

——— , *Spirit, Spirits and Spirituality* (Canyon County, Calif., 1977).

——— , *The Problem of Evil and the Judgments of God* (Canyon County, Calif., 1976).

Adolph Ernst Knoch, 1874-1965 (Saugus, Calif, 1965).

The Concordant Version in the Critics Den (Los Angeles, Calif., n.d.).

The Story of the Concordant Version (Saugus, Calif., n.d.).

Raymond E. Sloan, Jr. "A History of the Concordant Version," *The Bible Collector*, 8 (October–December 1966), 3–5.

KUHLMAN, Kathryn (May 7, 1907, Concordia, Missouri—February 20, 1976, Tulsa, Oklahoma); married Burroughs A. Waltrip, October 19, 1938 (div.).

Kathryn Kuhlman, spiritual healer and founder of the Kathryn Kuhlman Foundation, was born in Concordia, Missouri, where her father was mayor of the town. Her father was a Methodist and her mother a Baptist, and Kathryn attended both churches. At the age of fourteen she experienced a conversion while sitting in worship at the Methodist church. She claimed that the Holy Spirit moved through her and that Jesus came into her heart. After her sophomore year she dropped out of high school and headed west. She attended a boarding school for a while but soon began holding evangelistic services and filling the pulpit of small Baptist churches in Idaho.

Her itinerant life led her to Denver, where she preached at a small mission. As a result of her work, she was invited to become pastor of the independent Denver Revival Tabernacle. She was also ordained by the Evangelical Church Alliance. While at the tabernacle she invited evangelist Burroughs Waltrip to preach. He became so impressed with Kathryn that he divorced his wife and, on October 19, 1938, married her. The marriage ended in divorce several years later, and in the resulting scandal the congregation was dispersed.

When her work in Denver ended, Kathryn moved to Franklin, Pennsylvania, and became pastor of a small congregation that met at the Faith Temple. On her third evening there an event that was to change the course of her ministry occurred. During the service a woman reported that on the previous evening she had felt the power of God move through her and that she had been healed. Her doctor had confirmed the disappearance of a tumor. The following May a second extraordinary healing occurred, this time of a man who had been blind for twenty-two years.

On July 4, 1947, Kathryn moved her services to Pittsburgh, where she rented the Carnegie Auditorium from the city. She held weekly services there for the next twenty years. While the Carnegie Auditorium was being renovated, she moved to the First Presbyterian Church of Pittsburgh and held services every Friday evening.

As her ministry grew, she began to hold weekly services at Youngstown, Ohio, and monthly services at Los Angeles, California, as well as traveling widely, speaking, and conducting healing services for groups such as the Full Gospel Businessmen's Fellowship. A radio ministry, begun while at Franklin, expanded into regular shows heard across the United States and Canada, and in the mid-1960s she began a weekly television show that continued until her death. She founded the Kathryn Kuhlman Foundation, which helped fund foreign missions, two overseas radio stations, scholarship funds, and various ministries such as Teen Challenge, headed by Pentecostal minister David Wilkerson.

Kuhlman's fame experienced a major boost in 1962 with the publication of her first book, *I Believe in Miracles*, which sold over a million copies. The volume recounted the stories of a number of people who had been healed under her ministry. This was followed by a second volume in 1969, *God Can Do It Again*, which had a similar format.

As her fame spread, she was in great demand as a healer across the country. She became known for her flamboyant style and her speaking ability. She refused to use healing lines in which the sick were invited to come forward for the laying on of hands, a practice common at most Pentecostal healing services. She preferred that only people who professed a healing come forward.

She died of heart trouble after a lengthy illness.

Kathryn Kuhlman, *I Believe in Miracles* (Englewood Cliffs, N.J., 1962).

——— , *God Can Do It Again* (Englewood Cliffs, N.J., 1969).

——— , *Nothing Is Impossible with God* (Englewood Cliffs, N.J., 1974).

——— , *10,000 Miles for a Miracle* (Minneapolis, Minn., 1974).

Allen Spraggett, *Kathryn Kuhlman, the Woman Who Believes in Miracles* (New York, 1970).

Helen Kooiman Hosier, *Kathryn Kuhlman* (Old Tappan, N.J., 1976).

H. Richard Casdorph, *The Miracles* (Plainfield, N.J., 1976).

William A. Nolen, *Healing: A Doctor in Search of a Miracle* (New York, 1974).

LAKE, John Graham (March 18, 1870, St. Mary's, Ontario, Canada— September 16, 1935, Spokane, Washington); married Jennie Stevens, February 1898 (d. 1912); married Florence Switzer, November 27, 1913.

John Graham Lake, early Pentecostal healing minister and founder of a group of Apostolic churches on the West Coast, was born into a Methodist family and notes that he was converted as a child. He was one of sixteen children and in his sixteenth year moved to Michigan. When he was twenty years old, he moved to Chicago and in 1891 became a Methodist minister. Instead of taking a pastoral position, however, he founded a newspaper. In the late 1890s he began to attend the healing home established by John Alexander Dowie, founder of the Christian Catholic Church. He brought his brother, an invalid for twenty-two years, and saw him instantly healed. Then his sister was healed of cancer. Finally, his wife, who had become ill with a combination of tuberculosis and heart trouble, was healed as Lake prayed for her.

From these experiences Lake became a devoted advocate of spiritual healing and joined Dowie's church. He moved to Zion, Illinois, the community created by Dowie, and became the manager of the building department. During his years in Chicago he had entered the insurance business, and he continued that career.

In 1904 Dowie's enterprise fell apart, and Lake moved back to Chicago. He became a successful businessman and obtained a seat on the Chicago Board of Trade. He also attended the North Avenue Mission, where, in the fall of 1906, Miss Mabel Smith brought the experience of speaking in tongues as a sign of the baptism of the Holy Spirit from Azusa Street in Los Angeles. Pastor W. H. Durham received the baptism in March 1907; Lake received it in April of that same year. To his work as a lay healing evangelist, Lake added the emphasis upon the baptism of the Holy Spirit (Pentecostalism).

Shortly after casting his lot with the new Pentecostals, Lake divested himself of all his wealth and became a full-time evangelist. He also decided to go to Africa as a missionary. After spending the winter of 1907–8 in Indianapolis, he left for South Africa in 1908 accompanied by a group of Pentecostals.

This group, of which Lake was a part, were the first Pentecostals in Africa. At first they preached in conjunction with the Christian Catholic church in Zion, the group affiliated with Dowie's church in South Africa, but soon split over the issue of speaking in tongues. Lake returned to the United States briefly in 1909 but was back in South Africa in 1910 for the founding of the Apostolic Faith Mission. He became pastor of the Apostolic Tabernacle in Johannesburg.

In 1912 Lake joined an expedition into the Kalahari Desert. He returned to discover that during his absence his wife had died. Within a short time he resigned his pastorate and returned to the United States. He married again in 1913), and in 1914 he founded the Apostolic Church in Spokane, Washington. The church became a center for the revived movement of healing within the Evangelical churches. Lake spent the rest of his life ministering to the congregation in Spokane and traveling around the country as an evangelist. In 1920 as a result of his evangelistic efforts, an Apostolic Church was founded in Portland, Oregon, and a few years later in San Diego, California. Gordon Lindsey, who was to become a major force in the new surge of healing activity among Pentecostals in the 1950s, was converted in the Apostolic Church in Portland and for many years had a strong relationship with Lake.

John Graham Lake, *Adventures in God* (Tulsa, Okla., 1981).

———, *The John G. Lake Sermons on Dominion Over Demons, Disease and Death*, edited by Gordon Lindsey (Dallas, Texas, 1949).

———, *The New John G. Lake Sermons*, ed. by Gordon Lindsey (Dallas, n.d.).

———, *Spiritual Hunger*, ed. by Gordon Lindsey (Dallas, 1976).

Gordon Lindsey, *The Gordon Lindsey Story* (Dallas, Texas, n.d.).

Walter J. Hollenweger, *The Pentecostals* (Minneapolis, Minn., 1972).

DE LANDAS BERGHES et de Rache, duc de Winock, Rudolph Francis Edward St. Patrick Alphonsus Ghislain de Gramont Hamilton de Loraine-Brabant, Prince (November 1, 1873, Naples, Italy—November 17, 1920, Philadelphia, Pennsylvania); education: University of Cambridge; University of Paris; University of Brussels, Ph.D.

Rudolph, the Prince de Landas Berghes, was one of two men (the other being Joseph René Vilatte) to introduce Old Catholicism into the United States. Born of an aristocratic Austrian family, he received the best of educations and served on Lord H. H. Kitchener's staff in the Sudan for a short period (circa 1911). After retiring with the rank of lieutenant colonel, he returned to England. There he met Old Catholic Bishop Arnold Harris Mathew from whom he sought an episcopal consecration. It seems that Landas Berghes was among those wishing to strengthen the antipapal movement in his native Austria. The Austrian government had denied the Old Catholics a bishop for their national branch.

Landas Berghes affiliated with Mathew's church and on November 12, 1912, was ordained. Less than a year later, on June 29, 1913, he was consecrated and made Mathew's coadjutor. He was designated missionary bishop for Scotland. However, a year later, before any Scottish work developed, England was at war with Austria. Landas Berghes was not only a subject of the Austro-Hungarian Empire but related to several of the more prominent European families. He faced immediate internment; however, to avoid the problems that would be raised in holding him, the British government worked out an arrangement to send Landas Berghes to the United States.

He arrived in the United States on November 7, 1914, and soon found his way to Waukegan, Illinois, and the small independent Old Catholic Abbey of Saint Dunstan headed by one of Vilatte's priests, William Henry Francis Brothers. While there, he also contacted Carmel Henry Carfora, an independent Catholic bishop in Ohio. He enjoyed the hospitality of the Episcopal Church and assisted in the consecration of H. R. Hulse, the bishop-elect of Cuba, on January 12, 1915.

Once in the United States, he developed plans to form a branch of Mathew's church, which he called the North American Old Roman Catholic Church. He inaugurated the church in October 1916, when, on successive days, he consecrated Brothers (October 3) and Carfora (October 4). Much of the work proved unstable. Brothers broke with Landas Berghes and Carfora within a few months. He was replaced by Stanislaus

Mickiewicz, who had to be deposed within a year and who eventually joined Brothers.

With little to show for his work, Landas Berghes became disappointed and on December 22, 1919, after resigning as Primate of the N.A.O.R.C.C., made his submission to the Roman Catholic Church in St. Patrick's Cathedral in New York City in the presence of Patrick Cardinal Hayes. He did so with the understanding that his episcopal orders would be recognized. He, in turn, would retire and join an order.

On March 13, 1920, he became a novitiate with the Order of Saint Augustine and was appointed to teach French at Villanova University near Philadelphia for the academic year 1920–21. But he did not think the promises that had been made to him at the time of his submission had been kept. No acknowledgment concerning his status as a bishop came from Rome. Thus he decided to rejoin the N.A.O.R.C.C. and informed Archbishop Carfora of his intention. In November 1920, Carfora traveled to Philadelphia only to discover that Landas Berghes had died on November 17. He was buried in the community cemetery at Villanova.

Jonathan Trela, *A History of the North American Old Roman Catholic Church* (Scranton, Penn., 1979).

Peter F. Anson, *Bishops at Large* (London, 1964).

Karl Pruter and J. Gordon Melton, *The Old Catholic Sourcebook* (New York, 1983).

LEADBEATER, Charles Webster (February 16, 1854, Stockport, Cheshire, England—March 1, 1934, Perth, Australia).

Charles Webster Leadbeater, Theosophical writer and the second presiding bishop of the Liberal Catholic Church, was the only child of a railroad employee. Because of an error on his passport, his birthdate was incorrectly reported to be February 17, 1847, and some accounts of his life make him appear to be seven years older than he was.

Although unable to attend college, as a result of his father's early death and some financial reverses in the family, Leadbeater was able to become an Anglican priest through the assistance of his uncle, W. W. Capes, a reader in ancient history at Queen's College, Oxford. He was ordained deacon in 1878, became a curate at his uncle's church at Bramshott, Hampshire, and was ordained a priest the following year. At Bramshott, he pursued an early interest in psychic research. He met A. P. Sinnett and through him was introduced to the Theosophical Society and H. P. Blavatsky, its founder.

Within a few months of his joining the society in November 1883, he received two letters from a Mahatma, Koot Hoomi, one of the spiritual masters who Madame Blavatsky claimed made the hierarchy that ruled the cosmos. The letters advised Leadbeater to join Blavatsky in India. He quickly severed his ties and in November 1884 left for India. His arrival at his destination was delayed by a stop in Ceylon (now Sri Lanka), where he met Henry S. Olcott, the president of the Theosophical Society. Olcott had marshaled the society behind the spread of Buddhism and enlisted Leadbeater in the cause. Leadbeater took the vows as a Buddhist and joined Olcott on a trip to Burma. After the tour he settled in Adyar. He became the recording secretary of the society and the manager of its periodical, *The Theosophist.*

During the next twenty years, Leadbeater engaged in his own psychic development, writing books and speaking on behalf of Theosophy. After Annie Besant joined the society, they became close friends and collaborated on several projects of occult exploration and writing. Leadbeater wrote (or coauthored with Besant) over twenty books during this period. They include *Man Visible and Invisible* (1903); *The Inner Life* (1910); *The Astral Plane* (1910); *The Hidden Side of Things* (1913); *An Outline of Theosophy* (1915); and with Annie Besant, *Occult Chemistry* (1908); *Man, Whence, How and Whither* (1913); and *Talks on the Path of Occultism* (1930).

Leadbeater's role in the Theosophical Society was hampered by a scandal that grew out of some unorthodox counsel on sexual matters given to several young men in his charge. He was forced to resign from the society in 1906. At Besant's request he returned in 1909, but rumors and charges of sexual impropriety hounded him for the rest of his life.

In 1914 Leadbeater moved to Sydney, Australia. Two years later, J. I. Wedgwood, the presiding bishop of the newly formed Liberal Catholic Church, formed by men who withdrew from the Old Catholic Church in England when Archbishop Arnold H. Mathew had ordered them to leave the Theosophical Society, came to Australia. He introduced Leadbeater to the Liberal Catholic Church and on July 22, 1916 consecrated Leadbeater as regionary bishop for Australia. In characteristic fashion, Leadbeater threw himself into this new venture with great energy. He assisted Wedgwood in the editing of liturgical material. During the First World War, he wrote the two main theological works of Liberal Catholicism, *The Science of the Sacraments* and *The Hidden Side of the Christian Festivals*, both published in 1920. His advocacy of the church led to a split in the Theosophical Society in Australia because many members had brought to the society their dislike of religion, particularly liturgical religion. In 1923 Leadbeater succeeded Wedgwood as presiding bishop of the Liberal Catholic Church.

Although he never exercised direct authority over either American Theosophists or the American branch of the Liberal Catholic Church, Leadbeater's influence was significant for both groups (1) through his writings (he had over fifty titles to his credit), which were widely circulated in the United States, and (2) through individuals such as I. S. Cooper, the first American bishop of the Liberal Catholic Church and his former secretary.

Charles Webster Leadbeater, *The Christian Creed* (London, 1920).

——— , *The Hidden Side of Christian Festivals* (Los Angeles, Calif., 1920).

——— , *An Outline of Theosophy* (Chicago, Ill., 1903).

——— , *The Science of the Sacraments* (Los Angeles, Calif., 1920).

Gregory Tillett, *The Elder Brother: A Biography of Charles Webster Leadbeater* (London, 1982).

Hugh Shearman, *Charles Webster Leadbeater, a Biography* (London, 1980).

Arthur H. Nethercot, *The Last Four Lives of Annie Besant* (Chicago, 1963).

James Ingall Wedgwood, "The Beginnings of the Liberal Catholic Church," *Ubique* (February 1966).

EOP, 513.

LeBARON, Ervil Morrell (February 22, 1925, Colonia Juarez, Chihuahua, Mexico—August 16, 1981, Utah State Prison, Point of the Mountain,
Utah); married Delfino Salido.

Ervil Morrell LeBaron, polygamy-practicing Mormon leader and founder of the Church of the Lamb of God, was the eighth child of Alma
Dayar LeBaron, a polygamy-practicing Mormon living in Mexico. Raised
at Colonia Juarez, Ervil and his brother Joel went on a mission among the
Mexican Indians after finishing high school and, for some reason not
disclosed, were, as a result of their activities, excommunicated from the
Church of Jesus Christ of Latter-day Saints. In 1944, the same year that
Ervil's father decided to leave Colonia Juarez and found his own settlement, Colonia LeBaron, Ervil's brother Ben proclaimed himself a prophet
and Ervil became his chief disciple. Within a few years his enthusiasm
waned and he began to work with fundamentalist (polygamy-practicing)
leaders Margarito Bautista and Rulon Allred.

In 1951 Colonia LeBaron was organized under Bautista and Allred, and
both Ervil and his brother Joel were baptized by Bautista. Then in 1955 Joel
had a revelation that he was the "One Mighty and Strong" who Joseph
Smith had prophesied would come and set God's house in order. Joel
organized his Church of the First Born of the Fulness of Times in 1956 and
appointed Ervil president of the Mexican mission (in effect, head of
mission work in general) and acting secretary. In 1961 Bautista died. Joel
believed that Bautista had held the office of patriarch with authority from
Joseph Smith, which had been passed down through fundamentalist
leader Joseph Musser. Joel appointed Ervil patriarch.

Within a few years trouble began. Ervil began to "meddle" in the
family life of church members. He told people whom they should marry and
advised other people to get divorces. His activities became a public issue
when he told a church member, Anna Mae Morton, to divorce her
husband and marry him (i.e., Ervil). He also began to disagree with Joel on
the establishment of civil law. Joel had taught that obedience to the Ten
Commandments should be the basis of civil law. Ervil believed that this
civil law should be established through force. He preached that since the
law was obligatory, education in the law should be compulsory and hence
church attendance required.

In November 1969 Joel released Ervil from the patriarchal office. In
1971 he excommunicated Ervil for threatening violence. In August 1972
Ervil issued a Message to the Covenant People, an open letter in which he
asserted that to oppose an ambassador of the kingdom—that is, Ervil—is
treason and deserves the death penalty. On August 20 Joel was shot to
death by Ervil's followers.

Three months later Ervil surrendered to Mexican authorities. He was
tried and in November 1973 sentenced to twelve years for homicide. On
December 14, 1973, only a year after he entered jail, he was released when
his sentence was reversed by a higher court. On December 25 Ervil's
followers attacked and burned much of Los Molinos, a town in Baja,
California, where many of the Church of the First Born of the Fulness of
Times lived. Two were killed. In 1976 Ervil was arrested, tried, and
convicted for the raid on Los Molinos but served only eight months.

On May 10, 1977, under Ervil's direction, several members of his Church, which he had come to call the Church of the Lamb of God, entered the offices of fundamentalist leader Rulon Allred and shot him. Two years later, after an extensive manhunt, Ervil was arrested. On May 28, 1980, he was sentenced to life imprisonment for the Allred murder. On August 16, 1981, he was found dead in his prison cell in the Utah State Prison, the victim of a seizure. On the same day, Verlan LeBaron, his brother who had succeeded Joel as head of the Church of the First Born of the Fulness of Times, died in an automobile accident in Mexico City. Ervil had also been convicted of plotting to kill Verlan.

Ervil LeBaron, *Priesthood Expounded* (Buenaventura, Mexico, 1956).

———, *An Open Letter to a Former Presiding Bishop* (San Diego, Calif., 1972).

Verlan M. LeBaron, *The LeBaron Story* (Lubbock, Texas, 1981).

Ben Bradlee, Jr., and Dale Van Atta, *Prophet of Blood* (New York, 1981).

Michael Fessier, Jr., "Ervil LeBaron, the Man Who Would Be God," *New West* (January 1981), 80–84, 112–17.

LeBARON, Joel Franklin (July 9, 1923, Laverkin, Utah—August 20, 1972, Chapaltepec, Mexico); married Magdelena Soto, November 12, 1951.

Joel Franklin LeBaron, founder of the Church of the First Born of the Fulness of Times, was born into a polygamous Mormon family. His great-grandfather, Benjamin F. Johnson, had been a follower of Joseph Smith and the prophet married two of his sisters. His father, A. D. LeBaron, both believed in and practiced polygamy. Joel was the seventh child of his father's second wife (the first having divorced him). Joel was born in Utah just a few months before his father married for the third time, this time polygamously. That marriage led to the LeBarons' having to move to the Mormon settlement at Colonia Juarez in Mexico where polygamy was tolerated and openly practiced. Joel was raised at the Colonia and during his early life worked for his father.

In 1944 Joel's father sold his land at Colonia Juarez and began a new settlement, which became known as Colonia LeBaron near Galeana. That same year Joel's brother Ben proclaimed himself a prophet and Joel's brother Ervil began to work in his cause. Also during the years in Mexico, the LeBarons came to know Margarito Bautista, the most prominent polygamy-practicing Mormon leader in Mexico, and allowed him to organize Colonia LeBaron under his care. In 1951 both Joel and his brother Ervil were baptized by Bautista.

The smooth course of Joel's life was disrupted in 1955. While on a trip to Utah, Joel claimed that he had been visited by several heavenly messengers who told him that he, Joel, was the "One Mighty and Strong" whom Joseph Smith had prophesied would come speaking eternal words and set the house of God in order. On September 21, 1955, Joel responded to his visitation by incorporating a new church, the Church of the First Born of the Fulness of Times, in Salt Lake City. On April 3 of the next year, he formally organized the church and confirmed and ordained the first members and leaders. He appointed his brother Ervil head of the Mexican mission and acting secretary.

Joel proposed two unique teachings. First, he saw God as both creator and ruler. Through Moses, God gave the perfect law and this law, the Ten Commandments, was the basis of political order. Christ would only come again when a people existed who kept the commandments. He taught his followers to look for a time when God's kingdom would rule on earth.

Second, he proposed a distinct lineage of priesthood authority. The leadership of the Church that Joseph Smith had founded was, he claimed, placed in a "First Grand Head," an office that was self-perpetuating. According to Joel, that office had been passed to Benjamin Johnson by Joseph Smith and then to Joel's father and then to Joel. Under the First Grand Head is the patriarch, an office that is also self-perpetuating. Joel believed that the patriarch's office had been passed to Bautista. When Bautista died in 1961, Joel appointed his brother Ervil to that post.

During the 1960s Joel attempted to build networks of people who were not members of his church but believed in "God's standard for civil life"—that is, the Ten Commandments. In 1966 he began the Alliance for Pastors and Christian Teachers, which became the Christian Judaic Evangelical Brotherhood.

In November 1969 the growing trouble between Joel and Ervil led to Ervil's being removed from the patriarchal office and in 1971 excommunicated. Ervil established his own church and began to advocate violence, both to establish the civil order and to kill all who opposed him. On August 20, 1972, at his brother's direction, Joel was murdered by members of Ervil's church, which he called the Church of the Lamb of God.

Joel was succeeded by his brother Verlan M. LeBaron (1930–1981) as head of the Church of the First Born of the Fulness of Times. Ervil was tried and convicted for Joel's death but served only a few months before a higher Mexican court reversed his conviction. During the remainder of the 1970s, Ervil's church waged a war against the Church of the First Born of the Fulness of Times and other polygamy-practicing groups. In 1977 Ervil's followers killed Rulon Allred, a prominent polygamist. In 1979 Ervil was arrested and sentenced to life imprisonment. The Church of the First Born of the Fulness of Times continues as a small body with members primarily in Mexico, California, and Utah.

Verlan M. LeBaron, *The LeBaron Story* (Lubbock, Texas, 1981).

Lyle O. Wright, *Origins and Development of the Church of the Firstborn of the Fulness of Times* (Provo, Utah: Brigham Young University thesis, 1963).

Henry W. Richards, *A Reply to "The Church of the Firstborn of the Fulness of Times"* (Salt Lake City, Utah, 1965).

LEE, Ann (February 29, 1736, Manchester, England—September 8, 1784, Niskeyuna [now Watervliet], New York); married Abraham Stanley, January 5, 1762.

Ann Lee, founder of the United Society of Believers in Christ's Second Appearing, commonly known as the Shakers, was born Ann Lees daughter of a blacksmith. As a teenager she went to work in a textile mill where she developed a reputation as a serious-minded young woman and an ideal worker.

Ann's life began to change in 1758 when she joined a religious society led by James and Jane Wardley, two former Quakers who had been influenced by the French Prophets, a charismatic body that had come to England from southern France. Worship was spirited and included dancing, speaking in tongues, and singing. They professed no creed but had a strong belief in Christ's second coming.

In 1762 Ann was forced into a marriage by her father. She married a blacksmith who worked in her father's shop. It turned into a disastrous mating. Of the four children born to Ann, three died at birth and the other in childhood. She interpreted the deaths as judgments upon her own sin and concupiscence.

Her problems in childbirth and her continued association with the Wardley group led to the major event that changed her life. In 1770 she was arrested for sabbath breaking (a charge used to harass members of dissenting sects). While in prison she had a revelation in which Jesus appeared to her and showed her that the foundation of human sin originated in the sexual relationship between Adam and Eve and that the cardinal sin was the cohabitation of the sexes.

The group accepted her revelation and the authority that flowed from it. She entered a phase of public proselytizing. She was rearrested in 1772 and 1773. She was confined to Bedlam and while there had further revelations. She received her commission to finish Christ's work. She would later claim, "It is not I that speak, it is Christ who dwells in me." She professed to have an intimate, sensible feeling of Christ's continual presence with her. Her followers soon equated her experience with the second coming of Christ. They began to call her Mother Ann.

After her release from prison, Ann had a revelation that the group should go to New England. Accompanied by her husband, her brother, and six disciples, she journeyed to America in 1774. Upon their arrival they separated to find employment. Ann's husband soon began drinking and found another woman. The rest of the group acquired land near Niskeyuna, New York, and the group moved there in the spring of 1776. They remained there, quietly, during the Revolutionary War but immediately began to proclaim their message as soon as the war ended, slowed only by a brief arrest of Mother Ann. The authorities had confused her pacifist belief with sympathy for the British.

The next three years were spent in almost constant traveling throughout New York and New England, and everywhere she went she attracted followers from all segments of society. She preached a simple message calling for confession of sin and acceptance of a celibate communal life. She opposed war and slavery and argued for the equality of opportunity for both sexes.

From her preaching mission, eleven Shaker communities arose. After her death in 1784, her work barely begun, she was succeeded by James Whitaker who lived only three years more before he died. He was succeeded by Joseph Meacham and Lucy Wright, who built the small society into a major religious force in nineteenth-century America. It continued to exist into the twentieth century but had dwindled to fewer than ten members by the beginning of the 1980s.

Ann Lee, *Sound the Gospel Trumpet* (New Gloucester, Maine, 1850).

Whitson, Robley Edward, *The Shakers* (New York, 1983).

Henri Desroche, *The American Shakers* (Amherst, Mass., 1971).

Edward Deming Andrews, *The Gift to Be Simple* (London, 1940).

Marguerite Fellows Melcher, *The Shaker Adventure* (Princeton, N.J., 1941).

Rufus Bishop, *Testimonies of the Life, Character, Revelation and Doctrines of Our Blessed Mother Ann Lee and the Elders with Her* (Albany, N.Y., 1888).

NAW, 2, 385–87.

DRB, 255–6.

DAB, 11, 95–6.

WWWH, 308.

LEE (Byrd), Gloria (March 22, 1926, Los Angeles, California—December 2, 1962, Washington, D.C.); married William H. Byrd, 1952.

Gloria Lee, the founder of the Cosmon Research Foundation and flying saucer contactee, grew up in Los Angeles in the days of the burgeoning movie industry and as a child acted in the movies. She also had an early interest in flying and became an airline stewardess, a position she held until she met and married her husband. She settled down as a housewife but continued to work as a ground hostess at Los Angeles International Airport for several years after her marriage.

Her early adulthood coincided with the first great wave of interest in flying saucers. In 1952 George Adamski became the first of the prominent contactees, those who professed contact with the space aliens they claimed flew the saucers. In September 1953 Gloria Lee became a contactee, the first contact being made by automatic writing at the airport where she worked.

After the contact her interest in flying saucers increased, and she joined several psychic and occult (Theosophical) groups. She regularly received messages from the saucer being who identified himself as "J.W.," an inhabitant of Jupiter. He identified Lee as a reincarnated Venusian. Gradually the automatic writing by which they communicated gave way to telepathy. J.W. professed to come from a planet where vocal communication had evolved into telepathy and the people no longer had vocal cords.

Lee wished to prove J.W.'s existence, and recorded the reports of psychics who claimed to see him around her. One even sketched him. Then one day she received a message from him to look into the sky. Just as she did, a U.F.O. flew over her home near Santa Monica. Independently others reported seeing the same phenomenon.

In 1959 her continued communications resulted in the formation of the Cosmon Research Foundation and the publication of her first book, *Why We Are Here!* The book borrows heavily from Theosophy. The Theosophical spiritual hierarchy has been transformed into an interstellar command but otherwise remains largely intact. An emphasis is placed upon vegetarianism and a positive attitude toward sexuality. A second book, *The Changing Conditions of Your World*, appeared in 1962.

After her first book, Lee became a well-known figure in the contactee community. In 1960 she visited the Mark-Age Meta Center, headquarters of one of the larger contactee groups, and met Mark (public name of Charles Boyd Gentzel), the founder. Their work together disclosed that they were twin souls. She also met Jim Speed, who was later identified as the incarnated J.W. by Yolanda (public name of Pauline Sharpe), one of the Mark-Age psychic channels.

In September 1962 Lee, accompanied by Hedy Hood, a member of the foundation, traveled to Washington, D.C., to interest government officials and scientists in some plans for a spaceship given to her telepathically by J.W. On September 13, 1962, they took a room in the Hotel Claridge, and, following J.W.'s instructions, Lee began a fast (taking fruit juices only). On November 29 she went into a coma and died. No one had paid any attention to her plans.

Her death brought immediate reaction from other contactees. Verity, the public name of a medium in New Zealand with the Heralds of the New Age, claimed initial contact with Gloria on January 21, 1963. Eventually she produced a book supposedly dictated by Lee, who had joined the Ashtar Command, "an Etheric Band of Beings whose Commander-in-Chief is Jesus of Nazareth." Even before Verity, Yolanda, within minutes of learning of Lee's death in the newspaper, received a communication concerning future contact with her. Direct contact began on December 12 and resulted in the booklet *Gloria Lee Lives!* (1963).

For many years Lee was remembered as a martyr of the movement, but she was forgotten in the 1970s as personnel in the leadership changed.

Gloria Lee (Byrd), *Why We Are Here!* (Palos Verdes Estates, Calif., 1959).

The Changing Conditions of Your World by J. W. as instrumented by Gloria Lee (Palos Verdes Estates, Calif., 1962).

The Going and the Glory by Gloria Lee as instrumented by Verity (Auckland, N.Z., 1966).

Gloria Lee Lives! (Miami, Fla., 1963).

Brad Steiger, *The Aquarian Revelations* (New York, 1971).

LEWIS, Harvey Spencer (November 25, 1883, Frenchtown, New Jersey—August 2, 1939, San Jose, California); married Martha Morphier.

Harvey Spencer Lewis, founder of the Ancient and Mystical Order Rosae Crucis, was raised in New York City, where he was a Methodist and a member of the Methodist temple. He became an artist and writer and did feature artwork and columns for the *New York Herald*. In 1904 he formed the New York Institute for Psychical Research, which he served as president. The institute pursued a variety of occult studies but sought after Rosicrucian teachings. It was known internally as the Rosicrucian Research Society.

In 1908 he met Mrs. May Banks-Stacey, a British Rosicrucian, who had been appointed Legate of the Order in India. She put him in contact with the order in Europe. In 1909 Lewis traveled to France and was initiated and given authority to begin organizing work in America. Upon his return he gathered a group who would become the core of the new order. Mrs. Banks-Stacey presented him with further papers and the jewels of the order.

The group organized by Lewis met together for six years and in June 1915 issued the first publication, *The Great Manifesto of the Order*, which announced its formation. Lewis also began a magazine, *The American Rosae Crucis*. The order grew during the war years and in August 1917 held its first national convention in Pittsburgh. That convention proved decisive for the future, for it approved a plan for developing correspondence lessons. This course, written by Lewis, allowed the order to spread throughout the country (and eventually the world) to places where no group had been formed.

On June 17, 1918, police raided the headquarters of the AMORC in New York and arrested Lewis for selling fraudulent bonds and collecting money under false pretenses. Although the charges were later dropped, Lewis moved his headquarters to San Francisco later that year. During the years in San Francisco, Lewis built connections with several occult and Rosicrucian groups in Europe. In 1921 he received a charter from the Ordo Templi Orientis in Germany.

In 1925 Lewis moved the headquarters of the order to Tampa, Florida. During the two years there radio station WJBB was erected and managed by the order.

In 1927 Lewis returned to California, where land had been purchased for a headquarters complex. Shortly after the move, Lewis reincorporated the order in California and incorporated the Pristine Church of the Rose Cross, an affiliated religious group over which he served as bishop. The church survived only a few years because the order began to stress its nonreligious fraternal character and dropped its "religious" structure.

During the 1930s, the order expanded and the headquarters complex was developed by Lewis. The jurisdiction was enlarged to include all of the Western Hemisphere in 1934. In July of that year a Rosicrucian student research center, the Rose-Croix University in America, was dedicated by Lewis. Two years later a planetarium was opened. In 1939 he opened the Rosicrucian Research Library.

After moving to San Jose, Lewis began to write the large number of books on the occult for which he is most known outside of the order. They include *Rosicrucian Questions and Answers* (1929); *The Mystical Life of Jesus* (1929), a volume largely based upon *The Aquarian Gospel of Jesus the Christ* by Levi Dowling; *Self Mastery and Fate* (1929); *Rosicrucian Principles for the Home and Business* (1929); *Mansions of the Soul* (1930); *The Secret Doctrines of Jesus* (1937); and *Mental Poisoning* (1937). Lewis also wrote *Lemuria, The Lost Continent of the Pacific* (1931), which was published under a pseudonym, W. S. Cerve.

After Lewis's death, his son Ralph M. Lewis became head of the order.

Harvey Spencer Lewis, *Rosicrucian Questions and Answers* (San Jose, Calif., 1929).

———— , *Self Mastery and Fate with the Cycles of Life* (San Jose, Calif., 1929).

———— , *Rosicrucian Principles for the Home and Business* (San Jose, Calif., 1929).

———— , *Mansions of the Soul* (San Jose, Calif., 1930).

The Rosicrucian Manual (San Jose, Calif., 1952).

Christopher McIntosh, *The Rosy Cross Unveiled* (Wellingborough, 1980).

R. Swinburne Clymer, *The Rosicrucian Fraternity in America* (Quakertown, Pa., 1935).

EOP, 525.

LEWIS, Joseph (June 11, 1889, Montgomery, Alabama—November 4, 1968, New York, New York); married Fay Jacobs, 1914; married Ruth Stoller Grubman, 1952.

Joseph Lewis, founder of the Freethinkers of America, was at one point the foremost spokesperson for atheism in the United States and the author of best-selling books on the subject. Born into a Jewish family, he soon abandoned all beliefs in that religion. He was forced by the family's poverty to quit school at the age of nine to go to work. He was, nevertheless, determined to educate himself. He began a reading program that included the works of such great freethinkers as Robert G. Ingersoll and Thomas Paine. Ingersoll and Paine would remain his heroes for the rest of his life.

He moved to New York City around 1920 and soon made a sizable fortune in the dollar shirt business. In 1925 he helped incorporate the Freethinkers of America and became its first president, a role he was to maintain until his death. In the 1920s he began writing and publishing his own atheist literature. Among his early works were *The Tyranny of God*, *The Bible Unmasked*, and *Atheism*, each of which went through many printings over the next forty years (with some revisions). At this time Lewis founded his own publishing company, the Freethought Press Association, to publish his own and other atheists' books. In the early 1930s, he also began the Eugenics Publishing Company to put out sex education and birth control books. Many of the physicians who wrote for Eugenics were also freethinkers, although this was by no means a requirement. His publications did much to dispel the sexual ignorance that was widespread in the 1930–1950 period.

Among the other aims of Lewis's publications was that of showing that atheism was by no means unpatriotic. He did this by revealing that many of the nation's founders were freethinkers (if not outright atheists). Among his works (mostly pamphlets) on the subject were the ones on Lincoln, Franklin, Jefferson, and Paine, stressing their heterodox religious beliefs. His major work, a large book of 644 pages, was *The Ten Commandments*, in which he sought to show that they were an inadequate guide for moral behavior.

Perhaps Lewis's most polemical work was *An Atheist Manifesto*. It was marked by a significant emotional content—something not common in atheist literature. Lewis was also noted for reprinting editions of the works of Ingersoll (selected and edited by himself) and the works of Thomas Paine as well. He tried to make a case for Paine as the true author of the Declaration of Independence, a project usually credited to Thomas Jefferson. Although some of Lewis's evidence was suggestive, most historians did not believe that he had made his case.

The official publication of the Freethinkers of America was a magazine that went through a number of name changes. Perhaps its best known name was its last one, *The Age of Reason*. It was largely devoted either to the exploits of Lewis or to the memory of Paine or Ingersoll. The magazine died with Lewis in 1968. Another part of Lewis's project to rehabilitate the memory of Ingersoll and Paine was the production and erecting of statues to these two men all over the world. Lewis was successful in erecting statues of Paine in Thetford, England (Paine's birthplace); Paris; and Morristown, New Jersey. He failed in his long fight to have a statue of Robert Ingersoll erected in Washington, D.C. Lewis was also party to many lawsuits on church/state matters, most of them unsuccessful, although there were exceptions. After many years of trying, he was finally able to get the U.S. Post Office to issue a stamp in memory of Thomas Paine.

Joseph Lewis was, for quite a while, the nation's "public atheist." He appeared on a number of popular radio and television shows, being interviewed by Barry Gray, Mike Wallace, Long John Nebel, and others. He often appeared together with a clergyman, although these could not be called formal debates.

Lewis collapsed and died of a heart attack at his desk in the Freethought Press Association offices. There was no funeral service. Martin J. Martin, who had been the president of the New York chapter of the Freethinkers of America, attempted to continue the organization for a short time after Lewis's death but without notable success.

Joseph Lewis, *Atheism and Other Addresses* (New York, 1941).

——— , *An Atheist Manifesto* (New York, 1954).

——— , *The Bible Unmasked* (New York, 1926).

——— , *Ingersoll the Magnificent* (New York, 1957).

——— , *The Ten Commandments* (New York, 1946).

Arthur H. Howland, *Joseph Lewis: Enemy of God* (Boston, Mass., 1932).

Marshall G. Brown and Gordon Stein, *Freethought in the United States* (Westport, Conn., 1978).

Gordon Stein

LEWIS, Samuel Leonard (October 18, 1896, San Francisco, California— January 15, 1971, San Francisco, California).

Sufi Murshid Samuel L. Lewis more thoroughly than most American Sufi leaders embodied the belief in the essential unity of religions (at least on a devotional and mystical level) and of religious ideals (love, beauty, harmony). Lewis was born into a Jewish family. As a youth he showed an inclination to non-Jewish religious studies, much to the consternation of his parents. In 1915 he visited the World's Fair in San Francisco and discovered Theosophy. Four years later he discovered Sufism and began to study with American Sufi Murshid Rabia Martin, a disciple of Hazrat Inayat Khan, founder of the Sufi Order. Martin introduced him to Khan in 1923, and Lewis was formally initiated as a Sufi. The perspectives of the Sufi order gave focus to the rest of Lewis's life.

In 1920 Lewis had met Sogaku Shaku (a.k.a. M. T. Kirby), an early American convert to Buddhism, who introduced him to Nyogen Senzaki, an early Zen teacher in California. He attended Senzaki's lectures and assisted him in establishing his famous floating zendo. In 1930 Lewis traveled to New York to sit with Shigatsu (Sokei-an) Sasaki, who had opened the First Zen Institute of America. Sokei-an gave Lewis Dharma transmission, a recognition of Lewis as an accomplished teacher of Zen.

During the 1930s, Lewis also began to absorb elements of Hinduism. He met Paul Brunton and was initiated into the yoga of Ramana Maharshi.

Lewis did not let his explorations of other religions adversely affect his relation to Sufism. On Khan's last visit to the United States, Lewis had six private audiences with him. Khan pronounced Lewis "Protector of the Message." From 1927 to 1942, he assisted Rabia Martin at the center in Fairfax, California. During World War II he served in U.S. army intelligence (1942–5). In 1947 Rabia Martin died, but prior to her death she reoriented the group to Meher Baba. Lewis remained a member for two years but withdrew in 1949. He discovered that other Sufis did not recognize the status Khan had assigned him in 1926, and for many years he existed as an independent Sufi.

In 1956 Lewis made independent contact with Sufis in Pakistan and was initiated into the Naqshbandi order. He traveled on to India that same year and was initiated and ordained by the Nizami (Chishti) order, the group from which Khan had received his authority. His initiation took place at Amjer, the international center of the Chishti order.

In 1960 Lewis returned to Asia for two years. En route he stopped in Egypt, where he was initiated into both the Rifai and Shadhili Sufi orders. Traveling on to India and then Pakistan, in 1962 he was initiated into the Khalandar and Khidri-Chishti-Kadri orders. Then, Pir Sufi Barkat Ali of the combined Chishti, Kadiri, and Sabri orders gave full public ordination of Lewis as a murshid. He returned to the United States ready to reinitiate a Sufi movement.

During these years Lewis had not given up his associations with Hinduism and Buddhism. In 1953 he had been initiated by Swami RamDas (not to be confused with American guru Baba Ram Dass) of Kanhangad, India. In 1956 he was received and recognized by Zen masters of Japan and was initiated into Shingon Buddhism. In 1967 he was ordained a Zen master by Korean Zen master Kyung-Bo Seo.

Back in the United States in the mid–1960s, Lewis gathered disciples, the first of whom were initiated in 1966. (He also took off time to help start the Holy Order of MANS, an occult Christian order in San Francisco.) He named his first center the Mentorgarten, after the zendo established in the 1920s by Nyogen Senzaki.

During the last years of his life he traveled widely and became a popular figure within Eastern religious groups in the western United States. In 1968 he met Pir Vilayat Inayat Khan, the son and successor to Inayat Khan, who was in the process of reestablishing the Sufi Order in the United States. Lewis aligned his work with that of Pir Vilayat.

After Lewis's death, some of his students developed disagreements with Pir Vilayat. They left the Sufi Order and in 1977 formed the Sufi Islamia Ruhaniat Society, currently headquartered in San Francisco.

Samuel L. Lewis, *This Is the New Age, in Person* (Tucson, Ariz., 1972).

———, *Toward Spiritual Brotherhood* (Tucson, Ariz., 1972).

———, *In the Garden* (New York, 1975).

———, *The Jerusalem Trilogy* (Novato, Calif., 1975).

LINDSEY, Gordon (June 18, 1906, Zion, Illinois—April 1, 1973, Dallas, Texas); married Freda Schimpf, November 14, 1937.

Gordon Lindsey, founder of the Full Gospel Fellowship of Ministers and Churches and of Christ for the Nations and a leading figure of the Pentecostal-Deliverance (healing) movement of the 1950s, was born in Zion, Illinois, the town founded by John A. Dowie, founder of the Christian Catholic Church and early exponent of spiritual healing. After Zion collapsed financially, Lindsey's father, a teacher, moved the family west. He taught at Dale, Idaho; Portland, Oregon; and Scotts Mills, Oregon, prior to moving to California to join the short-lived Pisgah Grande community. The family finally settled in Portland, Oregon, where at the age of fourteen Gordon attended John G. Lake's church. Lake, also a former resident of Zion, had established a Pentecostal healing ministry on the West Coast. On his first visit to Lake's church, Lindsey heard Charles F. Parham, the founder of the Pentecostal movement, and was converted under his preaching. A few days later he spoke in tongues, the basic Pentecostal experience.

Lindsey felt a call to preach and, although unschooled, began to work in an informal street ministry. In 1924 he traveled to El Cajon, California, to begin life as an independent evangelist. He met John G. Lake, who was working in San Diego at that time, and took over his tent. He became a full-time evangelist and was able to cite several churches that grew from his initial preaching efforts.

In 1932 in Portland, Oregon, he met Freda Schimpf, his future wife. She was a member of the Four Square Gospel Church (founded by Aimee Semple McPherson). Lindsey became pastor of the Four-Square Church in the San Fernando Valley of California. He also pastored churches in Tacoma, Washington, and Billings, Montana (which he began). Evangelism, however, rather than the pastorate seemed to be his calling, and in the late 1930s he once again became an itinerant evangelist. Lindsey reentered the pastorate in 1944, when he accepted the call of the Assemblies of God congregation at Ashland, Oregon. He remained there until the occurrence of the events that were to change the course of his life and lift him out of obscurity.

In 1947 Lindsey met William Branham, a healing evangelist, and became his manager. He left his wife in charge of the church in Ashland and began a magazine, the *Voice of Healing*, that carried the news of a revival of the healing ministry among Pentecostals and reports by and about the evangelists who were promoting it. When Branham temporarily retired in 1948,

Lindsey began to work for Leon Hall, another evangelist, and expanded his work with the *Voice of Healing*. Headquarters were set up in Shreveport, Louisiana. In 1949 the first Voice of Healing Convention of the healing evangelists was held, and Lindsey's role in giving overall direction and leadership to the healing revival was institutionalized.

In 1952 the offices of the *Voice of Healing* moved to Dallas and a steady expansion began. The publishing venture grew in 1954 when Lindsey opened a printing plant adjacent to the headquarters. In 1959 Lindsey began a correspondence course. In conjunction with the readers of his magazine. Lindsey launched the Native Church Crusade, to build Pentecostal churches in Africa and overseas. As the work grew, the many evangelists formerly associated with Lindsey created their own self-supporting organizations. In 1961 the last of the Voice of Healing Conventions met. The next year, the ministers and congregations who still looked to Lindsey for leadership organized the Full Gospel Fellowship of Ministers and Churches.

Lindsey spent much of his last years writing. He had written his first book, *The Wonders of Bible Chronology*, in 1940. By the time of his death, he had penned more than 250 books and booklets.

The last decade of his life was marked by the growth of the work in Dallas. In 1966 a Christian Center was purchased and opened in Dallas. In 1970 a Bible school and bookstore opened. The new course that Lindsey's work had taken in the last years was signaled in 1967 when the name Voice of Healing gave way to Christ for the Nations, the name by which his work has been continued by his wife, who succeeded him as head of the complex of organizations.

Gordon Lindsey, *The Gordon Lindsey Story* (Dallas, Texas, n.d.).

———, *Bible Days Are Here Again* (Shreveport, La., 1949).

———, *The Bible Secret of Divine Healing* (Dallas, Texas, 1968).

———, *How You Can Be Healed* (Dallas, Texas, n.d.).

———, *Why Some Are Not Healed* (Dallas, Texas, 1967).

David Edwin Harrell, Jr., *All Things Are Possible* (Bloomington, Ind., 1975).

Mrs. Gordon Lindsey, *My Diary Secrets* (Dallas, Texas, 1976).

LLOYD, Frederic Ebenezer John (June 5, 1859, Milford Haven, South Wales—September 11, 1933, Chicago, Illinois); married Philena R. Peabody, February 7, 1917; education: Dorchester Missionary College, Oxon, graduated 1882; College of Church Musicians, graduated 1895.

Frederic Ebenezer John Lloyd, second primate of the American Catholic Church, was born in South Wales and raised in England. He was ordained a deacon in the Church of England in 1882 and soon left for Labrador and Newfoundland, where he served as a missionary for three years. In 1885 he was ordained as a priest by the Anglican bishop in Quebec and became rector of Holy Trinity Anglican Parish in Levis, Quebec. He served parishes in Quebec and Prince Edward Island until 1894, when he moved to St. Matthew's Episcopal Church in Bloomington, Illinois. He stayed there only a few months before becoming rector of Trinity Episcopal Church in Hamilton, Ohio. He served Trinity for four years and then moved to St. Mark's in Cleveland, Ohio (1898–1903), and then St. Peter's in Uniontown, Pennsylvania, in 1903. That year he also founded the Society of St. Philip the Apostle to train missionary priests.

The height of Lloyd's ecclesiastical career came in 1905 when he was elected bishop coadjutor of the Diocese of Oregon. He accepted, subject to the approval of the bishops and standing committees of the church. However, objections to his election were filed by a minority of the convention of the Diocese of Oregon, and Lloyd withdrew.

After a number of years of editing the American Church Directory (later retitled Lloyd's Clerical Directory), he left the Episcopal Church and became a Roman Catholic. Then a few years later he rejoined the Episcopal Church and from 1911 to 1914 served Grace Episcopal Church in Oak Park, Illinois. During his stay in Oak Park, he became actively involved in politics and was elected to a term in the Illinois senate.

In 1914 he left the Episcopal Church for the second time and the following year joined the newly formed American Catholic Church under Archbishop Joseph René Vilatte. On December 29, 1915, Vilatte consecrated Lloyd to the bishopric. In 1917 Lloyd married for the third time (his previous wives having died). His new wife was the widow of Hiram P. Peabody, millionaire real estate dealer.

Vilatte proved unsuccessful in building the church, and in 1920 he retired in favor of Lloyd who assumed the titles of archbishop, metropolitan, and primate of the miniscule group. Within a few years he had recruited several ex-Episcopal priests and consecrated them as bishops: Carl Nybladh (1921), Samuel Gregory Lines (1923), and A. Z. Fryxell (1924). Lloyd proceeded to build his church by recruiting priests (some of whom had congregations) and consecrating them. His bishops included Francis Kanski (1926), D. C. Hinton (1927), Leopold Peterson (1927), J. C. Sibley (1929), and Francis I. Boryzsewski (1932), most of whom left the church and became the leader of their own independent jurisdictions after Lloyd died.

Lloyd retired in 1932 for health reasons and died the following year. He was succeeded by Hinton, who gradually moved the church toward Theosophy. The American Catholic church has, in the intervening years, adopted the perspective of the Liberal Catholic Church.

Frederic Ebenezer John Lloyd, Editor, American Church Directory (a.k.a. Lloyd's Clerical Directory) (issued annually).

Peter F. Anson, Bishops at Large (London, 1964).

"Primate of American Catholic Church Dies," The Living Church (September 23, 1933).

Karl Pruter and J. Gordon Melton, The Old Catholic Sourcebook (New York, 1983).

WWW, 1, 737.

MACHEN, John Gresham (July 28, 1881, Baltimore, Maryland—January 1, 1937, Bismarck, North Dakota); education: Johns Hopkins University, 1898–1902, A.B.; Princeton Theological Seminary, 1902–1905, B.D.; University of Marburg, Germany; University of Göttingen, Germany.

John Gresham Machen, leading founder of the Orthodox Presbyterian Church, was raised in a cultured and educated atmosphere. His father was a lawyer who had mastered five languages. His mother pursued a strong interest in poetry through a close friendship with Sydney Lanier's sister and by writing a book on Robert Browning. He entered Johns Hopkins at the age of seventeen and graduated as valedictorian three years later. After a year of graduate studies, he entered Princeton Theological Seminary and earned a master's degree from the University in 1904 and a B.D. the following year. He spent a year in Germany before accepting a post at Princeton Theological Seminary as an instructor in theology.

Raised in a conservative Presbyterian-Calvinist atmosphere, Machen found his faith shaken by his education and the liberal theology he encountered in Germany. He struggled with his doubts during his early years as a teacher and delayed his ordination until 1914 after he had resolved them.

Machen emerged as both a defender of the faith and an example of scholarship placed in the service of Christian theology. He wrote a *New Testament Greek for Beginners* (1923), which became a standard text in many colleges and seminaries and eventually went through some forty editions. Other books included *The Origin of Paul's Religion* (1921); *Christianity and Liberalism* (1923); *What Is Faith?* (1925); *The Christian Faith in the Modern World* (1936); and *The Christian View of Man* (1937). Possibly his most famous book, *The Virgin Birth* (1930), is still considered the best conservative Protestant treatment of the subject.

During his stay at Princeton, Machen became deeply involved in the various controversies that were rending the Presbyterian Church. Theological controversy had been stirred by "Modernists," who denied many of what conservatives saw as essential doctrines of Christianity and by "Arminians" who denied the distinctives of Calvinist doctrines. Machen joined forces with those who attempted to stem the tide of theological drift within the church.

Following the capture of the church's organization by the "Modernists" in the mid-1920s, leaders made a decisive attack upon Machen and Princeton Theological Seminary, the most conservative in the denomination, to open it to a wide variety of theological views. A reorganization at the board level was accomplished in 1929. In response, Machen and several of the Princeton professors and supporters founded the independent Westminister Presbyterian Seminary.

No sooner had the issues at Princeton been resolved, however, than the same issues arose in mission work. A 1932 report, *Re-Thinking Missions*, was looked upon by Machen as denying the essential exclusiveness of Christianity in relation to world religions. Machen proposed to his presbytery that it petition the general assembly of the church to demand that members of the Board of Foreign Missions be orthodox believers. Getting no positive response, Machen led in the formation of the Independent Board of Foreign Missions in 1933. The 1934 general assembly condemned the new board as schismatic. Machen's presbytery, the Presbytery of New Brunswick, tried him, found him guilty of being schismatic, and suspended him from the ministry. Machen appealed, but the 1936 general assembly denied the appeal.

With others who stood by him, Machen met with his followers on June 11, 1936, and organized the Orthodox Presbyterian Church. (It was originally named the Presbyterian Church of America, but changed its name after a lawsuit with the parent body.) Machen lived only a few months after the formation of the church, which had formed to perpetuate his theological perspective.

John Gresham Machen, *The Origin of Paul's Religion* (New York, 1921).

———, *Christianity and Liberalism* (New York, 1923).

———, *What Is Faith?* (New York, 1925).

———, *The Virgin Birth of Christ* (New York, 1930).

———, *The Christian View of Man* (New York, 1937).

Henry W. Coray, *J. Gresham Machen, a Silhouette* (Grand Rapids, 1981).

Ned B. Stonehouse, *J. Gresham Machen: A Bibliographical Memoir* (Grand Rapids, Mich., 1954).

C. Allyn Russell, *Voices of American Fundamentalism* (Philadelphia, 1976).

DRB, 280–2.

WWW, 1, 762.

McGUIRE, George Alexander (March 26, 1866, Sweets, Antigua, West Indies—November 10, 1934, New York, New York); married Ada Eliza Roberts, December 20, 1892; education: Mico College for Teachers, Antigua (graduated 1886); Nisky Theological Seminary, St. Thomas, Virgin Islands (graduated 1888); Jefferson Medical College, M.D., 1910.

George Alexander McGuire, founder of the African Orthodox church, was born and raised in the West Indies. He was baptized an Anglican, the faith of his father, but was strongly influenced by his Moravian mother. After graduation from college, he attended the Nisky Theological Seminary of St. Thomas in the Virgin Islands, and for six years following graduation he pastored the Moravian congregation at St. Croix, Virgin Islands. In 1894 he migrated to the United States and joined the Protestant Episcopal Church. For over a decade he served in the Episcopal Church with distinction. He became the assistant pastor of the Church of the Crucifixion in Philadelphia. He was ordained deacon in 1896 and a priest a year later. In 1898 he became the priest for St. Andrew's Church in Cincinnati and returned to Philadelphia two years later to St. Thomas's Church.

In 1905 he began three years of work as archdeacon for Colored Work in Arkansas. With his growing knowledge of the role of the blacks in the Episcopal church, he opposed the plans of Arkansas bishop William Montgomery Brown for an independent branch of the Episcopal Church for black people.

In 1909 he became pastor of St. Bartholomew's Church in Cambridge, Massachusetts. In 1911 he moved to New York City to become the field secretary of the American Church Institute for Negroes. Increasingly frustrated over the Episcopal Church's unresponsiveness in opening leadership positions, in particular, the bishopric, to black people, McGuire left the United States and returned to his native Antigua and began a five-year pastorate at St. Paul's Church. While in Antigua he became a follower of black nationalist leader Marcus Garvey, founder of the Universal Negro Improvement Association. In July 1919 McGuire returned to the United States and became active in the U.N.I.A. He served as its chaplain-general, and in 1921 he wrote both the *Universal Negro Ritual* and *Universal Negro Catechism* for Garvey.

While working with the U.N.I.A., McGuire was licensed by the Protestant Episcopal church to assist at the Chapel of the Crucifixion in Harlem. However, in October 1919, he joined the Reformed Episcopal Church and established an independent congregation, the Church of the Good Shepherd, largely made up of former Episcopalians. Apparently McGuire had ambitions of building an international black church over which he would rule, and he planned to use the U.N.I.A. as the instrument of its development. To that end, he incorporated the Independent Episcopal Church in April 1920 and announced it as the harbinger of the African Episcopal Church. It was in his dual role as head of the Independent Episcopal Church and chaplain-general of the U.N.I.A. that he composed the *Ritual* and *Catechism*.

McGuire's vision was shattered almost as soon as it was created. Shortly after the 1921 U.N.I.A. convention, McGuire broke with Garvey who wanted nothing of McGuire's churchly plans for his association. McGuire resigned his office and then his membership in the U.N.I.A. On September 2, 1921, the Independent Episcopal Church became the African Orthodox Church, and McGuire was designated its bishop. Unsuccessful in obtaining consecration from Roman Catholic, Episcopal, or Orthodox sources, the church turned to Old Catholic Archbishop Joseph René Vilatte, who consecrated McGuire September 28, 1921, in Chicago. In 1924 McGuire was elevated to archbishop and spent the last decade of his life building his church.

In 1927 he consecrated Daniel William Alexander, the head of an independent South African church, and appointed him bishop of the province of South Africa. Alexander began to build the African branch of the church. McGuire also built the African Orthodox Church's hierarchy. In 1923 he turned to Vilatte's American Catholic Church and had Archbishop F. E. J. Lloyd consecrate William E. J. Robertson, who would succeed McGuire as head of the African Orthodox Church in 1934. McGuire, assisted by Robertson, in turn consecrated Arthur S. Trotman in 1924. McGuire also began Endich Theological Seminary, which, though it has had an existence always on the brink of dissolution, continues to train ministers for the small church McGuire left behind at his passing.

Arthur C. Terry-Thompson, *History of the African Orthodox Church* (New York, 1956).

Randall K. Burkett, *Garveyism as a Religious Movement* (Metuchen, N.J., 1978).

Gavin White, "Patriarch McGuire and the Episcopal Church," *Historical Magazine of the Protestant Episcopal Church* 38, 2 (June 1969), 109–41.

Karl Pruter and J. Gordon Melton, *The Old Catholic Sourcebook* (New York, 1983).

Randall K. Burkett, *Black Redemption: Churchmen Speak for the Garvey Movement* (Philadelphia, Penn., 1978).

WWW, 1, 813.

MACK, Alexander, Sr. (July 1679, Schriesheim, Palatinate, Germany—February 19, 1735, Germantown, Pennsylvania); married Anna Margaret Kling, January 18, 1701 (d. September 1720).

Alexander Mack, Sr., the organizer and leader of the movement that was to become the Church of the Brethren, was the son of a well-to-do miller in the German town of Schriesheim. His father had at one time been the mayor of the community. Alexander had been raised in the Reformed Church and was confirmed into membership in 1692. In 1702 his father left Alexander and his brother the mill that had been the basis of the family's prosperity.

Around 1703 Mack came under the influence of the Pietists, a group of individuals who emphasized the personal religious experience of the Christian. In particular Mack was attracted to Ernest Christopher Hochmann Von Hochenau, a charismatic Pietist leader. Mack opened his mill to the Pietists for meetings. In August 1706 the authorities, having become concerned over the increase of Pietist activity in Schriesheim, broke up a meeting at Mack's mill. In response to the repressive activity, Mack sold his half of the mill to his brother and moved his family to the more peaceful atmosphere of Schwarzenau in Wittgenstein, where many religious dissidents had found some degree of tolerance and protection.

At Schwarzenau, Mack found a close fellowship with a group of Pietists with whom he engaged in serious discussion about adult believer's baptism and the necessity of a church structure. In 1708 Mack was among eight people who conducted a formal rebaptism. In late summer they chose one by lot who was baptized first. That person then rebaptized each of the others. From this event the beginning of the movement known after 1908 as the Church of the Brethren is dated. News of the baptism spread through the separatist Pietists. The church at Schwarzenau grew, and Mack began to travel around Germany to preach and teach. Small congregations began to emerge in the area between Wittgenstein and the Palatinate. A large congregation was formed at Marienborn.

In 1713 and 1715 Mack wrote and published his two main works. The first, entitled *Basic Questions*, was structured as answers to forty questions supposedly asked by Eberhard Gruber, a Pietist leader who would the next year found the Community of True Inspiration, a rival group. Mack emphasized the necessity of baptism as an ordinance in which believers showed their obedience and faithfulness. He also advocated the use of the ban as a means of church discipline. His *Brief and Simple Exposition of the Outward Yet Sacred Rights and Ordinances of the House of God*, published two years later, laid out a more complete exposition of Brethren beliefs, emphasizing Christian discipleship. Mack advocated adult baptism by immersion. The believer is to be immersed three times in the name of the Triune God. Only the baptized were to be admitted to the Lord's Supper, which was held in the evening along with a full meal, called a love feast. Foot washing was also practiced. Their distinctive approach to the ordinances became the distinguishing characteristic of the Brethren.

In 1720, in anticipation of changing conditions in Wittgenstein, Mack and many of the Schwarzenau congregation moved to Surhuisterveen, Friesland, in the Netherlands. The year before this move, a group of Brethren under Peter Becker had already migrated to Pennsylvania. Mack chose to settle in the Netherlands in part because the Dutch had sent money to assist the Brethren, who had been in great need. Mack's personal fortune had been largely spent in supporting the congregation.

In 1728 Becker asked Mack to come to America. Mack had just settled an inheritance he had received from his wife's father, and in 1729 he led thirty families to Germantown. Once in Pennsylvania he helped reorganize three congregations and became the elder of the Germantown church. His remaining years were spent as the leader of the small but growing congregation and were disturbed only by the polemics with Conrad Beissel, who had split one Brethren congregation at Conestoga and led them into what became the Seventh-Day Baptist Church.

Alexander Mack, A Short and Plain View of the Outward Yet Sacred Rites and Ordinances of the House of God (Ashland, Ohio, 1939).

William G. Willoughby, Counting the Cost (Elgin, Ill., 1979).

Donald F. Durnbaugh, European Origins of the Brethren (Elgin, Ill., 1958).

Floyd E. Mallott, Studies in Brethren History (Elgin, Ill., 1954).

Donald F. Durnbaugh, The Believers' Church (New York, 1968).

McPHERSON, Aimee Semple (October 9, 1890, Ingersoll, Ontario, Canada—September 27, 1944, Oakland, California); married Robert James Semple, August 12, 1908 (d. 1910); married Harold Steward McPherson, February 28, 1912 (div. 1921); married David L. Hutton, September 13, 1931 (div. 1935).

Aimee Semple McPherson, the flamboyant founder of the International Church of the Foursquare Gospel and pioneer in the Pentecostal healing ministry, was born in Canada. Her father was a Methodist, but she got most of her early religious training from her mother, who was a member of the Salvation Army. Aimee had her conversion experience, however, at a Pentecostal meeting in 1907. At this time the newly born Pentecostal movement had not separated from the holiness movement (of which the Salvation Army was an integral part). The next year she married the evangelist who had converted her, Robert Semple, and joined him on his rounds as an itinerant revivalist. In 1909 in Chicago Aimee became a Pentecostal preacher.

In 1910 the Semples left for China to become missionaries, but three months after their arrival Robert died, leaving Aimee eight months pregnant. Aimee returned to the United States and joined her mother, who was working with the Salvation Army in New York City. In 1912 she remarried, but the marriage was not a happy one. Aimee left her husband in 1915 and returned to Ingersoll, Ontario, where she had been born.

In August 1915 she conducted a set of revival meetings at the Pentecostal mission at nearby Mount Forest. These meetings became the turning point in her life, because she felt the call to preach and decided to become an itinerant evangelist. She also began to practice healing by the laying on of hands, which came to be one of the characteristics of her work.

During the next few years she traveled between towns along the East Coast. Her husband left her, and her mother, "Minnie" Kennedy, joined her as a business manager. In 1918 she made a transcontinental tour that culminated in Los Angeles. She liked the city so much that she made it her headquarters, though she continued to tour the country for several years. She also began a monthly magazine, the *Bridal Call*.

The 1920s became the period of the institutionalization of Aimee's work. In 1921 she initiated construction on Angelus Temple adjacent to Echo Park in Los Angeles. It was opened on January 1, 1923, and was the center of Aimee's career for the rest of her life. In 1924 she became one of the pioneer radio preachers when she opened her own station, KFSG. Two years earlier she had become the first woman to deliver a radio sermon. In 1926 she opened the Lighthouse of International Evangelism (L.I.F.E.) Bible College to train the growing number of workers needed to lead her expanding organization. Finally in 1927 she founded the International Church of the Foursquare Gospel as a distinct Pentecostal denomination under which all her evangelistic and educational efforts were placed.

Aimee taught an orthodox Trinitarian Pentecostalism, with a strong emphasis upon the experience of speaking in tongues (*glossolalia*) as evidence that the believer had received the baptism of the Holy Spirit. She also practiced spiritual healing. Her message was presented in a personal but highly dramatized style, in a manner that made her the target of many of her more staid ministerial colleagues and also of the press. She called her message the *Foursquare Gospel*, a term she adopted from Albert Benjamin Simpson, holiness healing evangelist and founder of the Christian and Missionary Alliance. Simpson had preached a Fourfold Gospel by which he meant that he emphasized Christ as savior, sanctifier, healer, and coming Lord. Aimee simply substituted Christ as baptizer in the Holy Spirit for that of sanctifier.

The single most famous incident in Aimee's life occurred in May 1926, when she disappeared from a beach near Los Angeles. In June she reappeared in Mexico and claimed that she had been kidnapped. Many claimed that she had not been kidnapped at all but had planned to escape her career by going away with Kenneth G. Ormiston, the temple's former radio operator. She was indicted by the district attorney, but charges were dropped for lack of evidence.

By the time of her death in 1944, the International Church of the Foursquare Gospel had 400 congregations in the United States, 200 foreign mission stations, and 22,000 members. It continues as a major Pentecostal church.

Aimee Semple McPherson, *This Is That* (Los Angeles, Calif., 1923).

————, *The Story of My Life* (Los Angeles, Calif., 1931).

————, *Divine Healing Sermons* (Los Angeles, Calif., 1921).

————, *The Holy Spirit* (Los Angeles, Calif., 1931).

Aimee (Los Angeles, Calif., 1979).

Robert Bahr, *Least of All the Saints* (Englewood Cliffs, N.J., 1979).

Lately Thomas, *The Vanishing Evangelist* (New York, 1959).

Raymond L. Cox, comp., *The Foursquare Gospel* (Los Angeles, Calif., 1959).
NAW, 2, 477–80.
DRB, 278–79.
WWW, 2, 365.

MASON, Charles Harrison (September 8, 1866, near Memphis, Tennessee—November 10, 1961); married Alice Saxton (div.); married Lelia Washington, 1903 (d. 1936); married Elsie Washington, 1943; education: Arkansas Baptist College, 1897–98.

Charles Harrison Mason, founder of the Church of God in Christ, was born to Jerry and Eliza Mason, two tenant farmers. Young Charles was raised a missionary Baptist, but as a youth he developed a yearning for a religion such as he had only heard about from the older black people among whom he was raised. In 1878 he moved with his parents to the John Watson Plantation near Plummersville, Arkansas. While there in November 1878 he was converted and baptized by his brother I. S. Nelson, a Baptist preacher.

As Mason grew into adulthood, he felt a call to the ministry. In 1893, the year that was to be a turning point in his life, the Mt. Gale Missionary Baptist Church at Preston, Arkansas, licensed him to preach, and that same year he preached his first sermon at Preston. He was asked to speak at a revival meeting and had decided that his success as a preacher would be evidence to him of his conversion. His success was notable. Later that year Mason also professed to having been sanctified, made perfect in love by the Holy Spirit. Then, in November, he entered Arkansas Bible College to prepare himself for the ministry.

After only three months, Mason left school, as he had come to believe that education would be of no help to him in his work as a preacher. He became a holiness evangelist and conducted meetings throughout the southern states. Because of his holiness doctrine, he was gradually excluded from the Baptist Church. In 1895, along with C. P. Jones, he founded the Church of God in Christ as a holiness body. It grew and spread among the black people in Tennessee, Arkansas, and Mississippi. Mason became overseer for Tennessee.

Although the new church grew and prospered into the early twentieth century, Mason had come to feel that he did not yet have the fullness of the Holy Spirit. Having heard of the Pentecostal occurrences in Los Angeles, he traveled to California and under the ministry of W. J. Seymour, in March 1907, he received the baptism of the Holy Spirit and spoke in tongues.

After several weeks in Los Angeles, Mason returned to Memphis to share what he had found in California. He discovered that he had been preceded by Glenn Cook, a minister who also had been to Los Angeles. In August 1907 he presented his Pentecostal message to the church. As a result, Mason and Jones went their separate ways, and the church split. Those who accepted Mason met to reorganize the Church of God in Christ. They elected Mason general overseer and appointed D. J. Young, who had accompanied Mason on his California trip, editor of *The Whole Truth*, the church's periodical.

Mason, as general overseer (later designated senior bishop and chief apostle), had broad powers to appoint overseers and the head of national boards and agencies. He ruled the church with benevolent authority, and under his leadership it grew into one of the largest Pentecostal bodies in the United States. In 1945 a new headquarters building, the Mason Temple, was opened in Memphis.

Mason lived into his nineties. After his death the board of bishops of the church assumed a collective leadership of the organization.

J. O. Patterson, et al., *History and the Formative Years of the Church of God in Christ* (Memphis, Tenn., 1969).

Walter J. Hollenweger, *Black Pentecostal Concept* (Geneva, 1970).

Mary Esther Mason, comp., *The History and Life Work of Elder C. H. Mason and His Co-Laborers* (Memphis, Tenn., 1934).

Lucille J. Cornelius, *The Pioneer History of the Church of God in Christ* (Memphis, Tenn., 1975).

DRB, 292–3.

WWW, 4, 618.

MATHERS, Samuel Liddell (MacGregor) (January 8, 1854, London, England—November 20, 1918, Paris, France); married Mina Bergson, June 16, 1899 (d. 1928).

Samuel Liddell Mathers, one of the founders of the Hermetic Order of the Golden Dawn and literary leader of the magickal revival at the end of the nineteenth century, was born into a Scottish family in London. To assert his ancestry, he later added MacGregor to his name, claiming that Mathers was a name selected by part of the family when the MacGregor name was proscribed in 1604. He was raised a nominal Anglican.

Samuel's father died during his youth, and his mother moved to Bournemouth where Mathers was educated. He never attended college, but he received a good classical education and mastered a number of languages. In his teens he became a clerk in Bournemouth and continued to live with his mother until his thirty-first year. His two consuming interests during this period were the occult and the military. His first book was a military manual, *Practical Campaigning Instruction in Infantry Exercise*.

In October 1877 he became a Mason and reached the third degree within a year and a half. On his third-degree (III°) certificate he used the family title of Comte de Glenstrae for the first time. As a Mason he met Drs. Wynn Westcott and William Woodman. They introduced him to the Rosicrucian Society in Anglia, an occult order for Masons only. Mathers took his clan motto, *'S Riohail Mo Dhream* ("Royal is my race"), as his order motto and rose quickly to the ninth degree (IX°) and ruling elite of the S.R.I.A.

In 1885 he moved to London and encountered the occult world of the metropolis. He met Madame Blavatsky and joined the Theosophical Society. From Theosophical rebel Anna Kingsford, he absorbed feminism, antivivisection ideals, and vegetarianism. He also began his own research, the first product of which was a translation of Jewish magical texts, the Kabbalah, which appeared in an edited version in 1887 as *The Kabbalah Unveiled*. In 1888 he met the sister of philosopher Henri Bergson, whom he renamed Moina, and in 1890 they were married.

During these years in London, Woodman and Westcott had presented to Mathers a coded manuscript that turned out to be a set of occult rituals. They commissioned Mathers to edit the rituals in a usable format, and together the three formed the Hermetic Order of the Golden Dawn (OGD), a magical order built around the use of the edited rituals as the substance of the first order of degrees. The same year the OGD was formed, Mathers also published his next book, *Fortune-Telling Cards, the Tarot, Its Occult Significance and Methods of Play* (1888).

With the OGD in place, Mathers, assisted by Moina, established contact with the Secret Chiefs, the astral leaders of the order, and began receiving data for the second order of rituals and other teaching material. In 1891 he moved to Paris, claiming it to be a more conducive environment for work with the chiefs. In Paris he formed the Ahathoor Temple of the OGD.

Of the three founders, Mathers emerged as the leader of the order, largely because of his scholarly activities. He not only edited and/or wrote all the rituals and instructional materials, but he also produced a number of related works such as the translation of *The Greater Key of Solomon*, a model magical ritual instruction volume (1889), and *The Book of the Sacred Magic of Abra-Melin the Mage* (1896).

Mathers also took under his personal tutelage Aleister Crowley, then a young member of the London Temple. He admitted him to the higher grades of the order, only to split with him in 1903. The disruption of relations had vast negative results for Mathers, as Crowley kept and later published a manuscript that Mathers had translated and prepared, *The Goetia*, and many of the secret materials of the OGD. Mathers also compiled a *Book of Correspondences*, which he passed to Allen Bennett, an order member, who in turn passed it to Crowley. Crowley published it as *Liber 777*.

Shortly before his death, Mathers's military side reasserted itself. During World War I he opened a recruiting station in his home and helped train soldiers. After his death, Moina returned to England and established a temple, which she led.

Although Mathers never traveled to America, his work launched the magical revival in the United States. He chartered three temples, one of which survives as the present-day Builders of the Adytum founded by Paul Foster Case. His works, reprinted by occult publishers De Laurence & Company, circulated freely at the time that Rosicrucian and magical orders were just beginning.

S. L. MacGregor Mathers, with others, *Astral Projection, Ritual Magic and Alchemy* edited by Francis King (London, 1971).

———, *Kabbalah Unveiled* (London, 1907).

———, *Greater Key of Solomon* (London, 1888).

———, *Sacred Magic of Abramelin* (London, 1898).

Ithell Colquhoun, *Sword of Wisdom* (New York, 1975).

Ellic Howe, *The Magicians of the Golden Dawn* (London, 1972).

R. A. Gilbert, *The Golden Dawn* (Wellingsborough, 1983).

Francis King, *Ritual Magic in England* (London, 1970).

EOP, 5, 80.

MATHEW, Arnold Harris (August 6, 1852, Montpellier, Heraulh, France—December 20, 1919, South Mymms, England); married Margaret Duncan, February 22, 1892; education: College of the Holy Spirit, 1874–75; St. Peter's Seminary, Glasgow, D.D., 1876–77.

Although Old Catholic Bishop Arnold Harris Mathew had never exercised jurisdiction in the United States, he nevertheless had the major role, along with Joseph René Vilatte, in initiating the Old Catholic movement in North America. Mathew brought Old Catholicism, the movement centered in Holland that had protested the declaration of papal infallibility by the Roman Catholic Church in 1870, to England. He, in turn, consecrated bishops who brought several variations of Old Catholicism to North America.

Mathew was born into a mixed family, his father being Catholic and his mother an Anglican. He was baptized as a Roman Catholic but rebaptized as an Anglican. As a youth he attended both a Roman Catholic parish and a High Church Anglican parish and professed an inability to tell one from the other. Feeling a call to the ministry, he first decided to be an Anglican priest but left after only a year to pursue the Roman priesthood. He was ordained on June 24, 1877. For the next twelve years he served parishes across the width and breadth of England and even spent a short time as a Dominican novitiate (1878–79). Then, in 1889, he announced his conversion to Unitarianism.

After a year as a Unitarian he regained his faith in orthodox Christian doctrine and sought entry into the Church of England. He was never licensed as a curate because he refused to sign a renunciation of Roman doctrine; however, he was allowed to serve several Anglican parishes, including Holy Trinity, an Anglo-Catholic parish in London.

As an Anglican priest he was allowed to marry. On February 22, 1892, he married Margaret Duncan, an act that cut him off from the possibility of returning to the Roman Catholic Church. Thus, for over a decade he existed as an unattached cleric, neither Anglican nor Roman. Then in 1907 he opened correspondence with Bishop Edward Herzog of the Old Catholic Church in Switzerland about the formation of an Old Catholic Church in England.

The idea of Mathew's becoming an Old Catholic seems to have come from a priest, Richard O'Halloran, who had been defrocked but still led a small group of ex-Catholics. O'Halloran convinced Mathew that there was popular support for an Old Catholic movement and that a group of seventeen priests and sixteen laymen had designated him their bishop-elect. O'Halloran also composed a formal request to the Old Catholic bishops asking that they consecrate Mathew. In the midst of the negotiations, the bishops discovered that Mathew was married and had three children, a fact that almost stopped the proceedings. In the end, the problems were resolved and Mathew traveled to Holland; on April 28, 1908, Archbishop Gererdus Gul consecrated him.

Mathew returned to England to discover that O'Halloran had lied and that he was Bishop of a "paper church." He offered to retire, but the Old Catholic bishops authorized him to function as a missionary bishop. He began his task of building an ecclesiastical body, but then on June 10, 1910, Mathew consecrated two priests to the episcopacy, an action contrary to his agreements with his fellow bishops. The action led to a break with the Old Catholics on the Continent.

The break with the continental Old Catholics freed Mathew to consecrate other bishops, which he did freely in an attempt to build a church from the top down. He never gained more than a few hundred lay members. Among his important consecrations, that of the Duc de Landas Berghes, an Austrian nobleman, took place on June 29, 1913. During the first months of World War I, Landas Berghes found it convenient to leave England for the United States, where he became one of the founders of American Old Catholicism.

On October 28, 1914, he consecrated Frederick Samuel Willoughby, an Anglican priest who had lost his parish as the result of a morals scandal. Mathew soon had to depose Willoughby when the press made the story of the scandal public knowledge. Willoughby did not stop his episcopal functions but, in turn, consecrated other bishops who formed the Liberal Catholic Church. As one of his last acts, Mathew consecrated Bernard Mary Williams on March 5, 1916, to be his successor in the minuscule church.

During his lifetime Mathew was a prolific author and translator. Among his books are *Christianity and Agnosticism* (1898); *The Beginnings of the Temporal Sovereignty of the Popes* (1905); and *Faith and Scripture* (1912). The Mathew *Missal* is still used by many Old Catholic bodies in both England and the United States.

Arnold Harris Mathew, *Are Anglican Orders Valid?* (1910).

———, *Articles of Belief of the Old Catholics of Great Britain and Ireland, of the Western Orthodox Church* (Bromley, 1911).

———, *An Episcopal Odyssey* (Kingsdown, England, 1915).

———, *The Old Catholic Missal and Ritual* (London, 1909).

———, *The Catholic Scholar's Introduction to English Literature* (Dublin, 1904).

———, *Woman Suffrage* (London, 1907).

Peter Anson, *Bishops at Large* (London, 1964).

MATTHEW, Wentworth Arthur (June 23, 1892, Lagos, Nigeria—1973, New York, New York).

Born in West Africa, Wentworth Arthur Matthew, the founder of the Commandment Keepers and prominent black Jewish rabbi, grew up on St. Kitts, in the British West Indies, where his family moved when he was very young. At the age of twenty-one, Matthew moved to New York City. He worked at various jobs, including professional boxing and wrestling, and became a minister for the Church of the Living God, the Pillar and Ground of Truth, a small black Pentecostal group unique in that it was the only religious organization that officially endorsed the Universal Negro Improvement Association founded by Marcus Garvey. Garvey had moved to the United States in 1917 to organize black people.

In 1919 Matthew organized his own congregation, The Commandment Keepers: Holy Church of the Living God, with himself as bishop. Matthew began to absorb elements of Judaism, and by 1929 a newspaper could describe it as "Negro Sect in Harlem Mixes Jewish and Christian Religions." During this same period, Matthew came into contact with Arnold Josiah Ford, head of the black congregation Beth B'nai Abraham in New York City, possibly the source of his increasing adoption of Judaism through the 1920s. Like Matthew, Ford was a supporter of Garvey. Ford was also heavily influenced by knowledge of the existence of a tribe of Jews in Ethiopia.

In 1930 Ford turned his congregation over to Matthew and departed for Ethiopia. Matthew abandoned all trappings of Christianity. As Rabbi Matthew, he opened a synagogue on 131st Street in Harlem and incorporated the Commandment Keepers Congregation of the Living God. He also organized a social fraternal order, the Royal Order of Ethiopian Hebrews, the Sons and Daughters of Culture, Inc. Increasingly he identified black people as Falashas who had had their true identity taken away from them, and he denounced Christianity as the black man's worst enemy.

The coronation of Haile Selassie as emperor of Ethiopia in 1935 merely increased Matthew's attachment to the Falashas. In 1936 he declared himself the official representative of the Falashas in America and claimed credentials from Haile Selassie. The fact that Selassie was a Christian and had little regard for the Falashas did not alter Matthew's stance.

Matthew slowly adopted more and more traits of orthodox Judaism. In the early 1930s, he purchased an Ark, Torah scroll, prayer shawls, and yarmulkas. He learned some Hebrew and Yiddish and used a Jewish prayer book in his services. He adopted a traditional black Jewish position, that the lost sheep of the House of Israel were the black people and that the Old Testament personages such as Jacob (with the smooth skin) were black. An important part of the service for members of Matthew's congregation followed the removal of the scroll from the ark. Each male member approached Matthew who asked them, "What is your name?" Each replied with a name and tribe assigned by Matthew. Matthew also founded the Ethiopian Hebrew Rabbinical College and taught classes each Monday evening for his congregational leaders.

The Commandment Keepers moved to 123rd Street. The group expanded, and at the time of Matthew's death in 1973, there were an estimated three thousand members in congregations around New York and on the East Coast. Matthew was succeeded by his grandson, Rabbi David M. Dore. In 1977 Dore became the second black in history to receive a bachelor's degree from Yeshiva University.

Howard M. Brotz, *The Black Jews of Harlem* (New York, 1970).

Albert Ehrman, "Black Judaism in New York," *Journal of Ecumenical Studies* 8, 1 (Winter 1971), 103–13.

Ruth Landes, "Negro Jews in Harlem," *Jewish Journal of Sociology* (December 1967), 175–89.

MEHER BABA (Merwan Shehariarji Irani) (February 25, 1894, Poona, India—January 31, 1969, Guruprasad, Poona, India); education: Deccan College, Poona.

Indian guru Meher Baba began life as Merwan Shehariarji Irani, the son of a Persian couple who had migrated from their native land to Poona, Maharashtra State, India. His parents were Zoroastrians, and Merwan was born during the Zoroastrian month of Meher, the origin of the name given him in 1922 by one of his disciples. Merwan's formal education was curtailed in 1913 when, as a college student, he met Hazrat Babajan, a female guru. In the pluralistic religious environment of India, the Zoroastrian Merwan had little difficulty in becoming a student of this Islamic mystic, termed a Perfect Master by her followers. In January 1914, following an incident in which the guru kissed him on the forehead, Merwan experienced what he later described as "self-realization." He went home and lay unconscious for three days. He remained in a semiconscious state for nine months (during which time, it is claimed, he did not eat). After some awareness of his surroundings returned, he began to travel around the countryside and to meet other masters (spiritual teachers), the most famous being Upasani Maharaj (a Hindu), who, in 1921, pronounced Merwan a *Satguru*, one, who while living on earth, has come to full God-realization.

In 1922 he established an ashram in Bombay with a group of forty-five followers. The group included Muslims, Hindus, and Zoroastrians. The members of the ashram joined in a daily meditation at the ashram but also attended the nearby places of worship of their respective faiths. Disciples felt that Meher Baba's own experience was both compatible with and transcendent of their own particular religious path.

During 1923 Baba traveled with his disciples around India and Persia visiting various holy men and places. Finally in 1924 they settled at Aranaon, a small village near Ahmednagar, and established their center. A small village developed around Baba; it included an ashram, school, hospital, and dispensary and was known as Meherabad.

In 1925 Baba began a period of silence. He communicated through writing. Then, in 1927, he ceased even writing and from that time on communicated with the aid of an alphabet board. By this method he dictated his main works, the *Discourses* and *God Speaks*. In 1954 he gave up even the alphabet board and reduced communication to finger signs and gestures.

In 1927 Baba began the expansion of his movement in the West. He first sent a disciple to England to recruit English students for the school at Meherabad. While unsuccessful in this primary endeavor, the disciple did meet an Englishman, Meredith Starr, who later traveled to India and became Meher Baba's first Western disciple. In 1931 Baba made the first of numerous trips to the West, and during the remaining years of his life the number of his followers increased steadily.

Followers in the United States established the Meher Spiritual Center at Myrtle Beach, South Carolina. Baba visited the center for the first time in 1952. That same year he accepted a group of American Sufis, followers of Inayat Khan (d. 1927), and gave them a new direction as Sufism Reoriented. Since Meher Baba's death in 1969, a loosely organized movement built around many autonomous centers and groups, such as Meher Baba Information of Berkeley, California, and the Society for Avatar Meher Baba of New York City, has been formed.

Meher Baba claimed, and his followers (usually called Baba Lovers) believe, that he was an avatar, a god-man, the total manifestation of God in human form. The avatar's duty is to awaken humanity to a realization of its spiritual nature and quicken the whole life of the spirit of his time. Zoroaster, Rama, Krishna, Buddha, Christ, and Mohammad were all avatars of previous centuries.

As an avatar, Meher Baba's message was the metaphysical unity of all persons. By loving Baba, Baba lovers can learn to love others. In the highest, most intense, state of love, Divine Love, the distinction between the lover and the beloved ceases and one attains union with God.

Meher Baba, *The Path of Love* (New York, 1976).

————, *The Mastery of Consciousness*, edited by Allan Y. Cohen (New York, 1977).

————, *God to Man and Man to God*, edited by C. B. Purdom (North Myrtle Beach, S.C., 1975).

————, *Beams from Meher Baba on the Spiritual Panorama* (New York, 1958).

C. B. Purdom, *The Perfect Master* (North Myrtle Beach, S.C., 1976).

Jean Adriel, *Avatar* (Santa Barbara, Calif., 1947).

Naosherwan Anzar, *The Beloved* (North Myrtle Beach, S.C., 1974).

D.P. Sham Rao, *Five Contemporary Gurus in the Shirdi (Sai Baba) Tradition* (Bangalore, 1972).

EOP, 595.

METZ, Christian (December 30, 1794, Neuwied, Germany—July 27, 1867, Amana, Iowa).

Christian Metz, an unlettered carpenter from a small town in Germany, grew up within a small Pietist group called the Community of True Inspiration. Although not the founder of the group, he emerged in its second century as its reorganizer and led the persecuted group to a new life in the United States, where it would become popularly known by the settlement it built in Amana, Iowa. The Community of True Inspiration had been founded in 1714 by Eberhard Ludwig Gruber (d. 1728) and Johann Friedrich Rock (d. 1749). It was one among several groups growing out of the Radical Reformation that separated themselves from the state church. The community refused to take part in military service and would swear no oaths. It also emphasized the gifts of the spirit and the office of *Werkzeug*, an inspired person through whom the Lord spoke directly to his people. Both Rock and Gruber filled that role, but after their deaths no new *Werkzeug* appeared and the Community went into a period of decline.

No new *Werkzeug* appeared until 1817 when Michael Krausert, a tailor who had been converted by reading Rock's writings, arrived in Ronnesburg, the center of the community, and called for a revival. In response, two other *Werkzeugs* appeared—Barbara Heinemann, a servant girl not previously a member of the community, and Christian Metz. As a child of seven, Metz, whose family had been members of the community for several generations, had moved to Ronnesburg from his birthplace.

Shortly after Heinemann and Metz became *Werkzeugs*, Krausert defected from the community in the face of renewed persecution. Then, in 1823, Heinemann married and lost her status within the community for a number of years. Thus, Metz was left in charge of both the spiritual and temporal affairs of the community.

Increased persecution, attributed in no small part to the activity of the *Werkzeugs*, caused many of the group to move to Hessen in 1826 and to the cloister at Arnsburg in 1832. By 1834 four communities had been established near Arnsburg.

A solution was reached to the ongoing problems of the community in Germany in 1842 when the community received an inspired message (through Metz) to move to America. Metz led a small group to New York City to locate a place. They purchased the former Seneca Indian Reservation near present-day Buffalo, New York, and in 1843 founded Ebenezar (a name given in a revelation through Metz), the first of several villages in the area, including two in Canada. About eight hundred members of the community moved to America.

The land was purchased for the group as a whole with no idea of adopting a communal form of life; however, they gradually accepted a community structure as a practical means to organize the group. Resistance by some of the elders was dealt with by inspired messages from Metz.

By 1854 the community outgrew the land and faced the pressure of a growing Buffalo. Metz announced a move and headed a committee of four that went to Kansas to find land. Unsuccessful, a second committee located land in Iowa. The first village was laid out in 1855.

Metz had determined the name of the new community to be *Bleibe treu* ("Remain faithful") but in the end settled for the more easily pronounceable *Amana* ("Believe faithfully"). The community took ten years to move from New York, but gradually 1,200 members took up residence in the six towns Metz led in establishing. During the period, he traveled regularly between Iowa and New York.

Metz led the community through his inspired messages, said to number 3,654, plus numerous outpourings of the spirit in song and rhyme. Upon his death, Barbara Heinemann succeeded him and worked as the *Werkzeug* until her death in 1883. The industrious Amana Society, of course, continues to exist, although it has lost its communal organization and no *Werkzeug* appeared after Heinemann's death.

Christian Metz, *A Revelation of Jesus Christ Through the True Inspiration to the President of the United States* (1960).

———, *Inspirations* (1975).

Bertha Shambaugh, *Amana That Was and Amana That Is* (Iowa City, Iowa, 1932).

Francis Alan DuVal, *Christian Metz, German American Religious Leader and Pioneer* (State University of Iowa, Ph.D. dissertation, 1948).

Marjorie Wightman, "The Amana Story," in *The Iowan Visits Amana* (Shenandoah, Iowa, 1959).

DAB, 12, 586-7.

WWWH, 356.

MICHAUX, Lightfoot Solomon (November 7, 1884, Newport News, Virginia—October 20, 1968, Washington, D.C.); married Mary Eliza Pauline, 1906 (d. October 28, 1967).

Elder Lightfoot Solomon Michaux, founder of one branch of the Church of God, was the son of a former merchant seaman who had settled in Newport News, Virginia, and had become a successful merchant selling seafood and poultry. The large family was devoutly Baptist. As a teenager, Michaux left school and began to work for his father. In 1904 he opened his own store as well as a dance studio. He began to attend St. Timothy's Church of God (Holiness), a congregation affiliated with the Church of God (Holiness) founded by former Baptist preacher C. P. Jones. Michaux became the congregation's secretary-treasurer.

During World War I, Michaux's business flourished and he moved to Hopewell, Virginia. His wife became very religious during this period, and he built her a church called Everybody's Mission, over which she presided. The congregation affiliated with the Church of God (Holiness). Eventually Michaux was licensed and ordained in that church. After the war he returned to Newport News and entered business with his father. He also opened a Church of God congregation there.

Michaux felt both the measurable decline of business in the postwar years and the poverty of most black congregations in southeastern Virginia. He formed the Gospel Spreading Tabernacle Building Association to accumulate funds to support his ministry. In 1921 he left the Church of God (Holiness) after a disagreement with Jones, who wanted to move the successful Michaux to another congregation. As head of his own Church of God, Michaux began to expand his work. In 1922 he founded a congregation at Hampton, Virginia, and throughout the 1920s he spread the Church of God in the Chesapeake Bay area. In 1928 he moved to Washington, D.C., and the Gospel Spreading Tabernacle Building Association gave way to the Church of God and Gospel Spreading Association.

In Washington, Michaux developed the vision of a radio ministry. He had done a few broadcasts on a small mobile station in Virginia, but by 1928 he saw the potential of reaching a broad audience. He was finally able to get a spot on WJSV in 1929. When the station was sold to CBS, his popular show was expanded, so that by 1934 he was on more than fifty stations daily, with an estimated audience on Saturday evening of 25,000,000. His show was heard across the United States and carried internationally by shortwave; he became the first black minister to get such exposure. His programs blended both high-quality music (supplied by his church choir) and his own sermons, which mixed traditional holiness themes with positive thinking. He also began a magazine, *Happy News*.

Michaux's radio career peaked in the mid–1930s. His popularity prompted the managers of Madison Square Garden to turn over their facilities to him, the first black to have such access. By the end of the decade his audience began to decline. By the mid-1940s he remained on only a few stations in the East, in locations with congregations of his own church.

Over the three decades of ministry, he was able to penetrate the Washington establishment. He counted Eleanor Roosevelt and Mamie Eisenhower among his supporters, and President Eisenhower became an honorary member of his church. He also spurred the development of the largest privately owned black housing project in the United States: Mayfair Mansions and the Mayfair Extension First Commercial Site opened in 1946. He also developed community services to assist unemployed and homeless blacks as well as more traditional services to aid orphans and the aged.

In 1964, shortly before his death, he reorganized his work under the corporate name Gospel Spreading Church, although it remained popularly known as Elder Michaux's Church of God.

Lightfoot Solomon Michaux (as compiler), *Spiritual Happiness Making Songs* (Washington, D.C., n.d.).

———, *Sparks from the Anvil of Elder Michaux* (New York, 1950).

Lillian Ashcraft Webb, *About My Father's Business* (Westport, Conn., 1981).

Janette Houston Harris, "Elder Lightfoot Solomon Michaux," In Rayford W. Logan and Michael R. Winston, *Dictionary of American Negro Biography* (New York, 1982).

Marcus Boulware, *The Oratory of Negro Leaders: 1900–1968* (Westport, Conn., 1969).

Roscoe Lewis, *The Negro in Virginia* (Hampton, Va., 1940).

MILLER, William (February 15, 1782, Pittsfield, Massachusetts—December 20, 1849, Low Hampton, New York); married Lucy Smith, June 29, 1803.

William Miller, founder of the Adventist movement in the 1830s, was raised in a poor but pious home. When he was a child, his family moved from his birthplace to a small town, Low Hampton, in upstate New York. Except for a few years after his marriage, Miller lived on the family farmstead for the rest of his life. He had little formal schooling, but Miller educated himself and became a community scribe in his teen years. He also accepted deism as a personal theology.

After his marriage in 1803, Miller moved to Poultney, Vermont. He became a prominent community leader and served a short term as a deputy sheriff before joining the militia. He served as an officer during the War of 1812 (with the rank of captain) and stayed in the army after the hostilities ceased. In 1814 he returned to Low Hampton and became a farmer. Converted by the Baptists, he rejected his deism and joined the church. He also became a justice of the peace.

After joining the church, he began an intense period of Bible study. He was led to concentrate upon the prophetic sections of Scripture, and he attempted to understand how the figurative language was literally fulfilled in history. Of particular importance were the dream/visions of the Book of Daniel. From his study, he came to expect the imminent second advent of Jesus around the year 1843.

By 1831, after thirteen years of independent study, he was convinced that he should start teaching and preaching about his discoveries. His work found an immediate response. In 1833 he was licensed to preach. He compiled a series of articles he had written for the local newspaper and published his first booklet, *Evidences from Scripture and History of the Second Coming of Christ About the Year* A.D. *1843*. This publication served to spread his message, and he began to travel through New England lecturing (primarily at Baptist churches). In 1836 he published his lectures.

In 1839 he lectured at the Chardon Street Chapel in Boston. Among those who heard him was Joshua V. Himes, who joined Miller and immediately began to promote his message. In March 1840 he began a periodical, *Signs of the Times* (later *The Advent Herald*). In October 1840, with Miller in bed with typhoid fever, Himes led the conference of ministers who supported Miller. Within a year of his having met Himes, Miller's message had spread throughout New England, from which it would move west and south.

Miller had projected no definite date for the Second Coming, only that it would occur between March 21, 1843, and March 21, 1844. Hope was raised when a spectacular comet appeared without warning in February 1843, but March came and went without the predicted event. In the summer of 1843 agitation began for Adventists to come out of the denominations. Miller opposed the move.

When March 21, 1844, passed without the expected event, Miller confessed his error but then accepted a new date, October 22, 1844.

Miller, as did all of his followers, experienced the Great Disappointment on October 22. He went through a period of depression but soon revived. He retained a hope that Christ would come before March 21, 1845, but soon abandoned all attempts to set dates.

In the wake of the ridicule and community hostility directed toward his followers, he consented to their forming separate congregations (a process already begun), and Adventism moved from being a movement within the older churches to a distinct organization. Miller, in the end, took comfort in the effects, if not the accuracy, of his message. Because of the movement many were led to study the scriptures and many were reconciled to God. The preaching of a definite time for Christ's return had, he believed, been used providentially by God, but he warned his followers that other attempts at time setting might not have the same result.

Miller continued to lecture whenever health allowed but survived only a few years. After his death the group splintered into several factions. While some became content to wait for the hoped-for event, and some continued to set new dates, still others found a new prophet (Ellen G.

White) and a new cause (sabbatarianism). The Jehovah's Witnesses and Seventh-Day Adventists are the two largest bodies to grow out of Miller's work.

William Miller, *Evidences from Scripture and History of the Second Coming of Christ About the Year* A.D. *1843* (Troy, N.Y., 1836).

———, *Apology and Defense* (Boston, 1845).

———, *The Kingdom of God* (Boston, 1842).

———, *A Lecture on the Typical Sabbaths and Great Jubilee* (Boston, 1842).

———, *Synopsis of Miller's Views* (Boston, 1843).

Francis D. Miller, *The Midnight Cry* (Washington, D.C., 1944).

Sylvester Bliss, *Memoirs of William Miller* (Boston, 1853).

J. N. Loughborough, *The Great Second Advent Movement* (Washington, D.C., 1905).

Leroy Edwin Froom, *The Prophetic Faith of Our Fathers*, volume IV (Washington, D.C., 1954).

DAB, 12, 641–3.

WWWH, 358.

MONROE, Eugene Crosby (May 30, 1880, Sherman, New York— March 25, 1961, Sherman, New York); married Grace Marjorie Blanchard, October 8, 1902 (d. 1948); married Frieda Wiegand McFarland, November 15, 1949 (d. 1966).

Eugene Crosby Monroe, the founder of Shiloh Trust, a Pentecostal Christian community, was born the son of a carpenter-cabinetmaker in western New York. Although possessing an early desire to enter the ministry, he pursued a business career instead. After high school, he studied with the LaSalle Correspondence School. In 1906 he became a draftsman for the Artmetal Construction Company of Jamestown, New York. He was promoted to engineer two years later. In 1910 he moved to Youngstown, Ohio, where he worked for the General Fireproofing Company. As a cost estimator for the company, he developed a new method of estimating from analyzed cost records. In 1916 he moved to Cleveland and became an estimator for the Van Dorn Iron Works. After six months he was promoted to superintendent of operating. The plant was taken over by the government during World War I and ordered to manufacture tanks and battleship furniture. Monroe headed the furniture division.

In 1921 the company transferred Monroe to Philadelphia as branch manager of its Central Eastern territory. In Philadelphia Monroe encountered the pentecostal experience, that is, speaking in tongues as a sign of the baptism of the Holy Spirit. In 1923 he joined the Highway Mission. He also came into contact with the Apostolic Church, a British pentecostal body that had been brought to the United States after the war. In 1923 he was ordained as a minister and served as a pastor for their congregation in Philadelphia.

For the next two decades, Monroe led a double life. He continued his business career and served as a minister of "deeper life" truth. In 1928, when Van Dorn merged with Bergen Manufacturing Company, Monroe left the company and founded his own wood and metal shop, the Monroe Artcraft Shop in Philadelphia, which specialized in antique restoration and cabinetmaking. In 1938 he resumed his former occupation by becoming contract manager for the Marine Department of the Security Steel Equipment Corporation of Avenal, New Jersey, which was outfitting a new generation of warships, which would see action in World War II. In the same capacity, he moved to New York City in 1940 to work for James McCutcheon & Company.

In 1942 poor health forced Monroe to retire from both his business and ministerial duties. He purchased a farm outside his hometown and settled down to a life of writing and traveling. However, people to whom he had ministered came to Sherman and looked to Monroe for continued spiritual leadership. From this group, Shiloh Community evolved as a self-supporting entity. A bakery producing natural foods was begun. It expanded into a retail food market that sold cheese and meat products. A dairy farm, machine shop, and beef cattle ranch developed. Monroe assumed leadership of the community, which grew primarily by word of mouth. He conducted daily worship services to which visitors were welcomed but produced little in the way of literature.

After Monroe's death in 1961, his son Raymond became the leader, but he was killed in a plane crash in 1962. Raymond was succeeded by James Janisch, the present pastor and trustee.

During Monroe's time, although their business interests extended across the nation, the membership was confined to the farm at Sherman. During the period under Janisch, the center was reestablished at Sulfur Springs, Arkansas, which now functions as the group's headquarters. The basic principles of the founder have been followed and enlarged upon through the administration of the present trustee.

MORRIS, Joseph (December 15, 1824, Burwardsley, Cheshire, England— June 15, 1862, Kingston Fort, Utah); married Mary Thorpe, 1848 (div.); married Elizabeth Mills, 1855 (div.); married Elizabeth Jones, 1857.

Joseph Morris, Mormon prophet and founder of the Church of Jesus Christ of the Most High, was born into a poor family in England. He went to work early in life to help support the family. In 1848, an important year in his life, he married his first wife, converted to the Church of Jesus Christ of Latter-day Saints, and migrated to the United States, where he settled in St. Louis and worked on a riverboat. His years in St. Louis coincided with the work of Mormon prophet Charles Thompson, who was publishing his own periodical, *Zion's Harbinger and Baneemy's Organ*, and from whom Morris seems to have absorbed some of his unique ideas.

He moved on to Pittsburgh and for a short while served as a branch president for some Mormons, but there is no indication as to with which of the several Mormon factions the group was affiliated. In 1853 he moved to Salt Lake City and for the next few years moved around the state. The instability of his life at this period is further indicated by his first wife's leaving him, his remarriage and subsequent divorce, and his marriage to a third wife, all in less than five years.

At the time of his third marriage, he briefly served as a teacher in his ward, but was relieved of his duties when some disapproved of his excessive piety. That same year, 1857, he received his first revelation. He was told not to be discouraged; he was a chosen prophet of God.

In 1858 Morris wrote the first of a series of letters to Brigham Young. He outlined his new status as a prophet and called upon Young to support him. After two years of Young's rejection, Morris announced that God had rejected the leaders of the church and called for the righteous to gather around him. In the fall of 1860 he moved to South Weber, Utah, and there made his first converts, including Richard Cook, bishop of the South Weber Ward.

Cook's conversion led to intervention by the church. An investigation on February 11, 1861, led to the excommunication of Morris and seventeen of his followers. They began to gather at a nearby fort on the Weber River. On April 6 they formally organized the Church of Jesus Christ of the Most High. In May Morris issued a call for people to move to the settlement. More than three hundred had arrived by the summer.

As the followers of Morris gathered, the U.S. army troups that had been stationed in Utah were withdrawing to fight in the Civil War. Their movement east left Utah more firmly in control of the church, and tension between the Morrisites and their Mormon neighbors rose. In the spring of 1862, three former Morrisites tried to force the family of one of them, William Jones, to leave the encampment. The three were captured in the process and imprisoned. Utah authorities demanded their release. Morris saw his group as existing outside of the law and refused to receive the orders issued by the court.

In May 1862 the court ordered Morris's arrest and sent a detachment of militia to carry out the order. The militia attacked the fort, and in the process Morris and several of his aides were killed. The group was scattered; though it survived for a generation, it was never again united because it was continually subjected to the disruption of new prophetic claims.

Morris's mature thought had centered upon a belief in the imminent second coming of Jesus, for which the believers prepared from the summer of 1861 until the death of Morris. Even as the militia surrounded the settlement they believed that God would save them at the last minute. Morris believed himself a prophet and the successor to Joseph Smith. He taught a form of reincarnation, picked up from Charles Thompson, and identified himself with the Biblical Seth, with Moses, and with the seventh angel of the Book of Revelation. He also taught a community of property and opposed the church on the practice of polygamy.

Joseph Morris, *The Spirit Prevails* (San Francisco, Calif., 1886).

———— , *Gems of Inspiration, A Collection of Sublime Thoughts by Modern Prophets* (San Francisco, Calif., 1899).

C. LeRoy Anderson, *For Christ Will Come Tomorrow: The Saga of the Morrisites* (Logan, Utah, 1981).

James Dove, *A Few Items in the History of the Morrisites* (San Francisco, Calif., 1892).

"Morrisites" in Andrew Jenson, *Encyclopedic History of the Church of Jesus Christ of Latter-day Saints* (Salt Lake City, Utah, 1901–36), 540–41.

George Bartholomew Arbaugh, *Revelation in Mormonism* (Chicago, 1932), 183–94.

MUHAMMAD, Elijah (Poole) (October 10, 1897, Sandersville, Georgia—February 27, 1975, Chicago, Illinois); married Clara Evans, March 7, 1919 (d. 1972).

The man who became world famous as the Honorable Elijah Muhammad, founder of the Nation of Islam, was born Elijah Poole, the son of black tenant farmers in rural Georgia. After only a few years of farming, he left home at age sixteen. He lived in Atlanta for a while and worked at a variety of jobs. Several years after his marriage he moved to Detroit and worked in a car plant for six years until he was laid off by the depression of 1929.

The depression set the stage in Detroit for the emergence of a mysterious figure known variously as Professor Ford, Farrad Muhammad, W. D. Fard, and Master Fard Muhammad. He announced that he had come from Mecca to secure freedom, justice, and equality for North American black people. He formed an Islamic Temple in Detroit. Elijah Poole became one of its first members. In 1932 Fard sent Poole to Chicago to organize a temple. Later that year, Fard was arrested and the following year he moved to Chicago to live with Poole, who had been designated his chief minister.

Fard began to withdraw from contact with the members of the temples, and thus, when trouble arose in Detroit soon after Fard's move to Chicago, Poole was sent back to Detroit. It was about this time that Fard gave Poole his new name of Muhammad. Elijah Muhammad found the Detroit members split over the role of Fard. Some thought him to be a prophet. Elijah Muhammad and the majority believed him to be Allah incarnate and both the Madhi awaited by the Muslims and the second coming of Christ. Muhammad dealt with the dissidents; over the next year, as Fard disappeared completely from the movement, Muhammad emerged as the sole leader.

In 1934 Muhammad was arrested for keeping his children out of the public schools and educating them in the school founded by the group. He was charged with "contributing to the delinquency of a minor" and put on probation for six months. When the probation was over, he moved back to Chicago. Muhammad quietly led his followers until 1942, when he was arrested and convicted for inciting his followers to resist the draft. He spent four and one-half years in prison in Milan, Michigan.

Released in 1946, Muhammad returned to Chicago to reorganize the followers. During his absence, two new temples had been founded in Washington, D.C., and Milwaukee. A decade of steady growth followed, and by 1955 there were fifteen temples. The late fifties saw a sharp rise in the growth rate; and over 30 temples existed by the end of the decade.

As the Nation of Islam, the name Muhammad gave the movement, developed, Elijah Muhammad became known as the Messenger of Allah. Black people were seen as the descendants of Allah. White people were believed to have had a beginning only about 6,000 years ago. They were thought of as "devils." It was believed that the appearance of Master Fard Muhammad signaled the beginning of the deliverance of black people, the Lost-Found race, which would occur in the near future.

The program of the Nation of Islam included efforts to act upon the status of black people as the Divine Family. They dropped the white man's names and frequently replaced them with an X for unknown. Muhammad emphasized black capitalism, and members started numerous businesses.

The Nation of Islam, popularly called the Black Muslims, drew widespread media attention in the late 1950s as a result of their rapid growth, the emergence of the Civil Rights movement, and the discovery of their teachings on race. Three major books appeared about them in the early 1960s. The turbulence of the 1960s did not miss the Muslims, and Elijah Muhammad became the center of controversy because of his own actions (such as the 1962 alignment with Nazi leader George Lincoln Rockwell) and the violence that surrounded the movement (such as the 1965 slaying of ex-Nation of Islam minister Malcolm X).

Muhammad defended his teachings in several books, which began to appear in the mid-1960s. They include *Message to the Blackman* (1965); *How to Eat to Live* (1967); *The Fall of America* (1973); and *Our Savior Has Arrived* (1974).

After Elijah Muhammad's death, his son Wallace became the new leader. As Warith Deen Muhammad, he has dropped many of the unorthodox beliefs of the group, now renamed the American Muslim Mission. Several splinters have appeared that have continued the name Nation of Islam and the teachings of Elijah Muhammad. The splinters include one branch led by Wallace's brother John and a larger group led by Minister Louis X Farrakhan.

Elijah Muhammad, *The Supreme Wisdom* (Brooklyn, N.Y., 1957).

———— , *Message to the Blackman* (Chicago, 1963).

———— , *The Fall of America* (Chicago, 1973).

———— , *Our Savior Has Arrived* (Chicago, 1974).

Bernard Cushmeer, *This Is the One, Messenger Elijah Muhammad, We Need Not Look for Another!* (Phoenix, Ariz., 1971).

C. Eric Lincoln, *The Black Muslims in America* (Boston, 1963).

E. U. Essien-Udom, *Black Nationalism* (Chicago, 1962).

Louis E. Lomax, *When the Word Is Given* (Cleveland, Ohio, 1963).

DRB, 320–22.

MUKTANANDA, Paramahansa (May 16, 1908, Dharmasthala, India —October 2, 1982, Ganeshpuri, India).

The person known to the world as Paramahansa Muktananda, swami and founder of the Siddha Yoga Dham, was born to a well-to-do Hindu family in southern India. At birth he was named for the Hindu god Krishna. While intelligent and capable, he showed no interest in formal education and quite early developed a desire to be a *sudhu*, a wandering monk. At the age of fifteen, he ran away from home and began two decades of wandering around India. Among his first stops, The Math (monastery) of Siddharudha Swami in Hubli, Dharwar, became his temporary home. There he learned Sanskrit, yoga, and vedanta. When Siddharudha died in 1929, Muktananda began wandering again. During the

1930s, he made Yeola, Maharashtra, the center from which he launched his travels. He had begun to gather a group of disciples but he continued in the search for a guru, a teacher. He developed a close relationship with two teachers, Zipruanna, who lived at Nashirabad, Jalgaon, and Harigiri Baba of Vaijapur, Aurangabad, but could accept neither as his personal guru.

It was not until 1947 when he visited Bhagawan Sri Nityananda at Ganeshpuri that he knew he had at last found his guru. Nityananda taught as a siddha yogi. Rather than proposing specific disciplines for his disciples, he called upon them to put their reliance entirely in the guru and his grace. Once in that dependent relationship, spontaneous practices would spring up in the disciple as a result of the guru awakening the disciple's spiritual senses.

Muktananda visited Nityananda regularly for the next nine years, though he also developed his own center at Yeola and nurtured his own disciples. In 1955 he finally reached the point of full God-realization. Swami Nityananda built a home for Muktananda at Ganeshpuri and gave him his present name. In 1956, at Nityananda's invitation, he settled at Ganeshpuri and assisted Nityananda until his death in 1961.

After Nityananda's death Muktananda took over the center at Ganeshpuri, and the following year he turned the center into a public trust, naming it Shree Gurudev Ashram in honor of Nityananda. He also accepted Nityananda's work as his own. He saw his main role as a guru to impart *shaktiput*—that is, to awaken the *kundalini*, the serpentlike power in each individual. The *kundalini* is pictured as coiled in latency at the base of the spine. Upon awakening, the power travels up the spine to the crown of the head and brings enlightenment. In the siddha yoga system, the yogi uses his own power to awaken the followers' *kundalini*.

After World War II, of the many Americans turning to India for spiritual light, possibly the first to discover Muktananda was Albert Rudolph (1928–1973), who visited Nityananda in 1958 and subsequently became a disciple of Muktananda after Nityananda's death. As Swami Rudrananda, he returned to the United States and founded the Shree Gurudev Rudrananda Ashrams. He broke with Muktananda in 1971, but his centers continue as an American legacy.

A decade later, one of Rudrananda's students, Franklin Jones, traveled to Ganeshpuri and met Muktananda. He remained a student of his until 1971, when, as Bubba Free John (now Da Free John), he broke with Muktananda and became the head of the Dawn Horse Communion (now known as the Johannine Daist Communion).

In 1970 Muktananda made his first worldwide tour. Accompanied by popular American guru Baba Ram Dass (the former Richard Alpert, an associate of Timothy Leary), he spoke to audiences and gathered followers in New York, Dallas, Los Angeles, and San Francisco. He returned in 1974 and 1981. During the 1970s, the SYDA Foundation was established as a worldwide organization. At the time of Muktananda's death, there were more than a hundred centers (Siddha Yoga Dhams) in the United States.

Swami Muktananda, *Guru, The Play of Consciousness* (New York, 1971).

——, *Swami Muktananda in Australia* (Ganeshpuri, India, 1971).

——, *Siddha Meditation* (Oakland, Calif., 1975).

——, *Satsang with Baba*, 2 volumes (Oakland, Calif., 1974, 1976).

——, *Meditate* (Albany, N.Y., 1980).

Amma, *Swami Muktananda Paramahansa* (Ganeshpuri, India, 1969).

Franklin Jones (Bubba Free John), *The Spiritual Instructions of Swami Muktananda* (Lower Lake, Calif., 1974).

Shankar, *Muktananda, Siddha Guru* (Oakland, Calif., 1976).

EOP, 623.

MUSSER, Joseph White (March 8, 1872, Salt Lake City, Utah—March 29, 1954, Salt Lake City, Utah); married, 1892; married Mary Caroline Hill, 1909 (d. November 9, 1930); married Ellis Shipp, 19?; married again, 1930s.

Joseph White Musser, founder of the Apostolic United Brethren, one of the largest of the Mormon fundamentalist (i.e., polygamy-practicing) groups, was born into a prominent Utah family at the time the United States government was beginning its drive to stop polygamy as advocated by the Church of Jesus Christ of Latter-day Saints. His father, Amos Milton Musser, was the assistant church historian. His mother was his father's first plural wife, Mary Elizabeth White. Young Joseph received little formal education, but by his own effort he rose to the position of court stenographer in Salt Lake City and later chief clerk of the Utah Light and Railroad Company.

In 1890 the president of the Church of Jesus Christ of Latter-day Saints issued a manifesto stopping plural marriages in the church in the United States. Two years later Musser married for the first time. In 1895 he began a three-year mission for the church in the southern states. Upon his return to Salt Lake City, according to his own account, he was approached by the president of the church, Lorenzo Snow, and told that he had been selected to enter plural marriage. Despite the reluctance of his first wife, he married Mary Caroline Hill in 1909.

Unlike many who took plural wives, Musser did not move to the safe haven provided by Mexico. Rather he affiliated with sympathetic church members in the Granite Stake, near Forestdale, Utah, whose leaders were continuing to advocate and enter into polygamous marriages. He contracted his third marriage in 1909 while a member in the Granite Stake. In 1910 Musser was among a group of more than two hundred men who had contracted plural marriages whose names were listed in the *Salt Lake Tribune* as one of the new polygamists—that is, those who had taken plural wives in defiance of the church's prohibitions. At that time Musser was high councilor of the Granite Stake.

As years passed, Musser became openly militant in his defense of polygamy. He claimed that one of the church's apostles gave him the power to seal marriages in 1915 and commissioned him to marry couples and see that plural marriages did not die out. Then, on May 14, 1929, he claimed that an apostle secretly ordained him a high priest apostle and commissioned him to see that no year passed without children being born from polygamous marriages.

In 1930 Lorin Woolley, who claimed that he had a commission like Musser's, named Musser to the Council of Friends who were to head the United Effort, an informal name given to the polygamy-practicing Mormons associated with Woolley. Under the council a revival of fundamentalism occurred throughout the Mormon settlements. Woolley was succeeded by John Barlow. Under Barlow, Musser emerged as the major fundamentalist apologist. In 1934 he published the *Supplement to the New and Everlasting Covenant of Marriage* (coauthored with Leslie Broadbent). The next year he began *The Truth*, a periodical that for the next sixteen years was the fundamentalists' main forum. During the 1940s Musser wrote the several books that remain the most prominent defense of the fundamentalist position.

In 1951, upon the death of Barlow, Musser became head of the council. In 1949 he had suffered a paralyzing stroke, and many opposed his taking the new position. When he appointed Rulon Allred, his personal physician, and a Mexican, Margarito Bautisto, to fill vacant positions, opposition within the council arose. Musser retaliated by dismissing the council and appointing a totally new group, composed entirely of his supporters. The dismissed council members rejected his leadership and a schism resulted. Most members supported the old council. Musser reorganized his followers as the Apostolic United Brethren. He began a new periodical, *The Star of Truth*, which he edited until he died. He was succeeded by Rulon Allred, under whose leadership the Apostolic United Brethren grew into the second largest fundamentalist body in Mormonism.

Joseph Musser, *Celestial or Plural Marriage* (Salt Lake City, Utah, 1944).

———— , *The Law of Plural Marriage* (Salt Lake City, Utah, n.d.).

———— (with J. Leslie Broadbent), *Supplement to the New and Everlasting Covenant of Marriage* (n.p., 1934).

The Most Holy Principle, volume 4 (Murray, Utah, 1975).

Ben Bradlee, Jr., and Dale Van Atta, *Prophet of Blood* (New York, 1981).

Russell R. Rich, *Those Who Would Be Leaders* (Provo, Utah, 1967).

NACHMAN, Rabbi, of Breslov (Nisan 1, 5532 (1772), Medzibuz, Ukraine—Succos 4, 5570 (1810), Uman, Ukraine).

Rabbi Nachman was the direct descendent of the founder of Hasidism. His mother was the daughter of the Baal Shem Tov's only female child. His grandfather, for whom he was named, had been a student of the Besht. Thus, the founder of the Breslover Hasidic movement came from the heart of the Hasidic community.

Shortly after his Bar Mitzvah, the future rabbi married and went to live with his father-in-law, Rabbi Ephraim Baer at Husityn. Here both his learning and miraculous powers became known. It is reported that at a gathering to commemorate the passing of Rabbi Ephraim's wife, she appeared behind Nachman as he expounded the *Mishna*.

As his abilities grew and his fame spread, he moved to Modvedika and began to build a following as a Hasidic leader. He had been in Modvedika only a few years when he decided to make a pilgrimage to the Holy Land. That pilgrimage began in 1798 and lasted for almost a year. Upon his return in 1799, he settled in Zlotopli and began to expound the doctrines that were to set his followers apart from the mainstream of Hasidic thinking.

According to Breslover history, Rabbi Nachman's grandfather had delayed his proposed marriage to the woman who became Nachman's grandmother because of a vision. He believed that the one who would pave the way for the coming of the Messiah would come from among their children but that she would die in childbirth. His father-in-law Rabbi Ephraim had declared the youthful Nachman "the greatest of all the Tzaddikim" (i.e., "Hasidic teachers"). Upon his return from the Holy Land, Nachman began to accept the roles that had been prophesied about him. He declared to his followers that he was the leader of all the tzaddikim. He developed a very high view of the tzaddik, to whom he assigned almost Messianic qualities. Then at the end of his short life, he declared to his followers, "My light will glow till the days of the Messiah." His followers interpreted his words to mean that they would never need another living tzaddik to replace him.

In 1902 at the age of thirty, he moved to Breslov, the city that gave its name to his followers. Shortly after his arrival, Rabbi Nathan from the nearby city of Nemirov became his follower. Eventually Rabbi Nathan became Nachman's scribe and secretary; during the last few years of Nachman's life, he collected his teachings and stories for publication.

During the years in Breslov, Rabbi Nachman built a strong following. His work was characterized by devout pietism and mysticism and a loving relationship with those who gathered around him. He also became the center of controversy. The hostility came to him from fellow tzaddikim whom he had disparaged and from the learned enemies of the Hasidim in general. In 1809 the hostility led to his house being burned. Though still quite young, he took it as a sign of his approaching death.

He did not want to die at Breslov and moved to Uman, the site of a famous massacre of Jews. His move to Uman became a further teaching to his followers, to whom he claimed that the souls of the Uman dead remained hovering over the city and that when he, the true tzaddik, died, he would carry their souls to heaven by his strength. In death, he would still be the powerful tzaddik.

Nachman died in Uman in 1810 at the age of thirty-eight. Rabbi Nathan succeeded him as leader of the movement, but no new tzaddik was appointed, and to this day Rabbi Nachman's followers have survived without a living tzaddik. The continued belief in Rabbi Nachman's active leadership is shown in the practice of Tikun Haklali, the recitation of ten chapters of the Psalms as selected and edited by Nachman in 1808. He promised that their recitation would cleanse the soul and that any who would recite them at his grave and offer a gift to charity on his behalf would receive a gift from him in the life to come, even to pulling him by the hair from the fires of Gehenna.

At the time of the Nazi onslaught, the center of the Breslov Hasidim moved to Jerusalem. Nachman's chair was smuggled out of Europe to Jerusalem in the 1930s. It now resides in the Breslover synagogue, where it is used only for circumcision ceremonies when the infant is briefly laid upon it. Breslovers also went to Brooklyn, New York, and have become one of the prominent Hasidic groups in the United States.

Nachman left no writings himself, but thanks to Rabbi Nathan, his material was saved and later published as *L'Kutey Maharan* (*Selections from Rabbi Nachman*).

Rabbi Nachman of Breslov, *Rabbi Nachman's Fire* by Gedaliah Fleer (New York, 1975).

———, *Rabbi Nachman's Foundation* by Gedaliah Fleer (New York, 1976).

Arthur Green, *Tormented Master* (New York, 1911).

Ben Zion Bokser, *The Jewish Mystical Tradition* (New York, 1981).

Jacob S. Minkin, *The Romance of Hasidism* (New York, 1935).

NAKAYAMA, Miki Maegawa (June 2, 1798, Sammaiden, Yomato Province, Japan—January 26, 1887, Tenri City, Nara Prefecture, Japan); married Zembei Nakayama, 1811 (d. February 22, 1853).

Miki Nakayama, the founder of Tenrikyo, one of the "New Religions" of Japan, was born Miki Maegawa, the daughter of a prominent village leader in Yomato Province. Her family were Buddhists and she regularly attended the local Jodo Shu Temple. So devout was she in her practice of her religion that she, though only thirteen years of age, delayed the final confirmation of the marriage arranged by her father until she received assurance that neither her new husband or his family would interfere with her daily prayers. Twice a day she would repeat the *nembutsu*, a prayer calling upon the grace of the Amida Buddha.

The young wife proved a capable homemaker even by the high Japanese standards, and three years after she moved in with her husband's family, his mother and father announced their retirement from household life and turned over the home to her. Her continued devotion to Buddhism led three years later, when she was nineteen, to her initiation into the service of deliverance, *Gojusoden*, a rare event for one so young. In 1821 she became a mother for the first time.

Nakagawa seemed destined to the obscure life of a housewife remembered by only a few as a devout Buddhist laywoman. Then, suddenly in October 1838, she fell into a trance. The voice that spoke through her identified himself as *Ten no Shogun* ("the Heavenly General"). He said that he had descended from heaven to take Miki as a Shrine of God and a mediatrix between God the Parent and humankind. Her husband refused, but Miki stayed in the trance. Only after three days, on October 20, 1838, the generally accepted date for the founding of Tenrikyo, did he relent. As soon as the family accepted her destiny, she revived.

For the next fifteen years, life remained fairly normal, the main sign of Nakagawa's change manifesting itself in her continually giving family possessions away to the needy.

After her husband's death in 1853, she dedicated all to the service of God. Giving away her few remaining possessions, she was reduced to extreme poverty. She lived with her eldest son and young daughter, her sole companions since the community had abandoned her in her religious fervor. About this same time, her daughter began the first propagation of Nakagawa's teachings at Osaka. She proclaimed the name of God, *Tenri-O-no-Mikoto*, by repeating the mantra-like prayer, *Namu Tenri-O-no-Mikoto* (Save us, God). During these first years, Miki became known for her healing powers, especially for her granting of *ohiya yurushi* ("painless childbirth").

In 1853 Nakagawa was joined by Izo Iburi, a man grateful to Nakagawa for healing his wife of problems following a miscarriage. Convinced of Nakagawa's divine nature, he built a place of worship adjacent to the little two-room cottage in which she lived. The center opened in 1864, and the forms of worship that have come to characterize Tenrikyo were introduced, especially the sacred dance symbolic of the act of creation by God.

The next years were both difficult and eventful. Though able to get her center registered with the government temporarily, the Meiji Restoration returned Shintoism to its position as the state religion and led to persecution of others, including Tenrikyo. Nakagawa was arrested on numerous occasions over the remaining years of her life. During the 1870s, after one such arrest, she began to wear red clothes to signify her divine status. She also began to write the seventeen volumes of *Ofudesaki*, the Tenrikyo scriptures.

In 1875 while in her garden, she was unable to stand. Voices told her that the spot was the *jiba*, the cradle of the human race—the place where humanity was first created. Nakagawa then ordered the erection of the *kanrodai*, a column upon which a large cup was placed to receive the sweet dew from heaven that, upon its falling, would initiate a new era of happiness, wisdom, and virtue.

After Nakagawa's death, Iburi led the group and then her son became the first of a lineage of patriarchs. Not until 1908 was Tenrikyo recognized by the government and not until after World War II did it flourish. It came to the United States in 1929 and slowly spread through the Japanese community. After 1965 it experienced a spurt of growth, and Tenrikyo temples can now be found across the United States.

A *Short History of Tenrikyo* (Nara, Japan, 1956).

Tenrikyo, Its History and Teachings (Tenri, Japan, 1966).

Henry Van Straelen, *The Religion of Divine Wisdom* (Kyoto, Japan, 1957).

Harry Thompson, *The New Religions of Japan* (Rutland, Vt., 1963).

NEE, Watchman (Ni Shu-tsu) (November 4, 1903, Swatow, Kwangtung Province, China—June 1, 1972, Anhwei Province, China); married Charity Chang, 1934 (d. October 1971); education: Trinity College, Foochow, 1919–21, 1922–24.

Watchman Nee, founder of an Evangelical Christian group variously called the Little Flock and/or the Local Church, was born to a Christian family in mainland China. His grandfather, Nga U-cheng, had been a pastor with the Congregational Church's American Mission Board. His parents were Methodists. His father worked for the government as an officer in the Imperial Customs Service. Born Ni Shu-tsu (Henry Nee), he adopted a new name, To-Sheng (Watchman), proposed by his mother, to remind himself that he was to be a bell-ringer to raise up a people for God. As a youth, he was given both a classical Chinese and traditional Western Christian education. While at college, he rejected Christianity and became antireligious.

During his second year at Trinity, as a result of the ministry of Dora Yu, a Methodist missionary from Shanghai who visited Foochow, on April 29, 1920, he experienced a conversion. So radical was the change that he dropped out of school the following year to attend Yu's bible school. He returned the next school year to complete his course but decided against further schooling so he could enter a full-time ministry. During his last year at Trinity he began evangelistic work among his fellow students, on the city streets, and in the villages nearby. He initiated a meeting with a few people of like mind, but he soon left them as he developed his own unique theology.

Upon his return from the bible school in Shanghai, he had associated with Miss Margaret E. Barber, an independent missionary who introduced him to several strains of British Evangelicalism, most notably the writings of John Nelson Darby and the Plymouth Brethren. He formulated a picture of the true New Testament church, which he saw united by the principle of locality (i.e., one church per city), organized under the authority of elders rather than a pastor or rector, unstructured in its worship, and strongly evangelical. These ideas were spread through his magazine, *Revival* (later renamed *The Christian*). In 1927 he began to break bread (i.e., celebrate the Lord's Supper) with a small group who accepted his principles of church life. As others accepted his ideas, he found himself the leader of an indigenous Christian movement.

About this time, through Barber, he contacted the group of Exclusive Brethren headed by James Taylor. In 1930 some elders came to China and declared themselves in communion with Nee's group. They invited Nee to England. While there, in 1933, Nee met with and broke bread with a non-Brethren group headed by T. Austin-Sparks. When Taylor discovered what Nee had done, he broke relations with him. Nee returned to China, and his movement spread.

World War II brought financial difficulties. Thus in 1942, to keep himself from becoming a burden to the church, Nee took a job at his brother's chemical factory in Shanghai. He worked there for the next five years, meanwhile giving up his position as a teacher in the Shanghai congregation. After the war he returned to full-time church work. He also turned the factory over to the church to own, manage, and have use of the profits. Other members also turned over businesses to the church.

In 1949 the revolution established the People's Republic of China. Two years later the new government turned on Nee and the church, accusing them of imperialism. Nee ordered the group to divest itself of all business ties, but his efforts came too late. He was exiled from Shanghai and arrested on April 10, 1952. Two days later, charged with participating in corrupt business practices, he began serving a fifteen-year prison term. To protect itself, the congregation in Shanghai excommunicated him. Most of the movement on the mainland went underground. Nee remained in prison for the rest of his life.

The Local Church survived and spread among Chinese in Formosa and the West. Witness Lee, formerly an elder in Shanghai, emerged as the main leader and successor to Nee. He was leader of the Local Church in Formosa in the 1950s, but he has since moved to Anaheim, California, where he heads Living Stream Ministry. Local Church congregations can be found across the United States, but, as the movement has spread, it and Witness Lee have become the focus of intense controversy. Other Evangelical Christians have accused them of theological heresy and branded the Local Church as a cult, in part because of their exclusiveness. The controversy has generated a significant amount of polemical writing and several lawsuits.

In the spirit of the controversy that surrounds Lee, Nee has gained a wide audience in Evangelical Christian circles through his many books, most of which have been translated into English.

Watchman Nee, *The Normal Christian Church Life* (Washington, D.C., 1969).

——— , *Sit, Walk, Stand* (London, 1958).

——— , *The Normal Christian Life* (Fort Washington, Penn., 1961).

——— , *The Release of the Spirit* (Indianapolis, Ind., 1965).

——— , *The Latent Power of the Soul* (Hollis, N.Y., 1972).

Angus I. Kinnear, *Against the Tide* (Fort Washington, Penn., 1973).

Dana Roberts, *Understanding Watchman Nee* (Plainfield, N.J., 1980).

James Mo-Oi Cheung, *The Ecclesiology of Watchman Nee and Witness Lee* (Fort Washington, Penn., 1972).

James Chen, *Meet Brother Nee* (Hong Kong, 1976).

NEWBROUGH, John Ballou (June 5, 1828, near Springfield, Ohio— April 22, 1891, Shalam, New Mexico); married Rachel Turnbull, 1859 (div. October 6, 1886); married Frances Van de Water Sweet, September 28, 1887; education: Cincinnati Medical College, grad. 1849.

John Ballou Newbrough, the founder of the Faithists of Kosmon movement and spiritual channel for *Oahspe: A New Bible,* was born on a farm near Springfield, Ohio. His parents had moved to Ohio from Virginia because of their antislavery views. His father taught school, and young John was educated in the local schoolhouse. During the winter of his sixteenth year, he taught school.

He attended Cincinnati Medical College. As a student he lived with a dentist who taught him that profession, and he practiced both medicine and dentistry throughout his life. During his early years as a dentist in New York City, he invented a formula for dental plates that broke Goodyear Rubber Company's monopoly on the product.

In 1849 Newbrough migrated to California and struck it rich in gold mining. He teamed up with a Scotsman, John Turnbull, and the two went to Australia to mine. Again Newbrough found gold. In 1859 he returned home by way of Scotland. There he met and married Turnbull's sister. He settled in New York and took up his medical and dental practice again.

Once in New York he became associated with the Spiritualist movement. From childhood he had had experiences of seeing and talking to spirits and had learned to accept their guidance. He became a trustee of the New York Spiritualist Association, and his home became a site for numerous seances. In 1870 he also became a vegetarian.

His interest in Spiritualism led to a breakup of his marriage in the mid-1870s, though the divorce was not granted until 1886. For two years he lived at the Domain, a Spiritualist colony in Jamestown, New York. Increasingly, however, he was becoming upset with the quality of spirit contact that was the common fare of Spiritualist gatherings. He yearned for contact with higher spirits to learn the answer to the great metaphysical questions.

Then in 1881 he was guided to purchase a typewriter. It had been his practice to rise an hour before dawn each morning to meditate, but once he had the typewriter, the spirits took over. He described his next years: "For two years angels (good spirits) propounded to me questions relative to heaven and earth that no mortal man could answer intelligently. One morning lines of light rested on my hands, extending downward like wires. Over my head were three pairs of hands fully materialized, while behind me an angel stood with hands on my shoulders. My fingers played over the typewriter with lightning speed. I was forbidden to read what I had written and I had reached such religious ecstacy that I obeyed reverently. This same power visited me each morning. My hands kept on writing, writing. For fifty weeks this continued daily. Then I was told to publish the book which should be called OAHSPE" (pronounced o-ah-spay).

He presented his new revelation to the Spiritualists, a small group of whom responded. Among these was Andrew M. Howland, a graduate of Harvard and a wealthy Quaker, who was his chief associate for the rest of his life.

In 1883 a group of Newbrough's followers gathered in New York. They called themselves "Faithists of the Seed of Abraham," a name derived from *Oahspe*. They decided to found a communal colony to carry out a vision of the new bible of a place to care for foundlings and orphans. Land was purchased near Las Cruces, New Mexico, and the Children's Land, Shalam, began to emerge out of the desert. The first building was completed in 1885.

Newbrough chose a new wife from among the colonists, and she shared the leadership role with him. Shortly after their marriage, the first group of thirteen foundlings were received. In 1890 the Home, the children's resident house, was completed. Eventually approximately fifty children were to become residents of the colony.

In 1891 an epidemic of influenza struck the area and along with some of the children, it took the colony's leader. Howland assumed some of Newbrough's responsibilities and eventually married his widow. Shalam lasted until 1900, but eventually broke up after financial and doctrinal difficulties.

The Essenes of Kosmon, as Newbrough's followers were eventually called, continued to exist and spread, and today an international network of autonomous centers exists.

John Ballou Newbrough, *Oahspe* (1882; Los Angeles, 1950).

K. D. Stoes, *The Land of Shalam* (Evansville, Ind., 1958).

EOP, 648.

WWWH, 377–78.

NICHOLS, L. T. (October 1, 1844, Elkhart, Indiana—February 28, 1912, Battle Creek, Michigan); married.

L. T. Nichols, the founder of the Meggido Mission Church, was given only the initials of his father as a first name. When L. T. was only five, his father took his family into the wilderness of northern Wisconsin, where L. T. grew to manhood. During his teen years, his father became an invalid, and much of the family support depended upon L. T. Though he attended school when he could, his education was limited.

The frontier community in which L. T. lived had no permanent ministry but was served by visiting ministers who passed through the community. L. T. became an avid amateur Bible student. He soon became known as the local religious renegade, and he frequently confronted visiting pastors with his embarrassing questions.

His Bible study had convinced him that the truth of God was hidden beneath the fables (i.e., the teachings of the various denominations) of men. His study led him to a denial of many orthodox Christian beliefs— the Trinity, the immortality of the soul, hell, and the fall of humanity. He also came to believe that earth, not heaven, was the ultimate home of the saved of the human race. He began to preach in his community. He refused to accept a position with any denomination and chose never to preach for remuneration.

In 1874, with a group who accepted his ideas, Nichols moved to Oregon. He began to write tracts and pamphlets and to engage local ministers in debates on religious topics. At one such debate he met Maud Hambree, a Roman Catholic, who joined his small group and eventually succeeded him in leadership.

In 1880, after continual study of the Bible, Nichols announced his discovery of the truth that has distinguished his followers ever since. He taught that perfection of character (keeping the whole law) was necessary for salvation. Sin was the transgression of the law: no one could be saved apart from knowing and keeping every commandment of God. His followers saw the proclamation of this truth as the True Reformation.

In 1883 Nichols moved with his few followers to Dodge City, Minnesota. To support himself he engaged in a manufacturing business. He continued to write and traveled extensively throughout the Midwest, where several small congregations emerged. In 1901 Nichols decided upon a wider ministry and had a three-deck riverboat constructed. He called his followers to join him in a new life on the rivers (the Mississippi and its tributaries). Thirty families left their farms and businesses and moved onto the boat, called the *Meggido*, a biblical name meaning "God is in this place with a band of soldiers." From this time forward, Nichols and his followers were known as the Meggido Mission.

The mission sold the boat in the winter of 1903–4 and moved into permanent headquarters in Rochester, New York, with seventy-two people settling in the new home. Tithing was instituted as a means of supporting the mission's program of literature distribution as well as the missionaries. Nichols also announced a new discovery—the true date of Christmas is in the spring, Abib 1 on the Jewish calendar. In 1908 a church building was opened; it has served the group ever since.

Nichols developed heart trouble during his last years. He died of a heart attack at the sanitarium at Battle Creek, Michigan. The Meggido Mission Church has remained a small and almost unknown body, but it annually distributes a vast amount of literature, and its ads appear regularly in many mass-circulation magazines.

L. T. Nichols, *The Devil and Hell of the Bible* (Rochester, N.Y., n.d.).

———, *A Treatise on the Trinity* (Rochester, N.Y., 1966).

History of the Megiddo Mission (Rochester, N.Y., 1965).

NORRIS, John Franklyn (September 18, 1877, Dadeville, Alabama—August 20, 1952, Keystone Heights, Florida); married Lillian Gaddy, May 5, 1902; education: Baylor University, 1898–1903, A.B.; Southern Baptist Theological Seminary, Louisville, 1903–1905, Th.M.

J. Frank Norris, the flamboyant pastor of the First Baptist Church of Fort Worth, Texas, and founder of the World Baptist Fellowship, was born the son of a poor alcoholic sharecropper who frequently beat him. When he was eleven, he moved to Texas, where two years later he was converted and received a call to preach. During his teen years, he was shot by horse thieves when he came to the assistance of his father.

During his twenty-first year, he began his ministerial education at Baptist-sponsored Baylor University. He also served his first parish, Mt. Calm Baptist Church. After graduation he attended seminary in Louisville. He returned to Texas as pastor of the McKinley Avenue Baptist Church. There his native ability became evident as he took the thirteen-member church and added more than a thousand members in a few years. In 1907 he became editor of the *Baptist Standard*, the periodical for Southern Baptists in Texas. As editor he came into open conflict with many leaders in the denomination; he finally left his post to become pastor of First Baptist Church in Fort Worth, a position he was to hold for the rest of his life.

Norris's talents combined with his flamboyant style at his new parish made him one of the most successful and best-known ministers in America. Beginning with 1,200 members in 1909, First Baptist Church boasted 28,000 members in 1928. Norris pioneered the radio ministry in the Southwest and at his height spoke regularly over twenty-seven stations in every part of the country. He began his own magazine, the *Fence-Rail* (later known as *The Searchlight*, and more well known as *The Fundamentalist*), which not only overtook the circulation of the *Baptist Standard* but regularly circulated 80,000 copies throughout the South.

The most famous incident in Norris's life occurred in 1926. An outspoken foe of both alcohol and the Roman Catholic Church, Norris increased his campaign against "Rum and Romanism" in the mid–1920s by attacking H. C. Meacham, the Roman Catholic mayor of Fort Worth, Texas. One day a friend of Meacham's, D. E. Chipps, stopped by Norris's office. An argument ensued, resulting in Norris's shooting and killing Chipps. Norris was arrested, pleaded self-defense, and was acquitted, but the stigma marred his career.

Since the years as editor of the *Baptist Standard,* Norris experienced trouble with the Southern Baptist leadership. He was aggressive and at times set himself in competition with his colleagues. He began, soon after assuming the pulpit at Fort Worth, to accuse the denominational officials of interfering in local church affairs. He also publicized incidents of the convention's involvement in "modernist" tendencies and argued against their involvement in ecumenical organizations. For his efforts, he was successively excluded from the Pastors Conference of Fort Worth (1914), the Tarrant County Baptist Association (1922), and the state convention (1924). Finally in 1931 he left the Southern Baptist Convention and organized his own association of churches, the Premillennial, Fundamental, Missionary Fellowship (renamed Premillennium Baptist Missionary Fellowship and then World Baptist Fellowship).

During the 1930s Norris added to his role as pastor the tasks of building the fundamentalist movement nationally and of enlarging the World Baptist Fellowship. In 1935 he also became pastor of the Temple Baptist Church in Detroit, and held that pulpit jointly with his Texas charge for thirteen years. Among his first acts in Detroit was the removal of the congregation from the Northern Baptist Convention. In 1946 he claimed 25,000 members between the two congregations.

In 1948 he relinquished his Detroit post to G. Beauchamp Vick, an active leader in the World Baptist Fellowship. Two years later, Vick opposed Norris on matters before the fellowship and, with others dissatisfied with Norris, left and founded the Baptist Bible Fellowship, which has in the years since Norris's death outstripped the World Baptist Fellowship in size.

Norris died of a heart attack while attending a youth rally in Florida.

John Franklyn Norris, *The Gospel of Dynamite* (n.p., n.d.).

——— , *Inside History of First Baptist Church* (Fort Worth, Texas, n.d.).

——— , *Infidelity Among Southern Baptists Endorsed by Highest Officials* (n.p., n.d.).

Louis Entzminger, *The J. Frank Norris I Have Known for Thirty-four Years* (n.p., n.d.).

E. Ray Tatum, *Conquest or Failure? A Biography of J. Frank Norris* (Dallas, Texas, 1966).

George W. Dollar, *A History of Fundamentalism in America* (Greenville, S.C., 1973).

C. Allyn Russell, *Voices of American Fundamentalism* (Philadelphia, Penn., 1976).

ESB, 983.

WWW, 3, 644.

NOYES, John Humphrey (September 3, 1811, Brattleboro, Vermont— April 13, 1886, Niagara Falls, Canada); married Harriet A. Horton, June

1838; education: Dartmouth University, 1826–30; Andover Theological Seminary, 1931–32; Yale Divinity School, 1832–34.

John Humphrey Noyes, the founder of the Oneida Community, one of the most successful of the nineteenth-century communes, was born to a prominent Vermont family. His agnostic father, a successful businessman, served one term in Congress before retiring at the age of fifty-three. After retirement he settled in Putney, Vermont. At the age of nine, young John entered a private school. Six years later, in 1826, he began studies at Dartmouth with the idea of becoming a lawyer.

Noyes's law career ended with his conversion in 1831 and his resultant decision to enter the ministry. He entered the seminary at Andover but transferred to Yale after his first year. At New Haven he joined the Free Church and also became attracted to perfectionism, the belief that humans could, in some measure, become perfect in this life. Noyes began to identify with the perfectionists and traveled throughout New England preaching his ideas. In 1836 he settled in Putney and began to gather a group of followers, the first members of which were his own family. In 1837 he started *The Witness*, as a periodical to spread his views. Noyes believed that the second coming had already occurred and that man could thus be perfect; that once saved he could not fall from grace; and that church authority should not be allowed to overrule personal conviction.

Noyes had also developed some radical views on marriage. Some of these appeared in August 1837 in a letter published in *The Battle Axe and Weapons of War*, a periodical published by T. R. Gates. In this letter he declared that in heaven there will be no marriage and that sexual relations would not be restrained by law. The letter made him the center of controversy, and to punctuate his response that he was discussing heaven, not earth, he proposed marriage to a woman who had experienced sanctification while reading one of Noyes's writings. They were married the next year.

The next nine years were spent in spreading his views and gathering a close-knit cadre of followers around him at Putney. He published his first book, *The Way of Holiness*, which contained his collected articles. *The Witness* (1837–43) was followed by *The Perfectionist* (1843–44). In 1841 he created the Society for Inquiry as a covenant group that adhered to Noyes's views. In 1844 they formalized the communal nature of their life together with an incorporation that was widened to include all the adults the next year. Twenty-eight adults agreed to share work, living quarters, and finances.

In 1846 Noyes took the first step toward the complex marriage system he was later to develop. Noyes, his wife, and Mary and George Cragin agreed that it was God's will for them to share marriage partners. Two more couples, Noyes's sisters and their husbands, joined the arrangement before the year was out. Unfortunately, word soon leaked out to the community; in the face of the resulting hostility, Noyes was forced to flee.

Noyes reassembled his followers at Oneida, New York, where another group of his followers had begun a second community. He assumed leadership of what was to become his school for perfecting character. By 1851, under Noyes's theocratic leadership, about 275 people had come to reside at Oneida and its several branch communities.

At Oneida Noyes attempted to put into practice all of his perfectionist ideals, the most controversial of which was his system of complex marriage. Complex marriage involved the controlled sexual relations of a community where each male was considered married to each female. Noyes also developed a practice of birth control that he called "male continence," by which males controlled the emission of semen and prevented the production of unwanted children. (Noyes had been motivated to develop the practice, also known as *kerazza*, after his wife had borne five stillborn children.)

The Oneida community functioned well for one generation and was relatively free of persecution until the mid-1870s. At this time, when Noyes's health, particularly his hearing, began to fail, a group of primarily young adults who no longer believed in Noyes's perfectionist ideas emerged within the community. In the face of a crisis in which those who opposed Noyes's authority joined with outsiders bent upon suppressing the "immoral" community, Noyes fled to Canada in June 1879. A few months later the community voted to abandon complex marriage.

Although he kept in touch, Noyes never returned. He settled on the Canadian side of Niagara Falls and lived out his days surrounded by a small group of his most dedicated followers.

The members of the community settled down into more conventional lives. In 1880 the members reorganized as the Oneida Community, Limited, a joint-stock company, and continued to operate the community's industries, the most well-known being its silverworks.

John Humphrey Noyes, *Confessions of John H. Noyes* (Oneida Reserve, N.Y., 1849).

——— , *The Doctrine of Salvation from Sin, Explained and Defended* (Putney, Vt., 1843).

——— , *The Way of Holiness* (Putney, Vt., 1838).

——— , *Male Continence* (Oneida, N.Y., 1872).

——— , *History of American Socialisms* (Philadelphia, Penn., 1870).

Maren Lockwood Carden, *Oneida, Utopian Community to Modern Corporation* (Baltimore, Md., 1969).

Richard DeMaria, *Communal Love at Oneida* (New York, 1978).

Raymond Lee Muncy, *Sex and Marriage in Utopian Communities* (Bloomington, Ind., 1973).

Constance Noyes Robertson, *Oneida Community, the Breakup, 1876–1881* (Syracuse, N.Y., 1972).

——— , *Oneida Community, An Autobiography, 1851–1876* (Syracuse, N.Y., 1970).

DAB, 13, 589.

DRB, 335–37.

OBERHOLTZER, John H. (January 10, 1809, near Clayton, Berks County, Pennsylvania—February 15, 1895, near Quakertown, Pa.); married Mary Riehn, 1830s (d. October 6, 1871); married Susanna Moyer, November 1872.

John H. Oberholtzer, one of the founders of the General Conference Mennonite Church, was born on a farm in eastern Pennsylvania. Turning from farm life, he obtained an education and at the age of sixteen began to teach school, an occupation that engaged his winters for the next sixteen years. To support himself the rest of the year, he opened a locksmith shop. Along the way, he married and joined the Great Swamp Mennonite Church, a congregation in the Franconia Conference, near his home in Milford Square. Educated and articulate, he was chosen by the congregation to become one of their ministers in 1842.

Concerned, educated, and possessed of a progressive spirit, he almost immediately became the spokesperson for the younger generation and often came into conflict with the older and more conservative Mennonites. Many thought his sermons too scholarly. He also refused to wear the black straight-collar coat, the accepted ministerial dress. He began to introduce innovations. He preached in non-Mennonite congregations and often accepted honorariums for his services. He organized Bible classes, called *kinderlehre*, for the children. The classes grew into the first Mennonite Sunday school in America. In the *kinderlehre* he used a catechism developed by the Mennonites in Europe. As a minister he accepted into church membership Mennonites who had married non-Mennonites.

In 1847 the already controversial Oberholtzer introduced major issues in the Franconia Conference. He asked for a constitution, for the participation of the general membership in decision making, and for the keeping of minutes of meetings. He had previously introduced a constitution to the Big Swamp congregation, and he drew up an *Ordnung* for the conference. As a result of the debate on his demands, Oberholtzer and his followers withdrew and concurrently were excommunicated by the conference. They formed a new conference.

The first years of the new organization were tumultuous, and Oberholtzer found himself defending positions against attendance at revival meetings, foot washing, and membership in secret societies, each of which cost him small elements of his following. The total work progressed, however, and in 1852 he purchased a printing press and issued the first successful Mennonite periodical, the *Religioser Botschafter* (*The Religious Messenger*).

In 1860 he learned of three independent congregations in Iowa that seemed to share his "liberal" stance. He traveled to their conference, which was held over Pentecost, and worked out an agreement uniting his following with the Iowa group. Thus was the General Conference Mennonite Church, currently the second largest Mennonite group in America, formed. Oberholtzer was elected the first chairman. The new church formed a missionary society to evangelize the Indians; Oberholtzer served on the board until 1881. It also formed a historical society, planned a Christian training school for missionaries, and initiated a set of tracts for use in urban evangelism.

As chairman of the eastern conference from 1848 to 1872 and as the most prominent leader in the national body, Oberholtzer oversaw the steady growth of the General Conference. He actively raised money to support its seminary established in Ohio in 1867.

He retired in 1872, continuing to preach and lead in worship as health allowed. He preached his last sermon in October 1894, just four months before his death.

Samuel Floyd Pannabecker, *Open Doors* (Newton, Kans., 1975).

Edmund G. Kaufman, comp., *General Conference Mennonite Pioneers* (North Newton, Kans., 1973).

Cornelius Krahn and John F. Schmild, *A Century of Witness* (Newton, Kans., 1959).

Cornelius J. Dyck, *Twelve Becoming* (Newton, Kans., 1973).

ME, 4, 13.

OFIESH, (Aftimios) Abdullah (October 22, 1880, Mohiedhthet, Lebanon—1971); married Mariam, April 29, 1933; education: Middle Eastern Orthodox Ecclesiastical Seminary, graduated 1898.

Aftimios Ofiesh, the first bishop of the American Orthodox Catholic Church, was born Abdullah Ofiesh, the son of a small-town Orthodox priest in Lebanon. Only after overcoming strong family resistance was he allowed to enter the seminary from which he graduated as valedictorian. He selected Aftimios as his religious name. His early ecclesiastical career as the assistant to the bishop of Lebanon (1898–1900) and as the archdeacon of Latikia found him at the center of reform movements aimed at changing the administrative system of the church. Almost excommunicated for his efforts, he requested a transfer to the United States.

He arrived in the United States on December 13, 1905, and placed himself under the jurisdiction of Raphael Hawaweeny, the bishop of the Diocese of Brooklyn, a diocese under the Russian Orthodox Church that served Arab Orthodox Christians in North America. He assisted Bishop Raphael for a year and then began an eleven-year pastorate at St. Nicolas Church in Montreal. In Montreal he became involved in the attempts of Middle Eastern Orthodox to separate themselves from the Russian jurisdiction. Ofiesh sided against the independents.

In 1915 Bishop Raphael died, and Ofiesh was called to New York to replace him. He was consecrated bishop of Brooklyn by Russian Archbishop Evdokim. His efforts in reorganizing and strengthening the diocese led to his elevation to archbishop in 1923. This year also marked the beginning of significant troubles for the Russian Orthodox Church in America when pro-Soviet and anti-Soviet factions formed. That division had been preceded by the establishment of the Greek Orthodox jurisdiction and was followed by a splintering of the Arabs.

Upset by the splintering of Orthodoxy, which prior to World War I had been united under the Russians, Ofiesh, in 1926, proposed the formation of the independent American Orthodox Church, urging every Orthodox bishop in America to seek release from his foreign attachments so they would be free to unite. In 1927 he received the support of the Russian Orthodox bishops who granted Ofiesh authority to organize the Holy Eastern Orthodox Catholic and Apostolic Church in America (popularly termed the American Orthodox Catholic Church) as an independent body for American-born English-speaking Orthodox Christians.

The new church ran into trouble almost immediately. The patriarchs of Constantinople, Alexandria, Antioch, and Jerusalem rejected it. Then the Russian bishops, under pressure from the Episcopal Church, withdrew support. The Episcopalians saw Ofiesh's effort as direct competition and threatened to stop the financial support they were giving the Russian church. The Russians denounced Ofiesh and removed him as archbishop of Brooklyn. Ofiesh refused to give in. He asserted his authority and the authority of his church over all Orthodoxy in America.

Events came to a head in 1932. After a long lawsuit, the cathedral in Brooklyn was taken from him and returned to the Russian church. He in turn consecrated two bishops, Joseph Zuk and W. A. Nichols. He was left at the end of the year with a church of five bishops and only six parishes.

Then without warning, on April 29, 1933 Ofiesh went counter to all Orthodox practice and married a young Syrian woman. (It is against Orthodox practice for a priest to marry after ordination or for bishops to be married at all.) Then a month later, one of his bishops, Emmanuel Abo-hatab, died. Taking Ofiesh's marriage as a resignation, Zuk and Nichols met and elected Bishop Joseph as Ofiesh's successor.

The situation of the church deteriorated quickly after that action. In 1934 Zuk and another bishop, Sophonius Bashira, died and Nichols married. Though Nichols remained active as a clergyman and consecrated others who would in later decades attempt to revive Ofiesh's church, his effort died that year. Ofiesh retired quietly. He lived until 1971, no longer functioning as a bishop.

Aftimios Ofiesh, *The Orthodox Situation in America; A Practical Survey and Program for Unity* (Brooklyn, N.Y., 1931).

———, *Constitution of the Holy Eastern Orthodox Catholic and Apostolic Church in North America* (Brooklyn, N.Y., 1928).

John W. Morris, "Lest We Forget . . . The Episcopate of Aftimios Ofiesh," *The Word* 25, 2 & 3 (February and March, 1981).

Archimandrite Sarafim, *The Quest for Orthodox Church Unity in America* (New York, 1973).

Karl Pruter and J. Gordon Melton, *The Old Catholic Sourcebook* (New York, 1983).

OKADA, Mokichi (Meishu-sama) (December 23, 1882, Tokyo, Japan —February 10, 1955, Atami, Japan); married Taka Aihara, June 1907; (d. June 11, 1919); married Yosiko Ota, 1919 (d. 1962).

Mokichi Okada, known more popularly by his honorific title *Meishu-sama*, was the founder of the Church of World Messianity (in Japanese, *Sekai Kyusei Kyo*). He was born in poverty. His father was a dealer in secondhand goods. As a youth Mokichi did well in school but was sickly. Eventually eye trouble forced him to abandon a promising art career. He turned to business, and in 1906, with the small inheritance left him by his father, he opened a small store. The retail business thrived, and his store expanded. In 1917 he invented and patented an artificial diamond, which further increased his wealth.

During these early years only one factor—his poor health—marred Okada's success. Finally, in desperation, he visited a religious healer. His conclusion from the success of his visits was not that the healer had been effective but that medicine had caused his problem in the first place. He discontinued its use entirely from that time forward.

His recovery of health was followed by a period of tragedy and transition. In 1919 his first wife died and he soon remarried. He lost most of his money in the stock-market panic of 1920. Three years later his business was destroyed in an earthquake. In the midst of changes and misfortune, he began to turn toward religion.

Okada credited his illness for awakening his spiritual consciousness. After his financial losses and his wife's death, he joined Omoto, one of the several new religions that had emerged in twentieth-century Japan.

In 1926 he began to receive revelations himself. He spoke these revelations to his wife, who copied them down. Over three hundred pages were transcribed in the first three months. In the wake of these revelations he gave up his business altogether and became a healer. He saw himself as the channel for the Light of God, which flowed through him. He called his work of transmission *johrei*, which means the "purification of the spiritual body." Gradually he built a following.

On June 15, 1931, with his wife and twenty-eight followers on Mt. Nokogiri, he declared the beginning of the Daylight Age. Light was dawning in the spiritual realm after three million years of darkness. His independent course led to conflict with Omoto, and in 1934 he left the organization and founded Kannon Kai. In 1935 Omoto was suppressed by the Japanese government and its leaders jailed. As a former member, Okada was placed under heavy scrutiny and had to give up the practice of *johrei*. The movement prospered, however, and by Pearl Harbor day, there were ten churches.

The beginning of World War II brought further changes. Kannon Kai was suppressed (as were many religions). Okada moved to Hakone Province where he purchased a summer home. Okada carried into his new religion from Omoto the idea that the world was coming to a final judgment after which paradise would come to earth. Prior to the impending judgment, it was time for those who understood the course of the future to build model paradises on earth. The estate at Hakone became the site of the first such paradise. A second estate was purchased in Atami in 1944 to serve as a winter home. It became the site of the second and larger paradise.

After the war, *johrei* could be practiced again and Kannon Kai (name changed to Kippon Kannon Kai in 1947) began to flourish. At the same time Okada was attacked as the leader of a superstitious and corrupt organization, and in 1950 he was jailed on an $800 million tax-evasion charge. That same year, just a month before his arrest, he had chartered his movement as the Church of World Messianity, its present name.

While in prison he became ill and his health never returned after the experience. He died in 1955 and was succeeded by his wife and, after her death in 1962, his daughter, Fujieda Itsuki. He lived to see the church come to America and spread among the Japanese in Hawaii and the West Coast. In more recent years it has picked up a non-Japanese following but remains largely confined to the western part of America.

Mokichi Okada, *Teachings of Meishu-Sama*, I & II (Atami, Japan, 1967–68).

Light from the East, Mokichi Okada (Atami, Japan, 1983).

Harry Thomsen, *The New Religions of Japan* (Rutland, Vt., 1963).

OKADA, Yoshikazu (February 27, 1901, Tokyo, Japan—June 23, 1974, Tokyo, Japan).

Yoshikazu Okada, better known to his followers by his religious title *Sakuinushisama* ("Master of Salvation"), was the founder of Sukyo Mahakari, one of several Japanese religions brought to the United States in the 1970s. Okada was born into a Samurai family. His grandfather had been a tutor at Nakagama Castle. His father also began adult life as a tutor, but after the Meiji Restoration in 1868 he joined the army and rose to the rank of major general. Okada attempted to follow his father and after high school entered Rikugun Shikan Gakko, a military academy. After graduation he served in the imperial guards of the emperor.

Early in World War II, with the Japanese army in Indonesia, Okada fell from his horse and injured his back. He developed spinal tuberculosis, and the doctors gave him but three years to live. He returned to Japan and decided to devote the rest of his life to the service of God and humankind, and to carry out his vow he invested all his money in four factories that made planes for the Japanese air force. His business career ended abruptly in 1945 when all four factories were destroyed in the bombing of Tokyo.

Unlike the factories and his finances, Okada survived the war in good health, his back having healed despite his medical prognosis. He turned to religion and joined the Church of World Messianity, a religion founded by Mokichi Okada (no relation). The church taught a form of healing by the use of *johrei*, God's Direct Light. During the next years he concentrated on paying off his debts and practicing his faith.

By 1959 he had rid himself of debt. On February 22 of that year he had his first revelation of Su-God (the Lord God). He was told that a healing mission was about to be entrusted to him. On February 27 (his birthday) a voice woke him from his sleep and told him to change his name to *Kotama* (Jewel of Light). He began to work independently of the Church of World Messianity, although his teachings remained almost identical. He made his first converts among some bargirls in his neighborhood. By August 28, 1960, he had progressed to the point that he could launch his movement officially. Initially he called it the L. H. (Lucky and Happy) Sunshine Children but later changed it to *Sekai Mahikari Bunmei Kyodan* (Church of World True-Light Civilization).

Okada taught his followers the practice of *Mahikari-No-Waza*, the art of purification by God's True Light. Through *Mahikari-No-Waza* people can be cleansed of spiritual, mental, and physical pollution and eliminate misfortune, illness, and unhappiness. He initiated new members and gave them a pendant, an *Omitama*, which enables the wearer to focus and use the Light of God.

As the movement expanded, Okada's understanding of his role deepened. He came to view himself as God's "Proxy, Carbon Copy, and Robot." He assumed the titles of *Sukuinushisama* (Master of Salvation) and *Oshienushisama* (Spiritual Leader) and claimed to be the physical embodiment of the Shinto deity *Yonimasu-o-amatsu*. He received regular revelations, most by automatic writing. These have been collected into a large volume, the *Goseigenshu*, and constitute the scripture for *Mahikari*.

During the last years of Okada's life he was the leader of an expanding movement. On February 17, 1972, he was presented with the medallion of the Knight Commander of the Order of St. Denis by the American Academy of Science. In 1973 he had a private audience with Pope Paul VI. He saw his movement travel beyond Japan, first to France and then to Belgium, Switzerland, and Italy.

Ten days prior to his death, Okada named his daughter as his successor. Soon after his death, her role was challenged by a prominent member, Sekiguchi Sakae. The court ruled in favor of Sekiguchi and he took control of the headquarters of the group. Okada's daughter quickly reestablished new headquarters and adopted a new name, *Sukyo Mahikari* (True-Light Supra-Religious Organization). She received the support of most of the centers and members. Under her leadership the movement has become worldwide. In the United States, like the Church of World Messianity, it has been able to attract many non-Japannese followers.

Winston Davis, *Dojo* (Stanford, Calif., 1980).

A. K. Tebecis, *Mahikari, Thank God for the Answers at Last* (Tokyo, 1982).

Mahikari, Primary Initiation Text (Tujunja, Calif., 1978).

O'KELLY, James (October 1735 (?), Ireland (?)—October 16, 1826, North Carolina); married Elizabeth Meeks, 1759.

Information about James O'Kelly, founder of the Republican Methodist Church (later the Christian church), prior to his fortieth birthday is almost completely lacking. He regularly destroyed many records of his life; his widow burned many papers soon after his death; and his autobiography, which existed only in manuscript, was burned by Union soldiers in the Civil War. It is believed that he was born in Ireland in 1734 or 1735, had a modest education, and migrated to America in 1778.

At some point in his early years (circa 1775) he was converted, joined the Methodists, and began to preach. He received his first appointment in 1779 to New Hope, North Carolina. At the time O'Kelly entered the Methodist ministry, American Methodism was led totally by unordained lay ministers and considered itself an integral part of the Episcopal Church. Not being ordained, Methodist preachers could neither baptize members nor serve the Eucharist. Feeling the need of sacramental privileges, O'Kelly joined with a group of preachers that met at Fluvanna County, Virginia, and a four-man presbytery was appointed to ordain each other and others present. Though O'Kelly supported the dissidents, in the end he refused ordination. In spite of his refusing ordination, Bishop Asbury dropped him from the list of appointments in 1781. In turn, O'Kelly refused to sign the unity document that the ordained preachers signed when they returned to the discipline of the other Methodist preachers—in effect, denying their ordained status.

In 1784, at the Christmas conference when the Methodist Episcopal Church was organized and Francis Asbury was chosen as bishop, O'Kelly was finally ordained. Asbury appointed him to be presiding elder in southern Virginia, a post he held for the next ten years. O'Kelly's stable position attests both to his ability and his increasing role as the voice of the loyal opposition within the church. That voice first appeared in force in 1787, when Richard Whatcoat arrived from England with authority from John Wesley, the founder of Methodism, to function as a superintendent (i.e., bishop). Led by O'Kelly, the church refused to acknowledge Whatcoat until several years later when they voted him into the bishop's office.

In 1789 Asbury organized a council to manage the growing church. The council consisted of Asbury-appointed presiding elders, including O'Kelly. After attending the first meeting, O'Kelly became its vocal enemy. He saw it as an instrument of Asbury's tyranny in running the church. He led the Virginia Conference of 1780 in rejecting the council and in supporting the idea of a general conference of all the preachers. His idea was eventually accepted, and the first General Conference met in 1792.

At the General Conference, O'Kelly opposed the exclusive appointive powers of the bishop and argued for the right of ministers to appeal unsatisfactory appointments to the conference. When his motion was defeated, he and his supporters left the conference and, without leaving the church, organized informally as the Republican Methodists. O'Kelly tried to find a means of reconciliation with Bishop Asbury, but in the face of unresolved differences, he met with his supporters on August 4, 1794, at Surrey County, Virginia, and organized the Republican Methodist church. Seven years later the church underwent reorganization. It took the name Christian Church, accepted the Bible as its sole rule of faith and practice, and organized congregationally.

The reorganization occurred in the midst of a pamphlet war that had begun in 1798. O'Kelly had seen the need to justify his position, and, under a pseudonym, Christicola, he wrote *The Author's Apology for Protesting Against the Methodist Episcopal Government*. He argued for the freedom of the Christian citizen of Zion and for an egalitarian church. Two years later, Asbury's supporter Nicolas Snethen answered with *A Reply to an Apology for Protesting Against the Methodist Episcopal Government*, which prompted O'Kelly to respond with *A Vindication of the Author's Apology with Reflections on the Reply* (1801). Snethen eventually issued the last word: *An Answer to James O'Kelly's Vindication of His Apology*.

In the course of the polemics, O'Kelly was accused of denying the Trinity, an accusation seemingly based on the Unitarian stance of a group in New England that had formed separately from O'Kelly's group and took the same name, the Christian Church.

O'Kelly traveled among the congregations in his charge until his death. After his death, his congregations splintered. Most eventually became part of the larger Christian church, which had merged with the Congregational Church in the 1930s and is today known as the United Church of Christ.

James O'Kelly, *Essay on Negro Slavery* (Philadelphia, Penn., 1784).

——— , *The Author's Apology for Protesting Against the Methodist Episcopal Government* (Richmond, Va., 1798).

——— , *A Vindication of the Author's Apology with Reflection on the Reply* (Raleigh, N.C., 1801).

——— , *The Divine Oracles Consulted* (Hillsboro, N.C., 1820).

——— , *Letters from Heaven Consulted* (Hillsboro, N.C., 1822).

——— , *The Prospect Before Us* (Hillsboro, N.C., 1824).

Charles F. Kilgore, *The James O'Kelly Schism in the Methodist Episcopal Church* (Mexico City, 1963).

J. F. Burnett, *Rev. James O'Kelly, A Champion of Religious Liberty* (Cincinnati, n.d.).

F. A. Norwood, "James O'Kelly, Methodist Maverick," *Methodist History* 4, 3 (April 1966), 14–28.

DRB, 341–2.

EWM, 2, 1805.

DAB, 14, 7–8.

WWWH, 386.

OLAZABAL, Francisco (October 12, 1886, El Verano, State of Sonora, Mexico—June 9, 1937, Alice, Texas); married Macrina Orozco, 1914; education: Wesleyan College, San Luis, Poposi, Mexico, 1907–1910; Moody Bible Institute, 1911.

Francisco Olazabal, founder of the Latin American Council of Christian Churches, was born to a prominent family in a small town in Mexico. His father was the mayor and judge in the village. Under the impact of the mission of the Methodist Episcopal Church, South, his mother had become a lay missionary. As a youth, Francisco frequently accompanied his mother on her journeys to nearby towns to preach. When he was eighteen, however, he rebelled against his mother and her faith and left home and went to live with his grandmother in San Francisco. While in the Bay Area, he met George and Carrie Montgomery, ministers with the Christian and Missionary Alliance, who were preaching in Oakland. Under their ministry, he accepted Christ.

With his newly found faith came a new appreciation of his mother. He returned to Mexico, attended Wesleyan College, and entered the Methodist ministry. After completing his education he pastored in Durango and then was sent to the Spanish-speaking congregation in El Paso, Texas. He left the pastorate in 1911 to attend Moody Bible Institute, but after only six months he left to initiate missionary work in Southern California. The Methodists appointed him missionary/evangelist for the Compton area and then in 1913 sent him to Pasadena as pastor of the Spanish-speaking mission.

After three successful years in Pasadena, during which time a new church was built, he was sent to assist the Mexican missions that had been started by the Methodist congregations in San Francisco and Sacramento. During his tenure, the Methodist Episcopal Church, South, ordained him as an elder.

About the same time he was ordained, he revived his relationship with the Montgomerys. Since he had left them to return to Mexico, they had become Pentecostals and were preaching the Pentecostal experience of speaking in tongues as a sign of the baptism of the Holy Spirit. Although initially hostile to Pentecostalism, before the year was completed he had accepted it and he left the Methodists to become an independent Pentecostal evangelist. The success that had marked his pastoral career followed him as a Pentecostal. He had revivals at Danville and Los Angeles, and he joined the Assemblies of God. In 1918 he returned to El Paso, the site of his former pastorate, and began meetings that grew into the first Latin American Assemblies of God congregation. He pastored the church for several years, during which time more than three hundred regularly attended. He also assisted in the growth of other Spanish-speaking congregations around the country.

In the early 1920s, a feeling grew within many of the Spanish-speaking congregations, then under the overall direction of Henry C. Ball, that they were being controlled by "outsiders" who did not really understand their particular culture and needs. The issue was focused at the Mexican convention that met at the 1922 Texas–New Mexico District sessions at Victoria, Texas. The Mexican pastors assembled, expecting to be able to organize as a separate Spanish-speaking district. Ball announced to them that they would have to wait. They refused, and on March 4, 1923, gathered at Houston, Texas, and organized the Latin American Council of Christians. Olazabal, who had terminated his membership in the Assemblies of God in January, became president of the new organization, a post he retained for the rest of his life. He directed his ministry to both Mexico and the United States and in 1934 opened work in Puerto Rico.

During the 1930s, Olazabal came into contact with A. J. Tomlinson of the Church of God. In 1936 fraternal relations between the two organizations were formalized and discussions begun on uniting the two churches. Before the merger could be arranged, however, Olazabal was killed in an automobile accident. The merger talks that relied heavily on the personal relationship between Tomlinson and Olazabal were discontinued.

Homer A. Tomlinson, *Miracles of Healing in the Ministry of Rev. Francisco Olazabal* (Queens Village, N.Y., 1939).

Victor De Leon, *The Silent Pentecostals* (privately printed, 1979).

OLCOTT, Henry Steel (August 2, 1832, Orange, New Jersey—February 17, 1907, Adyar, Madras, India); married Mary Eplee Morgan, April 26, 1860 (div. 187–); education: New York University, 1847–48.

Henry Steel Olcott, one of the co-founders of the Theosophical Society, was born in New Jersey but grew up in New York City. His college education was cut short by his father's business failure. At sixteen, he found himself in Elvira, Ohio, working on a farm with his uncles. They introduced him to both agriculture and Spiritualism. After five years in Ohio, he went to New Jersey and studied agricultural chemistry on the model farm of Professor J. J. Mapes. In 1855 he opened his own school. He wrote several books during the four years before his school failed.

He moved to New York City and became the assistant agricultural editor for the *New York Tribune*. On the eve of the Civil War, he married and shortly thereafter joined the army. In 1862 he obtained the rank of colonel and became a special investigator to search out corruption and war profiteers. His success led to his being invited to join the team investigating the Booth conspiracy, and he made the first arrest in the case, that of Ned Spangler.

After the war Olcott studied law, and in 1868 he was admitted to the New York bar. He also continued to dabble in journalism.

In July 1874, his latent interest in Spiritualism reasserted itself. He made a visit to Chittenden, Vermont, to investigate the phenomena produced by the famous Eddy brothers. On a second visit he met Helena Petrovna Blavatsky, the event that was to change his life.

Upon his return to New York, he began to write a book, *People from the Other World*, an account of his Spiritualist adventures, which was published in 1875. He also joined the circle that began to form around Madame Blavatsky. In September he joined Blavatsky and William Q. Judge in forming the Theosophical Society. He was elected president, a position he was to hold for the rest of his life. The following year, he and Blavatsky moved into an apartment together during the time she was working on her major work, *Isis Unveiled*. In 1878 the two decided to go to India. They settled in Bombay, where Olcott engaged in the import/export business to support them.

In October 1879, they began *The Theosophist*, a periodical, which by the end of the year was turning a profit and providing their income. In 1880 Olcott began the first of his world-roaming tours on behalf of the Theosophical Society. He traveled to Ceylon, where he formally became a Buddhist and opened seven branches of the society. In 1881 he made a return trip, primarily to raise money for Buddhist schools. He also wrote the *Buddhist Catechism*, for many years one of the most popular English-language introductions to Buddhism.

The remainder of Olcott's life was divided between the two separate but somewhat interrelated goals of launching a worldwide Buddhist mission thrust to the West and building the Theosophical Society. In the former cause, he came to believe that the mission must necessarily be preceded by the production of a common platform upon which all Buddhist sects could agree. To that end, he held a meeting in Adyar in 1891 that produced a fourteen-point document. While the colonel found general acceptance among Buddhists to whom he presented the document, it had no real authority and was little used. Olcott's most significant contributions to the spread of Buddhism were his promotion of contact between Japanese and Ceylonese Buddhists and his assistance in the appearance of Anagarika Dharmapala at the World Parliament of Religions in Chicago in 1893.

On behalf of the society, Olcott traveled throughout India, southern Asia, and Australia founding and strengthening branches. He attempted to hold the increasingly independent American and European sections within the organization, but he eventually broke with Judge who took most of the American group into an independent Theosophical Society in America.

During his last years he wrote the multivolume *Old Diary Leaves*, his memoirs of the developing movement. He continued his travels when his health permitted. He died in 1907.

Henry Steel Olcott, *The Buddhist Catechism* (Adyar, India, 1947).

———, *Old Diary Leaves*, 6 volumes (Adyar, India, 1972–75).

———, *People from the Other World* (Hartford, Conn., 1875).

Howard Murphet, *Hammer on the Mountain* (Wheaton, Ill., 1972).

Bruce F. Campbell, *Ancient Wisdom Revived* (Berkeley, Calif., 1980).

Josephine Ransom, *A Short History of the Theosophical Society* (Adyar, India, 1938).

Marion Meade, *Madame Blavatsky* (New York, 1980).

DRB, 342–3.

DAB, 14, 10–11.

EOP, 666.

WWW, 1, 913–14.

OWEN, Robert Dale (November 9, 1801, Glasgow, Scotland—June 17, 1877, Lake George, New York); married Mary Jane Robinson, April 12, 1832 (d. 1871); married Lottie Walton Kellog, June 23, 1876.

Robert Dale Owen, though not the founder of any group or movement, became a leading exponent of three alternative traditions in America—free thought, communalism, and Spiritualism. He was the son of Robert Owen, the wealthy industrialist and utopian visionary. Educated by private tutors, he finished his formal education in Switzerland. Urged by his father to assist in the establishment of his utopian ideals in the United States, Owen migrated to the community at New Harmony, Indiana, which his father had established in 1825. There he taught and edited the colony's newspaper, *The New Harmony Gazette*. At the colony, young Owen was influenced by fellow Scot and social reformer Frances Wright, who had just founded a colony of her own for freed slaves at Nashoba, Tennessee. Owen joined Wright in Tennessee, and they traveled to Europe together. Upon their return, they went back to New Harmony and jointly edited the newspaper.

By the time of their return, the communal vision of both New Harmony and Nashoba had failed. On February 1, 1828, the two issued a "Communication from the Trustees of Nashoba" in which they announced their abandonment of communitarianism. Wright, and later Owen, went on a lecture tour and by the end of 1829 ended up in New York. They continued the newspaper from New Harmony as *The Free Enquirer*, a free-thought newspaper that was actively hostile to Christianity. They also opened a hall of science in which they expounded their views on religion and other issues such as free love, in which Wright was a believer.

In 1830 Owen's book, *Moral Physiology*, an early work on birth control, was published. Owen married in 1832. He took his wife to Europe and then returned to settle in New Harmony. He served five years in the Indiana legislature; in 1839 he ran for the U.S. House of Representatives but was defeated, partially because of reaction to his early radicalism. He ran again in 1843 and was elected to the House as a Democrat. After failing to be reelected, Owen was made consul to the Kingdom of the Two Sicilies (Naples) in 1853. In 1858 he returned to the United States and later served as a member of President Buchanan's committee to determine policies toward the freed slaves.

While in Naples, Owen became curious about spiritual phenomena, and in 1856 he attended his first demonstration of animal magnetism. His curiosity led him to Spiritualism; eventually he was converted to the movement. Once back in the United States, he wrote his classic work, *Footfalls on the Boundary of Another World*, which appeared on the eve of the Civil War. His approach in this volume focused upon his investigation and observation of psychic phenomena. His third book, *Debatable Land Between This World and the Next* (1871), made him a recognized leader in the Spiritualist movement.

A few years before his death, Owen penned his last book, a partial autobiography, *Threading My Way* (1874).

Robert Dale Owen, *Moral Physiology* (New York, 1830).

———— , *Footfalls on the Boundary of Another World* (Philadelphia, Penn., 1860).

———— , *Debatable Land Between This World and the Next* (New York, 1871).

———— , *Twenty-seven Years of Autobiography, Threading My Way* (New York, 1874).

Richard William Leopold, *Robert Dale Owen, a Biography* (Cambridge, Mass., 1940).

Arthur Bestor, *Backwoods Utopias* (Philadelphia, Penn., 1970).

George B. Lockwood, *The New Harmony Movement* (New York, 1905).

DNB, 14, 1346–47.

WWWH, 390.

Gordon Stein

PALMER, Elihu (August 7, 1764, Canterbury, Connecticut—April 7, 1806, Philadelphia, Pennsylvania); married (d. 1793); married Mary Powell, 1803; education: Dartmouth College, graduated 1787.

Elihu Palmer, founder of the Deistical Society, was the first major American deist leader. He was raised on a farm, and the turbulent times of the American Revolution delayed his education. After his graduation from Dartmouth, he read theology while serving as a Presbyterian minister at Pittsfield, Massachusetts, and New Town, Long Island, New York. He began to develop liberal views and was forced out of the pulpit. In 1789 he moved to Philadelphia and joined the Baptists, but again he was forced out of his pulpit in March 1791 for his liberal views. With a few followers he joined the Universal Society, which had recently been founded by John Fitch (the inventor of the steamboat), and became the society's minister. His religious views had become deistic, and he preached a sermon denying the divinity of Christ. The reaction was so condemnatory that he had to leave the city. For the next two years, Palmer read law with his brother in western Pennsylvania, and in 1793 he was admitted to the bar in Philadelphia. That same year he lost his first wife and was himself left blind by the yellow fever epidemic that ravaged the city.

Realizing that a career in law was now beyond any real possibility, Palmer became a deist preacher. He settled in Augusta, Georgia, for a year. In 1794, on a trip to Connecticut, he visited New York City. He was asked to lecture and, because of the great response, remained in the city and organized the Deistical Society of New York. The Society became the base for his future lecturing, though he made appearances on the platform in a number of towns up and down the Hudson River and in Baltimore, New Jersey, and Philadelphia. It was while lecturing in Philadelphia that Palmer died in 1806.

Palmer was the author of only one published book (several of his lectures and sermons were printed as pamphlets). It was entitled *Principles of Nature; or A Development of the Moral Causes of Happiness and Misery Among the Human Species*. First published in 1801, the book went through several American editions, although it was not especially influential at first. Then the book was republished by Richard Carlile in England in 1819 and, again, there were several editions. All these editions are very rare today. In this book Palmer makes the original claim that the powers of man are sufficient for all the great purposes of human existence. This idea would later form the basis for humanism. He can also be considered the father of American philosophical naturalism. Yet another original idea of Palmer's was that the personality of Jesus, and his teaching as well, contained flaws that "poisoned" Western theology. He much preferred Eastern and Roman philosophers and held that the world was worse morally because of Jesus' teachings. He also rejected the idea of human immortality. Palmer's antipathy to Christianity extended to the point where he concluded that progress and Christianity were incompatible.

Palmer was also editor of the magazine *Prospect, Or View of the Moral World* (New York, 1803–05), a deistic publication that he founded. He also edited the deistic magazine *The Temple of Reason* (New York and Philadelphia, from 1802–03). Some of the sections of an unpublished book on politics, which Palmer was writing at the time of his death, were later published in England by Richard Carlile under the title *Posthumous Pieces* (London, 1824). They are preceded by a biographical introduction by Palmer's friend John Fellows.

Palmer has been largely forgotten in the twentieth century but remains important for both his philosophical originality and his emergence as the first American to make a career of public unbelief.

Elihu Palmer, *Principles of Nature; or, a Development of the Moral Causes of Happiness and Misery Among the Human Species* (New York, 1801).

———, *Posthumous Pieces* (London, 1824).

G. Adolph Koch, *Republican Religion* (New York, 1933).

Paul Kurtz, ed., *American Thought Before 1900* (New York, 1966).

Herbert M. Morais, *Deism in Eighteenth Century America* (New York, 1934).

Marshall G. Brown and Gordon Stein, *Freethought in the United States* (Westport, Conn., 1978).

DAB, 14, 177–79.

DRB, 348–9.

Gordon Stein

PALMER, Phoebe Worrall (December 18, 1807, New York, New York—November 2, 1874, New York, New York); married Walter C. Palmer, September 28, 1827 (d. 1883).

Phoebe Palmer was one of the creators of the nineteenth-century holiness movement that in the decade after her death led to the founding of the first of the holiness denominations in America. She was raised in the Methodist Episcopal Church in a family that practices a daily worship hour. She had her initial experience of grace as a child. In 1827 she married, and she and her husband became members of Allen Street Methodist Episcopal Church, New York City. Their attempts at raising a family were frustrated by the deaths of all three children soon after birth.

In 1832 Phoebe's life was changed by the events that began at Allen Street. The minister announced a series of four special meetings to begin in April. The meetings continued for more than two years. One result of this revival was the formation of a weekday prayer meeting for the women. In 1835 the Allen Street women united with the women of the Mulberry Street Church and began holding their joint prayer meeting each Tuesday in the Palmer home. As a result of these meetings, several of the women, including Phoebe in 1837, were sanctified, an experience of grace in which they were made perfect in love. That same year Phoebe's pastor invited her to begin a Young Ladies Bible Class at the church.

The growth of the Tuesday afternoon meetings and the sanctification experienced by several of the members led, in 1839, to the invitation for men to join in the gatherings. Thus came into existence the Tuesday Afternoon Union Meeting for the Promotion of Holiness. That same year Phoebe was invited to become a class leader at Allen Street, a role usually reserved for men.

Both the Tuesday meetings and the Palmers soon became two of the major focuses of a growing movement to emphasize holiness and sanctification within the Methodist Episcopal Church (in which it had been central but was being neglected). In the 1840s the two began to travel around the country promoting holiness, and Phoebe became a popular speaker at churches and revival meetings. In 1845 her first book, *Way of Holiness*, originally a series in the Methodist *Christian Advocate and Journal*, appeared.

Besides keeping up her normal church work and her travels to speak on holiness, Phoebe persisted in a round of evangelistic and social endeavors. She regularly visited the sick, the poor, and the inmates of the local prison. She founded the New York Female Assistance Society for the Relief and Religious Instruction of the Sick Poor. She assisted in the founding of several new Methodist congregations. It was in pursuit of the latter activity that she transferred her membership at Allen Street to the Norfolk Street Church in 1848.

During the 1850s the several holiness efforts grew into a national movement. Phoebe's books *Faith and Its Effects* (1848) and *Incidental Illustrations of the Economy of Salvation* (1855) played no small part in that growth. At the height of the revival in 1859, the Palmers took their long-delayed trip to England and Ireland. Partially as a result of the Civil War that had begun in the States, they extended their visit for four years.

Upon their return, they began immediately to revive a flagging holiness movement whose momentum had been blunted by the war. They purchased Timothy Merritt's *Guide to Holiness*, the main prewar holiness periodical. Within a decade they had increased its circulation from 7,000 to 40,000. As soon as the war ended, the movement revived and Phoebe became, for the second time, a popular speaker, especially at the numerous camp meetings and holiness associations that sprang up around the United States. She wrote her two major books, *Pioneer Experiences* and *Promise of the Father*, both of which appeared in 1868. She continued to write and speak, though slowed by illness in the 1870s, until her death in 1874.

Neither Phoebe nor her husband formed a new group. However, through their pioneering effort in the holiness ministry and their promotion of the independent camp meetings and associations, they helped create the groups that were to break completely from Methodism in the 1880s and 1890s and become the first holiness churches.

Phoebe Worrall Palmer, *The Way of Holiness* (New York, 1845).

——— , *Present to My Christian Friend: Entire Devotion to God* (New York, 1845).

——— , *Faith and Its Effects* (New York, 1848).

——— , *Promise of the Father* (Boston, 1868).

Richard Wheatley, *The Life and Letters of Mrs. Phoebe Palmer* (New York, 1876).

DRB, 349–50.

EWM, 2, 1852.

NAW, 3, 12–14.

PARAMANANDA, Swami (Suresh Chandra Guha Thakurta) (February 5, 1885, Banaripura, East Bengal, India (Now Bangladesh)—June 21, 1940, Cohasset, Massachusetts).

The person known to his American followers as Swami Paramananda, the founder of the Ananda Ashrama, was born into a wealthy and influential East Bengali family as Suresh Chandra Guha Thakurta. His early life was spent in Calcutta and Dacca. His father, a devout Hindu, introduced him to the writings of Sri Ramakrishna, and Suresh had contact as a youth with the Ramakrishna Math (monastery) located at Belur, a Calcutta suburb. In 1900 the young Suresh ran away from home, and despite the opposition of his parents, he joined the Math. In January 1902, shortly before his death, Swami Vivekananda, the founder of the Vedanta Society and student of Ramakrishna's, led Suresh in the taking of the vows of a *sannyasin*, the renounced life; Suresh became Swami Paramananda.

Paramananda spent the next four years in Madras with Swami Ramakrishnananda. During this time the vision of a mission in the West was impressed upon Paramananda, and Ramakrishnananda encouraged his young colleague. The opportunity to travel to America occurred in 1906; Paramananda accompanied Swami Abhedananda to New York as his assistant at the Vedanta Center, which had been established several years before. They arrived on December 23, 1906. Because of the growth of the Vedanta movement and the need of the Swamis in other places, Paramananda became acting head of the New York Vedanta Center in September 1907 and held the post until he moved to Boston at the end of 1908.

During his years in New York, Paramananda wrote the first of over forty books. *The Path of Devotion* (1907) consisted of numerous extracts of letters he had written to a member of the Center, Sister Devamata, who would become his close associate and in the 1920s write his biography.

Paramananda had first traveled to Boston to hold classes and speak at the invitation of Mrs. Ole Bull. He finally moved to Boston, where in January 1909 he opened the Boston Vedanta Center. In December 1909 he went to Washington, D.C., and started a center there. During the next few years he divided his time between Boston and Washington, with Devamata taking leadership in his absence. He also traveled widely throughout the United States and made several trips to Europe beginning in 1911. After his return from the 1911 trip, which included a visit to India, he initiated a program of expansion of the Boston center. He began his own periodical, *Message of the East*, and his own publishing effort, which issued not only his books but those of Sister Devamata as well.

In 1915 Paramananda made his first trip to Los Angeles, where an earlier attempt to found a Vedanta Center had failed. He found an immediate audience, and, beginning in 1917, he divided his time between Boston and Los Angeles. In 1923 he opened the Ananda Ashrama, at La Cresenta, California, north of Los Angeles. In 1929 Paramananda opened Ananda Ashrama at Cohasset, Massachusetts, as a retreat center. His three centers (Boston, La Cresenta, and Cohasset) consumed his time until his death in 1940. During these years he continued to write and publish. He moved the Ashrama's publishing center to California.

During the Swami's life, his centers were intimately connected with the larger Vedanta movement in America, although it was corporately independent. He had built a personal following and had developed an independent publishing concern. After his death the three centers severed their connection with the Vedanta movement, and Sister Devamata succeeded Paramananda as the leader. In 1952 the Boston center merged with the Cohasset center, and the Ananda Ashrama survives to this day in its two rural locations.

Swami Paramananda, *The Path of Devotion* (Boston, 1907).

——— , *Christ and Oriental Ideals* (Boston, 1912).

——— , *Emerson and Vedanta* (Boston, 1918).

——— , *The Vigil* (Boston, 1923).

——— , *My Creed* (Boston, 1929).

Sister Devamata, *Swami Paramananda and His Work*, volume I (La Cresenta, Calif., 1926), volume II (La Cresenta, Calif., 1941).

Levinsky, Sara Ann, *A Bridge of Dreams* (West Stockbridge, Mass., 1984).

WWW, I, 933.

PARHAM, Charles Fox (June 4, 1873, Muscatine, Iowa—January 29, 1929, Baxter Springs, Kansas); married Sarah Thislethwaite, December 31, 1896.

Charles Fox Parham, founder of the modern Pentecostal movement, was born to a pioneer farming family that moved to rural Kansas in 1885. There was no church in the area, but the sickly Charles did have a Bible that he read avidly. At the age of thirteen, he was converted at a revival meeting being held at the local schoolhouse. The youthful Parham became a Sunday school teacher, and the next year he was licensed as an exhorter by the Methodist Episcopal Church. He soon began preaching and preparing himself for a life as a minister. At age sixteen he left home to attend Southwestern Kansas College.

During his short stay at the college, two important events happened, both of which he related to his backsliding from his Christian faith and to an earlier promise to God to do mission work. He became ill with rheumatic fever and was given up by the doctors. But he was healed and consequently made a firm commitment to spend his life as a minister. He left school and accepted an appointment to the Eudora/Linwood circuit as a Methodist preacher.

In 1894, after two years as a Methodist preacher, he left the Methodist Church and denominationalism; for the next four years he worked in the area as an independent evangelist. During his years as a Methodist he had been deeply affected by the holiness movement and had joined the "come out" movement articulated by those who lived in tension with the Methodists because of their involvement with holiness.

During the years as an evangelist, he married a woman whom he had met some years earlier at a revival meeting. Together they opened Bethel, a healing home, in Topeka, Kansas, in 1898. The home became the center of Parham's evangelistic teachings and a training center for Bible students. Parham had developed a dislike for doctors and taught his followers to rely upon God alone for healing and health. He also began a periodical, *The Apostolic Faith*. Parham's ministry proved fruitful, and a following grew up around him. He laid emphasis upon salvation, healing, sanctification, the second coming of Jesus, the baptism of the Holy Spirit, immersion, and a noneternal hell.

In 1900 Parham made a trip east and visited other holiness ministers who had a healing ministry—John Alexander Dowie and Albert B. Simpson. He returned to Topeka only to find his work taken over by some colleagues. Rather than fighting for his center, he opened another Bible school in October 1900 and began anew.

Over the holiday season of that year, the events that were to change the direction of Parham's life and ministry occurred. In December 1900 Parham gave his students the task of interpreting the second chapter of Acts. He left for services in Kansas City and returned on New Year's Eve and asked for a report. The students agreed that the coming of the Holy Spirit, as at Pentecost, was always signified and evidenced by the speaking in unknown tongues. One student, Agnes Oznam, asked that hands be laid upon her to receive the Holy Spirit. As the group prayed over her, she began to speak in Chinese and was unable to speak English for three days. The experience was repeated in the lives of other students as they too began to speak in tongues.

During January 1901, Parham and some of his students held meetings in Kansas City to share what they had discovered. The meetings were preceded by newspaper articles and drew an immediate response. Later that year Parham moved to Kansas City, where he opened a bible school. He wrote *A Voice Crying in the Wilderness*, a book recounting his experiences and his new teaching about the baptism of the Holy Spirit being evidenced by the speaking in tongues.

During the next five years he held meetings throughout Kansas and Missouri, preaching primarily to holiness groups. In 1905 he traveled to Orchard, Texas, where he received an invitation to come to Houston. He spent the winter of 1905-6 in Houston and opened a Bible school there. Among his students was a black man, W. J. Seymour. Seymour took Parham's teachings to Los Angeles to a small holiness mission. As a result of Seymour's work Pentecostalism spread to several churches, white and black, in the Los Angeles area.

While Seymour was in Los Angeles, Parham moved from Houston back to Kansas. He also traveled to Zion, Illinois (the home of J. A. Dowie), to hold a meeting. Hearing of the spread of Pentecostalism in Los Angeles, he then went to California but did not find what he had expected. He denounced Seymour and the leaders of the Los Angeles groups and decried their involvement with Spiritualism and hypnotism. As the revival spread, he also rejected the move to organize the Pentecostal people into denominations, preferring free churches that were only loosely associated. He rejected a leadership role in Pentecostalism and chose to remain a traveling evangelist. From this point he and those who chose to follow him separated themselves from the main body of the Pentecostals. In 1911 Parham settled in Baxter Springs, Kansas, which became his permanent home and the center of his itinerant ministry. Congregations sprang from his work and continue to this day as a loose unincorporated association called the Apostolic Faith Church.

Charles Fox Parham, *A Voice Crying in the Wilderness* (Baxter Springs, Kans., 1944).

Sarah E. Parham, *The Life of Charles F. Parham, Founder of the Apostolic Faith Movement* (Joplin, Mo., 1930).

Vinson Synan, Jr., *Aspects of Pentecostal-Charismatic Origins* (Plainfield, N.J., 1975).

Carl Brumback, *Suddenly From Heaven* (Springfield, Mo., 1961).

PARKER, Daniel (April 6, 1781, Culpepper County, Virginia—December 3, 1844, Elkhart, Texas).

Daniel Parker, founder of the Two-Seed-in-the-Spirit Predestinarian Baptists, came from a family of Baptist preachers, a calling of both his father and grandfather. Soon after his birth the family moved to Georgia, where he grew up in poverty and received no formal education. In 1802 he experienced conversion, was baptized, and joined the Nails Creek Baptist Church in Franklin, Georgia. The following year he was licensed to preach, moved with his wife and parents to Dickson County, Tennessee, and united with the Trumbull Baptist Church. That church ordained him in 1806, and he began an eleven-year period as a Baptist pastor in Tennessee.

Around 1810 he heard a brother minister preach on the peculiar ultra-Calvinist predestinarian view, which he later popularized and with which he became everafter identified. According to the theory, after God created humankind, Satan was allowed to implant his seed in Eve, who brought forth not only the elect children of God (Abel) but the children of Satan (Cain) as well. The elect are of God and go to Him, while the seed of Satan are his and are without hope of salvation. Parker's ultrapredestinarian

views served to counter the influence of the Free-Will Baptist theology
that was growing in the South, but it also gave a rationale for his opposition to missions.

During the early nineteenth century, Baptists had begun to advocate
and organize cooperative missionary societies by which several congregations, or an association, would fund missionaries to preach to the un-
saved. Conservative Baptists opposed missionary societies as unscriptural
usurpations of the power of the local church. Parker, who became a
leading voice in the antimission controversy, saw the entire human race as
predestined according to the seed with which any individual happened to
be born. To send missionaries to the children of Satan was useless, and the
elect had no need of mission societies for their salvation.

Though Parker was uneducated and uncouth in manner, his native
abilities as an eloquent speaker and able debater pushed him into leadership roles. In 1815 he became moderator of the Concord Baptist Association in Tennessee, which provided him with a position from which he
could condemn not only mission societies but also theological seminaries,
benevolent and Bible societies, and all religious newspapers, tracts, and
books (except his own).

In 1817 he moved to Illinois. In 1820 he published his first pamphlet, a
thirty-eight-page attack on missions. His main theological works appeared
in 1826, in the form of three pamphlets: *Views on the Two Seeds*; *A
Supplement, or Explanation of My Views*; and *The Second Dose of Doctrine*. In
these he developed the two-seed theory as a commentary on Genesis 3:15.
His views were further expanded in the *Church Advocate*, a periodical he
edited for two years (1829–30). During the years in Illinois, he found time
not only to pastor and write but also to become active in politics. He
served one term in the Illinois senate (1826–27).

In Illinois Parker had organized and pastored the Lamatte Baptist
Church in Crawford County. In the 1830s he decided upon another
move—to Texas—and in 1832 he and three brothers made the trip south.
They encountered a Mexican law forbidding the formation of a non-
Roman Catholic church, but Parker found a loophole. The law did not
forbid the migration of a preexisting congregation into Texas. He returned
to Illinois and organized the Pilgrim Predestinarian Regular Baptist
Church of Jesus Christ. In August 1833, one month after their formation,
the church members began migrating to Texas. They arrived in 1834. A
second congregation was organized in 1837, and the Union Association of
Regular Predestinarian Baptists was formed in 1840. Parker died four years
later.

After Parker's death, his ideas spread throughout the South and the
West. Membership in the late nineteenth century peaked at approximately 13,000 but sharply declined during the twentieth century. In the
1970s, only seven congregations—organized in three associations, with a
combined membership of less than two hundred—could be found.

Daniel Parker, *The Authors' Defense* (Vincennes, Ind., 1824).

———, *A Public Address to the Baptist Society of the Baptist Board of Foreign Missions*
    (Vincennes, Ind., 1820).

———, *Views on the Two Seeds* (Vandalia, Ill., 1826).

O. Max Lee, *Daniel Parker's Doctrine of the Two Seeds* (Nashville, Tenn., 1962).

Burrilla B. Spencer, ed., *A History of Kentucky Baptists from 1769 to 1885* (Cincinnati, Ohio, 1885).

Arthur C. Piepkorn, *Profiles in Belief*, II (New York, 1978).

DRB, 351–52.

ESB, 1071.

PERCIVAL, Harold Waldwin (April 15, 1868, Bridgetown, Barbados, British West Indies—March 6, 1953, New York, New York).

Harold Waldwin Percival, one of the founders of the independent Theosophical Society of New York and later the Word Foundation, was born on his parents' plantation in the West Indies. The devout Christianity of his parents did not satisfy Percival, and at an early age he began a personal religious quest. His father died when he was ten, and Percival moved with his mother to Boston and later to New York City.

As a young man he became interested in Theosophy and in 1892 joined the Theosophical Society headed by William Q. Judge. After Judge's death in 1896, the society split into several factions. Along with J. H. Salisbury and Donald Nicholson, Percival formed the Theosophical Society of New York. Largely self-educated, Percival began the Theosophical Publishing Company of New York and soon became a major writer, publisher, and distributor of Theosophical literature. He authored his first books, *The Zodiac* (1906), *Karma, the Law of Life* (1910) and *Hell and Heaven, on Earth and After Death* (1911).

During his first decades as a Theosophist, Percival became best known as the editor of *The Word*, a monthly periodical that he edited from 1904 to 1917. It was the official organ of the Theosophical Society of New York. Both languished and died during the war years.

Percival had already, as a Theosophist, begun to develop his own independent system. In 1893 he had for the first time a personal mystical experience that he described as being "conscious of Consciousness." Being conscious of Consciousness reveals the hidden and unknown and places an obligation to share the new knowledge revealed. By 1902 he had begun to systematize his new findings in dialogue with Theosophy. In 1912 he began to outline material for a book that would contain his complete synthesis. He dictated the material to a colleague, Benoni B. Gattell, intermittently for two decades. In 1932, the first draft, entitled *The Law of Thought*, was completed. For the next fourteen years he edited and rewrote the volume. After retitling it *Thinking and Destiny*, he published the thousand-page volume in 1946. Subsequently he published three books dealing in greater detail with selected subjects: *Man and Woman and Child* (1951); *Masonry and Its Symbols* (1952); and *Democracy Is Self-Government* (1952).

In 1946 Percival and several associates formed the Word Publishing Company to print and distribute his books. Four years later he formed the Word Foundation to perpetuate his teachings. The foundation continues to distribute Percival's books.

Percival had put his own ideas and perceptions to the test in writing his books. He taught that in the state of being conscious of Consciousness one could know about any subject simply by thinking. Thinking, he defined, is the "steady holding of the Conscious Light within on the subject of the thinking. Briefly stated, thinking is of four stages: selecting the subject; holding the Conscious Light on that subject; focussing the Light; and, the focus of the Light. When the Light is focussed, the subject is known."

Harold Waldwin Percival, *Thinking and Destiny* (New York, 1946).

——— , *Man and Woman and Child* (New York, 1951).

——— , *Masonry and Its Symbols* (New York, 1952).

——— , *Democracy Is Self-Government* (New York, 1952).

The Theosophical Movement, 1875-1950 (Los Angeles, 1951).

WWW, 4, 744.

PLUMMER, George Winslow (August 25, 1876, Boston, Massachusetts—January 26, 1944, New York, New York); married Grace Francis Waite (d. 1935); married Gladys E. S. Miller; education: Rhode Island School of Design; Brown University.

George Winslow Plummer, one of the founders of the Societas Rosicruciana in America, was raised in New England as a member of an old pre-Revolutionary family. After finishing college, he moved to New York City where he became an artist and an art director for several periodicals and where he met and married his first wife. He also joined the Masons.

In 1907 Sylvester C. Gould, a member of the Boston College of the Societas Rosicruciana Republicae Americae, decided to form a new Rosicrucian group open to the general public and not limited to Masons. That same year he began a periodical, *The Rosicrucian Brotherhood*, and the following year started the new group, the Societas Rosicruciana in America (S.R.I.A.). Plummer worked with Gould on the formation of the S.R.I.A., and in 1909, when Gould died, Plummer assumed leadership of the group—a position he held for the next thirty-five years. The S.R.I.A. was incorporated in 1912.

For the next decade, Plummer combined his career as an artist and free-lance adman with his leadership of the S.R.I.A. In 1916 he founded the Mercury Publishing Company and began publishing *Mercury*, a quarterly, as the official magazine of the society. In 1920 he went full-time with the society. It had chartered six colleges (groups) in the United States plus one in Sierre Leone by that time. Two more were added in 1921.

During the 1920s a long-standing interest in Christian mysticism became manifest in the formation of the Seminary of Biblical Research. In 1926 Plummer began a series of lessons on *Christian Mysticism*, which were distributed through the seminary and the society. Plummer also became head of the Anglican Universal Church, a small independent Catholic jurisdiction. He was consecrated bishop by Puerto Rican bishop Manuel Ferrando, a former Roman Catholic.

In 1934 Plummer was reconsecrated by Archbishop William Albert Nichols of the American Orthodox Church and assumed the ecclesiastical name Archbishop Georgius. Shortly thereafter he reconsecrated three of the Anglican Universal Church bishops, Harry Van Arsdale Parsell, Adrian C. Grover, and Marcus Allan Grover, who took the episcopal names of Irenaus, Patricius, and Marcus, respectively. In 1936 he consecrated Stanislaus Witowski (de Witow), who took the name Theodotus. In 1936 the new church, renamed the Holy Orthodox Church in America, reported congregations in New York City; Birmingham, Alabama; Scranton, Pennsylvania; and Chicago, Illinois—all locations that also had S.R.I.A. colleges or study groups.

Plummer authored the lessons of the S.R.I.A. as well as a number of books and booklets, many published posthumously, including *Rosicrucian Fundamentals* (1920); *Principles and Practice for Rosicrucians* (1947); *The Art of Rosicrucian Healing* (1947); and *The Science of Death* (1978).

After his death, Plummer was succeeded as head of the Holy Orthodox Church in America by Archbishop Theodotus, who eventually married Plummer's widow. After Theodotus's death, Gladys Plummer de Witow became head of both the society and the church. She is known as Mother Serena. On November 9, 1980, she was consecrated by Archbishop Herman Adrian Spruit of the Church of Antioch and became Archbishop Serena of the Holy Orthodox Church in America.

George Winslow Plummer, *Consciously Creating Circumstances* (New York, 1939).

——— , *The Art of Rosicrucian Healing* (New York, 1947).

——— , *Principles and Practice for Rosicrucians* (New York, 1947).

——— , *The Science of Death* (New York, 1978).

——— , under pseudonym Khei, *Rosicrucian Fundamentals* (New York, 1920).

Christopher McIntosh, *The Rosy Cross Unveiled* (Wellingborough, 1980).

Peter Anson, *Bishops at Large* (London, 1964).

Harold V. B. Voorhis, *Masonic Rosicrucian Societies* (New York, 1958).

PRABHUPADA, Abhay Charan De Bhaktivedanta Swami (September 1, 1896, Calcutta, India—November 14, 1977, Vrindavan, India); married Padharani Satta, 1919; education: Scottish Churches College, 1916–1920.

The one whom the world knows as A. C. Bhaktivedanta Swami Prabhupada, founder of the International Society for Krishna Consciousness, was born Abhay Charan De in India at the height of British colonial rule. His father was a cloth merchant and a daily visitor to the Radha-Govinda Temple just across the street from Abhay's boyhood home. He taught his son deity worship from childhood. Abhay's mother wanted to send him to England to study law, but his father refused, not wanting his son to be corrupted by Western society. Instead Abhay entered the Scottish Churches College in 1916. While a student, he married an eleven-year-old girl, a marriage arranged by his father. He was not happy with the marriage and was intent upon taking a second wife, but was dissuaded by his father.

In 1920 he finished his college work but refused his degree as a means of responding to Gandhi's call to boycott British goods. He became the manager of a pharmaceutical company, an occupation by which he was to make his living for the next four decades. He also met Sri Srimad Bhaktisiddhanta Sarasvati Gosvami, the head of the Guadiya Math, an India-wide Caitayna-Vaishnava religous movement, who would become Abhay's guru (teacher). Under his influence, he began to move away from his political leanings.

After the birth of his first son and with the press of family responsibilities upon him, he moved to Allahabad to expand his business. Though his business prospered, he was somewhat cut off from contact with the Guadiya Math until 1928, when a mission was opened in Allahabad. This action increased Abhay's devotion. In October 1932 he traveled to Vrindavan, and for the second time he met Sri Bhaktisiddhanta Sarasvati; one month later he was initiated. He was given the name Abhay Charanaravinda (meaning "one who fearlessly takes shelter at the feet of the Lord").

In 1936, shortly before his guru died, Abhay wrote him and asked how he, a businessman and householder, could best serve. He was told to prepare himself to spread the teachings of Krishna worship in the West. He put the suggestion aside, however, because of his family. After his guru's death, he found the Gaudiya Math split by various factions fighting over the succession to leadership. He stayed aloof from the internal battles but stayed in contact with many disciples of his guru. He spent his time writing his first books, an *Introduction to the Geetopanishad* and the *Bhagavad Gita As It Is*. For his accomplishment, his fellow disciples gave him the title Bhaktivedanta (*bhakti*, "devotion," and *vedanta*, the "knowledge of God").

During the 1940s Abhay found himself saddled with an unhappy marriage and family responsibilities, the turbulence of World War II, and the postwar independence struggles in India, and an unfulfilled desire to spend all of his time as a Krishna devotee. During the war he had begun a magazine, *Back to Godhead*, but it floundered in the wartime paper shortage. After the war he continually experienced business failures, because of lack of interest and inattention to business concerns; he gradually made the transition to full-time work in spreading devotion (*bhakti-yoga*) to Krishna.

During the 1950s he moved from place to place in various efforts to organize support for a worldwide Krishna-consciousness movement. He organized a short-lived League of Devotees. He revived *Back to Godhead* in 1952 and again in 1956. Finally, in 1956, he had for the third time a vision of his guru telling him to take *sannyassa*, the renounced life, to break with his family, and spend his life in Krishna devotion. He took his vows in November 1956 and emerged A. C. Bhaktivedanta Swami.

He spent the remaining years in India writing and obtaining funds to publish his books, *Easy Journey to Other Planets* and three volumes of his commentary on the *Srimad-Bhagavatum*. As soon as the last volume was published he migrated to New York City and took up his mission as given by his guru in 1936. He began work on New York's Lower East Side, where he experienced his first success among the hippies. In 1966 he opened a storefront center and revived *Back to Godhead*, which has been reprinted regularly since. The movement spread rapidly and a San Francisco center opened in 1967.

During the last days of his life Srila Prabhupada (as he came to be called honorifically) divided his time between his writing and leading and organizing a growing worldwide movement. He continued his commentary on the *Srimad-Bhagavatum* and began translating the *Caitanya-caritamrta*, a classic work of the Bengali Krishna devotional tradition. Over sixty volumes of his writings were published by the Bhaktivedanta Book Trust, which he founded in 1972.

The International Society for Krishna Consciousness, which he headed, became one of the most prominent of the alternative religions to emerge during the 1970s in America, from which it has since spread to every continent. Prior to Srila Prabhupada's death, the society included more than one hundred centers around the world, as well as a number of children's schools, rural communities, and major cultural centers in Bombay, Vrindavan, and Mayapur, India.

A. C. Bhaktivedanta Swami Prabhupada, *Bhagavad-Gita As It Is* (New York, 1972).

———, *KRSNA, The Supreme Personality of Godhead*, 3 volumes (New York, 1970).

———, *The Path of Perfection* (Los Angeles, 1979).

———, *The Science of Self-Realization* (New York, 1977).

———, *The Nectar of Devotion* (New York, 1970).

Satsvarupa dasa Goswami, *Srila Prabhupada-lilamrta*, 3 volumes (Los Angeles, 1980–81).

Steven J. Gelberg, ed., *Hare Krishna, Hare Krishna* (New York, 1983).

Faye Levine, *The Strange World of the Hare Krishnas* (Greenwich, Conn., 1974).

J. Stillson Judah, *Hare Krishna and the Counterculture* (New York, 1974).

EOP, 106.

PURNELL, Benjamin (March 27, 1861, Greenup City, Kentucky— December 16, 1927, Benton Harbor, Michigan); married Angelina Brown, 1877; married Mary Stoddard, 1880.

Benjamin Purnell, the founder of the House of David, became the most successful leader in the United States to derive from the lineage of British prophetess Joanna Southcott. We know little about his early life. He married at the age of sixteen, but he soon deserted his wife and applied for a divorce. However, he never pursued the divorce decree and both he and his first wife remarried without it being granted. The 1880s became a mobile decade with Purnell and his second wife moving from town to town. He worked at odd jobs, including broommaking. Along the way, he obtained a copy of *The Flying Roll*, a book written by Southcottite prophet James J. Jazreel (d. 1885).

In 1882 the Purnells joined a Jazreelite commune in Detroit. The year before, its leader, "Prince" Michael Mills, had proclaimed himself the Seventh Angel of Revelation 8:6. Jazreel had emphasized the role of the succession of leaders to Southcott as fulfillment of the prophecy of the angels in Revelation. Prince Michael received Purnell and soon made him a "Pillar," a leader within the community.

In 1895 Purnell proclaimed Michael an imposter and himself as the Seventh Angel. Purnell was expelled from the Detroit colony and began a period of itinerant preaching. He finally settled in Fosteria, Ohio, with Silas Mooney, who became his devoted disciple and assistant. While in Fosteria, he wrote his first book, *Star of Bethlehem*, published in 1902. He gethered a following and built a tabernacle.

About the time his book appeared, Purnell made contact with a group of Jazreelites in Benton Harbor, Michigan. Michael had returned to England to try to take leadership of the followers of Jazreel there, and no one remained in the United States to challenge Purnell. He moved to Benton Harbor in March 1903 with a small group of followers from Fosteria.

In 1904 Purnell left the new colony and went to Australia. He had great success there in recruiting members for what he now called the House of David from among the followers of John Wroe, another Southcottite prophet. During this trip he established a center in Australia and brought eighty converts with him to the United States. Upon his return in 1905, he purchased land outside Benton Harbor and began to establish the House of David. The next few years were spent in creating a stong self-supporting community. In 1908 an amusement park, which for many years was a major tourist attraction, was opened. The House of David also had a band and a baseball team that toured the country giving exhibition games.

Members of the community accepted Purnell as the Seventh Angel (or Messenger) of Revelation; the other six being: Joanna Southcott, Richard Brothers, George Turner, William Shaw, John Wroe, and James Jazreel. Members took Nazarite vows and did not cut their hair. They were also vegetarians and adopted a celibate life. Although celibacy was a community norm, Purnell continually faced charges of sexual immorality with the many female members of the community. He usually met such charges with a ceremonial mass marriage of community members (1910, 1914) and periods in which he disappeared altogether.

In 1922 he made his last public appearance. Four years later, on November 26, 1926, state police raided the community and caught the aging leader in his night clothes with four female group members. Purnell was arrested and an extensive investigation began. In November 1927 the colony was moved into receivership after being declared a public nuisance; Purnell and his wife were excluded from further association with the colony. Five weeks after the judge's decision, Purnell died.

In the power vacuum created by Purnell's arrest and death, H. T. Dewhist, a member, took control of the House of David. Mary Purnell began to fight in court for the colony, claiming that most members were loyal to her. In 1930 a settlement was reached, and she and her supporters moved down the road to begin a new colony, called the House of David as Reorganized by Mary Purnell. Both groups continue to circulate the books of Benjamin Purnell, including his *Book of Wisdom*; *The Ball of Fire* (6 volumes), and *Book of Dialogues* (1906).

Benjamin Purnell, *Book of Dialogues*, 3 volumes (Benton Harbor, Mich., 1912).

——— , *The Book of Wisdom*, 7 volumes (Benton Harbor, Mich., n.d.).

——— , *Prove All Things* (Benton Harbor, Mich., n.d.).

——— , *Shiloh's Wisdom* (Benton Harbor, Mich., n.d.).

———, *Benjamin's Last Writing* (Benton Harbor, Mich., 1927).

Milo M. Quaife, *Lake Michigan* (Indianapolis, Ind., 1944).

The What? Where? When? Why? and How? of the House of David (Benton Harbor, Mich., 1931).

G. R. Balleine, *Past Finding Out* (New York, 1956).

Richard Mathison, *Faiths, Cults & Sects of America* (Indianapolis, Ind., 1960).

QUIMBY, Phineas Parkhurst (February 16, 1802, Lebanon, New Hampshire—January 16, 1866, Belfast, Maine); married Susannah Haraden.

Phineas Parkhurst Quimby, the discoverer of mental healing whose teachings are the source for the New Thought movement, grew up in Belfast, Maine, a small town to which his parents had moved when he was only two years old. He had little formal schooling and was apprenticed to a clockmaker from whom he learned his trade.

Two events in the 1830s led to Quimby's becoming a healer. First, he developed tuberculosis and cured himself without going to a doctor. Secondly, in 1838 Quimby attended a lecture on Mesmerism that a Doctor Collyer gave. He then enthusiastically studied the subject until he became a proficient hypnotist. He also met Lucius Burkmer, a person who could quickly and easily slip into a hypnotic trance. In trance, Burkmer could diagnose and prescribe for the ill who came to hear Quimby lecture. Quimby also became a magnetic healer.

During the years as a magnetist, Quimby explored and pondered the phenomena of hypnotism. He saw the tricks of the mind. He also saw people get well from drugs prescribed by Burkmer that had no medicinal potency. He came to believe that disease was merely the mistaken notion of the sick and that the mind was the major factor in sickness and health. If the mind of the patient could be changed, the cure would result. He reached this conclusion without reference to either biblical or religious consideration.

In 1859, having developed his ideas about mental healing, he opened an office in Portland, Maine. He began to write down his teachings, which were recopied and edited by some of his students. He also accepted students who came to him for healing and to learn his practices. Among his prominent students and patients were Warren Felt Evans, Annetta Seabury Dresser and Julius Dresser, who would later found the New Thought movement, and Mary Baker Eddy, the founder of the Church of Christ, Scientist.

Quimby was neither formally educated nor a systematic thinker. He developed his teaching from the observation that disease was a disturbance of the mind diverted by error. He was not a religious man in any traditional sense and denounced priests and doctors as the two classes of people most leading the masses into error. While not associated with a church, he did develop theological thoughts around which he built his healing work.

He asserted that the only religion he knew was God, or Wisdom. Jesus was simply a man like any other man. But Quimby did, however, distinguish between Jesus and the Christ. The Christ was the Science that Jesus had tried to teach and the God that is within each person. Jesus was also the great healer and founder of the science of healing, which Quimby had rediscovered.

Quimby did not publish any of his writings during his lifetime. His students had the copies that had been circulated privately. Only in 1921 did a copy of his writings appear as *The Quimby Manuscripts*. It was also left to his students to turn his teachings into a popular movement.

A major controversy erupted in the 1800s when Julius and Annetta Dresser accused Mary Baker Eddy of publishing Quimby's ideas as her own. In the light of her having been a student of his and having praised him and his work at one time, the question has remained a hotly debated item. The publication of Quimby's papers have done much to settle the debate. It is obvious that Quimby and Eddy shared some common language and a few opinions and that he had used the term Christian Science on occasion, but not as a formal name to describe his work. However, it is equally the case that Eddy's teachings and practice departed radically from those of Quimby, the distinction being partially obscured by the development of a variety of syntheses of their ideas within the New Thought movement of the early twentieth century.

Phineas Parkhurst Quimby, *The Quimby Manuscripts*, edited by H. W. Dresser (New York, 1921).

——— , *The Healing Wisdom of Dr. P. P. Quimby*, ed. by Mason Alonzo Clark (Los Altos, Calif., 1982).

——— , *Immanuel* (Mokelumne Hill, Calif., 1960).

Ann Ballew Hawkins, *Phineas Parkhurst Quimby* (Los Angeles, Calif., 1951).

Horatio W. Dresser, *A History of the New Thought Movement* (London, 1919).

Annette Gertrude Dresser, *The Philosophy of P. P. Quimby* (Boston, 1895).

Charles S. Braden, *Spirits in Rebellion* (Dallas, Texas, 1963).

WWWH, 428.

RAMAKRISHNA, Sri (Gadadhar Chattopadhyay) (February 18, 1836, Kamarpukur, Bengal, India—August 16, 1886, Calcutta, India); married Saradamani Devi, May 1859 (d. July 21, 1920).

Gadadhar Chattopadhyay, who came to be known as the priest of a temple of the Goddess Kali and who was called by his followers Sri Ramakrishna, founded no movement and established no organization. However, he became the inspiration of a generation of Indian Hindus and his influence spread throughout the world through the Vedanta Society, founded by a student of his, Swami Vivekananda.

He was born to a poor family in an obscure village, but as a child he showed a mystic bent and entered into spontaneous trancelike states. He neglected studies and spent his time in solitary meditation, group singing, and putting on theatrical performances of Hindu stories. When his elder brother established a Sanskrit school in Calcutta, he called Gadadhar to join him.

On May 31, 1855, still a youth of nineteen, he got the opportunity to become a priest at a temple of Kali at Dakshineshwar, five miles north of Calcutta. He reluctantly accepted the post, which at least allowed him many hours for meditation. Soon after taking up his duties, he developed an overwhelming desire for union with the Divine Mother. One day the Divine Mother revealed Herself to him and he fell into a trancelike state. He followed this experience with attempts to identify with the forms of other Hindu deities.

His behavior was odd even for India, and many people thought him mad. His parents called him home for a rest and cure. To complete his cure, they arranged his marriage to Saradamani Devi, a child of five years.

In 1861 Gadadhar returned to the Kali Temple to resume his duties. He studied with several teachers, but in 1865 he again began the search that would eventually lead to identity with God. He resolved to immerse himself in identity with Brahman and remained in a state of trance for six months. At the end of this period, he received the command of the Divine Mother: "Remain on the threshold of relative consciousness for the sake of humanity."

Having tasted the mystical awareness through Hinduism, he decided to expand his awareness of the divine life outside of Hinduism. He took instruction in Sufism (Islamic mysticism) and Christianity. His mystical experiences led him to a realization of the harmony of all religions. "Different creeds are but different paths to reach the one God."

In 1872 his wife joined him at Dakshineshwar. Though she had married him as a child and he had not lived with her for eleven years, they found an immediate spiritual union and oneness of mission. He worshipped her as the embodiment of the mother of the universe and trained her in spiritual leadership.

During the last decade of his life, the speculation concerning his sanity continued; but while some speculated, others saw him as Sri Ramakrishna, the God-intoxicated priest. A group gathered around him. Narendranath Datta, later known as Swami Vivekananda, his most important disciple, joined the group in 1881 and quickly became its leading figure.

In October 1885 Ramakrishna became ill. He died the following August. After his death Narendra took over and organized the disciples into an order, known in the West as the Vedanta Society. After a short while Ramakrishna's wife also began to assert the leadership role that he had pressed upon her and became known as the mother of the movement that Ramakrishna inspired.

Sri Ramakrishna, *The Gospel of Ramakrishna* (New York, 1947).

Christopher Isherwood, *Ramakrishna and His Disciples* (New York, 1965).

Swami, Nikhilananda, *Ramakrishna: Prophet of New India* (New York, 1948).

Romain Rolland, *The Life of Ramakrishna* (Mayavati, India, 1931).

Swami Gamhirananda, *History of the Ramakrishna Math and Mission* (Calcutta, India, 1957).

EOP, 763.

RANDOLPH, Paschal Beverly (October 8, 1825, New York, New York—July 29, 1875, Boston, Massachusetts); married.

Paschal Beverly Randolph, the founder of the Rosicrucian Fraternity in America, was the son of William Beverly Randolph (of the Virginia

Randolphs) and Flora Randolph, a woman of mixed blood. Because of his mother's partial descent from Madagascan royalty, Randolph was frequently charged with being part negro, a claim he constantly refuted. His mother died of smallpox when he was a child, and he was raised an orphan by an actress acquaintance of his mother's half-sister. He had only a year of schooling and at the age of sixteen ran away to sea. His life at sea ended five years later when he was severely injured while chopping wood. He learned the barber's and dyer's trades, making his living with those occupations while studying medicine; he began to practice medicine in the 1850s.

In 1850 he traveled to Europe and became an initiate of the Rosicrucian Fraternity at Frankfurt on Main, Germany. He also met General Ethan Allen Hitchcock, an American Rosicrucian and hermeticist. He was briefly active in the Reform party in 1852 and 1853, when he met Abraham Lincoln for the first time, but returned to Europe in 1854 to continue his occult studies. There, it is claimed, he met many of the Rosicrucian leaders in France and England—Eliphas Levi, Kenneth MacKenzie, and Edward Bulwer-Lytton. In Paris in 1858 he was made Supreme Grand Master of the Western World and a Knight of L'Ordre du Lis. He returned to the United States and founded the American branch of the Rosicrucians.

As the Civil War was approaching, Randolph began a two-year world tour during which he was initiated by the Ansaireh in Syria and into the Order of the Rose, headed by Hargrave Jennings, in London. Upon his return to the United States, he spent a year in the recruitment of black soldiers before journeying, at Lincoln's personal request, to New Orleans to begin three years of work as a teacher among the freed slaves. In 1866 he attended the Southern Loyal Convention, a gathering of anti-Johnson radicals, and spoke on behalf of the blacks, calling for their being given the vote. Following the convention he joined the pilgrimage to Lincoln's tomb, but had such a negative experience with many of the delegates that he left politics entirely.

After the convention Randolph moved to Boston and opened a medical practice, which he continued until 1870. He also reorganized the Rosicrucian work and began writing and publishing his many books. In February 1872 he was arrested and accused of writing and circulating books on free love. The arrest was part of a plot by some former business partners of Randolph's to obtain his copyrights. He was acquitted of all charges after a well-publicized trial.

Randolph was the author of numerous books, including *Dealing with the Dead* (1861) (later republished as *Soul, the Soul World*); *The Grand Secret or Physical Love in Health and Disease* (1862); *Ravalette, the Rosicrucian's Story* (1863); *Seership* (1868); *Love & the Master Passion* (1870); *Eulis, the History of Love* (1874) (later republished as *Eulis, Affectional Alchemy*); and *The Book of the Triplicate Order* (1875).

As can be implied from the titles of several of his books, Randolph explored at some depth the occult perspective on love and sex. His teachings formed the content of the inner teachings of the Rosicrucian

Fraternity. He also had a group of disciples in France and his work on sex magic, *Sexualis Magia*, has survived only in a French edition. The work he initiated continues at the Rosicrucian Fraternity, which is headquartered at Beverly Hall, Pennsylvania.

Randolph shot himself, in reaction to his discovery of his wife's involvement in an adulterous affair.

Paschal Beverly Randolph, *The Grand Secret* (1860–61).

——, *Eulis, the History of Love* (Toledo, Ohio, 1874).

——, *The Book of the Triplicate Order* (San Francisco, Calif., 1875).

——, *Sexualis Magia* (Paris, 1931).

——, *Ravalette, the Rosicrucian's Story* (Quakertown, Penn., 1935).

The Rose Cross Order (Allentown, Penn., 1916).

R. Swinburne Clymer, *The Rosicrucian Fraternity in America* (Quakertown, Penn., 1935).

Francis King, *Sexuality, Magic and Perversion* (Secaucus, N.J., 1972).

EOP, 765.

RAPP, George (November 1, 1757, Iptingen, Württemberg, Germany— August 7, 1847, Economy, Pennsylvania); married Christine Benzinger, 1783.

George Rapp, who led a group of German Pietists to America and founded communities at Harmony, Indiana, and Economy, Pennsylvania, was the son of a farmer and vine-dresser in a small German town. He received a common school education and left school to work as a vine-dresser and weaver. He married in 1783 and fathered two children, John and Rosina. At about the age of thirty, he took a deeper interest in religion. He found a conflict between what he saw at the local parish and what he found described in the New Testament. He also began to develop some distinct theological opinions.

In 1787 he began to preach, gathering a circle of pious believers at his home. His followers soon felt the brunt of persecution, though the ruler of the land tolerated them as they were generally law-abiding citizens. Rapp was called before the king because he refused to attend church.

Around the turn of the century, Rapp, whose following consisted of several hundred families, seeking a more friendly social setting, decided to move his followers to America. To that end, he traveled with his son John to Pennsylvania and in 1803 purchased land at Zelienople. The next year some six hundred of Rapp's followers settled on the land and created the community of property that was to be one of their characteristics. At first, they agreed among themselves to return the investments without interest to any who left but abrogated that practice in 1808. Henceforth, they gave a voluntary gift to any who left the community.

In 1807 Rapp suggested that celibacy be adopted and marriage renounced. The community agreed to live as if unmarried. Both Rapp and his son John led the way in treating their wives as sisters. In the freedom of America, Rapp's ideas were allowed to reach their logical conclusions, and he was allowed to put them into practice in the community. In his Bible study, Rapp had come to believe that Adam was created as an androgynous being, both male and female. When he became discontented, God removed his female side and created Eve. The separation of Adam and Eve was the true fall. Rapp also believed that Jesus was an androgynous person. He concluded from his reading of scripture that celibacy was the most acceptable state in this life, especially since the second coming was near.

In reading the New Testament, he discovered that the early church practiced a community of goods, and as a result he organized his followers as a commune. He taught them values of hard work with their hands, honesty, humility, self-sacrifice, and simplicity. He believed that his community should be self-sufficient. From the beginnings in Germany, Rapp taught his followers to separate from the world but to remain law abiding. They paid their taxes (even their religious taxes) but did not attend the Lutheran Church. In general, that practice was followed in America, where they refused to vote. Rapp's adopted son represented the community in worldly affairs and served in various capacities outside the community. He, for example, helped write the first constitution for the state of Indiana.

In 1815 Rapp led his community in selling its property in Pennsylvania and settling on the Wabash River. Here his followers created their most famous settlement, Harmony. During the ten years there, Harmony became the largest city in Indiana, but in 1824 Rapp decided to abandon it and move back to Pennsylvania. A new town, Economy, was created; it became the permanent home of Rapp and the community.

Rapp rose to a position of complete authority at Harmony and Economy. He was considered a prophet and saint by his followers and seems to have ruled with a benevolent paternalism. He preached three times each week, at two Sunday services and on Thursday evening. He placed great reliance upon confession of sins and admonished each person to confess daily. Each evening he set aside time to listen to those confessions. He loved music and flowers and promoted musical education for all. Flower gardens were a common sight in the community; an elaborate labyrinth was constructed at Harmony.

Rapp was active until the end of his life; he preached from his sickbed through a window just a few days before his death at the age of eighty-nine.

George Rapp, *Thoughts on the Destiny of Man* (Harmony, Ind., 1824).

Karl J. R. Arndt, ed., *A Documentary History of the Indiana Decade of the Harmony Soceity*, 1814–1824, 2 volumes (Indianapolis, Ind., 1975, 1978).

Hilda Adam Kring, *The Harmonists* (Metuchen, N.J., 1973).

Karl J. R. Arndt, *George Rapp's Harmony Society, 1785–1847* (Philadelphia, Penn., 1965).

Donald E. Pitzer and Josephine M. Elliott, "New Harmony's First Utopians," *Indiana Magazine of History* LXXV, 3 (September 1979).

George B. Lockwood, *The New Harmony Movement* (New York, 1905).

DRB, 373–4.

DAB, 15, 383–4.

WWWH, 432.

REES, Seth Cook (August 6, 1854, Westfield, Indiana—May 22, 1933, Pasadena, California); married Hulda Johnson, December 1876 (d. 1898); married Frida Marie Stromberg, November 1899.

Seth C. Rees, one of the founders of the Pilgrim Holiness Church (now a constituent part of the Wesleyan Church), was born to devout Quaker parents in Westfield, Indiana, the same Quaker community that a generation later produced Pentecostal leader A. J. Tomlinson. He attended the Friends' Westfield Academy, which provided Rees with all of the formal education he possessed. At the age of nineteen, he was converted at a protracted meeting in his hometown. A short time later, he took the occasion of a quarterly meeting at the Friend's Church to preach his first sermon. Having felt a call to preach, he ministered at various churches in the area. His future wife, described as a "backslider," was won anew to faith under his preaching.

After his marriage he became a pastor and served a number of different churches in the Midwest. For two years in the 1880s he became a missionary to the Modoc, Cherokee, and Peoria Indians in Kansas.

In 1883, while serving his first pastorate, he experienced sanctification, an experience that characterized the holiness movement of the late nineteenth century. Holiness doctrine taught that after an initial salvation-justification experience (conversion) a believer could, by a second work of God's grace, be cleansed from inbred sin and made perfect in love. After his sanctification, Rees became closely associated with Albert B. Simpson, founder of the Christian and Missionary Alliance. He preached for Simpson at his summer camp in Old Orchard, Maine. While pastoring a church in Raisin Valley, Michigan, he served as president of the Michigan Auxiliary of the Christian and Missionary Alliance.

From 1894 to 1896 Rees pastored the independent holiness congregation, Emmanuel Church, in Providence, Rhode Island. Despite his success, he felt confined and left the church to enter full-time evangelistic work. On a trip to Cincinnati, he met Martin Wells Knapp and discovered the work he was building. In 1897 he joined with Knapp in the formation of the International Holiness Union and Prayer League. He became its first president and is credited with giving it a strong vision of a worldwide ministry. He led the union, first as president and then as superintendent until 1905. Following Knapp's death in 1901, disagreement arose over the use of funds sent in by readers of *The Revivalist*, the periodical associated with the union. Rees's minority opinion that they should all go to foreign missionaries led to his resignation.

Rees spent the next seven years in evangelistic work, with the usual marked success. He promoted missions and initiated the organization of ten rescue homes for women in various cities (the first of which had been founded in Chicago in 1901). Then in 1912 he became pastor of the University Church of the Nazarene, located adjacent to the Nazarene University in Pasadena, California. He developed a close relationship with Dr. H. Orton Wiley, president of the university. However, within the Church of the Nazarene, opposition developed to both Rees and Wiley. In the midst of the controversy, Rees and his congregation were excommunicated. Thus in 1917 Rees organized the Pentecostal Pilgrim Church (name later changed to Pilgrim Church of California). No sooner had the new church been organized than Rees found support from other congregations who left the Nazarenes and joined him. His congregation became a denomination. Rees founded a periodical, *The Pilgrim*, opened Pilgrim Bible College, and continued to lead his congregation, whose 325 members supported over twenty foreign missionaries.

In 1922 the Pilgrim Church of California merged with the Union that Rees had helped found in Cincinnati, and the new organization took the name Pilgrim Holiness Church. Rees became one of three superintendents and upon its reorganization in 1930 was elected its sole general superintendent, a position he held for the rest of his life.

In 1968 the Pilgrim Holiness Church merged with the Wesleyan Methodist Church to become the Wesleyan Church.

Seth C. Rees, *The Ideal Pentecostal Church* (Cincinnati, Ohio, 1897).

———— , *Fire from Heaven* (Cincinnati, Ohio, 1899).

———— , *Back to the Bible: or, Pentecostal Training* (Cincinnati, Ohio, 1902).

———— , *The Holy War* (Cincinnati, Ohio, 1904).

———— , *Wings of the Morning* (Greensboro, N.C., 1926).

Paul Westphal Thomas and Paul William Thomas, *The Days of Our Pilgrimage* (Marion, Ind., 1976).

Paul S. Rees, *Seth Cook Rees, the Warrior Saint* (Indianapolis, Ind., 1934).

REMEY, Charles Mason (May 15, 1874, Burlington, Iowa—February 4, 1974, Florence, Italy); married Gertrude Heim Klemm, July 17, 1931 (d. August 5, 1932); education: Cornell University, 1893–96; Ecole des Beaux-Arts, 1898–1902.

Charles Mason Remey, for many years a leading figure in the Baha'i faith and claimant to be the second Guardian of the Faith, was born of a distinguished family. His father, Rear Admiral George Collier Remey, had been a Civil War veteran and a distinguished naval officer for over forty years. The destroyer *U.S.S. Remey* was named in his honor. As the eldest son, Charles Mason chose a career in architecture and traveled to Paris to complete his graduate work. While in Paris he joined a Baha'i group and two years later in 1901 traveled to Haifa for his first meeting with Abdu'l-Baha who had succeeded his father as leader of the faith.

After his education was completed, Remey moved to Washington, D.C., to become a lecturer and then assistant professor of architecture (1906–1910) at George Washington University. He left his position to become an architect and to devote time to the spread of the Baha'i message. His first main task occurred in 1908. He toured the many scattered Baha'i communities in the Middle East and, at Abdu'l-Baha's request, wrote an account of his travels. He also became a major writer of English-language materials on the Baha'i faith at a time when it was little known in the West. *The Baha'i Movement* (1912) became for many people their first exposition of the history and teachings of the faith.

In 1920, the year before his death, Abdu'l-Baha appointed Remey to design the Baha'i Temple to be built on Mount Carmel in Israel. He would later become the architect for the temples at Kampala, Uganda, and Sidney, Australia.

Abdu'l-Baha was succeeded as leader of the faith by his grandson, Shoghi Effendi. Effendi called Remey to Haifa to assume an international leadership role. In 1951 Effendi institutionalized the international administration of the Baha'i faith by creating the International Baha'i Council. Remey was named to the council as its president. In December 1951 Effendi turned the informal title, Hands of the Cause, into a formal leadership group charged with administratively overseeing the faith. Remey was among the first group named as Hands of the Cause.

In 1957 Effendi died without leaving a will and testament or naming a successor as Guardian. No member of the family remained alive who was loyal to the faith. Remey joined with the other Hands of the Cause in proclaiming the formation of a Baha'i World Center made up of nine Hands of the Cause to assume the function of the Guardian. Remey was one of the nine. During the next few years, however, Remey dissented from the position of the Hands. He argued that the Guardianship was a necessary feature of the structure of the faith. He also asserted that, as president of the International Baha'i Council (a position assigned Remey by Effendi), he was the only one in a position to become the Second Guardian. After waiting for two years for the Hands to accept his position, he left Haifa in 1959 and came to America. In April 1960 he issued a proclamation to the Baha'is of the world and circulated it prior to the annual gathering of American Baha'is that year. He also issued a pamphlet, *A Last Appeal to the Hands of the Faith*, asking them to abandon plans to elect members to the International Baha'i Council in 1961. The Hands rejected his claims and expelled him from the faith.

Through the 1960s Remey continued to assert his opinions, and in 1968 he appointed the first five elders of the Baha'i Epoch. He announced the organization of those loyal to him as the Second Guardian under the name The Orthodox Abha World Faith. Remey retired to Florence, Italy, and lived the last ten years of his life there. After his death two men claimed that Remey had appointed them to be the Third Guardian: Donald Harvey and Joel Marangella. Harvey's followers are represented by the Charles Mason Remey Society, and Marangella's followers are now known as the Mother Baha'i Council of the United States.

Charles Mason Remey, *The Baha'i Movement* (Washington, D.C., 1912).

───── , *Observations of a Baha'i Traveller* (Washington, D.C., 1914).

───── , *Extracts from Daily Observation of the Baha'i Faith Made to the Hands of the Faith in the Holy Land* (n.p., 197–).

───── , *Twelve Articles Introductory to the Study of the Baha'i Teachings* (New York, 1925).

───── , *Universal Consciousness of the Baha'i Religion* (Fuenze, Italy, 1925).

Francis Cajetan Spataro, *The Lion of God* (Bellerose, N.Y., 1981).

───── , *The Remeum* (Bellerose, N.Y., 1980).

WWW, 6, 341.

RICHMOND, Olney H. (February 22, 1844, St. John's, Clinton County, Michigan—March 30, 1920, Chicago, Illinois); married.

Olney H. Richmond, founder of the occult Order of the Magi, was born and raised in Michigan. At the age of seventeen, he enlisted in the 14th Michigan Infantry and served throughout the War Between the States. In the spring of 1864, while stationed in Nashville, Tennessee, he encountered a mysterious stranger who called him Yenlo (Olney spelled backward). The stranger introduced him to the ancient Egyptian Order of the Magi and told Richmond that he had been picked as the stranger's successor to carry on the work. The following evening Richmond was initiated and invested with the secrets and work of the order. He was designated the "keeper of the word." He never saw the stranger again. After the war Richmond returned to Michigan and settled successively at Cedar Springs, Pierson, and Grand Rapids. He became a successful businessman as head of a drug and chemical manufacturing company. He married and had two daughters.

Richmond admitted in later years to understanding almost nothing of what took place in Nashville. In 1871, however, he had a sudden urge to visit Chicago. While there, he encountered a man from Charleston, South Carolina, who gave him a book that contained some of the words given him in Nashville. This book provided the key he needed to understand the information he had previously received and to direct his studies for the next eighteen years. Mathematics, astrology, and cartomancy were the focuses of his efforts.

In 1889 Richmond felt sufficiently accomplished in his occult studies to open the first Temple of the Magi in Grand Rapids, Michigan. Interest in his work was increased by a series of articles in the *Grand Rapids Daily Democrat* in the spring of 1890 in which Richmond first expounded his teaching publicly. The articles were picked up and reprinted by the Chicago occult newspaper *The Progressive Thinker*. The response was so great that Richmond sold his business in Grand Rapids and moved to Chicago. For the rest of his life he devoted his full time to teaching and the building of the order.

By 1893 he had published his first two books, *Temple Lectures*, the most systematic exposition of his teachings, and *The Mystic Test Book*, his study of cartomancy and astrology. In 1896 a third book, *Evolutionism*, appeared. In 1901 he organized the Church of the Veritans for those occultists who were not initiates of the order but wished to benefit from the order's teachings.

Richmond's teachings and the order pioneered the revival of occultism and occult religion that began in the late nineteenth century in the United States. He taught the ancient wisdom; that is, he claimed that his work directly descended from an ancient order that had been transmitted from Atlantis to Egypt, where it flourished, and from where it came into early Christianity. Centuries ago, it had gone underground only to reemerge through its modern-day exponent.

For Richmond the ancient wisdom was based upon astrology, the observation of the planets and their effects on human life. From that observation, and the observation of nature in general, humankind can learn the mystic properties of matter and spirit and of the occult potencies and forces of nature. Once known, they can be exploited for human betterment.

Like most occultists, Richmond saw his teachings as completely scientific in nature. He espoused evolution as a key element in the order's worldview. He also claimed to teach only what could be proved and demonstrated. He rejected belief in bodily resurrection, a material heaven, and an eternal hell and taught a belief in reincarnation.

After Richmond's death in 1920, his daughter, Arline L. Richmond, succeeded him as leader of the order. She kept it going until the 1940s, but it disbanded after her death.

Olney H. Richmond, *Religion of the Stars or the Temple Lectures* (Chicago, 1891).

———— , *The Mystic Test Book or the Magic of the Cards* (Chicago, 1893).

———— , *Evolutionism* (Chicago, 1896).

Arline L. Richmond, *Yenlo and the Mystic Brotherhood* (Chicago, 1945).

RIGDON, Sidney (February 19, 1793, Piny Fork, Pennsylvania—July 14, 1876, Friendship, New York); married Phoebe Brooks, June 12, 1820 (d. 1886).

Sidney Rigdon, Mormon leader and founder of a short-lived branch of the Mormon movement, was the son of a staunch Baptist farmer. Largely self-educated, Sidney had to support his family after his father died in 1810. In 1817 he professed a conversion and joined the United Baptists. The following year he began to study for the ministry and was licensed to preach in 1819. He moved to Warren, Ohio, and became known as a powerful preacher. He helped organize the Mahoning Baptist Association, a fellowship of Baptist churches in northeast Ohio. In 1822 he became pastor of the First Baptist Church in Pittsburgh (in the Redstone Association), a position he held for two years. He then worked as a tanner until he was called to Mentor, Ohio, as pastor.

During the 1820s Rigdon had become heavily influenced by the various religious options available on the American frontier. His early contact with the Shakers convinced him of the rightness of Christian communal living. He also met Alexander Campbell, who had in 1823 moved his church into the Mahoning Association where he could develop the ideas that would lead to the founding of the Disciples of Christ with less opposition than in the Redstone Association. Although Rigdon had been initially impressed with Campbell, the two disagreed on the issue of communal living. They split with each other in 1830 when Rigdon assisted in the formation of a community of about one hundred of his church members on a farm at Kirkland, Ohio.

In the fall of 1830, Rigdon received a visit from Parley P. Pratt, a young man Rigdon had converted several years earlier. Pratt introduced Rigdon to the *Book of Mormon* and the Church of Jesus Christ of Latter-day Saints. Rigdon was converted, and in December 1830, he journeyed to New York to meet Joseph Smith, the Mormon prophet. During his brief visit, he became a leader in the church. Smith received a revelation for Rigdon personally and had Rigdon assist him in the preparation of what became his "Inspired Version" of the Bible. Before Rigdon left, Smith received a revelation that the Saints, the Mormons, should move to Kirkland.

Because a number of Rigdon's parishioners followed him into the Latter-day Saints, and others were attracted because of his efforts and reputation, the church experienced a major growth. He also helped initiate the Mormon settlement in Missouri. All was well until March 1832 when both Smith and Rigdon were attacked by a mob and tarred and feathered. Rigdon was traumatized, and his resultant mental problems led to Smith's revoking his license to preach. When he did recover, he was accepted back into the leadership and in 1833 was named to the first presidency, a position second only to Smith. Rigdon remained Smith's closest adviser during the 1830s until the expulsion of the Saints from Missouri and the establishment of the settlement at Nauvoo, Illinois.

In 1839 Rigdon fell ill for a long period and lost Smith's ear. In 1841 he was released from the first presidency, ostensibly because of his illness. In fact, he and Smith were having strong disagreements, which came to light in 1842 when he accused Smith of trying to seduce his daughter. The resulting scandal occurred at the very time that Smith was introducing the church's leaders to his ideas about polygamy. Smith tried to have Rigdon expelled from the church. Before that could be accomplished, Smith was killed by a mob who broke into the Carthage county jail where he was being held in protective custody. Rigdon moved to assert his right to head the church but lost out in a power struggle to Brigham Young. On September 8, 1844, Young excommunicated Rigdon and all his supporters.

Rigdon moved back to Pittsburgh. He gathered up the anti-Young, antipolygamy Saints, and in April 1845 established his own branch of the Church of Christ. The group settled on a farm near Greencastle, Pennsylvania. The entire enterprise came to an end two years later when the church went bankrupt and was unable to meet the payment on the farm. The group members drifted into other splinters, although most found their way into the one formed by William Bickerton.

After the bankruptcy Rigdon moved to Friendship, New York, and lived in retirement for his remaining years. He did not join any of the other Mormon factions. He discussed his life as a Mormon very rarely. He did occasionally defend his reputation against the charges that he had worked in a printing office where he had found a manuscript by Solomon Spaulding. Anti-Mormons accused him of delivering that manuscript to Smith who used it as a basis for the *Book of Mormon*. Rigdon asserted to the end that he had known neither Smith nor the *Book of Mormon* until 1830, and reputable scholarship that has examined the Spaulding hypothesis extensively supports Rigdon and has found no evidence of a prior connection.

F. Mark McKiernan, *Voice of One Crying in the Wilderness: Sidney Rigdon, Religious Reformer* (Lawrence, Kans., 1971).

DRB, 380–1.
DAB, 15, 600–01.
WWWH, 443.

ROBERTS, Benjamin Titus (July 25, 1823, Cattaraugus, New York— February 27, 1893, Cattaraugus, New York); married Ellen L. Stowe, May 3, 1849; education: Wesleyan University, Middletown, Connecticut, 1845–48.

Benjamin Titus Roberts, founder and first general superintendent of the Free Methodist Church, grew up in the famous "Burned-Over District" of western New York. He originally chose law as a profession and in 1842 moved to Little Falls to study in the office of a Mr. Link. Two years later he returned to his hometown and during a meeting at his home church gave his life to God. He gave up the study of law and redirected his life into the ministry. Early in 1845 he began two terms at Lima Seminary (a high school) to prepare himself to enter Wesleyan University. During his years at Wesleyan he taught Sunday school at a black church, which greatly influenced his opinions on slavery. Daniel Steele, later an outstanding holiness theologian, was his classmate, but he found himself most stirred by the preaching of J. W. Redfield, a Methodist evangelist who conducted an extended meeting in Middletown.

In 1848 he was admitted to the Genesee Conference of the Methodist Episcopal Church and married the niece of George Lane, the church's book agent. He was assigned successively to Careyville (1848); Pike (1849); Rushford (1851); Niagara Street, Buffalo (1852); Brockport (1853); Albion (1855); and Pekin (1857). During the pastorate at Pike, Roberts attended a revival led by Phoebe Palmer and experienced sanctification, the second work of grace that holiness advocates believe makes one perfect in love. Soon afterwards he began to oppose innovations within the Methodist church, such as the pew rentals, the wearing of gold and costly apparel, and the use of organs. Gradually two groups within the conference appeared, the reformers who wished to return to old standards and a larger group that favored change.

In 1857 Roberts wrote an article for the *Northern Independent* that he called "New School Methodism." He attacked all of the innovations that he felt were sapping Methodism. At the Genesee Conference later that year, he was tried for immoral and un-Christian conduct in condemning his fellow ministers. He was censured publicly by the bishop. During 1857–58 the "New School Methodism" article was reprinted as a pamphlet. In 1858 he was retried, as was his colleague Joseph McCreedy, and expelled.

Roberts appealed to the Methodist Episcopal General Conference (due to meet in 1860). Meanwhile, denied an appointment, he traveled and spoke to audiences whenever allowed. Groups of lay followers held meetings to protest the Genesee Conference's action. In August 1860, after the General Conference refused to accept Robert's appeal, they met and formed the Free Methodist church. They elected Roberts general superintendent, a post he held for the rest of his life. He organized the first society three days later, August 26, 1860, at Pekin, New York.

Roberts wrote the constitution and *Discipline* for the new church and edited a hymnal. He wrote an apology entitled *Why Another Sect* and became the editor of a monthly periodical, the *Earnest Christian*. From his Rochester home he roamed throughout the conference and nation to found Free Methodist congregations. In 1866 he sold his home in Rochester in order to purchase a farm at North Chili, New York, which became the site of the church's first school. He personally carried the mortgage for the next twenty years.

In 1910 the Genesee Conference of the Methodist Episcopal Church reviewed the case of Roberts and returned his credentials to his son, thus publicly admitting its error of 1858.

Benjamin Titus Roberts, *Why Another Sect* (Rochester, N.Y., 1879).

———, *Fishers of Men* (Rochester, N.Y., 1878).

———, *First Lessons on Money* (Rochester, N.Y., 1886).

———, *Holiness Teachings* (North Chili, N.Y., 1893).

Benson Howard Roberts, *Benjamin Titus Roberts: A Biography* (North Chili, N.Y., 1900).

Wilson T. Hogue, *History of the Free Methodist Church*, 2 volumes (Winona Lake, Ind., 1915).

Leslie R. Marston, *From Age to Age a Living Witness* (Winona Lake, Ind., 1960).

DAB, 16, 2–3.

EWM, 2, 2029–30.

WWWH, 446.

ROBINSON, Frank B. (July 5, 1886, New York, New York—October 19, 1948, Moscow, Idaho); married Pearl Leavill, 1919 (d. 1982); education: Bible Training School, Toronto; College of Divine Metaphysics, Indianapolis, Indiana, 1915–1916.

Frank B. Robinson, the founder of Psychiana, although he wrote two autobiographies, left much of his life vague and ill-defined. He claimed to have been born in New York, though his brother claimed he was born in Bucks, England. He was raised by a British Baptist minister. His mother died when he was eight, and his father remarried. When he was sixteen, he was given a boat ticket to Canada and a letter of introduction to a Baptist minister. During the next several decades he moved about both Canada and the United States and held a wide variety of jobs. No verification has been found of his having attended and graduated from McMaster University in Toronto, but he did attend the Baptist Bible Training School and was ordained a Baptist minister. He also spent some time in the Salvation Army.

During those early years in Canada, he worked in several pharmacies, a profession that he followed for much of his life, and spent a brief time in the Northwest Mounted Police.

In his autobiographies, Robinson recounts numerous bad experiences with churches and church leaders. Collectively they led him from what he termed "orthodox" faith but spurred his search for God. Two experiences became the turning point in his life. The first occurred in Hollywood, California. He gained the courage to disbelieve everything the church had taught him and to try to find God by other means. Instead of feeling condemned, he felt a deep sense of peace and rest. A few years later, in

Portland, Oregon, after a period in which he had been reading New Thought literature, he had an encounter with God, ". . . God Opened the veil which is supposed to separate us mortals from God, and though God and I are very close now, I shall never forget that day."

Robinson became a follower of New Thought. He attended the College of Divine Metaphysics, an early New Thought school, and earned a Doctor of Divinity degree.

In the decade after his college graduation, he lived on the West Coast and worked at different jobs. In 1928 he became the manager of a pharmacy in Moscow, Idaho, and began his career as a metaphysical teacher. Soon after his arrival in Moscow, he and his family joined the Presbyterian church. He began in the evenings, however, to write a series of lessons that followed the main New Thought emphases of health, happiness, and material prosperity through atunement to God's universal laws. He offered a series of lectures in Moscow and in the spring of 1929 received his first two students. In the summer of 1929 he began to advertise in several national periodicals and developed Psychiana, as he had come to term his teachings, as a mail-order school and religious-teaching organization.

Robinson became a prolific author. His first book, *The God Nobody Knows*, appeared in 1930. It was followed by others including *God and Mr. Bannister* (1941); *The Pathway to God* (1943); and *What God Really Is* (1935). He wrote two accounts of his life: the *Life Story of Frank B. Robinson* (1934) and the *Strange Autobiography* (1941).

In his movement from traditional Christianity to New Thought, Robinson accepted the free-thought critique of Christianity. In 1933 he authored *Crucified Gods Galore*, an attack upon the uniqueness of Jesus' passion, almost entirely paraphrased from the free-thought classic, *The World's Sixteen Crucified Saviors* by Kersey Graves. He also published editions of two works by Joseph Wheless, *Is It God's Word?* and *Forgery in Christianity*.

Within a few years Psychiana grew into one of the largest New Thought organizations, with students in every state and around the world. It continued until Robinson's death and dissolved soon after.

Frank B. Robinson, *Life Story of Frank B. Robinson* (Moscow, Idaho, 1934).

——— , *The Strange Autobiography of Frank B. Robinson* (Moscow, Idaho, 1941).

——— , *The God Nobody Knows* (Moscow, Idaho, 1930).

——— , *God and Mr. Bannister* (Moscow, Idaho, 1941).

——— , *The Pathway to God* (Moscow, Idaho, 1943).

Charles S. Braden, *These Also Believe* (New York, 1949).

ROERICH, Nicholas Konstantinovitch (September 27, 1874 (old calendar), October 9, 1874 (new calendar), St. Petersburg, Russia—December 13, 1947, Kulu Valley, Punjab, India); married Helena Ivanovna Shaposhnikov, 1901; education: University of St. Petersburg, 1893–1895; Academy of Fine Arts, St. Petersburg, 1893–1897.

Nicholas Roerich, co-founder with his wife, Helena Ivanovna Roerich, of the Agni Yoga Society, was the son of a well-to-do lawyer in St. Petersburg, Russia. A precocious youth, young Nicholas developed an early interest in art, archeology, and writing. In his midteens he wrote and illustrated adventure stories that were published and brought him to the attention of art teachers. He also excavated some mounds on the family estate and discovered artifacts from the tenth century. After graduating from the gymnasium, at the age of nineteen he, at the insistence of his father, entered the university to study law. However, he had decided on a career in art, and he continued to study painting above and beyond his university work.

Upon finishing his law degree, he studied full time at the Academy of Fine Arts but left in 1897 out of loyalty to his teacher, who had resigned his position in a dispute with the academy's council. During the next twenty years Roerich became one of Russia's outstanding artists. His work became known throughout Europe and even in America. In 1901 he became secretary to the Society for the Encouragement of the Fine Arts in Russia and five years later became director of their school. He was honored in 1909 by his election to the Russian Imperial Academy of the Fine Arts.

Roerich left Russia in 1917, at the time of the Revolution. He lived in Finland for a few months and then moved to Sweden and England. In 1920 he was invited to the United States by the director of the Art Institute of Chicago. He began a national tour in New York City in December.

Roerich found an immediate response not only to his paintings but to the ideas he had been developing about the unity of the arts. Upon the completion of the tour, he returned to New York and founded the Master Institute of the United Arts on November 17, 1921. Under its motto, "Art will unify all humanity," the Institute began a program of classes in a wide variety of artistic endeavors. The Institute's concerns were embodied in the Roerich Museum founded in 1924.

Roerich, always of a mystic and artistic temperament, encountered the Theosophical Society, founded by H. P. Blavatsky, and he and his wife joined. They subsequently became associated with several Theosophical organizations, such as the Arcane School headed by Alice A. Bailey. Theosophy teaches the existence of a divine hierarchy whose role it is to guide the course of human history and to instruct the human race in spiritual truths. Madame Blavatsky and Alice Bailey claimed to have received personal instruction from the members of the hierarchy.

The Roerichs became devoted students of Theosophy, and Helena translated Blavatsky's major work, *The Secret Doctrine,* into Russian. Shortly after their acceptance of Theosophy, Helena also claimed to have encountered Master Morya, designated by Madame Blavatsky as one of the masters of the Seven Rays, representative of the aspect of Will. Morya gave teachings to Helena, which were published in a series of books, the first being *Leaves of M's Garden,* volume I (1924). Eventually thirteen volumes were published. The Agni Yoga Society began as a group of students gathered informally to study the material.

In 1924 Roerich began a tour of Asia that lasted for five years and culminated in his settling in the Punjab in 1929. He founded Urusvati, the Himalayan Research Institute, in 1928 to carry on archeological and related research. It is headquartered in Naggar, Punjab. Roerich continued to travel during his last years. During the 1930s he promoted the idea of a Peace Pact to protect cultural treasures in time of war. The interest in the Peace Pact was lost during World War II.

The headquarters of the Agni Yoga Society is located in the same building that houses the Roerich Museum (which keeps a vast display of Roerich's art on display). It circulates the Agni Yoga books and promotes study groups built around them.

Nicholas Roerich, *Adamant* (New York, 1922).

——— , *Flame in Chalice* (New York, 1929).

——— , *Heart of Asia* (New York, 1929).

——— , *Realm of Light* (New York, 1931).

——— , *The Banner of Peace* (Calcutta, 1933).

Garabed Paelian, *Nicholas Roerich* (Agoura, Calif., 1974).

Nicholas Roerich, 1874-1974 (New York, 1974).

Message of 1929 (New York, 1930).

Jean Duvernois, *Roerich, Fragments of a Biography* (New York, 1933).

Roerich, a Monograph (New York, 1924).

WWW, II, 455-56.

RUSSELL, Charles Taze (February 16, 1852, Pittsburgh, Pennsylvania—October 31, 1916, Pampa, Texas); married Maria Frances Ackley, 1879 (legally separated, 1906).

Charles Taze Russell, founder of the Watch Tower Bible and Tract Society, was nine when his mother died and was raised a Presbyterian by his father, who was a businessman. In his youth he rejected his Presbyterian training and spent a time in complete unbelief. Charles also seemed destined for a prosperous business career; by the age of fifteen, he was in partnership with his father retailing men's clothes. His career was interrupted by his attendance at some meetings conducted by Adventist Jonas Wendall, and by his acceptance of the belief that the world's end was near and that Christ would come in 1874. In 1868 Russell formed his own Bible study group to explore Scripture in the light of Wendall's teaching.

Over the next decade, working with this group and reading other Adventists, Russell developed his own views: that hell meant annihilation not eternal torment; that humanity had been ransomed from death not eternal hell; that there was no biblical basis for the Trinity; and that Christ did return in 1874, but as an invisible presence. In 1876 he made contact with Nelson H. Barbour, an Adventist and editor of *The Herald of the Morning*, who shared his views on the 1874 date. Russell became co-editor of *The Herald*, and his Bible study group aligned itself with Barbour's in Rochester, New York.

In 1879 Russell broke with Barbour over the doctrine of the ransom atonement and began issuing his own magazine, *The Watch Tower and Herald of Christ's Presence*. He began to issue tracts expounding his position, and a booklet, *Food for Thinking Christians*, appeared the following year. Over one million copies of the booklet were distributed during the next four years. Russell totally gave up secular work in 1877 to work with

Barbour, and he was able to attract some thirty groups of worshippers to his cause by the end of 1880. In 1881 he sent two people to England to distribute *Food for Thinking Christians.*

The remainder of the century consisted of years of steady growth. In 1884 he incorporated Zion's Watch Tower Tract Society (later the Watch Tower Bible and Tract Society). In 1886 he began issuing the *Millennial Dawn* series (later the *Studies in the Scripture*), six more volumes of which appeared through 1904. These volumes contained the most systematic presentation of his mature teachings. In 1889 he opened the Bible House in Pittsburgh as the new headquarters of the society. A trip to Europe in 1891 led to his decision to publish foreign-language editions of his tracts and books and marked the beginning of the spread of his work in Germany and Scandinavia. By 1893 the first national assembly (convention) was held in Chicago, concurrently with the World's Fair.

As Russell's work progressed and his following grew, he became a focus of controversy. A major thrust of his work was the attempt to convert members of the larger churches to his unique doctrinal stance. The increasing tension between Russell and church leaders led directly to the debates with prominent Methodist pastor E. L. Eaton (1903) and Disciples of Christ Elder L. S. White (1908).

In 1909 the society's headquarters were moved to Brooklyn and a second corporation was formed, the People's Pulpit Association. Russell had long predicted that the end of the Gentile sovereignty over the nations would occur in 1914. With that year approaching, Russell increased the activity to reach the public with his message. A new set of tracts, the *People's Pulpit,* was begun and his weekly sermons were syndicated (eventually to 3,000 newspapers).

The beginning of World War I in 1914 seemed to confirm Russell's prediction, but its continuance into 1915 and 1916 did not fit. In the midst of the confusion, Russell died while returning east from a talk in Los Angeles. He was succeeded by Joseph Franklin Rutherford, who led the society through its darkest hours of schism, government persecution, and change into what came to be known in the 1930s as the Jehovah's Witnesses.

Charles Taze Russell, *Food for Thinking Christians* (Pittsburgh, Penn., 1881).

———, *Millennial Dawn* (a.k.a. *Studies in the Scriptures,* 7 volumes (Alleghany, Penn., 1886–99, 1904).

———, *Pastor Russell's Sermons* (Chicago, 1917).

———, *What Pastor Russell Said* (Chicago, 1917).

———, *What Pastor Russell Taught* (Chicago, 1919).

The Laodicean Messenger (Chicago, 1923).

Timothy White, *A People for His Name* (New York, 1967).

Jehovah's Witnesses in the Divine Purpose (Brooklyn, N.Y., 1959).

Alan Rogerson, *Millions Now Living Will Never Die* (London, 1969).

Stan Thomas, *Jehovah's Witnesses* (Grand Rapids, Mich., 1967).

DRB, 385–6.

DAB, 16, 340–1.

WWW, I, 1067.

RUTHERFORD, Joseph Franklin (November 8, 1869, Morgan County, Missouri—January 8, 1942, San Diego, California); married.

"Judge" Joseph Franklin Rutherford, who took the loosely organized Bible Students associated with the Watch Tower Bible and Tract Society and welded them into the Jehovah's Witnesses theocratic organization, was raised on a farm in Missouri. His Baptist father opposed his leaving the farm for a career in law, but Rutherford worked his way through school, in part as a court reporter, and was finally admitted to the bar in Missouri in May of 1892. He began with a law firm in Booneville, Missouri, spent four years as the public prosecutor, and occasionally served as the "special judge" for the 14th Circuit. (He actually served a total of four days in place of the regular judge.)

He first became associated with the Bible Students led by Charles T. Russell in 1894 when he bought a set of Russell's *Millennial Dawn* volumes. He was so impressed that he bought other copies to give away. It was not, however, until 1906 that Rutherford was baptized. He became the society's attorney in 1907 and two years later was admitted to the bar in New York and oversaw the move of the society to Brooklyn. The first of his many writings as a Bible student appeared in 1906. His important work, *A Great Battle in the Ecclesiastical Heavens* (1915), was a defense of Russell.

In 1916 Rutherford was elected president of the Watch Tower Society, but his leadership was immediately challenged by Paul S. L. Johnson and others, including several members of the board of directors. It was secured only after an internal organizational struggle that lasted over a year and cost the society approximately one-fourth of its membership.

No sooner had the trouble over succession begun when even more serious problems fell upon Rutherford. In February 1918 Canada banned the society. Then U.S. army intelligence began an investigation of society activities. Finally, on May 7, 1918, Rutherford and seven other leaders of the society were arrested and charged with advising people against serving in the military. In the midst of the charged emotional climate of the war, Rutherford and the others were sentenced in June to begin eighty-year prison terms. Rutherford remained in federal prison until March 25, 1919, when he was finally released on bail pending appeal. The sentence was reversed.

The war years had been hard on the Bible Students. The expected changes predicted for 1914 had not occurred. The internal battle had sapped its strength, and the imprisonment of its leaders had led to widespread disorganization. Rutherford was determined to build a new organization out of the remnant and to form a tightly-organized society out of the loosely knit Bible student congregations.

As a first step, Rutherford began a new magazine, *The Golden Age* (now *Awake*). He also appointed directors in each congregation to oversee its distribution. The appointment of the directors signaled the gradual change from elected to appointed officers at the congregational level.

Rutherford wrote most of the reorganized society's literature. Beginning in 1922 he annually produced several booklets and usually a book and increasingly organized the membership into campaigns to get the literature read and into the hands of a waiting public. In 1931 he gave the Bible Students a new name: Jehovah's Witnesses. By 1938 he had completed the reorganization of the Witnesses into the theocratic organization.

Whereas Russell had targeted the churches as major institutions toward which proselytization should be attempted, Rutherford saw the churches, that is, Christendom, as the enemy of God's purpose and people. He openly and vehemently attacked them, especially the Catholic Church whom he took pains to identify with Nazism as World War II was beginning. In contrast to the human organizations, Rutherford called the Witnesses to remember their nonaligned status. The increase of nationalistic feelings in the 1940s caused severe persecution to Jehovah's Witnesses, who were viewed as subversives and disloyal in almost every nation.

Throughout World War II the Witnesses followed Rutherford's lead, though he died in 1942 at the age of seventy-two in the society's home in San Diego.

Joseph F. Rutherford, *Man's Salvation from a Lawyer's Viewpoint* (1906).

————, *Millions Now Living Will Never Die* (Brooklyn, N.Y., 1920).

————, *The Harp of God* (Brooklyn, N.Y., 1921).

————, *Deliverance* (Brooklyn, N.Y., 1926).

————, *Children* (Brooklyn, N.Y., 1941).

Timothy White, *A People for His Name* (New York, 1967).

Jehovah's Witnesses in the Divine Purpose (Brooklyn, N.Y., 1959).

Alan Rogerson, *Millions Now Living Will Never Die* (London, 1969).

Chandler W. Sterling, *The Witnesses* (Chicago, 1975).

Edward Curran, *Judge "for Four Days" Rutherford* (Brooklyn, N.Y., 1940).

DRB, 387–8.

SAI BABA of Shirdi (1856?, Hyderabad, India—October 15, 1918, Shirdi, Maharashtra State, India).

Almost nothing about the early life of this Indian holy man is known. He is believed to have been born to a Brahmin family in a small town in Hyderabad State, India, but the name of his family, even his name at birth, and the facts of his early life were never discovered. What is known is that he became one of the most influential fakirs in early twentieth-century India and, without founding a new organization, he influenced numerous teachers who did build large worldwide movements.

Sai Baba left home when he was eight years old to follow a Muslim teacher. When his teacher died, he associated himself with a Hindu guru named Venkusa. As a young lad of sixteen he appeared in the village of Shirdi in Maharashtra State, where he stayed for three years, living under a margosa tree. He disappeared for a year and then returned. No one knew his name, but the priest of a local temple called him Sai and the people began to call him Sai Baba. He wore only meager clothing and no shoes. He kept to himself and spoke only in answer to questions. He took up residence in a small mud-walled mosque and begged food in the town, distributing most of what he collected to the poor.

One incident changed the townspeople's attitude toward him. It grew out of his fondness for light. He would beg oil in the village and keep his lamps burning far into the night. One day the shopkeepers decided to tease him by not giving him any oil. The shopkeepers then went to the mosque to see what Sai Baba would do. Much to their amazement, he filled his lamps with water. They burned as if with oil.

In 1886, about ten years after he settled in Shirdi, a second incident led the townspeople to believe that they had someone unusual in their midst. He entered *samadhi*, the highest state of meditative consciousness in which wakefulness is transcended, and he remained in the state for three days. After this incident he began to be known outside of Shirdi. Also after this incident, accounts of miracles began to grow. People claimed to experience spontaneous ecstacy in his presence. They reported that he visited them in their dreams. Incidents of his clairvoyance circulated. Most importantly, many claimed that Sai Baba had healed them. Frequently he used the *udhi*, the ash from the sacred fire he kept burning in the temple. As the stories circulated, people began to come from all over India to visit him.

People quite naturally began to see Sai Baba as their guru. In 1908 he began to be worshipped as a god. The practice started with a child of four who spontaneously placed some flowers on him in a manner proper to a temple deity.

As a teacher, Sai Baba advocated a system of devotion to the guru. He merged qualities of both Hinduism and Islam. He advocated vegetarianism (from Hinduism), while using Muslim mantras and prayers. He admonished followers to remain in the faith in which they were raised but to attend the festivals of others.

Sai Baba stayed in Shirdi all the last years of his life. He died and was buried there; his resting place has become a shrine and place of pilgrimage. He is still remembered decades later as one of India's most famous holy men. His influence has been extended, however, by the several gurus who were influenced by him. Meher Baba spent time with both Sai Baba and another of Sai Baba's followers, Sri Upasani Baba. Satya Sai Baba considers himself the reincarnation of Sai Baba. Both Meher Baba and Satya Sai Baba have growing movements in North America.

Arthur Osborne, *The Incredible Sai Baba* (New Delhi, India, 1957).

D. P. Sham Rao, *Five Contemporary Gurus in the Shirdi (Sai Baba) Tradition* (Madras, India, 1972).

EOP, 794.

SANDFORD, Frank Weston (October 2, 1862, Bowdoinham, Maine—March 4, 1948, Hobart, New York); married Helen Finney, July 12, 1892 (d. November 24, 1941); education: Bates College, graduated 1886; Cobb Divinity School.

Frank Weston Sandford, founder of the Kingdom, Inc. (popularly known as the Church of the Living God and as the Holy Ghost and Us Society), was born in rural Maine. His father was a farmer. Sandford became a schoolteacher while still in his teens. At the age of eighteen, he attended some evangelistic services and was converted. Becoming serious about a career, he began classes at Nichols Latin School in February 1880 to prepare for college. He played baseball in college but gave it up for a law career, which he, in turn, relinquished for the ministry. After finishing his divinity schooling, he served Free Baptists congregations at Topsham and at Somersworth, Maine. While at Somersworth he began to hear the voice of God speaking to him. The first of several crucial messages from God, the single word "Go," led him to resign his pulpit on January 1, 1893, and begin life as an independent evangelist. He briefly associated with A. B. Simpson of the Christian and Missionary Alliance, who had a summer camp at Old Orchard, Maine. He also went on his first round-the-world tour in the winter of 1890–91 to learn about the state of missionary endeavors.

During his years as an evangelist, many people were attracted to Sandford, and with six students, he began building a Bible school on land donated to him outside of Durham, Maine. The school opened in 1897 and slowly grew into a complete community. Within a few years a hospital building, a children's building, and residence center were completed. The center was named Shiloh, and a Post Office was designated by the government.

In November 1901 Sandford had the second of the crucial messages from God, "Elijah is here—testify." Based upon these words, Sandford came to believe that he was Elijah returned as one of the witnesses to the events of the last days as mentioned in Revelation 11. By virtue of that authority, he established the Kingdom, an act believed to answer the petition in the Lord's Prayer, "Thy Kingdom come." His temporal authority over the Kingdom was firmly established in 1903 when, through a message from God, Sandford was named as David, that is, designated as king. The Kingdom was formally incorporated in 1904.

Sandford ruled the Kingdom as an autocrat, and his often harsh and arbitrary use of power led to significant opposition. Exposés were published in the local newspapers. In 1903 he lost the support of Rev. N. H. Harriman, a leader in the Kingdom, and his printer, M. A. Ledger, who left and claimed his printing press. The year climaxed with Sandford's indictment for cruelty to children and manslaughter (responsibility for a minor who died from neglect). He was convicted of cruelty and fined one hundred dollars.

Recovering from his trial, Sandford purchased two ships and in 1906 left for Palestine to begin the establishment of the Kingdom in Jerusalem. While one ship returned to Maine, in early 1907, Sandford set out on a two-year voyage around the world, the first of several missionary tours in the next few years. Trouble awaited his return in the fall of 1911, however, as he was again charged with manslaughter in the case of six crew members who had died at sea. In December 1911 he was convicted and began serving a ten-year sentence in the federal penitentiary at Atlanta, Georgia. He quietly accepted his fate, and during the years in jail he taught a prison Bible class. He kept up with his followers through correspondence and their visits to Atlanta.

Released in August 1921, he returned and assumed control of Shiloh. Two years later he disbanded the community and moved the headquarters to Boston, to the Kingdom center called "Elim." Sandford lived in semiretirement, teaching occasionally and writing. He died in his eighties at Hobart, New York, where he lived most of his retirement years.

Decentralized, the Kingdom survives to the present as a small group scattered in congregations around the United States.

Frank Weston Sandford, *Seven Years with God* (Mt. Vernon, N.Y., 1957).

Arnold L. White, *The Almighty and Us* (Ft. Lauderdale, Fla., 1979).

E. P. Woodward, *Sandfordism: An Exposure of the Claims, Purposes, Methods, Predictions and Threats of Rev. F. W. Sandford, the "Apostle" of Shiloh, Maine* (Portland, Me., 1902).

SASAKI, Shigatsu (1882, Japan—May 17, 1945, New York City); married Tomoko Sasaki, 1906; married Ruth Fuller Everett, 1944; education: Imperial Academy of Art, Tokyo, Japan.

Shigatsu Sasaki, the founder of the First Zen Institute of America, was better known as Sokei-an, a name he took from the home of the temple of Zen Buddhism's Sixth Patriarch. During his early life in Japan, he was an artist and, at the age of sixteen, he went to work as a dragon carver for temples undergoing restoration. As a student at the Imperial Academy of Art, he met Sokatsu Shaku, the student of Imakita Kosen and Soyen Shaku. Sokatsu had been sent to Tokyo by Kosen's successor Soyen to revive the Ryomokyo-kai, the lay movement of Zen practitioners.

Sasaki was among a small group of Sokatsu's disciples invited to accompany him in 1906 on a mission to spread the Ryomokyo-kai to the United States. Just prior to their leaving for America, Sasaki married, also at Sokatsu's request, one of the female disciples. The group settled first in Berkeley, California (where some of Sokatsu's former disciples were students), but soon moved to a farm near Hayward. The failure of the farm caused a split, as Sasaki left the group when he disagreed with Sokatsu over trying to continue the farm. The two were reunited when the group gave up the farm and opened the Ryomokyo-kai in San Francisco. In 1910 Sokatsu returned to Japan permanently along with all of the group except Sokei-an and his wife.

Sokei-an wandered north on foot and finally settled in Seattle. His marriage, never a happy one, despite the two children it produced, broke up; his wife returned to Japan in 1914. Sokei-an soon headed east and settled in New York City. He made his living as an artist until he suddenly returned to Japan in 1919. He rejoined his wife and decided to complete his Zen training. For the next decade, he traveled back and forth between the United States and Japan and became a successful writer.

In 1928 Sokei-an completed his Zen training and returned to America permanently. He established the Buddhist Society of America (changed to the First Zen Institute of America in 1945). As the only Zen master in New York, Sokei-an became the teacher of many of the popular Zen proponents of the next generations such as Alan Watts.

The Zen Institute prospered through the 1930s; in November 1941 its headquarters opened on East Sixty-fifth Street in New York City. At the first meeting, Sokei-an announced to his students that after more than ten years of spreading Buddhism in the United States, "Now I commence the second period of my work in New York City." Unfortunately the next month the Japanese bombed Pearl Harbor. Japanese Buddhist priests were among the first put under surveillance. Six months later, Sokei-an was interned for a period of more than a year (June 15, 1942–August 15, 1943).

Among Sokei-an's students was Ruth Fuller Everett, who had been introduced to D. T. Suzuki on a trip to Japan in 1930. In 1932 she spent three months in Nanzen-ji Monastery. In 1938 she settled in New York City and became a staunch member of the Institute and editor of its magazine, *Cat's Yawn*. After Sokei-an's internment Ruth Everett obtained the help of George Fowler, a former student and then commander in the navy, to assist in his release. In 1944 she married Sokei-an to help stabilize the Institute.

Sokei-an's health suffered from the period of internment; he died in 1945 never having recovered his strength. He left to his second wife the task of finding a replacement for him at the Institute and of completing the translation of the *Rinzai-roku* (*Collected Sayings of Rinzai*). She soon moved to Japan to pursue the studies that would allow her to complete the translation work, which was all but finished at the time of her death in 1967. Since Sokei-an's death, the Zen Institute has existed as a lay Zen organization. It has been headed by Mary Farkas, one of Sokei-an's students.

Mary Farkas, "Footsteps in the Invisible World," *Wind Bell* VIII, 1–2 (Fall 1969), 15–19.

Rick Fields, *How the Swans Came to the Lake* (Boulder, Colo., 1981).

SCHWENCKFELD von Ossig, Caspar (1489, Ossig, Silesia, Germany—December 10, 1561, Ulm, Germany); education: University of Cologne, 1505–1507; University of Frankfurt, 1507.

Caspar Schwenckfeld von Ossig, founder of what has come to be called the Schwenckfelder Church, was born into an old noble family that had moved into Silesia at the beginning of the thirteenth century. Caspar was well educated; for ten years (1511–21) he served as an adviser to the successive dukes of Silesia. He emerged into prominence with the beginning of the Reformation.

The Lutheran movement forced Schwenckfeld to give serious study to religion for the first time in his life. After several years of studying the Scriptures and the early church fathers he sided with the reformers and convinced Friedrich II of Liebnitz, the Duke of Silesia, to back the Reformation in his land. He had already formed a brotherhood of Christian men who met together to pray, study the Bible, and discuss religious topics. With a distinctly mystical bent, Schwenckfeld advocated the interpretation of Scripture in a spiritual sense. God is Spirit, he suggested, and the kingdom of God is a spiritual kingdom. He became a lay preacher and was very active in educating the people.

He published his first books in 1523–24. These were followed by twelve theses on the Sacrament sent to Luther in 1525. Schwenckfeld denied the presence of Christ in the Eucharist. He termed the Eucharist not the Body of Christ but the bread and wine of the Lord. Luther rejected his views, and the two reformers parted ways. Schwenckfeld began to see the Eucharist as a source of schism in the church; he decided to suspend observance of it until his spiritual interpretation was accepted as the correct one and unity and peace within the Church were attained.

Schwenckfeld's work led to increased pressure on the government in Silesia from the Holy Roman Emperor. Hence, in 1529, he moved to Strassburg and then to Ulm in 1534. During this period in southern Germany, he continued to preach and teach. He established many conventicles, informal groups that met for prayer and study. He wrote more than a dozen books, mostly of a controversial nature. He asserted, contrary to Lutheran teachings, that the risen Christ had put aside all earthly limitations and had become a new divine man, coequal to the Father.

After moving to Ulm, Schwenckfeld increasingly became the center of controversy. In 1536 he rejected the agreement that the reformers at Strassburg had worked out with the Lutherans. Further conflict with the ministers at Ulm led, in 1539, to their condemnation of his books. In 1540 Philip Melanchthon led a group of theologians meeting at Schmalkalden to condemn his teachings, after which Schwenckfeld went into hiding, where he remained for most of the rest of his life.

In response to the condemnation at Schmalkalden, he wrote his Great Confession. It had little effect in reducing pressure, and the list of theological condemnations continued to grow. In 1542 he began a stay at Justingen under the protection of Philip von Hesse, but the relative freedom ended when Philip was defeated in battle by the Holy Roman Emperor and taken prisoner in 1546. During his years there he penned almost fifty books and wrote several hundred letters.

In 1547 he left Justingen and began a period of clandestine movement. He met with followers, continued to write and publish, and, as the Reformation was consolidated, became wanted throughout Germany. Toward the end of the 1550s his health failed, and in 1561 he settled quietly in Ulm. After his death, his body was buried secretly (according to the most accepted tradition) in the basement of the home where he was hiding.

Followers survived in southern Germany for about a century and in Silesia until the early 1700s. A renewed period of persecution in the 1730s caused all the Schwenckfelders to migrate to Pennsylvania where five congregations and 2,700 members can be found today.

Selina Gerhard Schultz, A Course of Study in the Life and Teachings of Caspar Schwenckfeld von Ossig Pennsburg, Penn., 1964).

Peter C. Erb, Schwenckfeld and His Reformation Setting (Valley Forge, Penn., 1978).

Rufus M. Jones, Spiritual Reformers in the 16th and 17th Centuries (New York, 1914).

George H. Williams, The Radical Reformation (Philadelphia, Penn., 1962).

SCOTT, Orange (February 13, 1800, Brookfield, Vermont—July 31, 1847, Newark, New Jersey); married Amy Fletcher (d. 1835); married Eliza Dearborn, October 6, 1835.

Orange Scott, co-founder of the Wesleyan Methodist Church, was born into a poor family in rural New England. His father made a living as a woodsman and a day-laborer on farms. As a result the family moved frequently. Orange had little education, though he did learn to read. Unable to buy proper clothes, he never attended church. As a teenager he followed his father as an itinerant farmer.

Orange's religious consciousness was awakened in 1820, when, one summer day while working on a farm, he pledged himself to a determined effort to find God. He began to read his Bible and attend church. In September 1820 he experienced a conversion at a Methodist camp meeting in Barre, Vermont, as a result of which he joined the Methodist Episcopal Church. Six months later he was a class leader, and in 1821 he was asked to assist on circuit as a preacher. Thus began a spectacular rise to leadership in the Methodist Church. He was admitted on trial in the New England conference in 1822, and while serving his several charges, he educated himself. In 1830 he began a four-year appointment as presiding elder of the Springfield (Massachusetts) district. He followed that tenure with two years as presiding elder for the Providence (Rhode Island) district. He was elected a delegate to the General Conference for the first time in 1832. In 1836 and 1840, he chaired the delegation.

Trouble with the church, however, began in 1833. He was introduced to abolitionism and the issue of slavery by a colleague, Rev. H. H. White. Once aware of the plight of the slaves, he saw slavery as a chief moral evil. He was embarrassed that the Methodists had left their abolitionist stance of the previous century for a milder policy that simply opposed slavery. He purchased copies of *The Liberator*, William Lloyd Garrison's periodical, circulated them to his fellow ministers in New England, and won them to his position.

Scott rose to national prominence by championing the cause of abolitionism at the 1836 Methodist General Conference. Unfortunately the conference adopted a resolution opposing the abolitionist position, which the bishops then used to silence Scott and his colleagues. Scott retaliated by starting an abolitionist periodical, *The Wesleyan Quarterly Review*. He also began to call for reform of the church's government, having seen the power of the bishops and presiding elders to stop discussion of slavery-related issues.

Because he refused to remain silent on slavery, Scott was released from his post as presiding elder and appointed to the church at Lowell. In 1837 he took a supernumerary status, for health reasons, and for the next two years lectured for the Anti-Slavery Society. He returned to Lowell in 1839.

The 1840 General Conference again took a position against abolitionism. Following the conference Scott again left the parish and moved to Newbury, Vermont. He founded *The True Wesleyan* as a forum for his position. He transferred to the New Hampshire Conference in 1842, just months before he left the church altogether on November 8. He finally lost hope of the Methodists' accepting reform.

In December 1842, joined by others who had also left, Scott called a convention to meet at Andover, Massachusetts, in February 1843 for the purposes of organizing a new church. The group adjourned to Utica, New York, where, in June 1843, they organized the Wesleyan Methodist Connection of America (name changed in 1947 to Wesleyan Methodist Church). Scott became the first president of this abolitionist nonepiscopal Methodist denomination. *The True Wesleyan* was adopted as the new church's periodical.

Scott threw all of his energy into the new organization. Unfortunately, he was already sick with tuberculosis, and the long hours and travel throughout the connection quickly took their toll. In 1846 he moved to Newark, New Jersey, to be nearer the publishing office. He refused to slow down, his health failed, and he died in 1847.

The Wesleyan Methodist Church merged in 1968 with the Pilgrim Holiness Church to form the Wesleyan Church. Having carried the emphasis on personal holiness from the Methodist Episcopal Church, to which it added an emphasis on social holiness. The church easily identified with and became a strong supporter of the holiness movement in the late nineteenth century.

L. C. Matlack, *The Life of Orange Scott* (New York, 1848).

Ira Ford McLeister and Roy S. Nicholson, *History of the Wesleyan Methodist Church* (Marion, Ind., 1959).

EWM, 2112–13.

SENZAKI, Nyogen (1876, Siberia—May 7, 1958, Los Angeles, California).

Nyogen Senzaki, teacher of Zen Buddhism and founder of the Mentorgarten Meditation Hall in Los Angeles, was born in Siberia of a Japanese mother and a father of either Russian or Chinese origin. As a child, he was found next to his frozen mother by a Japanese monk and was subsequently adopted by a shipwright named Senzaki, whose name he took. The shipwright placed him under the care of a scholar trained in both Soto Zen and Kegon Buddhism. The scholar gave the youthful Nyogen a good education. In his teen years, Senzaki began a correspondence with Soyen Shaku and in 1896 he presented himself at Shaku's Engakuji monastery at Kamakura.

When he first moved to the monastery, Senzaki was found to have tuberculosis and was forced to live in semiisolation for a year while he recovered his health. Then, as a student, he roomed with D. T. Suzuki. He studied at Engakuji for five years before leaving to found a nursery school, which he called the Mentorgarten and modeled on the German kindergartens.

In 1905 he left Japan for the United States. He cited at least three reasons: he was unhappy with the state of Japanese Zen, which he saw as in a period of decline; he was unhappy with the militancy of the government then in the midst of the war with Russia; and he also wanted to raise money for his Mentorgarten. Upon arriving in San Francisco, he took a job as a houseboy at the home of the Alexander Russells. They were at that time entertaining his teacher, Soyen Shaku, and beginning to practice Zen. He stayed only a short time, until Soyen Shaku sent him into San

Francisco with the admonition, "Just face the great city and see whether it conquers you or you conquer it."

For several years he worked at odd jobs. In 1910 he became a hotel porter and worked himself up to manager. Eventually, in 1916, he was able to purchase a hotel, but he was a poor businessman and the project failed. He then became a cook.

During the seventeen years after leaving Shaku, he occasionally wrote an article on Zen but taught very little and took no students. Then in 1922, with money saved from his job, he rented a hall and gave a lecture on Zen. Out of this first gathering developed what came to be known as the floating zendo. As money allowed, he would rent a hall, set up his painting of Manjusri, the *bodhisattva* of wisdom, and lecture and teach. On alternate evenings he would direct his attention to first Japanese-Americans and then to non-Japanese Americans.

In 1928 he took the floating zendo to Los Angeles; for three years he moved between San Francisco and Los Angeles. Finally in 1931 he found a permanent location in Los Angeles and established the Mentorgarten Meditation Hall. His efforts stabilized over the next decade, but, like all Japanese-American institutions, the Mentorgarten was disrupted by World War II. In 1942 Senzaki was interned and sent to Heart Mountain, Wyoming. He took the floating zendo with him and established it in a temple at the camp. He also sent monthly lessons to his students in Los Angeles. In 1945 he was released; he returned to Los Angeles to teach for the remaining years of his life.

When Senzaki died, his work disbanded, and he left no continuing organization. Thus Senzaki's significance lies not in his zendo so much as in: (1) his having carried the banner of Rinzai Zen during the years that the Oriental Exclusion Act prevented many Buddhist teachers from coming to the United States; (2) his bringing other Zen teachers, such as Nakagawa Soen, to America; and (3) his inspiring the organizations founded by his students, such as Robert Aiken's Maui Zendo.

Nyogen Senzaki, *Like a Dream, Like a Fantasy,* edited by Eido Shimano Roshi (Tokyo, 1978).

———, *A Lecture on Meditation* (Los Angeles, Calif., n.d.)

——— and Saladin Reps, *The Gateless Gate* (Los Angeles, Calif., 1934).

——— and Ruth Strout McCandless, *Buddhism and Zen* (New York, 1953).

——— Soen Nakagawa and Eido Shimano, *Namu Dai Bosa, A Transmission of Zen Buddhism to America* (New York, 1976).

Rick Fields, *How the Swans Came to the Lake* (Boulder, Colo., 1981).

Emma McCloy Layman, *Buddhism in America* (Chicago, 1976).

Wind Bell, VIII, 1–2 (Fall 1969).

SEYMOUR, William Joseph (May 2, 1870, Centerville, Louisiana— September 28, 1922, Los Angeles, California); married Jenny Evans Moore, May 13, 1908.

William Joseph Seymour, founder of the Pacific Apostolic Faith Movement, and one of the most important figures in the origin of the modern Pentecostal movement, was born in rural Louisiana, the son of former slaves. Little is known of his early life. In 1895 he moved first to Indianapolis, where he joined the Methodist Episcopal Church, and then in 1900 to Cincinnati, where he fell under the influence of Martin Wells Knapp, the holiness preacher who had separated from the Methodists. He joined the Church of God (Anderson, Indiana), the group founded by Daniel S. Warner, popularly known as the "evening light saints," who taught that the holiness movement of the late nineteenth century represented the "evening light" or last spiritual outpouring on God's people before the second coming. While in Cincinnati, Seymour caught and survived smallpox but suffered some facial scarring and loss of the use of one eye. The experience with smallpox led Seymour into the ministry, and he began the life of a traveling evangelist. He moved to Houston, Texas, as a base of operation.

In 1905 Charles F. Parham came to Houston with his new message that proclaimed the possibility of the baptism of the Holy Spirit signified by speaking in tongues. He opened a Bible school. Seymour made contact with Parham through a black woman, Lucy Farrar, who had attended Parham's meetings in Kansas and had experienced the baptism. Seymour attended Parham's classes and slowly came to believe his teachings concerning the necessity of speaking in tongues.

Meanwhile, in Los Angeles, a group of Baptists who had become holiness people were kicked out of their church and began to hold independent services. Among their number was Neely Terry, a black woman who had also attended Parham's classes in Houston. She convinced the group to invite Seymour to become their pastor. With the assistance of Parham, Seymour traveled to Los Angeles in March 1906. As the text for his first sermon, Seymour chose to speak on Acts 2:4 and expound the new doctrine concerning the baptism of the Holy Spirit. The new idea offended some of the holiness people, and they locked Seymour out of the church. Richard and Ruth Asberry then invited him to hold a meeting in their home at 214 North Bonnie Brae Street. There on April 9, 1906, just nine days before the San Francisco earthquake, the Spirit fell, and the first person spoke in tongues. She was Jenny Moore, who eventually married Seymour, who in turn spoke in tongues three days later.

The Bonnie Brae location soon proved too small, and Seymour located an abandoned Methodist church building at 312 Azusa Street. For the next three years meetings were held daily. Seymour led the meetings, though most descriptions agree that he subordinated himself to the spontaneous occurrences in the congregation. He generally sat behind the cardboard box pulpit in an attitude of prayer.

Seymour organized the Pacific Apostolic Faith movement as an outpost of the work being built by Parham in the Midwest and the South. He began a magazine, the *Apostolic Faith*, which listed Parham as the "projector" of the movement. And it was to Parham he turned when in August 1906 he developed expectations of a great revival. Parham arrived in October, but instead of a revival he and Seymour quarreled and parted company. Parham accused Seymour of allowing fanaticism to reign. Seymour accused Parham of an unidentified indiscretion and disagreed with him over the necessity of sanctification prior to receiving the baptism of the Holy Spirit, which Parham rejected. Despite Parham's departure and even Seymour's establishing rival meetings across town, the work at Azusa Street became known across the United States, and individuals, both black and white, came to witness the revival and to claim the baptism. Many of the people who were to spread the message across the country—C. H. Mason, Glenn Cook, G. B. Cashwell—sat under Seymour.

The break with Parham, however, signaled the loss of the major leadership role that Seymour briefly enjoyed. In 1907 Florence Crawford, who served as the state director of the movement, moved the periodical to Portland, Oregon, where she established a separate apostolic faith work. Then in 1911 Seymour broke with Chicago pastor Wiilliam H. Durham, who had also come to reject Seymour's position on the believer's progression from salvation (justification) to sanctification to baptism in the Holy Spirit.

The breaks with Parham, Crawford, and Durham cost Seymour most of his white members. He remained as the pastor of a predominantly black congregation, largely separated from the major thrust of the movement that by the beginning of World War I had spread to every section of the United States. Seymour became a largely forgotten figure, though his initial contribution to the Pentecostal movement was vital. He also seems to have been among the first to articulate the Pentecostal-Holiness or "three experience" position within Pentecostalism.

William J. Seymour, *The Doctrine and Discipline of the Azusa Street Apostolic Faith Mission of Los Angeles* (Los Angeles, 1915).

Douglas J. Nelson, *For Such a Time as This, The Story of Bishop William J. Seymour and the Azusa Street Revival* (Birmingham, Eng., 1981).

James S. Tinney, "William J. Seymour: Father of Modern-Day Pentecostalism," in Randall K. Burkett and Richard Newman, eds., *Black Apostles* (Boston, 1978).

Leonard Lovett, "Black Origins of the Pentecostal Movement," in Vinson Synan, ed., *Aspects of Pentecostal-Charismatic Origins* (Plainfield, N.J., 1975).

Charles Edwin Jones, *A Guide to the Study of the Pentecostal Movement* (Metuchen, N.J., 1983).

SHAKU, Soyen (1859, Japan—;1919, Kamakura, Japan); education: Keio University, 1884–86.

Soyen Shaku, the first person to bring Rinzai Zen Buddhism to America and to direct Zen toward non-Japanese Americans, was born in Japan in 1859. In 1871 at the age of twelve he was ordained a monk in the Rinzaishu Engakujiha, A Rinzai Zen sect founded in 1282 by Mugaku-Sogen (1213–1278). The leader of the group was Imakita Kosen Roshi (1816–1892), who had developed a unique interest in having his monks university trained and in promulgating Zen among a lay public. During his early years as a monk, Soyen was recognized as an outstanding student; in 1884 he received the dharma transmission from Kosen who declared of Soyen, "He is a born *bodhisattva*."

That same year Soyen began two years of study at Keio University. On completion of his studies, he traveled to Ceylon to study Hinayana Buddhism and Sanskrit. Between his university training and travel abroad,

Soyen began to develop the cosmopolitan perspective that was to characterize his life's work. On his return to Japan, he became the teacher at the Nagata Zendo, a position he held until Kosen's death in 1892, when he succeeded his teacher at Engakuji, the monastery at Kamakura.

That year he received an invitation to speak at the World Parliament of Religions that was being organized by the League of Liberal Clergymen in Chicago, Illinois. It was considered improper for a Zen monk to travel abroad, especially to a "barbarian" country such as the United States. Most advised against it, but true to his cosmopolitan stance, he accepted the invitation.

In Chicago he delivered two addresses, both read by Dr. J. H. Burrows, the president of the parliament, since Soyen could not speak English. He gave one address on Buddhist thought, "The Law of Cause and Effect as Taught by Buddha," and a second on war, "Arbitration Instead of War." More important than his speeches, however, was that Soyen met Paul Carus and after the parliament stayed at his home in LaSalle, Illinois. Carus, the owner of the Open Court Publishing Company, developed an interest in Buddhism as a result of Soyen's visiting the Parliament. The following year he wrote and published the first popular English-language book by an American "advocate" of Buddhism, *The Gospel of Buddhism.*

After the parliament, Soyen returned to Japan to resume his duties at Engakuji. Among his students were the three who would be most important in spreading Zen in the United States, Nyogen Senzaki, Sokatsu Shaku, and D. T. Suzuki. He pursued a normal course as teacher, abbot, and leader of the Rinzaishu Engakujiha until 1905, when Mr. and Mrs. Alexander Russell came to Engakuji to study Zen. The Russells were accepted as students, and they, in turn, persuaded Soyen to return to America with them the following summer.

He lived outside San Francisco at the Russell residence and led the family and servants in the daily practice of Zen. He introduced Mrs. Russell to the practice of the koans, and she became the first American to experience them. While living with the Russells, Soyen also gave lectures in their home and traveled to a number of localities to speak to both Japanese and non-Japanese audiences. D. T. Suzuki joined him as his interpreter. After nine months in San Francisco, accompanied by Suzuki, Soyen journeyed across the United States, lecturing, and returned home by way of Ceylon.

For the remaining years of his life, he lived quietly at Kamakura. Not only did he serve as head of the Rinzaishu Engakujiha but he also assumed leadership of the Rinzaishu Kenchojiha, another Rinzai sect, and became president of Rinzai College. He died in 1919.

Soyen Shaku, *Sermons of a Zen Buddhist Abbot* (Chicago, 1906), reprinted as *Zen for Americans* (LaSalle, Ill., 1974).

———, "The Law of Cause and Effect as Taught by Buddha," in *The World's Congress of Religions*, edited by J. W. Hanson (Chicago, 1894).

Rick Fields, *How the Swans Came to the Lake* (Boulder, Colo., 1981).

Wind Bell, VIII, 1–2 (Fall 1969).

SHOGHI EFFENDI Rabbani (March 1, 1897, Akka (now Acre, Israel)—November 4, 1957, London, England); married Mary Maxwell (Ruhiyyih Khanum), 1937; education: American University, Beirut, Lebanon; Oxford University.

Shoghi Effendi Rabbani, the Guardian of the Baha'i World Faith from 1921 to 1957, was the grandson of Abdu'l-Baha, the second leader of the faith. His mother, Diyaiyyah Khanum, was Abdu'l-Baha's daughter. He was named Abdu'l-Baha's successor when he was about ten years of age and appointed his successor at the age of twenty-four upon the death of Abdu'l-Baha in 1921. He attended college both in Beirut and Oxford, where he was studying when he received the news of Abdu'l-Baha's death. He returned to Haifa to assume leadership of the faith.

It had been his great grandfather's (Baha'u'llah) accomplishment to found and establish the faith, and his grandfather (Abdu'l-Baha) had built it into a worldwide movement. One of Shoghi Effendi's tasks was to organize the loosely knit movement efficiently to carry out the aims and purposes of the religion—the unification of the human race and the establishment of universal and lasting peace. Almost immediately Shoghi Effendi began to develop the organizational structure of the faith. He encouraged the formation, already begun by Abdu'l-Baha, of local spiritual assemblies wherever there were nine members in one location. Where sufficient numbers of Baha'is warranted it, national spiritual assemblies were elected by delegates who had been locally elected. By the mid–1920s, nine such national assemblies were functioning.

To aid the organizational development, he emphasized the distinctiveness of the Baha'i faith. During the time of Baha'u'llah and Abdu'l-Baha, members of the Baha'i faith in the West often (erroneously) continued to be members of other religions. He disavowed dual memberships. He also clarified Baha'i membership: In order to become a Baha'i, an individual must accept the revelations of the Bab and Baha'u'llah and the terms of the Will and Testament of Abdu'l-Baha. The development of the Baha'i administration had few negative repercussions. While some members who held joint memberships withdrew, the vast majority followed the leadership of Shoghi Effendi.

Shoghi Effendi contributed immensely to the literary growth of the religion. Fluent in English, he was able to translate many of the works of Baha'u'llah including *Gleanings from the Writings of Baha'u'llah; Prayers and Meditations; The Hidden Words of Baha'u'llah; The Kitab-i-Iqan; The Seven Valleys and the Four Valleys;* and *Epistle to the Son of the Wolf.* He also translated the *Narrative of Nabil* (English title, *The Dawnbreakers*), an early Baha'i contemporary of the Bab and Baha'u'llah. He wrote many works including a centennial Baha'i history, *God Passes By,* covering the years 1844–1944. His many shorter works—letters, directives, and words of encouragement—have been collected and published in several volumes: *Messages to America; The World Order of Baha'u'llah; Baha'i Administration; The Advent of Divine Justice; Messages to the Baha'i World;* and *The Promised Day Is Come.* While not regarded as scripture, as are the words of his predecessors, Shoghi Effendi's writings carry the weight of authority second only to theirs.

Shoghi Effendi was also responsible for the shaping of the Baha'i faith's identity as an independent world religion on a par with Islam, Christianity, and Judaism. His work on the beautification of the gardens in the precincts of the shrine of Baha'u'llah; his supervision of the construction of the shrine of the Bab and the International Baha'i Archives and their attendant gardens on Mount Carmel; his documentation of Baha'i developments worldwide in *The Baha'i World* volumes; his appointment of representatives to various international congresses; all these steps aided the Baha'i faith's recognition as a world religion.

Shoghi Effendi took his last steps to develop the international organization in the years just prior to his death. In 1951 he appointed "Hands of the Cause of God," a group that reached twenty-seven in number, who assisted him in the propagation and protection of the faith worldwide. Further, he appointed nine Baha'is to serve on the International Baha'i Council, a forerunner of the Universal House of Justice, the international administrative authority that directs the Baha'i world community and administers the international affairs of the religion. After Shoghi Effendi's death, the Hands of the Cause served as an interim governing body until the first Universal House of Justice, who currently guide and administer the affairs of the Baha'i World Faith, was elected in 1963.

Shoghi Effendi Rabbani, *The Advent of Divine Justice* (Wilmette, Ill., 1938).

———— , *Baha'i Administration* (Wilmette, Ill., 1928).

———— , *God Passes By* (Wilmette, Ill., 1944).

———— , *The Promised Day Is Come* (Wilmette, Ill., 1941).

———— , *The World Order of Baha'u'llah* (Wilmette, Ill., 1932).

Amatu'l-Baha Ruhiyyih Khanum, "The Guardian of the Baha'i Faith," in *The Baha'i World*, 1954–1963 (Haifa, 1970), 59–205.

William McElwee Miller, *The Baha'i Faith* (South Pasadena, Calif., 1974).

Jessyca Russell Gayer, *The Baha'i Faith* (New York, 1967).

SIMONS, Menno (1496, Witmarsum, Friesland, Netherlands—January 31, 1561, Wüstenfelde, Germany); married Geertruydt.

Menno Simons, leader of the northern wing of the Anabaptists, from whom the Mennonite Church takes its name, emerged out of obscurity in 1524 when he was ordained to the priesthood at Utrecht and assigned to Pingjum, near his hometown, as vicar. Little is known of his parentage (his father's name was Simon), childhood, or education.

During his first year as a priest he began the questioning that would lead him away from the Roman Catholic Church. While saying the Mass, he began to doubt transubstantiation, that the bread and wine were changed into the body and blood of Christ, an essential Catholic doctrine. In this doubt he was possibly influenced by a group of Dutch reformers called the Sacramentists. Menno turned to the Bible, and through its study became convinced that the Sacraments were to be viewed as symbolic.

His Bible study led to his reading Luther, Zwingli, and the other reformers. His opinion about the Sacraments raised a second issue: the conflict of authority between the Bible and the Catholic Church. Through reading Luther, Menno decided in favor of the Bible. Once having made the change in authority, the path of reform was completely open before him.

Around 1530 Melchior Hofmann introduced the Anabaptist view into East Friesland. News of his work raised the issue of the appropriateness of adult believer's baptism versus infant baptism. Menno turned to the Scripture and finding no mention of infant baptism as practiced by his own church, he concluded that believer's baptism was the proper practice.

Instead of joining the Anabaptists, however, he accepted the assignment as priest in his hometown of Witmarsum in 1531. He also accepted Anabaptist ideas on crucial issues but rejected the Anabaptist apocalyptic vision and their violent and revolutionary activities. He denounced them in his sermons. Then came the defeat of the Anabaptist community at Munster in 1535; the torture and death of the leaders changed Menno. He began to identify with Anabaptism and openly preach its views at Witmarsum.

In January 1536 he left Witmarsum and entered the Anabaptist underground of the Netherlands and northern Germany as an itinerant evangelist. For the next two decades he moved from place to place, preaching and writing pamphlets. At a time and place unknown, he was rebaptized and ordained an elder; during the 1540s he became recognized as the leader of the Anabaptists in the north. In 1542 a reward was offered for his arrest.

As the leader of the Anabaptists, Menno steered a mediating course. He rejected those who were lax in discipline and advocated waiting until the persecution ended before organizing congregations. He also refuted the apocalyptic visions that had so often led to disaster and violent activity. He advocated a strict use of the ban though not the harsh enforcement that would later characterize the Amish.

The year 1554 was an important year for Menno. He participated in the writing of the Wismar Articles, an agreement by the northern Anabaptist leaders on many points of belief and practice. He also wrote and published his most substantive book, *Een Klare beantwoodinge*, a response to the charges of Gellius Faber. Shortly after this book went to the printer in Lubeck, Menno moved to Oldedloe, Holstein, where he found protection at Wustenfelde, the estate of Bartholemew von Ahlefeldt. Here he lived the final years of his life in relative peace.

Menno's leadership pulled together and gave new direction to the Anabaptists in Holland and northern Germany; they became known as Mennonites in recognition of the decisive influence his leadership had given to them. In the eighteenth century they began their migration to the New World and eventually became a worldwide movement.

Menno Simons, *The Complete Writings of Menno Simons*, edited by John Christian Wenger (Scottdale, Penn, 1956).

H. S. Bender and John Harsch, *Menno Simons' Life and Writings* (Scottdale, Penn., 1936).

John Horsch, *Menno Simons, His Life, Labors and Teachings* (Scottdale, Penn., 1916).

Irvin B. Horst, *A Bibliography of Menno Simons* (Nieuwkoop, 1962).

ME 3, 577–84.

SIMPSON, Albert Benjamin (December 15, 1843, Cavendish, Prince Edward Island, Canada—October 29, 1919, Nyack, New York); married Margaret Henry, September 13, 1865; education: Knox College, Toronto, graduated 1865.

Albert Benjamin Simpson, founder of the Christian and Missionary Alliance, was born in Canada's Maritime Provinces, where his father was a shipbuilder and merchant. A few years after Albert's birth, his father lost his business in a general depression, and the family moved to Chatham, Ontario, where Albert was brought up on a farm. At the age of fourteen he decided to prepare for the ministry in the Presbyterian Church in which he had been raised. His father had provided him with a good education, but he realized after he had made the decision to be a minister that he had not experienced salvation. He experienced that salvation a short time later while reading a book, the *Gospel Mystery of Salvation*. At the age of sixteen, be began teaching school to earn the money to attend college. Two years later he appeared before the Presbytery of London in Ontario. He passed his exam and was recommended to attend Knox College, where he proved an outstanding student. After graduation he was ordained and accepted a call to Knox Church in Hamilton.

In 1873, after eight successful years, he moved to Louisville, Kentucky. There, as pastor of a Presbyterian church, he came in contact with the holiness movement and was influenced by its teachings. These years were also marked with success; during his pastorate he led the congregation in the building of the Broadway Tabernacle, which had a seating capacity of two thousand.

In 1880 Simpson moved to New York City as pastor of Thirteenth Street Presbyterian Church. He remained as pastor only two years, for all of the new influences that had come into his life began to culminate. In 1881 he was sanctified and openly identified with the holiness movement. Then, while attending a summer resort at Old Orchard, Maine, he experienced a physical healing of a long-standing condition and so emerged also as a strong advocate of spiritual healing. Finally he had come to believe in adult baptism by immersion. Rather than split his parish over his new convictions, he withdrew.

With a few like-minded people, he formed an independent congregation in 1882. Besides accepting Simpson's doctrinal perspective, the church embodied Simpson's ideal of a missionary-oriented church. Within a few years, it had organized a missionary training college, a ministry to "fallen women," two rescue missions, an orphanage, a mission to sailors, and a medical clinic for the poor. In 1884 the first five missionaries were sent to Africa. Regular meetings that focused upon healing were held on Fridays.

In 1886 Simpson held his first national convention for colleagues who shared his basic evangelistic and missionary interests at Old Orchard. The group decided to organize a mission to Tibet and other places that were without any Christian witness. The following year they formalized their plans by organizing the Evangelical Missionary Alliance. A Canadian branch was formed in 1889 as the International Missionary Alliance. These two bodies merged in 1897 to form the Christian and Missionary Alliance.

By 1893, when Simpson took his first international mission tour, the alliance had missionaries in twelve fields. He visited most of them on a trip that took him through Europe to Egypt, the Holy Land, India, Burma, Singapore, Japan, and Hong Kong.

Simpson was a prolific writer. He began a periodical, *Word, Work and World*, in 1882. It continues today as the *Alliance Weekly*. He wrote more than seventy books, including *The King's Business* (1886); *The Fullness of Jesus* (1886); *Christ in the Bible* (1889); and *The Fullness of Jesus* (1890). A small volume, *The Four-Fold Gospel* details the doctrinal perspective that dominated Simpson's life, the affirmation of Christ as Savior, Sanctifier, Healer, and Coming King. In later years Aimee Semple McPherson would revise it as the Four-Square Gospel. Simpson was also a poet and hymn writer and published two volumes of his work: *Hymns of the Christian Life* (1891) and *Millennial Chimes* (1894).

Simpson lived to see his movement become established as a strong body in America that supported several schools to train missionaries and that had missionary stations around the world in Asia, Africa, and Latin America.

Albert Benjamin Simpson, *The Christian Life* (London, 1911).

———— , *Ernests of the Coming Age* (New York, 1921).

———— , *The Four-Fold Gospel* (New York, 1890).

———— , *The Self Life and the Christ Life* (New York, 1897).

A. Thompson, *The Life of A. B. Simpson* (New York, 1921).

WWW, I, 1128.

SINGH, Jaimal (July 1839, Ghuman, Punjab, India—December 29, 1903, Beas, Punjab, India).

Jaimal Singh, founder of the Radhasoami Satsang Beas, was born into a pious Punjabi Sikh family. According to the biography written by his twentieth-century disciple Kirpal Singh, founder of the Ruhani Satsang, Jaimal Singh was at the age of five placed in the charge of Bhai Khem Das, a learned vedantin. Within the first year, it is claimed, he read the entire *Guru Granth Sahib*, the holy scriptures of the Sikhs. He showed a decided aptitude for the spiritual life, and even after his daily work as a sheep-herder for his father, he practiced his disciplines with his teacher before retiring to sleep. His father tried to temper Jaimal's enthusiasm for religion and sent him to live with his sister in another town. There Jaimal merely found another teacher, a master of *pranayana*, the breathing disciplines of yoga, and continued his studies.

When Jaimal was fourteen, his father died. His years of study of the scriptures and practice of yoga had given Jaimal a desire to find someone who could explain the secret of the "five shabds," *panch nam*, mentioned in the *Guru Granth Sahib*. In his search for a teacher, Jaimal happened to meet an aged sadhu at Hardwar who told him of a sage at Agra who had mastered the practice. Immediately he went to Agra and eventually took initiation at the age of seventeen from Shiv Dayal Singh, the founder of the Radhasoami faith.

Shiv Dayal taught Jaimal Singh the practice of *surat shabd yoga*, "union of the soul with the divine sound current," which enables one to transcend the physical body and enter the higher realms of consciousness. Jaimal, accordingly, was ripe for the discipline and became spiritually adept at meditation almost immediately. However, since Shiv Dayal admonished his disciples to make their own living in the world, Jaimal joined the twenty-fourth regiment of the Punjabi army.

In 1877, shortly before his death, Shiv Dayal gave Jaimal Singh his own turban and commissioned him to preach *Nam* in the Punjab. During the years immediately after the death of his master, Jaimal remained in the army and gave occasional initiations to those souls he deemed fit. However, Jaimal did not begin giving formal initiations until 1884 after Radhaji, Shiv Dayal's wife, had reminded him that his master had left orders for him to give *satsang* and spread *Nam*. He retired from the army in 1889 and eventually settled on the banks of the Beas River. He lived in a little mud hut and taught the path of *Sant Mat* to a small group of disciples.

The later years of his life were marked by two significant events. First, in 1894 while on a *satsang* tour that took him through the town of Murree, he met Sawan Singh who was to become his foremost disciple and successor. Second, though Jaimal Singh had close connections with the Radhasoami groups in Agra, he did not agree to the formation of the central administrative council in 1902. He thought that Rai Saligram, one of the gurus who had succeeded Shiv Dayal at Agra, and his successors, such as Brahm Shankar Misra, the organizer of the council, were twisting the real teachings of Shiv Dayal Singh. Instead of believing that Shiv Dayal was but one of many perfect saints who had taught the path of *shabd* and that Radhasoami was but a simplified version of the *Sant Mat* tradition, Rai Saligram and the Agra *satsangs* had elevated Shiv Dayal as the first complete incarnation of the highest lord, Radhasoami Purush, who had brought to manifestation a new and higher revelation. This change, as he perceived it, he could not accept. He refused the invitation to join the council. He also refused to submit the list of his initiates to the council and instructed Sawan Singh to follow his course, unless a change appeared at Agra. Finally, he opposed the construction of the *samadh*, an elaborate building honoring Shiv Dayal Singh in Agra, because it lent itself to idol worship.

Before his death in 1903, Jaimal Singh appointed Sawan Singh as his spiritual successor. He left behind only a small movement (he had initiated approximately 2,350 disciples), substantially fewer than the number related to Agra. However, when Sawan Singh took leadership of the group and built it into an international movement, it became the largest of all the Radhasoami organizations in the world.

Jaimal Singh, *Spiritual Letters* (Beas, India, 1976).

Kirpal Singh, *A Great Saint, Baba Jaimal Singh, His Life and Teachings* (Delhi, India, 1960).

Seth Shiv Dayal Singh, *The Sar Bachan* (Beas, India, 1955).

SINGH, Kirpal (February 6, 1894, Sayyad Kasran, Rawalpindi, Pakistan—August 21, 1974, Delhi, India).

Kirpal Singh, spiritual master and founder of the Ruhani Satsang, was born in a small village in what is now Pakistan. He was a precocious child who began the practice of meditation at the age of four. He was a good student and a voracious reader. After graduating from high school in 1911, he went to work for the Indian government in the military services department; after thirty-six years of service, he retired in 1947, as the deputy assistant controller of military accounts.

At the time of his graduation, he was faced with a major question of what was to be his aim in life. He took seven days of intense meditation to reach his decision: "God First and the world next." He set his life in pursuit of self-knowledge and God-knowledge. He also decided, through his searching of scriptures, that a living master was necessary for him to realize his goal. He began to search for such a living master. During his spiritual quest, he was granted a vision of one whom he believed to be Guru Nanak, the founder of the Sikh religion. Finally in 1924, on a visit to Beas, India, he was told of Sawan Singh, the Great Master who had succeeded Jaimal Singh as head of the Radhasoami Satsang Beas. The Radhasoami movement was a modern manifestation of the Sat Mat tradition, which, through a number of mystic poets, had emphasized the practice of surat shabd yoga.

Upon meeting Sawan Singh, Kirpal Singh immediately recognized him as the person who had appeared in his vision seven years previously and many times since. He became a disciple and took initiation. For many years he worked as a follower of Sawan Singh and rose to a prominent position in the Dera at Beas. It is claimed by Kirpal Singh that during this period he was instrumental in the writing of *Gurmat Siddhant* (*The Path of the Masters*), a two-volume survey of spirituality later published under Sawan Singh's name.

Shortly after his retirement and decision to devote his life entirely to the work of his master, Kirpal Singh claims he was summoned to the bedside of ailing Sawan Singh who told him: "Kirpal Singh! I have allotted all other work but have not yet entrusted the task of bestowing *Naam*—initiation into mystical experience—to anyone. That I confer upon you today, so that this holy and sacred science may flourish throughout the world from end to end." He took these words as his commissioning.

After Sawan Singh died in April 1948, Jagat Singh was appointed the new satguru of the Radhasoami Beas. Subsequently, Kirpal Singh left Beas for Delhi to begin his own spiritual work. He founded the Ruhani Satsang, and, in 1951, established its headquarters at the Sawan Ashram in Delhi.

From the beginning of the Satsang, Kirpal Singh saw his work as reaching beyond India to the West. In 1949 he appointed Mr. and Mrs. T. S. Khanna as his representatives to introduce the Ruhani Satsang in the West. They moved to Virginia and gathered disciples for their master. In 1955 Kirpal Singh made the first of his several tours to the West and initiated his first American disciples.

Kirpal Singh wrote many books in English, which were published by the Ruhani Satsang and circulated freely in the West. Among these were *A Brief Life-Sketch of Param Sant Baba Sawan Singh Ji Maharaj* (1949); *Man! Know Thy-Self* (1954); *Prayer* (1959); *Godman* (1967); *The Mystery of Death* (1968); and *The Crown of Life* (1971). He also began a monthly periodical, *Sat Sandesh*.

Among his several projects was the World Fellowship of Religions, which held its first meeting in 1957 in Delhi. He served as president at its several gatherings during the rest of his life.

After his death in 1974, he was succeeded by his son Darshan Singh. An intense controversy arose, however, and the Ruhani Satsang split into three organizations. The largest group of followers recognize Darshan Singh and his Sawan Kirpal Mission. Thakar Singh, another disciple, took charge of the Sawan Ashram and now heads the Kirpal Ruhani Satsang. The Sant Bani Ashram is headed by Ajaib Singh, another disciple. All three groups have followings in the United States. The Sant Bani Ashram, headquartered in New Hampshire, has been most active in compiling and publishing Kirpal Singh's writings.

Kirpal Singh, The Godman (Delhi, India, 1967).

——— , The Japji (Delhi, India, 1959).

——— , Morning Talks (Delhi, India, 1970).

——— , The Way of the Saints (Concord, N.H., 1976).

George Arnsby Jones, The Harvest Is Rich (New York, 1965).

Emil J. Christesen, Eye Opener (New York, 1969).

T. S. Khanna, Pioneer of the New Age, Sant Kirpal Singh Ji Maharaj (Alexandria, Va., n.d.).

Bhadra Sena, The Beloved Master (Delhi, India, 1963).

Message of the Great Master and His Ashram (Delhi, India, n.d.).

SINGH, Sawan (July 27, 1858, Mehmansinghwala, Punjab, India— April 2, 1948); married Krishna Vanti Ji (Shrimati Kishan Kuar), 1883.

Param Sant Baba Sawan Singh Ji Maharaj, who succeeded Jaimal Singh (1839–1903) as head of the Radhasoami Beas, took the small organization and turned it into a national body with centers across India and an international body with centers in Europe and North America. He was the only son in a Grewal jat (agricultural) family. He lived with his family for the first twelve years of his life, and shortly before he left them to attend school, he was married to a child like himself. He never lived with his bride, for years later, just twenty days before the final ceremony consummating their marriage, she died. After graduating from school he became an instructor at the Military School at Farrukhabad. In 1884 he entered the Thompson College of Engineering at Rooki. He completed the engineering course and joined the government's engineering service. For many years he served as a subdivisional officer in various locations around India. Shortly before entering college, he married again, but saw little of his wife during the years because of his devotion to his spiritual quest.

In 1894 Sawan Singh was stationed at Murree. He had spent many years visiting gurus in search of a satisfying teacher. As Murree was on the pilgrims' route to the cave of Amar Nath, he had the opportunity to meet and talk with many holy men. In October 1894 he met Jaimal Singh, founder of the Radhasoami Beas. According to the account transmitted by his followers, Sawan Singh was riding through the countryside in his normal course of duties. He encountered Jaimal Singh and one of his disciples but paid little attention to either. The disciple was offended that Sawan Singh had failed to greet Jaimal Singh, but the master told his traveling companion that he had come to Murree just to find Sawan Singh and that he would come to him in four days. As predicted, four days later Sawan Singh came to Jaimal Singh and, on October 15, 1894, was initiated by him. He soon became Jaimal Singh's most prominent disciple.

Sawan Singh wanted to resign his post with the engineering office, but Jaimal Singh forbade it, as he believed that followers of the path should earn their own living. Thus, even in 1903, when Jaimal Singh died and passed his succession to Sawan Singh, the latter stayed at his job until his retirement in 1911.

After his retirement Sawan Singh moved to Beas and took charge of the development of the modest establishment of his master. Jaimal Singh had only initiated 2,350 persons. Sawan Singh began to hold weekly *satsangs*, discourses for gatherings of followers. The attendance grew; within a few years the modest satsang hall proved inadequate. Sawan Singh moved outdoors into an open field. He devoted the remainder of his life to the spread of Radhasoami Beas. He initiated more than 125,000 disciples into the path, the largest number of any Radhasoami master up to the present time (1983), and second only to Charan Singh, the present leader of the Radhasoami Satsang Beas, who has initiated more than 900,000 disciples.

In the early 1930s, Sawan Singh constructed the famous Satsang Ghar, a huge building used for meetings and initiations. The original foundation stone had been laid by Jaimal Singh shortly before his death. Sawan Singh also helped develop the spiritual colony, Dera Baba Jaimal Singh, in honor of his guru on the banks of the Beas River.

Sawan Singh eventually attracted disciples from around the globe, the most notable of whom were Dr. Julian P. Johnson (who lived at Beas from 1932 to 1939 and wrote the most influential of all Radhasoami works, *The Path of the Masters*); Harvey Meyers; Sir Colin Carbett; Flora E. Wood; Dr. Pierre Schmidt; and Dr. Louis Bluth (who later became a disciple of Paul Twitchell and served as chairman of the board of ECKANKAR).

Two weeks before his death, Sawan Singh appointed Sardar Bahadur Jagat Singh as his spiritual successor via a registered will. Others, most prominently Kirpal Singh, founder of the Ruhani Satsang, also claimed succession and formed their own splinter groups.

Sawan Singh, *My Submission* (Beas, India, n.d.).

———, *Philosophy of the Masters*, 5 volumes (Beas, India, 1963–72).

———, *Tales from the Mystic East* (Beas, India, 1961).

———, *Spiritual Gems* (Beas, India, 1976).

Kirpal Singh, *A Brief Life-Sketch of Hazur Baba Sawan Singh Ji Maharaj* (Delhi, India, 1949).

Julian P. Johnson, *With a Great Master in India* (Beas, India, 1953).

Daryai Lal Kapur, *Call of the Great Master* (Beas, India, 1964).

SINGH, Seth Shiv Dayal (August 25, 1818, Agra, United Provinces, India—June 15, 1878, Agra, India); married Narayan Dei.

Seth Shiv Dayal Singh, better known to his followers as Soamiji Maharaj, the founder of what has become known as the Radhasoami (Sikh) faith, was born into a family who were disciples of Tulsi Sahib, a master of the yoga of the sound current (*surat shabd yoga*) in northern India. As a boy Singh sat at the feet of Tulsi Sahib and began the practice of meditation. By the age of six he was giving public talks. Some claim that he was initiated by Tulsi Sahib, who passed his spiritual succession to him in 1843.

As a young man, Singh worked as a tutor in Persian. He gave up his career, however, and spent fifteen (some accounts say seventeen) years in deep meditation in a small room in his house. Around 1860 he began to hold *satsang* (teaching sessions) for a few select disciples, and in 1861 he opened these to the general public.

Singh taught that the path to God was within the human body, not in any temple, mosque, or *gurdwara* located in the world. He placed emphasis on three cardinal practices: *simran*, repetition of the Holy Name(s) of the Supreme Being, which should be done with the mind and not the tongue; *dhyan*, contemplation of the living master's form or the inner light at the eye center; and *bhajan*, listening to the sound current reverberating within the higher regions of consciousness, which ultimately enables one to leave the body at will and journey directly back to the abode of the Supreme Lord.

Shiv Dayal Singh initiated approximately 3,000 to 4,000 individuals. He wrote two main works (both published posthumously): *Sar Bachan Radhasoami Chand-Band* (a collection of Hindi hymns); and *Sar Bachan Radhasoami Bartik* (a collection of discourses delivered in *satsang*).

After Shiv Dayal's death, four devotees served as gurus. They were Rai Saligram; Baba Jaimal Singh; Baba Gharib Das; and Seth Pratap Singh. Of these, Rai Saligram and Baba Jaimal Singh eventually founded the two largest Radhasoami centers. However, both gurus had divergent opinions on the true nature of their master's teachings. Rai Saligram claimed that Shiv Dayal Singh was the first full incarnation of the Supreme Lord, Radhasoami, and had instigated a new religion for the benefit of mankind. Baba Jaimal Singh, however, believed that Shiv Dayal Singh was unique only because he had simplified the method by which *Sant Mat*, the path of the saints, was taught and that Shiv Dayal Singh was but one of the many masters who had appeared on the earth since time immemorial. To Jaimal Singh, Radhasoami was not a new religion but a modern manifestation of an ageless tradition.

The teachings of Shiv Dayal Singh have come to America primarily through the lineage of masters founded by Jaimal Singh at Beas, in particular Sawan Singh, Jagat Singh, and Charan Singh. Kirpal Singh, a noted disciple of Sawan Singh, has also been instrumental in conveying Shiv Dayal's teachings through his organization, the Ruhani Satsang, possibly the most successful Radhasoami group in America.

Seth Shiv Dayal Singh, *The Sar Bachan* (Beas, India, 1955).

Seth Pratap Singh, *Biography of Soamiji Maharaj* (Agra, India, 1970).

David Christopher Lane, *Radhasoami Mat: Parampara in Definition and Classification* (Berkeley, Calif., 1981).

SIVANANDA, Swami (Kuppuswami Iyer) (September 8, 1887, Pattamadai, India—July 14, 1963, Rishikish, India); education: Society for the

Propagation of the Gospel College, Tiruchirappalli, India, 1903–05; Tanjore Medical Institute, 1905–06.

Swami Sivananda Saraswati, the Indian saint and yoga teacher, was born Kuppuswami Iyer, the son of a pious Hindu government official. His parents encouraged his education and sent him to college and medical school to prepare him for a career as a doctor. Before he could finish his medical training, however, his father died, and he was forced to leave school. Undeterred in his desire to serve the sick, in 1909 he started a medical journal, Ambrosia, a monthly that specialized in preventive medicine and the Indian Ayurvedic system.

In 1913 he moved to Malaya and administered a hospital for a rubber plantation. While there the chance encounter with a wandering holy man, a sadhu, started Iyer on his spiritual quest. In 1923 he resigned his post and returned to India. He traveled around the country on a spiritual pilgrimage until he met Swami Viswananda Saraswati at the holy city, Rishikish. Viswananda initiated Iyer as a sanyasin. The sanyasin are ascetics who dedicate their whole lives to the quest for oneness with God. He also donned the ochre robe, traditionally worn by those who take the vow, and in the process became Sivananda Saraswati, the name by which he is known around the world.

After a brief stay in Rishikish, Sivananda settled in the Swargashram across the river at Lackshmanjhula, where many sanyasins dwelled. Here his desire for serving people with his medical skills and his ascetic vow melded into the particular form of the "Divine Life" that was to characterize his mature years.

At Swargashram, Sivananda spent his time in meditation and study. He met with pilgrims and individuals who came to the ashram for spiritual guidance. He also wrote his first articles and books. The Practice of Yoga appeared in 1929, the first of more than two hundred books that he would write in his lifetime. He gathered around him a core of disciples and students. Accompanied by his students, he made his first pilgrimages and teaching tours around India. To his audiences he emphasized bhakti (devotional) yoga and karma (service) yoga. Unable to forget his medical past, he opened a dispensary to serve the many people who lived at the ashram.

In 1934 he made the decision to establish his own ashram and, with his students, moved back across the river to Rishikish. He founded Ananda Kutir (the abode of bliss) in an abandoned cowshed. This was the beginning of what was to become the Sivanand Ashram. True to his vision, he set aside one of the four rooms of the cowshed as a dispensary to serve the local community.

As the work grew, Sivananda founded the Divine Life Trust in 1936 with the stated goal of spiritualizing the subcontinent of India. In 1939 an open-membership Divine Life Society was organized as an auxiliary to the trust. He had already begun The Divine Life, a monthly periodical, the first of six that the Ashram would eventually produce. He also founded the Forest Academy to train disciples in his teachings. The dispensary, which grew into a major medical facility, eventually adopted a leper colony as a means of further exemplifying Sivananda's life of service.

Sivananda remained in active charge of the Ashram until his death in 1963. Though he never visited the West, his teaching spread even prior to World War II, as copies of his writings found their way to Europe. A planned trip to Europe and North America in 1950 was canceled because of Sivananda's health. His inability to come to the West did not, however, prevent him from becoming one of the most influential forces in the spread of Hinduism and yoga through the many students who came and established ashrams and teaching centers across the continent.

Even before Sivananda died, Swami Sivananda Radha (Sylvia Hillman) founded the Yosodhara Ashram Society in Vancouver. Another former resident of the Sivanand Ashram, Swami Vishnu Devananda, arrived in San Francisco in 1958 on a world tour. He settled in Montreal the next year and built a chain of Sivananda Vedanta Yoga Centers. In 1959 Swami Chidananda, who succeeded Sivananda as head of the Divine Life Society in 1963, organized the society in the United States. They were followed in succession by Swami Jyotir (1962, Yoga Research Society) and Swami Satchidananda (1966, Integral Yoga Institute), both with disciples across North America.

Swami Sivananda, *Sadhana* (Sivanandanagar, India, 1958).

————, *Science of Yoga*, 18 volumes (Durban S.Afr., 1977).

————, *Yoga Asanas* (Sivanandanagar, India, 1969).

Swami Venkatesananda, *Gurudev Sivananda* (Sivanandanagar, India, 1961).

N. Ananthanarayanan, *From Man to God-man* (New Delhi, India, 1970).

Swami Krishnananda, *Swami Sivananda and the Spiritual Renaissance* (Sivanandanagar, India, (1959).

K. A. Tawker, *Sivananda, One World Teacher* (Rishikesh, 1957).

SMITH, Charles Lee (1887, near Ft. Smith, Sebastian County, Arkansas—October 26, 1964, San Diego, California); education: University of Oklahoma; Harvard University.

Charles Lee Smith, founder of the American Association for the Advancement of Atheism, was born in Arkansas but spent most of his youth in Missouri and the Oklahoma Indian Territory. He attended the preparatory school at Epworth University, and for a while he considered becoming a Methodist minister. He chose law instead; after several years as a law clerk at Guthrie, Oklahoma, and two years at the University of Oklahoma, he passed his bar exam and was admitted to the Oklahoma bar. He also attended Harvard University but withdrew during his junior year when his funds ran out.

Around 1912 Smith discovered Thomas Jefferson's book of extracts from the New Testament and learned that Jefferson was an infidel. His reading in Jefferson led to the discovery of free-thought literature and eventually culminated in his conversion to atheism.

After leaving Harvard Smith traveled around the United States for about three years, doing odd jobs. When World War I began, he enlisted in the army. He spent much of the war in an isolated outpost in Vladivostock, Russia. After the war he moved to New York and began selling and writing for *The Truth Seeker*, a prominent atheist–free-thought periodical.

In 1925, with his friend Freeman Hopwood, Smith founded the American Association for the Advancement of Atheism. The "4As," as it was commonly called, was initially denied incorporation papers in New York State on the grounds that it was "against the public interest." After obtaining their papers on a second attempt, Smith launched an aggressive propaganda campaign. It led to the founding of many 4A chapters at college and university campuses and a Junior Atheist League, which attempted to appeal to those of high school age and under. Even though most of the campus organizations were weak and short-lived, the 4A thrived nationally; by the end of the decade, it had more than three thousand members.

In 1928 he returned to his home state of Arkansas to oppose the possible adoption of an antievolution law. He rented a storefront in Little Rock and began to give away proevolution and antireligion literature. Eventually Smith was arrested, tried, convicted, and fined twenty-five dollars plus costs for distributing "obscene, slanderous or scurrilous literature." He went to jail to work off his fine and began a hunger strike. The case was dismissed. Smith reopened the store and was again arrested, this time for blasphemy. He was convicted and released on bail. Several years later the charges were dismissed in the midst of an appeal process.

Smith argued, during the months of the actions in Arkansas, that he was trying to nullify the various antiatheist laws, such as those that in many states denied an atheist the right to hold office. He had no success in either that goal or the more prominent attempt to stop the adoption of the Arkansas antievolution law, which had passed soon after his second conviction.

Under Smith's guidance, the 4As attempted a variety of lawsuits on atheist issues, such as stopping the employment of chaplains in Congress or the reading of the Ten Commandments in schools. Such suits were usually lost in the lower courts, and Smith was unable to raise money for the appeal.

In 1930 Smith became editor of *The Truth Seeker*, the oldest freethought periodical in the United States. The 4As became largely a paper organization, and Smith began to focus on his new endeavor. In the 1950s antiSemitism and antiblack attitudes gained prominent space in *The Truth Seeker* and led to Smith's alienation from many atheists and the loss of subscriptions. In 1964 James Hervey Johnson purchased the paper, and Smith moved the offices to San Diego. He remained as editor, though a few months after the move he died of a heart attack.

Charles Lee Smith, *Sensism: The Philosophy of the West* (New York, 1956).

———, "In Darkest Arkansas," *Third Annual Report of the American Association for the Advancement of Atheism* (New York, 1928), 7–10.

———, *A Debate Between W. L. Oliphant . . . and Charles Smith . . . Shawnee, Oklahoma, August 15 and 16, 1929* (Nashville, Tenn., 1952).

———, *There Is a God!, Debate Between Aimee Semple McPherson and Charles Lee Smith* (Los Angeles, n.d.).

Homer Croy, "Atheism Beckons to Our Youth," *World's Work* 54 (1927), 18–26.

———, "Atheism Rampant in Our Schools," *World's Work* 54 (1927), 140–47.

Marcet Haldeman-Julius, "Is Arkansas Civilized?" *The Debunker* 9, 1 (December 1928), 3–16, 113–20.

——— , "Arkansas Defends Its God," *The Debunker* 9, 2 (January 1929), 3–15.

James Hervey Johnson, "Charles Smith: 1887–1964," *The Truth Seeker* 91, 11 (November 1964), 161–62.

Gordon Stein

SMITH, Joseph, Jr. (December 23, 1805, Sharon, Vermont—June 27, 1844, Carthage, Illinois); married Emma Hale, January 18, 1827.

Joseph Smith, Jr., founder of the Church of Jesus Christ of Latter-Day Saints, popularly called the "Mormons," was born in New England. During his eleventh year the family moved to Palmyra, New York, and a few years later to a farmstead south of Palmyra on the road to Manchester. Western New York was, during the early nineteenth century, an area in which the many factions of Protestantism warred for the allegiance of a largely irreligious community. This heightened religious rivalry formed the backdrop for Smith's early life. Several members of his family joined the Presbyterian Church, while young Joseph was partial to the Methodists.

In 1820 Smith experienced the first of a series of visions that led him away from the existing churches and eventually caused him to found a new church. (These visions, a century and a half later, remain a matter of intense controversy. Mormon scholars, anti-Mormons, and others who have examined the accounts of the visions still disagree on matters of both interpretation and content. There is even some doubt concerning the date of the initial vision.) In that first vision, Smith saw two personages, Jesus and, according to a later account, God the Father. He asked them which church he should join. They told him to join none of them because they were all wrong. Then on September 21, 1823, he was visited by the Angel Moroni who told him of gold plates buried on a hill nearby. Written upon the plates was an account of the ancient inhabitants of North America. Moroni also told him of two stones, called the Urim and Thummin (Exodus 28:30), the possession of which would make of Smith a seer capable of translating the plates. (The accounts of the visions and the stones must be seen against Smith's short career as a seer with a stone that assisted him in locating gold and lost objects.)

In 1827 Moroni allowed Smith to have the plates, which he translated over the next two years. (The physical reality of the plates, questioned by many non-Mormon scholars who have examined Smith's life, was attested to by eleven witnesses who claimed to have seen them. Though some left the church, none ever retracted his statement.) The translation was published in 1830 as the *Book of Mormon*; it told the story of some Israelites who had migrated to North America and were the ancestors of the American Indians.

Meanwhile, as the translation proceeded, Smith and Oliver Cowdery had a vision on May 15, 1826 in which John the Baptist gave them the Priesthood of Aaron, the authority to establish the temporal affairs of the church. They, in turn, baptized each other. In a second vision they met Peter, James, and John, who conferred upon them the higher priesthood as Apostles. On April 6, 1830, Smith led in the formal organization of the Church of Christ (the name soon changed to the Church of Jesus Christ of Latter-day Saints). Smith and Cowdery ordained each other as elders and in turn ordained others present at the occasion.

The new church began to attract followers almost immediately; it also attracted hostile community response. In January 1831, Smith established headquarters farther west at Kirkland, Ohio, but persecution followed. On March 24, 1832, a mob tarred and feathered Smith. He recovered quickly and led his growing group in the building of a large temple, which was finished in 1836. There was little time to enjoy the temple, however, because the financial collapse in 1837 forced Smith to lead his followers to Missouri in January 1838. He joined the Mormons who had already established a settlement near Far West. Smith found no peace there either because the governor of Missouri ordered the group out of the state in October 1838. In November, as his followers hurriedly left for Illinois, Smith was arrested and spent the next six months in jail. He escaped after he had bribed the sheriff and was reunited with his church in Quincy, Illinois.

Smith led in the establishment in Illinois of the new Mormon community, named Nauvoo, which quickly grew into the second largest city in the state. While there he began to introduce the practice of polygamy. Plural marriage fit intellectually into the idea of celestial marriage, in which a couple were sealed for eternity as well as being married until death. The exact number of plural wives of Smith is unknown, and estimates range from twenty-seven to eighty-four, though many of these were merely sealed to Smith and never lived with him as a wife.

During the years at Nauvoo, Smith reached the height of power as the church's leader and virtual ruler of the community. He also made enemies both outside Nauvoo and among the church members. Dissent became focused in a series of incidents in the summer of 1844 that ended his career. Disgruntled ex-members founded an independent newspaper, *The Nauvoo Expositer*. After the first issue, Smith ordered the paper destroyed. The resulting controversy led to Smith's arrest and confinement in the jail at Carthage, Illinois. There on June 27, 1844, a mob broke into the jail and killed Smith.

After his death the Mormons split into several groups, the largest of which followed Brigham Young to Utah. In the Midwest, a number of factions regrouped as the Reorganized Church of Jesus Christ of Latter Day Saints, the second largest group.

Joseph Smith, Jr., *The Book of Mormon* (Palmyra, N.Y., 1830).

———— , *Doctrines and Covenants* (Kirkland, Ohio, 1835).

———— , *History of the Church of Jesus Christ of Latter-day Saints*, 6 volumes (Salt Lake City, Utah, 1902–12).

———— , *The Holy Scriptures, Translated and Corrected by the Spirit of Revelation* (Plano, Ill., 1867).

Fawn M. Brodie, *No Man Knows My History* (New York, 1945).

Donna Hill, *Joseph Smith, the First Mormon* (Garden City, N.Y., 1977).

Lawrence Foster, *Religion and Sexuality* (New York, 1981).

Keith Huntress, *Murder of an American Prophet* (San Francisco, Calif., 1960).

Lucy Mack Smith, *Biographical Sketches of Joseph Smith and Progenitors* (Lamoni, Iowa, 1912).

John H. Evans, *Joseph Smith: An American Prophet* (New York, 1946).

DRB, 411–13.

DAB, 17, 310–12.

SOUTHCOTT, Joanna (April 25, 1750, Tarford, Devonshire, England—December 27, 1815, London, England); married John Smith, November 12, 1815.

Joanna Southcott, apocalyptic prophetess whose work has led to the formation of several millennial religious bodies, was born the humble daughter of a poor farmer in rural England. Her father saw that she received basic education and a deep religious training. Joanna was raised as an Anglican, an affiliation she never left despite the official disapproval of the movement that grew up around her. She forsook marriage; she learned the upholstery trade, by which she supported herself most of her life.

Her life was quite mundane until 1792 when, at the age of forty-two, she began to hear a voice that she came to believe was that of God. She wrote down what the voice told her and transcribed other material through a practice called "automatic writing." The material warned that the time of the end was near and that Christ would soon return. It saw the world as heading for a time of trouble. She sought to convince people of the truth of her prophecies, especially Rev. Joseph Pomroy, the Vicar of St. Kew, Cornwall; in this regard, she began to make a number of individual prophecies. To Pomroy, whom she believed was to be her voice to convince the church of her communications, she gave a written prediction of the death of the Bishop of Exeter, at a time when he seemed in perfect health.

In 1794 Joanna began to make a place for herself in the cosmic scheme. She described herself as the bride mentioned in Revelation 19. By 1800 she had made no converts, and so she took her total savings and some borrowed money to publish some of her communications. The first of six pamphlets, *The Strange Effects of Faith*, appeared in February 1801, and the remaining five over the next year. The pamphlets produced the response for which she had looked and attracted some clergymen to her cause. With a following and some capable assistants, she was able in 1802 to move to London. Once there, she gained a significant convert in Elias Carpenter, the owner of a papermill and a wealthy philanthropist.

With Carpenter's first gift, a ream of paper, Joanna began to prepare seals. She cut the paper into small squares onto which she put a brief message and her signature. These seals were given to followers as a sign of their renunciation of the devil and soon became the distinctive mark of her movement. Joanna told her followers that the world was controlled by Satan and that conditions would not change until a sufficient number of people were sealed.

From the middle of 1803 until the end of 1804, the first period of sealing, more than eight thousand seals were given out. Most of her support, however, came from the followers of fallen apocalyptic leader Richard Brothers, who was languishing in an insane asylum. Among those who associated with Joanna were would-be leaders who offered prophecies that threatened to divide her movement. In response her closest followers rallied her supporters and opened chapels at which they could gather. The first opened in London in 1805, with others soon appearing in Leeds, Stockport, Bath, Bristol, and Exeter. In 1807 she began sealing again and gave out fourteen thousand in one year.

The climax to Joanna's career began in 1814. Her voice told her that in 1815, her sixty-fifth year, she would bear a child. Early in 1815 she announced that she was pregnant and that the baby was identical with the one called Shiloh, a biblical figure (Genesis 49: 100) popularly identified with Christ. The birth of her baby would, in effect, be the second coming of Christ.

As 1815 progressed, many eminent physicians pronounced Joanna pregnant. She decided to marry so that her child would have a legal name and father. Unfortunately her pregnancy was hysteric in origin, and no baby emerged from her womb. By mid-December every sign of pregnancy had disappeared. Joanna did not recover from the disappointment and died before the year was out.

The disappointment over the baby and the death of their prophetess threw the movement into chaos. Several leaders arose to provide an explanation for the failure and a new direction for the movement. Most supporters finally gathered around George Turner, who adopted the theory that Joanna, as the woman of Revelation 12: 1–6, had given birth but, as Scripture had announced, the child had immediately been taken up into heaven. Shiloh lives and will return at the proper moment. Turner saved Joanna's movement. After his death, others arose to lead segments of her followers. In the United States, three groups emerged that trace their lineage directly to Joanna—the Christian Israelite Church, the House of David, and the House of David Reorganized; more than one prophet has drawn on Joanna's prophecy and career for inspiration.

Joanna Southcott, *The Strange Effects of Faith*, 6 volumes (Exeter, England, 1801–02).

———, *Sound An Alarm in My Holy Mountain* (Leeds, England, n.d. [1804]).

———, *The True Explanation of the Bible*, 6 volumes (London, 1804–05).

———, *Prophecies Announcing the Birth of the Prince of Peace* (London, n.d. [1814]).

G. R. Balletine, *Past Finding Out* (New York, 1956).

James K. Hopkins, *A Woman to Deliver Her People* (Austin, 1982).

Eugene Patrick Wright, *A Catalogue of the Joanna Southcott Collection at the University of Texas* (Austin, Texas, 1968).

Jack Gratus, *The False Messiahs* (New York, 1975).

J. F. C. Harrison, *The Second Coming, Popular Millenarianism, 1780–1850* (London, 1979).

DNB, 18, 685–87.

SPAULDING, Baird Thomas (May 26, 1872, Kohocton, New York— March 18, 1953, Tempe, Arizona); married.

Baird Thomas Spaulding, independent Spiritualist teacher and author, did not found a new group; rather he became the author of a single set of books that became best-sellers throughout the metaphysical, Spiritualist, and occult communities of the United States. His books, the five volumes of *The Life and Teachings of the Masters of the Far East*, sold over one million copies. They claim to be the factual report of Spaulding's visit to India in 1894, but in fact they seem to be a fictionalized story that provides a setting for Spaulding's metaphysical speculations.

Little is known of Spaulding's early life. His grandfather, John Spaulding, spent much of his life in India and seems to have been the inspiration for his grandson's interest. Although he claimed an age of ninety-five at the time of his death, thus setting a birthdate in the 1850s, more recent research has established that he was born in upstate New York in 1872. Spaulding hid much of his early life, even from his close friends, in an effort to add to the aura of mystery about his contacts with the "masters."

Spaulding became famous within the psychic community in 1924, when the first volume of his book appeared. In the preface he claimed to have taken a trip to India in 1894 as part of a scientific expedition sponsored by a famous university. In reply to the university's response that no such expedition had occurred, the revised edition stated that Spaulding was merely an independent member of "a research party."

In the book, Spaulding claimed contact with the Great Masters, spiritual teachers who lived in India, Tibet, and China. They, according to Spaulding, accept the Buddha as the Way to Enlightenment but teach that Christ is Enlightenment, the Christ Consciousness. The content of the book closely resembles the ideas and concepts of popular New Thought and Christian Science. The response to the first volume led to a second volume in 1927.

No evidence of Spaulding's ever having made a trip to India in the 1890s has surfaced, and close associates claim that he did not go until 1935 when he visited the subcontinent briefly. Just prior to this trip, he published a third volume of his series, a volume largely plagiarized from books and newspapers. A fourth volume appeared in 1948.

Spaulding spent his last years lecturing before Spiritualist and psychic-interest groups and dabbling in various mining adventures. He died en route to Los Angeles. After his death his publisher brought out a fifth volume in the series, which consisted of transcripts of lectures that Spaulding had given during the last two years of his life.

Baird T. Spaulding, *Life and Teachings of the Masters of the Far East*, 5 volumes (1924–1948).
David Bruton, *Baird T. Spaulding—As I Knew Him* (Marina Del Rey, Calif., 1980).

SPENCER, Peter (1779, Kent County, Maryland—July 25, 1843, Wilmington, Delaware).

Peter Spencer, founder of the Union Church of Africans, was born a slave in rural Maryland. After his master's death, Spencer received his freedom and moved to Wilmington, Delaware, where he made his living as a mechanic. He was also able to get some education.

While in Maryland, Spencer had been converted to Methodism, and in Wilmington he joined Asbury Methodist Episcopal Church. Spencer was among one hundred black members at Asbury in 1805 when trouble arose in the congregation. The white members accused the black members of being too noisy and raucous in the worship service (they had supposedly broken several benches), and of tracking dirt into the sanctuary. The black members were "exiled" to the balcony. Spencer rose to the fore as a leader of the black members during this crisis.

Resenting their new position, the black members decided to form a separate congregation. In connection with this action, Spencer's first written words have been preserved: "In the year 1805 we, the colored members of the Methodist Church in Wilmington, thought that we might have more satisfaction of mind than we then had if we were to unite together and build a house for ourselves, which we did the same year. The Lord gave us the favor and the good will of all religious denominations, and they all freely did lend us help, and by their good graces we got a house to worship the Lord in."

The new church did not solve all the problems, since the church was still under the control of the Methodist Episcopal Church. The minister from Asbury was also assigned to be the minister of Ezion, as the black church was called. The members of Ezion were denied the right to manage their own business affairs. The issues continued for several years and eventuated in a lawsuit in 1812. The court ruled in favor of the Methodist Episcopal Church and ordered the members to either submit to the court's decision or vacate the church building.

In 1813 Spencer led most of the members out of Ezion with the intention of founding an independent congregation. The group met June 1, 1813, for their first worship service. They purchased a new lot, upon which they erected a building. They incorporated as the Union Church of Africans, with Spencer as their minister. Three years later Spencer traveled to Philadelphia to take part in the deliberations that led to the formation of the African Methodist Episcopal Church. He participated fully in the conference and preached the closing sermon, but he then refused to bring his congregation in Wilmington into the new denomination. Spencer remained as leader of the Union Church of Africans for the rest of his life and is credited with having founded approximately thirty congregations.

Twenty years after his death, the Union Church united with the First Colored Methodist Protestant Church to create the African Union First Colored Methodist Protestant Church. A schism in the United church led to the formation of the Union American Methodist Episcopal church.

Daniel James Russell, *History of the African Union Methodist Protestant Church* (Philadelphia, Penn., 1920).

Lewis V. Baldwin, *Invisible Strands in Methodism, A History of the African Union Methodist Protestant and Union American Methodist Episcopal Churches* (Evanston, Ill., Ph.D. dissertation, Northwestern University, 1980).

EWM 2, 2226.

SPURLING, Richard G., Jr. (1858, Germany—May 24, 1935, Turtletown, Tennessee); married Barbara Hamby.

Richard G. Spurling, Jr., one of the founders of what today is known as the Church of God (a Pentecostal group that exists in several branches), came to the United States as an infant. Just as the Civil War began, the large Spurling family settled near Cumberland Gap in Kentucky. One of Richard's older brothers joined the Union army and two joined the Confederate. Richard's father, a miller, tried to remain neutral. After the war, Spurling moved his family south, eventually settling in Monroe County, Tennessee, just across the North Carolina border. Richard's mother died while he was still in childhood, and his father remarried.

The elder Spurling built a lumber mill and gristmill, and from him young Richard learned the trade that remained his occupation for the rest of his life. Richard Spurling, Sr., was also a Baptist minister and passed along his deep piety to his youngest son. In 1881 the two laid the foundation for a building in which to conduct worship services adjacent to their mill.

During the 1880s Spurling had been among many Christians who were upset by the splintering of denominations and the spiritual deadness of the churches. Finding his pleas for revival rejected by the Baptists, Spurling met with his followers on August 19, 1886, and formed an independent congregation. Its title, the Christian Union, reflected the initial desire to unite the various church bodies. Richard Spurling, Jr., though hesitant at first, joined the new congregation and on September 26, 1886, was ordained as a minister. His father, now in his seventies, had decided to retire and turn both the mill and the church over to his son. He had planned to move north to live with one of his other sons but died before he could relocate.

Richard, Jr., assumed the duties of pastoring the small flock whose membership grew but little over the next decade. Then in 1896 Spurling learned of a revival being conducted by a group of independent holiness preachers in a schoolhouse across the line in Cherokee County, North Carolina. Spurling, who had emphasized the necessity of holy living to his congregation, quickly accepted the new holiness teaching. The preachers taught the possibility of a second work of the Holy Spirit in the life of Christians by which they were sanctified and freed to live a holy life. Many who attended the revival also experienced *glossolalia*, speaking in tongues, though they did not understand what was happening to them.

As a result of the revival, Spurling moved the Christian Union to North Carolina and joined with the group meeting at the schoolhouse.

Spurling remained as one of the ministers of the new group, although W. F. Bryant became the leading minister. Spurling's leadership was reasserted in 1902, when, faced by a disturbance in the congregation who were being led astray by some fanatical teachers, he called together the leaders and reorganized the church. A simple plan of church government was adopted and the name changed to Holiness Church of Camp Creek.

Thus the situation stood when Ambrose J. Tomlinson, who traveled the area for the American Bible Society, discovered the church. Tomlinson joined it and soon rose to dominate its life and leadership. Spurling remained active but became increasingly disaffected as the church grew and changed. He lived the remainder of his life at Turtletown, Tennessee, and preached in the mountains. He lived to see the split in the church in 1922–23. Though little involved in the church's leadership at that time, he remained a member of the Church of God (Cleveland, Tennessee). Some years later one of his granddaughters willed the family cemetery to the faction that had followed A. J. Tomlinson, the Church of God of Prophecy.

Today numerous Church of God groups trace their origin to the work begun by Spurling and his father in the rural mountains of east Tennessee.

Richard G. Spurling, Jr., *The Lost Link* (Turtletown, Tenn., 1920).

June Clover Marshall, A *Biographical Sketch of Richard G. Spurling, Jr.* (Cleveland, Tenn., 1974).

Charles W. Conn, *Like a Mighty Army* (Cleveland, Tenn., 1955).

STEINER, Rudolf (February 27, 1861, Kraljevic, Hungary—March 30, 1925, Dornach, Switzerland); married Anna Eunicke, October 31, 1899 (d. March 17, 1911); married Marie von Sievers, December 24, 1914; education: Technical University, Vienna; University of Rostock, Rostock, Germany, Ph.D., 1891.

Rudolf Steiner, founder of the Anthroposophical Society and the Christian Community, lived a very mobile early life as the son of a railroad worker. His family moved from his birthplace to Pottschach, Austria, at the age of two and to Neudoerfl, Hungary, six years later. The family finally settled in Vienna when it became time for Rudolf to attend college. At the age of eighteen he seemed destined to follow his father in a career with the railroad and entered the Technical University. But even as a child, he had had perceptions of what he called supersensible reality and broadened his own studies to include the arts and the humanities. While sitting in on classes at the University of Vienna, he became familiar with the work of Goethe.

In 1883 he was invited to edit and write the introduction to the scientific writings for the Kuerschner edition of Goethe's *Works*. Over the next decade he became known for his scholarly work on Goethe, and in 1888 he was invited to work at the Goethe Archives at Weimar. From 1890 to 1897 he worked on the Weimar edition of Goethe's works.

During his years at Weimar, he had also pursued the more underlying interest of his life—the search for a bridge between the world of sense experience and the spiritual world. In 1894 he published his first important independent work, *The Philosophy of Spiritual Activity*, in which he explored the role of thinking as a spiritual activity and conscience as a moral reality.

New realms of experience were opened for Steiner in 1897. He moved to Berlin to edit a literary magazine. He also encountered the Theosophical Society, for which he was soon giving regular lectures. He went through a period of inner struggle that ended in 1899 with what he noted was a profound experience in which he witnessed the crucifixion of Christ on

Golgotha. From this experience he was, he believed, able to understand the true meaning of Jesus' mission and the truth of Christianity.

The first twelve years of the new century provided time for the development of his independent ideas. He wrote several of his most important books: *Knowledge of the Higher Worlds and Its Attainment* (1904); *Theosophy* (1904); and *Occult Science, an Outline* (1909). His new approach to Christianity was presented in *Christianity as Mystical Fact* (1901) and in a series of other works.

Meanwhile, in 1902, Steiner became leader of the German section of the Theosophical Society even though he disdained their Eastern philosophical emphases. A growing conflict became open in 1909, when he clashed with Annie Besant at a society convention. She spoke of Buddha over Christ and Steiner responded with a lecture on Buddha announcing Christ. Then in 1910 Besant announced the formation of the Order of the Star of the East to promote Krishnamurti as the coming world savior. Steiner refused to promote the Order of Krishnamurti.

In 1912 he proposed the formation of Anthroposophy as an anti-Oriental section of the society but soon saw the need to leave altogether, and with his supporters he formed the Anthroposophical Society on February 3, 1913.

During his years in Berlin, Steiner became directly involved in drama. He wrote several mystery plays for the Theosophical Society and eventually married an actress after his first wife died. At the time that the break with Theosophy became apparent, the need for a place to perform the plays and give them the proper atmosphere arose. Steiner designed a building, using all his spiritual and mundane knowledge, and the infant society built it at Dornach, Switzerland, just as World War I began. It was appropriately named the Goetheanum.

Steiner spent the years after World War I expanding the society and putting his spiritual ideals into practical use. His educational ideas were embodied in the Waldorf School in Stuttgart. In 1922 he founded the Christian Community to give form to a liturgical and communal approach to Christianity. In 1923 he reformed the society; the following year he added an esoteric section as a school for self-development through spiritual science.

After his death in 1925, the society began to spread throughout Europe and America. It was carried initially by German-speaking immigrants to England and the United States. The society came to the United States as early as 1925 and soon spread across the country. Although the first Christian Community liturgy was performed in 1928, there was little response and the movement was not formally established until 1948.

Rudolf Steiner, *The Course of My Life* (New York, 1951).

――――, *The Philosophy of Spiritual Activity* (New York, 1932).

――――, *Theosophy* (New York, 1932).

――――, *Cosmic Memory* (West Nyack, N.Y., 1959).

――――, *Christianity as Mystical Fact* (West Nyack, N.Y., 1961).

Stewart C. Easton, *Rudolf Steiner: Herald of a New Epoch* (Spring Valley, N.Y., 1980).

Johannes Hemleben, *Rudolf Steiner* (East Grinstead, Sussex, England, 1975).

Friedrich Rittelmeyer, *Rudolf Steiner Enters My Life* (London, 1929).

A. P. Shepherd, *A Scientist of the Invisible* (New York, 1959).

Guenther Wachsmuth, *The Life and Work of Rudolf Steiner* (New York, 1955).

EOP, 882.

STETSON, Augusta Emma Simmons (October 12, 1842, Waldoboro, Maine—October 12, 1928, Rochester, New York); married Frederick J. Stetson (d. 1901); education: Lincoln Academy, New Castle, Maine.

Augusta Emma Simmons Stetson, one of the first independent Christian Science teachers, was raised in an old New England family of Pilgrim descent. Showing an early talent for music, while she was still a teenager Augusta became the organist for the Methodist church her family attended. After high school, she attended Lincoln Academy where she majored in public speaking. She married Frederick J. Stetson, who was in the shipbuilding business. He and Augusta subsequently lived in such diverse places as England, India, and Burma. However, after several years, they returned to Boston because of her husband's failing health. He had never recovered from the years spent in Libby Prison as a Confederate prisoner during the Civil War.

Stetson had intended to work as a public lecturer, but while finishing her training, she discovered Christian Science. She attended the November 1884 class. She left for Maine soon after finishing the class and worked as a Christian Science practitioner with phenomenal success. Mary Baker Eddy responded by appointing her as one of the five preachers in the mother church pulpit in Boston and then in November 1886 by sending her to New York City to take over a group of unorganized Christian Science faithful.

On February 3, 1888, Stetson brought the members together and incorporated the First Church of Christ, Scientist in New York City. They elected her pastor (after 1895 called first reader). She was formally installed and ordained on October 21, 1890. The work grew steadily under her talented leadership. By the turn of the century, the church had grown to the point that its rented quarters were inadequate. A million-dollar granite building was erected on Central Park West, with an adjoining home for Stetson. It was dedicated November 29, 1903. Twelve years earlier she had begun the Christian Science Institute as a training school for practitioners in association with the church. Through the institute she had built a large group of practitioners and an inner core of dedicated church members, all with a strong personal loyalty to herself.

Her success, the opulence of the new church building, her oratorical skill, and the obviously strong personal attachment of her students caused many to see her as a rival to Eddy. In 1902 Eddy limited the term of first readers to three years. Stetson resigned but retained the dominant position in the church in New York. She proposed plans to build a large branch church to the New York church, but she was prevented by Eddy's direct order.

Stetson's steady rise was called into question in 1909 when Eddy ordered an investigation of rumors that she had built a personal following within the church. The then first reader at the New York church charged her with deviating from Christian Science teaching. When the board of directors of the mother church made its report, it revoked Stetson's license as a practitioner and teacher. It called her to Boston for a hearing after which, at Eddy's direction, it dismissed her from membership.

Stetson accepted her fate but continued to profess her innocence. Loyal to Eddy, she told people that she was merely being tested and that she would be reinstated in the near future. The next year, however, Eddy died without any move to vindicate her ousted New York leader. Stetson remained in charge of the Christian Science Institute and of the home next door to the church, which became the institute's headquarters. She continued to teach those loyal to her for the remainder of her days.

When it became obvious that the mother church would not move to accept her back into its fold, she began to reinterpret her fate as a victory, a trial she had to go through as a test. Her role in the material organization of the Church of Christ, Scientist, prepared her to continue as a teacher independent of any material organization. She referred to her activity after 1910 as the "Church Triumphant." Also, as late as 1927, she remained loyal to Eddy, who she believed would return to life, as did Christ, and vindicate her.

Stetson began to write pamphlets attacking the mother church as the material organization and issued the two books defending her position, *Reminiscences, Sermons and Correspondence* (1913) and *Vital Issues in Christian Science* (1914). In 1924 she published her major work, *Sermons Which Spiritually Interpret the Scriptures and Other Writings of Christian Science*. In the 1920s she became identified with several questionable causes, including a magazine, the *American Standard*, which espoused Nordic supremacy, and a daily radio show that focused upon Christian Science and the "Protestant" principle and the traditional "Americanism" that stood against Catholicism.

She died of edema while visiting a nephew in Rochester, New York. Her cremated remains were interred at Damariscotta, Maine, where she had lived most of her childhood years.

Augusta E. Stetson, *Give God the Glory* (New York, 1911).

———, *Vital Issues in Christian Science* (New York, 1914).

———, *Reminiscences, Sermons, and Correspondence* (New York, 1926).

———, *Sermons and Other Writings* (New York, 1926).

Altman K. Swihart, *Since Mrs. Eddy* (New York, 1931).

Report of the Board of Trustees of First Church of Christ, Scientist of New York City (New York, 1909).

Charles S. Braden, *Christian Science Today* (Dallas, Texas, 1958).

NAW, 3, 364–6.

DRB, 431–2.

WWW, I, 1179.

STORRS, George (December 13, 1796, Lebanon, New Hampshire—December 28, 1879, Brooklyn, New York?).

George Storrs, one of the founders and the first president of the Life

and Advent Union, was born into a community of staunch Congregationalists, but showing an independence of spirit and thought, he waited until
he was nineteen before he joined. He married during his twenty-second
year, but his wife lived only six and a half years. During her illness Storrs
was befriended by a Methodist Episcopal Church minister, as a result of
which he joined that church and entered the ministry. He was admitted on
trial to the New England Conference in 1825 and was accepted into full
connection the following year. He served successively charges at Landaff
(1825), Sandwich (1826–27), Gilmanton–Northfield (1828–29), Great Falls
(1830), Portsmouth (1831), Great Falls (1832), and Concord (1832–34). All
his appointments were in New Hampshire during a time in which Methodism was experiencing significant growth. New Hampshire was set off as a
separate conference in 1832, and Storrs was a charter member. In 1835
Storrs, who had become active in the abolitionist movement, was arrested
at a meeting of the Sanbornton Bridge Anti-Slavery Society. That same
year he was reported as supernumerated (too ill to take an appointment)
at the Methodist conference. The following year he was located—that is,
dropped from the role of conference membership. Both his health and his
abolitionist sentiments led to his withdrawal from the conference and the
church in 1840.

In 1837 Storrs had picked up a pamphlet someone had dropped on a
railcar floor. It was written by Rev. Henry Grew and was concerned with
the destruction of the wicked. He concluded that immortality was conditional upon faith in Christ and that the wicked would not exist in hell but
rather would be totally destroyed after the final judgment. Storrs's own
Bible study in the light of Grew's writings convinced him that Grew was
correct. In 1841, the year after he left the Methodists, he published *An
Inquiry: Are the Souls of the Wicked Immortal? In Three Letters*. He had
originally written the letters to a minister colleague in the hopes that
Grew's argument might be refuted.

The year 1842 was a turning point in Storrs's career. He became pastor
of a small independent congregation in Albany, New York. He preached a
series of six sermons on conditional immortality, which were later republished as *An Inquiry: Are the Souls of the Wicked Immortal? In Six Sermons*.
That same year Calvin French, a minister who had become involved in the
Adventism of William Miller, introduced Storrs to the movement. Before
the year was out, Storrs left his new pastorate to become an Adventist
evangelist. The reprinting of his *Six Sermons* and the conversion to his
opinions of several leading ministers, such as Charles Fitch, made conditional immortality and Storrs the focus of controversy through Adventism.

In 1843 Storrs started an Adventist periodical, *The Bible Examiner*, in
Albany. He also authored a book, *The Second Advent*. After the disappointment when Christ failed to return in 1843, Storrs became a leading
advocate of the seventh-month expectation, which looked for the return
in 1844. After this Great Disappointment, he refused to engage in further
date setting. On April 29, 1845, the discouraged Adventists reorganized at a
conference held in Albany in the church formerly pastored by Storrs.

Storrs aligned himself with those who eventually formed the Advent Christian Church, which accepted Storrs's views on conditional immortality.

In 1859 Storrs introduced another issue into the Adventist cause, the so-called "life theory." He argued that there would be no general resurrection; only the righteous would be raised. This new doctrine led to a separation by Storrs and his followers and the formation in 1863 of the Life and Advent Union. Storrs became its first president and remained an active minister in the union for the rest of his life. He continued to publish the *Bible Examiner* until a few months before his death, when illness overtook him.

In 1964 the Life and Advent Union merged again with the Advent Christian Church.

George Storrs, *The Bible Examiner* (Boston, 1843).

———, *An Inquiry: Are the Souls of the Wicked Immortal? In Six Letters* (Montpelier, Vt., 1841).

———, *An Inquiry: Are the Souls of the Wicked Immortal? In Six Sermons* (Albany, N.Y., 1942).

Mob, Under Pretense of Law, or the Arrest and Trial of Rev. George Storrs at Northfield, N.H. (Concord, N.H., 1835).

Leroy Edwin Froom, *The Prophetic Faith of Our Fathers*, volume IV (Washington, D.C., 1954).

Seventh-Day Adventist Encyclopedia (Washington, D.C., 1976), 1428.

STRANG, James Jesse (March 21, 1813, Scipio, Cayuga County, New York—July 9, 1856, Burlington, Wisconsin); married Mary Pierce, November 30, 1836; married Elvira Eliza Field, July 13, 1849; married Betsy McNutt, January 19, 1852; married Sarah Adelia Wright, July 15, 1855; married Phoebe Wright, October 27, 1855; education: Fredonia Academy.

James Jesse Strang, Mormon leader and prophet, was born Jesse Strang, the son of a farmer. He was a sickly child and as a result attended school only rarely. He was an avid reader and was able to educate himself. He attended Fredonia Academy briefly and taught school for a while. In 1836 he was admitted to the bar. That same year, he married the daughter of a Baptist minister. They moved to Ellington, New York, where Strang practiced law, edited the local newspaper, and served as postmaster.

In 1843, with their four children, Strang and his wife moved to Burlington, Wisconsin, where her brother was in business. Her brother's partner was Moses Smith, a Mormon, who introduced Strang to the *Book of Mormon* and the Church of Jesus Christ of Latter-day Saints. Strang was so impressed with this new religion that, in early 1844, he traveled to Nauvoo, Illinois, and met Joseph Smith. On February 25, 1844, he was baptized by Smith; a week later he was ordained by Hyrum Smith, the prophet's brother. Strang returned home with a mission to explore southern Wisconsin as a possible location for a new church center. After two months Strang wrote a favorable report and asked to begin a new stake for the church in the Racine area.

On June 27, 1844, both Joseph and Hyrum Smith were killed. On the same day, according to Strang's claim, he had a visitation from an angel. The angel told him of Smith's death and ordained him to carry on the work of the church as the new prophet. Then on July 9, he received a letter from Smith written shortly before his death. Strang claimed the letter confirmed his role as prophet and president of the church and commanded the Saints to move to Voree, just outside Burlington, Wisconsin. (Critics of Strang assert that he failed to relate the angel's visit to anyone until sometime after Smith's death was generally known, and he was merely attempting to take over the church. They also charge that the letter, now considered by scholars to be a forgery, at best authorized Strang to establish a stake in Wisconsin, not to succeed Smith as prophet.)

Strang presented his claims at a meeting of the church's elders at Florence, Michigan, on August 5. Elder Crandall Dunn rejected his claims and excommunicated him. That action was upheld by the Twelve Apostles, who also excommunicated Strang, on August 24, 1844.

Gathering those that did believe his claims at Voree on January 5, 1845, Strang organized his church and called all the Saints to Voree. He also announced a second revelation he had had that promised that Strang would receive the "plates of the ancient records." On September 1, 1845, the Lord's messenger told him where the plates were located and on September 12, accompanied by four witnesses, he dug up the plates, which were lodged in the roots of an oak tree. Harkening back to Joseph Smith's translation of *The Book of Mormon*, Strang translated these plates by means of the Urim and Thummim given him by the angel. The following week he published the translation and issued them as the "sealed plates" that Smith had not been allowed to publish. Smith was reduced to the "forerunner" and Strang given the title of the "Mighty Prophet."

In 1847, as leader of a growing church, Strang had a revelation appointing Beaver Island, Michigan (in the middle of Lake Michigan), as the new gathering place for the Saints. He moved his followers there; over the next nine years, almost three thousand joined him. The Beaver Island settlement prospered. While there, Strang ran for the legislature, where he served two terms. In 1849 he began secretly to practice polygamy. He eventually took four additional wives. The practice soon became known and accepted, but only about twenty men followed the practice.

Strang began to extend his authority on Beaver Island. He had himself proclaimed king. His kingdom began to disintegrate, however, when on June 16, 1856, two men shot him. They escaped aboard the U.S.S. *Michigan*, whose captain, apparently in on the plot, took the men to the authorities in Mackinac where they were soon freed.

Strang was taken back to Voree, where he died. He was buried at Burlington. After his death the church dwindled quickly. Most members joined other Mormon factions, primarily the Reorganized Church of Jesus Christ of Latter-day Saints. The several hundred that survived carried on the tiny church, which today has but two congregations, one in New Mexico and one at Voree, Wisconsin.

James Jesse Strang, *The Book of the Law of the Lord* (Saint James, Mich., 1850).

———, *The Diary of James J. Strang*, trans. by Mark A. Strang (East Lansing, Mich., 1961).

———, *The Prophetic Controversy* (Saint James, Mich., 1856).

———, *James J. Strang, Teachings of a Mormon Prophet* (Burlington, Wisc., 1977).

————, *The Diamond: Being the Law of Prophetic Succession, and a Defense of the Calling of James J. Strang as Successor to Joseph Smith* (Voree, Wisc., 1848).

George Bartholomew Arbaugh, *Revelation in Mormonism* (Chicago, 1932), 146–58.

Henry E. Leger, *A Moses of the Mormons* (Milwaukee, Wisc., 1897).

Milo M. Quaife, *The Kingdom of St. James* (New Haven, Conn., 1930).

Robert P. Weeks, *King Strang* (Ann Arbor, Mich., 1971).

Lawrence Foster, "James J. Strang: The Prophet Who Failed," *Church History* 50, 2 (June 1981), 182–92.

DAB, 18, 123–5.

WWWH, 511–12.

SUZUKI, Daisetz Teitaro (October 18, 1870, Kanazawa, Japan—July 12, 1966, Kamakura, Japan); married Beatrice Erskine Lane, 1911 (d. 1939); education: Ishikawa College, 1888–91, Tokyo Imperial University, 1891–94.

Daisetz Teitaro Suzuki, the single person most responsible for the spread of Buddhism among Westerners in the twentieth century, was born to a poor couple in a small village in northern Japan. Upon completion of his high school work, the young Suzuki became a teacher. After his mother died (his father had died during his childhood), he moved to Tokyo and attended the Imperial University (though he never enrolled in a degree program). He also began Zen training.

Shortly before the death of Imakita Kosen Roshi (1816–1892), Suzuki became a student at his Engakuji monastery in Kamakura and thus began his personal recovery of the Rinzai Zen Buddhism, which was his Samurai family's heritage. He was recognized as an able student, and in 1897 Soyen Shaku, who succeeded Kosen as abbot of the monastery, suggested that Suzuki go to the United States to assist Paul Carus, whom Shaku had met at the World Parliament of Religions in 1893, in the translation and publication of Buddhist materials in the West. Suzuki moved to LaSalle, Illinois, and became an editor at Carus's Open Court Publishing Company. His first tasks were the translations of the *Tao Te Ching* and Ashvaghosho's *The Awakening of Faith in the Mahayana*. He also began to work on his own first book, *Outlines of Mahayana Buddhism*.

In 1905–06 he accompanied Soyen Shaku during his American visit and served as his interpreter. He returned to Japan in 1909 by way of London, where he stopped to translate Emmanuel Swedenborg's writings into Japanese. He then settled in Japan as a lay disciple at Kamakura.

In 1911 he married Beatrice Erskine Lane. They continued to live at the Engakuji monastery until 1919, when Suzuki accepted a post to teach philosophy of religion at Otani University in Tokyo. While in Tokyo, he and his wife began *The Eastern Buddhist*, an English-language journal that they jointly edited until her death in 1939. Suzuki also began to write the many books in which he explained Mahayana Buddhism, particularly Zen, to the Western mind. The first of these, his *Essays in Zen Buddhism*, was published in 1927 by Rider. Other titles that appeared over the years included *Essays in Zen Buddhism*, series two and three; *The Training of the Zen Buddhist Monk; Zen and Japanese Culture; The Field of Zen; On Indian Mahayana Buddhism;* and *Manual of Zen Buddhism*.

Suzuki did not return to the United States until 1949, when he went to Honolulu and taught at the University of Hawaii for the school year 1949–1950. From Honolulu he moved to Claremont, California, for a year at the Claremont Graduate School before beginning six years at Columbia University. During these years in New York, partially because of his books and the popularity of Zen among the Beatniks, he became a well-known personality and was in high demand for media appearances. The growth of interest in Zen created by his presence led to the formation of the Zen Studies Society.

In 1957 Suzuki retired from Columbia, but before returning to Japan, he spent six months in Cambridge, Massachusetts, at the request of colleague Shinichi Hisamatsu, who was teaching at the Harvard Divinity School. The two helped start the Cambridge Buddhist Association, and Suzuki served briefly as its president. In 1958 he returned to Japan and lived out the last years of his life quietly at Engakuji.

D. T. Suzuki, through his writings and to a lesser extent his teaching, has been credited with leading more Westerners to Zen than any other single force. Most importantly, his writings made many of the people who were to become the leaders of Zen in the West initially aware of Buddhism as a serious life option.

Daisetz Teitaro Suzuki, *Essays in Zen Buddhism*, 3 volumes (London, 1927–34).

———, *The Training of the Zen Buddhist Monk* (Kyoto, Japan, 1934).

———, *Manual of Zen Buddhism* (Kyoto, Japan, 1935).

———, *Zen Buddhism and Its Influence on Japanese Culture* (Kyoto, Japan, 1938).

———, *The Field of Zen* (London, 1969).

Rick Fields, *How the Swans Came to the Lake* (Boulder, Colo., 1981).

Emma McCloy Layman, *Buddhism in America* (Chicago, 1976).

Charles S. Prebish, *American Buddhism* (North Scituate, Mass., 1979).

"On Dr. Daisetz Teitaro Suzuki (1870–1966), "*Wind Bell*, VIII, 1–2 (Fall 1969), 29–30.

DRB, 444–46.

WWW, IV, 919–20.

SWEDENBORG, Emmanuel (January 29, 1688, Stockholm, Sweden—March 29, 1772, London, England); education: University of Uppsala, graduated 1709.

Emmanuel Swedenborg—scientist, inventor, theologian, and seer—was born Emmanuel Swedberg, the son of a professor at the University of Uppsala. Emmanuel grew up in the university community and stayed in Uppsala after 1702 when his father moved to become bishop of Skara. He had a pious upbringing and a good education. His thirst for knowledge was coupled with a wide-ranging encyclopedic interest in nature. After graduation, he traveled abroad for five years, returning to Sweden in 1715 ready to begin a career. Through a friend, physicist Christopher Polhem, he obtained an appointment as special accessor with the Board of Mines. In 1718 he turned down a professorship at Uppsala to continue his mining work.

Also in 1718, the family was ennobled. As was customary, their name was changed, and Swedberg became Swedenborg. Emmanuel, as the eldest son, also received a seat in the Diet, in which he remained active for half a century.

Swedenborg's two decades with the Board of Mines revealed a man dominated by a ceaseless pursuit of knowledge of the world, who tried in many ways to put that knowledge to work for the service of king and country. He found only a minor appreciation for his work. This period was marked by the publication of several books, the most notable being the *Opera Philosophica et Mineralis* (1734); *OEconomia Regni Animalis* (1740–41); and *Regni Animalis* (1743–45). In the *Economy of the Animal (Soul) Kingdom*, he first suggested the nebular hypothesis of the origin of the universe, which was later popularized by Immanuel Kant and scientists William Herschel and P. S. de LaPlace.

In 1743 Swedenborg's life began to change. He had his first experiences intimating contact with the spiritual world. In 1745 he had fully developed that contact and conversed freely with angelic beings. He came to believe through his spiritual experiences that the Lord had commissioned him to restore knowledge of the spiritual realm, humanity's true home, to the church.

Swedenborg discovered that there were two realms of created existence: the spiritual realm, which was real and substantial, and the physical realm, which was the reflection of the spiritual. Between the two realms was an exact correspondence. Swedenborg saw the main task of restoration to lie in explaining the Scripture; most of his remaining work consisted of the spiritual interpretation of the Bible in the light of his knowledge of the angelic worlds and the law of correspondence.

In 1747 he was offered a position as councillor of the Board of Mines. Instead, he asked for retirement. He left for Holland and began work on his multivolume *Arcana Coelestia* (Heavenly Secret), a commentary on the books of Genesis and Exodus. It was published in twelve volumes from 1749 to 1756. From this commentary flowed five theological treatises, the most famous being the one on *Heaven and Hell*, published in 1758.

The most famous incident in Swedenborg's career occurred in 1759. In Gothenburg, three hundred miles from Stockholm, Swedenborg had a vision of the great fire of July 19, which he described to a number of people. News of the fire only reached the town two days later. The fame generated by this incident led to an audience with the queen, to whom Swedenborg communicated a secret that she had shared only with her brother, recently deceased.

The remainder of his life was spent writing and overseeing the publication of his works, the most important being the *Treatise on the Four Doctrines* (1760–61) and *Conjugal Love* (1768), the first of his religious writings to have his name on the title page. He died in London in 1772 on the date he had predicted in a letter to John Wesley, the Methodist founder.

In England Swedenborg's teaching found the following that had eluded him in Sweden. His work was translated into English in the 1770s; what was to become the Church of the New Jerusalem was founded in 1774. Members brought the church to America in 1792, where it currently exists in three branches, the largest being the General Convention of the New Jerusalem in the United States of America.

Emmanuel Swedenborg, *The Spiritual Diary* (Boston, 1871).

———— , *Arcana Coelestia* (Standard edition, New York, 1949).

———— , *Angelic Wisdom Concerning the Divine Love and the Divine Wisdom* (Standard edition, New York, 1949).

———— , *The Four Doctrines* (Standard edition, New York, 1949).

———— , *The True Christian Religion* (Standard edition, New York, 1949).

George Trowbridge, *Swedenborg: Life and Teachings* (New York, 1944).

William White, *Life of Emmanuel Swedenborg* (Philadelphia, Penn., 1880).

John Howard Spalding, *Swedenborg's Religious Thought* (New York, 1977).

EOP, 897.

TEED, Cyrus Read (October 13, 1839, Moravia, New York—December 22, 1906, Estero, Florida); married; education: Eclectic Medical College, New York, graduated 1868.

Cyrus Read Teed, founder of the Koreshan Unity, lived in upstate New York and spent most of his youth working on the Erie Canal. After nine years of work, he quit in 1859 to begin his study of medicine in Utica. He married in 1860 and moved to New York City in 1862 with the intention of completing his education. He enlisted in the army instead and became a private in the 27th Regiment of the New York Volunteers. His superior officers soon learned of his medical experience, and he was transferred to field hospital service as an assistant surgeon. After the Civil War, he finished his education. In 1868 he opened an office in Deerfield, New York.

During the next several years he became absorbed in some "electro-alchemical" experiments and had some revelations from the "superior celestial spheres." The essence of Teed's revelation was called *Cellular Cosmology*, the title of Teed's 1899 book. Teed taught that the sun was the center of the universe and that the earth was hollow. We live on the inside of a sphere with the central sun located at the midpoint. The sun (God Almighty) emits heat, light, and the descending influence of gravity—all of which are limited by the point where metallic and mineral substances materialize. We live in the midst of a cosmic egg. Teed also taught alchemy, reincarnation, celibacy, and communism.

Teed began to share his views with his patients; during the 1870s he traveled around New York State spreading his teachings. In 1880 he established a small community in his hometown of Moravia, New York, and began publishing a periodical, *Herald of the New Covenant*. Very early in the movement, Teed assumed the name Koresh, derived from the Greek form (*Kyros*) of his name, Cyrus.

In 1888 Teed moved to Chicago and formally established the Koreshan Unity and its associated church, the Assembly of the Covenant. Teed began the *Guiding Star* as a monthly periodical in May 1889, and six months later he issued a weekly, the *Flaming Sword*. In 1888 Beth-Ophra, a cooperative home for Teed's followers, was opened at Washington Heights in Chicago. It grew to include 150 residents. Teed also established groups in various cities across the United States, from Portland, Oregon, to Lynn, Massachusetts.

In 1894 Teed moved with his followers to Estero, Florida, where a commune that soon numbered over two hundred members was created. The group attained some fame for the various experiments they conducted to prove the correctness of Teed's cellular cosmology. In 1903 the Koreshan Unity was incorporated in New Jersey. Teed also established a publishing house in Estero, and from its presses his many books flowed: *The Immortal Manhood; Reincarnation-Resurrection of the Dead;* and *The Great Red Dragon.*

Teed died in 1906. His followers expected a resurrection and placed his body in a bathtub on the bank of the Estero River. It was washed away in a flood several months later.

During the twentieth century, the Unity has dwindled and today has only a few members. In 1949 the publishing house was destroyed in a fire. In 1962 more than three hundred acres known today as the Koreshan State Park were deeded to the state of Florida.

Cyrus Read Teed, *The Cellular Cosmology* (Chicago, 1899).

——— , *The Illumination of Koresh: Marvelous Experiences of the Great Alchemist Thirty Years Ago at Utica, N.Y.* (Chicago, 1899).

——— , *Shepherd of Israel* (Chicago, 1896).

——— , *The Law of Optics* (Estero, Fla., 1912).

Howard Fine, "The Koreshan Unity: The Chicago Years of a Utopian Community," *Illinois History* (June 1975).

"An Unusual New Park on the Tamiami Trail," *The New York Times,* March 5, 1967.

The Koreshan Foundation, *Koreshanity, the New Age Religion* (Miami, Fla., 1971).

THOMPSON, Charles Blanchard (January 27, 1814, New York?— 189–?, Philadelphia, Pennsylvania?).

Charles Blanchard Thompson, founder of the Congregation of Jehovah Presbytery of Zion, was at one time a staunch member of the Church of Jesus Christ of Latter-day Saints (Mormons). Little is known of his life prior to his joining the church in 1835 in Kirkland, Ohio, where he became a leading member. In 1841 he published in Batavia, New York, a defense of the church, *Evidences in Proof of the Book of Mormon, Being a Divinely Inspired Record.* In 1843 he was in Nauvoo, Illinois, where he remained until after the murder of Joseph Smith, Jr., the church's founder. After Smith's death he affiliated with J. J. Strang's group, but he left after little more than a year. Thompson then moved to St. Louis, where he established himself as a tailor.

Thompson began to receive revelations soon after he moved to St. Louis, and in 1847 he founded the Congregation of Jehovah Presbytery of Zion. On New Year's Day 1848, he issued a revelation that served as an apology for his new organization. He argued that God had rejected the church because of its failure to complete the Nauvoo Temple in the appointed time. The congregation was but a temporary substitute for the real Zion in Independence, Missouri. On January 13 he issued a further revelation noting that, because of the polygamy of Joseph and Hyrum

Smith, their progeny could not inherit the priesthood and the keys to the kingdom and the sure redemption of Zion had been transferred to him (Thompson).

Thompson gathered a following of some fifty to sixty families, and in 1853 a committee was appointed to locate a spot for the group to settle. They chose a site in Monona County, Iowa, and began to build the settlement, called Preparation. Thompson moved to the new settlement and became the leader of a commune. He claimed to be the reincarnation of the biblical character Ephraim, and he took the title of Baneemy, the Patriarch of Zion. In 1857 he issued a collection of his revelations, *The Laws and Covenants of Israel*. He also issued a book of regulations for the kingdom of God (all copies of which, with the exception of one with a missing title page, have been lost). Thompson proposed an elaborate kingdom order built around the Ecclesis or congregation, the treasury, and the state.

Preparation lasted only two years. Members accused Thompson of mismanaging funds and in 1857 drove him from the community, along with his chief steward. Thompson moved back to St. Louis and tried to reestablish his following. A lengthy litigation over the property in Iowa began. It was finally settled in 1867 in favor of the members, and the assets were divided among them. In 1860 Thompson wrote and published *The Nachash Origin of the Black and Mixed Races* in which he defended slavery with an elaborate and mythical anthropology. He argued that blacks were not the descendents of Adam. He believed that they were of a race of the children of the gods who did not keep their first estate and were punished with Nachash, or black bodies.

Thompson tried yet another time to gather a following and by the end of the 1870s he was established in Philadelphia. He also began to publish a periodical, *Cyips Herald*. The group broke apart in 1888 over the issue of whether they should sell or give the paper away. Thompson was listed in the Philadelphia directory as late as 1892, but his eventual fate is unknown.

Charles B. Thompson, *The Laws and Covenants of Israel* (Preparation, Iowa, 1857).

——, *The Nachash Origin of the Black and Mixed Races* (St. Louis, Mo., 1866).

George Bartholomew Arbaugh, *Revelation in Mormonism* (Chicago, 1932).

Denominations That Base Their Beliefs on the Teachings of Joseph Smith (Salt Lake City, Utah, 1969).

Russell R. Rich, *Little Known Schisms of the Restoration* (Provo, Utah, 1962).

TINGLEY, Katherine Augusta Westcott (July 6, 1847, Newburyport, Massachusetts—July 11, 1929, Visingso, Sweden); married Philo B. Tingley, 1889.

Katherine Augusta Westcott Tingley, American Theosophical leader, became known in her middle years when, as the wife of Philo B. Tingley, she began to work for various social-reform causes in New York in the late 1880s. Little is known of her early life. One side of her family were Congregationalists, and she attended that church, and the other side were "materialists." She was married twice before her wedding to Tingley. In 1887 she formed the Society of Mercy; in 1889 the Martha Washington

Home for the Aged; and in 1891 the Do-Good Mission, an emergency-relief agency on New York's East Side.

During her years in social work, she also became interested in Spiritualism, which in 1894 led to a meeting with William Q. Judge, head of the American branch of the Theosophical Society, who brought her into Theosophy. Judge, who was leading the schism of the American branch from its European and Indian connections, recognized Tingley's abilities and quickly groomed her for a leadership role. Judge died in March 1896, and Tingley succeeded him. In June she began a ten-month round-the-world crusade for Theosophy. While on the tour she conceived the plan she would follow as Theosophy's leader. She authorized the purchase of land on Point Loma in San Diego, California. She ended her tour at Point Loma, where she laid the cornerstone for the School for the Revival of the Lost Mysteries of Antiquity, the first step in her goal of making Theosophy visible in the educational, artistic, and social realms.

In January 1896 she formed the Universal Brotherhood Organization, and at the Theosophical Society's convention the next month she took complete control of the society as leader and official head. The Universal Brotherhood Organization merged with the society, which was renamed the Universal Brotherhood Organization and Theosophical Society. In 1900 she moved to Point Loma and established permanent headquarters there.

Tingley's rise to leadership of the society came just as the Spanish-American War was at its height. She responded to the war by organizing the War Relief Corps and establishing an emergency hospital on Long Island for soldiers wounded in Cuba. In 1899 she initiated relief efforts in Cuba under the auspices of the International Brotherhood League, the humanitarian department of the society. In 1901 Tingley visited Cuba and selected a group of children to be brought to Point Loma for education. Upon their arrival in the United States, the Immigration Department detained them under accusations that the school at Point Loma was both financially and morally incompetent. These events occurred just as Tingley was pursuing a lawsuit against the *Los Angeles Times* for libel. After several weeks, the Immigration Department, finding no substance to the charges concerning the school, released the children. In 1903 she won the lawsuit and was awarded $7,500.

During the early years of the century, Tingley attempted to create a total community at Point Loma. She invited members of the society to move to California, and as a result many groups around the country languished. The community, never a financial success, continually drained energy from the membership nationally. To the school, established in 1896, she added the Isis Temple of Art, Music and Drama, which moved from New York to California in 1900.

While work in the United States foundered, Tingley expanded activities abroad. In 1903 she founded the Raja Yoga Academy, a boarding school, in Cuba, the first of four. In 1907 she visited Sweden, met King Oscar, and purchased property on the island of Visingso, which became a European headquarters.

The Point Loma community was held together by Tingley during her lifetime because she was able to raise the financial resources to keep the many activities alive.

Tingley died six weeks after being in an automobile accident in Germany in 1929. She was succeeded by Gottfried de Purucker, who oversaw the dismantling of the community. During his years in office, all the Point Loma property was sold and the name of the organization again became the Theosophical Society (not to be confused with the Theosophical Society in America, headed at that time by Annie Besant).

Katherine Tingley, *The Gods Await* (Point Loma, Calif., c 1926).

———, *The Mysteries of the Heart Doctrine* (Point Loma, Calif., c 1902).

———, *Theosophy: The Path of the Mystic* (Point Loma, Calif., 1922).

———, *The Voice of the Soul* (Point Loma, Calif., 1928).

———, *The Wisdom of the Heart, Katherine Tingley Speaks*, compiled by W. Emmett Small (San Diego, Calif., 1978).

Emmett A. Greenwalt, *California Utopia: Point Loma, 1897–1942* (San Diego, Calif., 1978).

Robert V. Hine, *California's Utopian Colonies* (New Haven, Conn., 1966).

Lauren R. Brown, *The Point Loma Theosophical Society: A List of Publications, 1898–1942* (La Jolla, Calif., 1977).

The Theosophical Movement, 1875–1950 (Los Angeles, 1951).

NAW, 3, 466–8.

WWW, I, 1242.

TOMLINSON, Ambrose Jessup (September 22, 1865, near Westfield, Indiana—October 2, 1943, Cleveland, Tennessee); married Mary Jane Taylor, April 24, 1889 (d. March 22, 1945).

Ambrose Jessup Tomlinson, one of the founders of the Church of God, now existing in several branches, was born in rural Indiana in a Quaker community. His parents were not religious people, and he had little religious training as a child. He married a devout Quaker, however, and she led him into a conversion experience soon after their marriage. He became an active layman in the Chester Quaker Meeting and helped build their Sunday school.

In 1895 J. B. Mitchell, a colporteur for the American Bible Society and the American Tract Society, invited Tomlinson to accompany him on his travels to eastern Tennessee and western North Carolina. Tomlinson did and soon became a colporteur himself. Traveling through the hill country in 1896, he came in touch with the Holiness church at Camp Creek, North Carolina. This congregation had been founded in 1886 by Richard Spurling, and in the decade of its existence, it had experienced many phenomena later to be identified with the Pentecostal movement.

In 1899 he moved his family to North Carolina, and for several years he continued an informal relationship with the church, which he joined in 1903. He was soon ordained as a pastor. In 1904 he moved to Cleveland, Tennessee, and there led an independent congregation in affiliating with the Camp Creek church. Another church also united, and by the time a convention was called in 1906, the three congregations constituted a growing movement. Tomlinson was selected as the moderator for the gathering. In 1907 the small group of churches changed its name to the Church of God, and the work spread to locations in the tristate area.

In January 1908, following the annual convention, G. B. Cashwell accepted Tomlinson's invitation to come to Cleveland to conduct a revival and share the Pentecostal experience he had brought from Azusa Street in Los Angeles. Among the first to respond was A. J. Tomlinson, who spoke in tongues (he claimed he spoke in twelve different languages) on January 12. During the year the entire Church of God became a Pentecostal body.

In 1909 Tomlinson was named general moderator of the church and the next year general overseer. He was given the power to appoint pastors. In 1914 he was made general overseer for life. He also became editor of the church periodical, *The Church of God Evangel*, which was started in 1911. In 1917 he helped found the church's training school and became its superintendent; two years later he assumed the same role for the orphanage and home for children.

As the 1920s began, Tomlinson was the unquestioned leader of a growing church. Then trouble arose. In 1922 he was accused of mismanaging church funds. A committee was appointed to investigate the state of the church in all its departments. As a result, a number of charges were filed against him. They ranged from disloyalty to the Church of God to misappropriation of funds. In June 1923 he was tried and impeached, an action confirmed by the church's judicial body the next month.

Although cut off from the church for which he had labored for twenty years, Tomlinson refused to acknowledge the validity of the impeachment action. In August 1923 he held a conference in Chattanooga, Tennessee, of all his supporters, and in a November general assembly he picked up the work as if nothing had happened. Only a minority followed Tomlinson into what is today called the Church of God of Prophecy.

In the summer of 1937, Tomlinson's health began to fail, and he had to limit his travels and duties. After his death in 1943, his sons, Milton and Homer, inherited leadership of the church but soon parted ways as each claimed sole authority as general overseer.

Ambrose Jessup Tomlinson, *Diary of A. J. Tomlinson*, 3 volumes (Queens Village, N.Y., 1948, 1953, 1955).

———, *God's Twentieth Century Pioneer* (Cleveland, Tenn., 1962).

———, *Historical Notes* (Cleveland, Tenn., 1943).

Lillie Duggar, *A. J. Tomlinson, Former General Overseer of the Church of God* (Cleveland, Tenn., 1964).

Homer A. Tomlinson, *The Great Vision of the Church of God* (Queens Village, N.Y., 1939).

Charles W. Conn, *Like a Mighty Army* (Cleveland, Tenn., 1955).

DRB, 468–9.

TOMLINSON, Homer Aubrey (October 25, 1892, near Westfield, Indiana—December 4, 1968, Queens, New York); married Marie Wunch, November 22, 1919; education: University of Tennessee, Knoxville, 1910–1912.

Homer A. Tomlinson, founder and bishop of one branch of the Church of God, was one of the most colorful individuals on the American religious scene in the twentieth century. He was also instrumental in the founding and growth of three different branches of the Church of God.

Homer was the son of A. J. Tomlinson, founder of the Church of God, with headquarters at Cleveland, Tennessee—one of the early Pentecostal bodies to form in the South after the turn of the century. In 1904 he moved with his parents to Cleveland and was present when the church was organized with his father as moderator (later general overseer). Prior to moving from Indiana, he had experienced salvation at the age of eight. Shortly after settling in Tennessee, at the age of fourteen, he was sanctified; the following year he experienced the baptism of the Holy Spirit. At this time he was at a revival meeting and spoke in tongues for five hours.

While supportive of his father's work, Homer did not want to be a preacher. In 1912 he left home and spent two years at college. He was a school principal for a year and then moved to Indiana for three years. In 1916 he went to New York City where he engaged in the public relations and advertising business. Along the way he served in the army tank corps for a brief period.

Homer's decision to join the ministry was precipitated by his father's impeachment and removal from office in 1923. (Although his father, A. J. Tomlinson, was removed from the church he had led for twenty years, he called his supporters around him and started over again.) In June 1923 Homer opened a church in Jamaica, New York, and began to actively expand the following in the Northeast. He eventually became state overseer for New York and secretary of foreign languages for the Church of God. He did much of his work among the immigrant groups, particularly the Spanish-speaking groups, in New York City. After building a large tabernacle in Jamaica, he lost it in 1937 as part of the continuing litigation that encumbered the church well into the 1940s.

In 1943 A. J. Tomlinson died. Shortly after his death, a group of state overseers gathered and elected Homer's younger brother Milton as the new general overseer, subject to the approval of the 1944 assembly of the church. Homer rejected this action, claiming that his father had appointed him as early as April 8, 1942, to carry on the work. His father had reaffirmed and added to that appointment in September 1943, when he commissioned Homer to carry the Church of God flag to every nation on earth.

In December 1943 he called an assembly of his supporters and "reorganized" the Church of God. The assembly confirmed him as general overseer. Using his advertising skill and willingness to engage in numerous publicity stunts, he began to build both the Church of God and his own reputation as its leader. Immediately after World War II, he traveled to Jerusalem to begin fulfilling his commission to plant the church's flag in every nation. In 1950 he announced his first campaign for the presidency of the United States. He ran on the Theocratic party ticket in 1952, 1960, and 1964.

In 1954 he declared himself "King of All Nations of Men in Righteousness," and, at the assembly of the Church of God that year, had himself crowned. He saw his action, which he frequently repeated as he traveled the globe, as a symbolic act that pointed toward the day when all the nations would be gathered together as one in righteousness.

Bishop Tomlinson remained active in writing, traveling, speaking, and preaching until shortly before his death at the age of seventy-six. His last book, *The Shout of a King*, was an autobiographical reflection on the history of the Church of God.

Homer A. Tomlinson, *The Shout of a King* (Queens Village, N.Y., 1968).

——— , *The Great Vision of the Church of God* (Queens Village, N.Y., 1939).

William Whitworth, "On the Tide of the Times," *New Yorker* (September 24, 1966), 67–108.

WWW, V, 727.

TOWNE, Elizabeth Lois Jones (May 11, 1865, Portland, Oregon—June 1, 1961, Holyoke, Massachusetts); married J. Holt Struble, 1880 (div. 1900); married William E. Towne, May 26, 1900.

Elizabeth Towne, though not the founder of any religious group herself, is remembered as one of the major advocates and publishers of the New Thought movement during the first decades of the twentieth century, when the various groups were attempting to stabilize the loosely organized movement into several national churches. As owner/editor of one of the movement's largest publishing houses and widely read periodicals, she provided the means through which the many churches and other New Thought groups reached their potential members.

Towne grew up in the Willamette Valley of Oregon. Her parents were Methodists. She quit school when she was fourteen and married when she was fifteen. The marriage was not a happy one, and the energetic and talented Elizabeth felt confined by the role of dependent housewife. She also had left Methodism behind and became a follower of the burgeoning New Thought movement. She found a way toward the economic independence she sought, and her new religious enthusiasm led her to start a New Thought magazine, the *Nautilus*. Using money borrowed from her father and a mailing list given to her by another magazine editor, she printed the first issue in October 1898. It became an immediate success.

In 1900 she moved to Holyoke, Massachusetts. She divorced her first husband and married William E. Towne. She incorporated as the Elizabeth Towne Company, with herself as president and treasurer. Her new husband became the associate editor. Her children and ex-husband formed the early staff.

The move to Holyoke launched Towne's career as a leading New Thought lecturer, author, and publisher. Among her many books were *Joy Philosophy* (1903); *Meals without Meat* (1903); *Practical Methods for Self-Development* (1904); *How to Concentrate* (1904); *How to Grow Success* (1904); *Happiness and Marriage* (1904); *How to Wake the Solar Plexus* (1904); *How to Train Children and Parents* (1904); *You and Your Forces* (1905); *Experiences in Self-Healing* (1905); *The Life Power* (1906); and *Lessons in Living* (1910). Her publishing house also published many of the outstanding New Thought writers, such as W. W. Atkinson, Browne Landone, and Annie Rix Militz. The progress of her publishing venture was steady and suffered only one setback when a fire destroyed the offices in 1910, although not a single issue of the *Nautilus* was missed.

As the New Thought movement coalesced, Towne became active in several cooperative groups. In 1918 she became a charter member of the New England Federation of New Thought Centers. Her prominence led to her being elected president of the International New Thought Alliance in 1923. From 1923 to 1932 she served as honorary president of the Alliance. In 1924 she accepted ordination in the Church of Truth, the small New Thought denomination founded by Albert Grier in Spokane, Washington.

Unlike many New Thought leaders, Towne became active socially and politically. She was a charter member of the Holyoke Women's Club as well as the Business and Professional Women's Club, and served a time as president of both. From 1924 to 1933 she was president of the Holyoke League of Women Voters and a director-at-large during the last five years of her time in office. She became a charter member of the Holyoke Council on World Relations and for several years was a delegate to the National Federation on the Cause and Cure of War.

Towne remained active into her 80s and lived past her ninety-fifth birthday.

Elizabeth Towne, *Joy Philosophy* (Holyoke, Mass., 1903).

———— , *Experiences in Self-Healing* (Holyoke, Mass., 1905).

———— , *The Life Power* (Holyoke, Mass., 1906).

———— , *Lessons in Living* (Holyoke, Mass., 1910).

———— , *Democracy's Dividends* (Holyoke, Mass., 1935).

Thomas Dreier, *The Story of Elizabeth Towne and the Nautilus* (Holyoke, Mass., 1911).

William E. Towne, *Health and Wealth from Within* (Holyoke, Mass., 1909).

Charles S. Braden, *Spirits in Rebellion* (Dallas, Texas, 1963).

WWW, 4, 949-50.

TWITCHELL, John Paul (October 22, 1908?, Paducah, Kentucky— September 17, 1971, Cincinnati, Ohio); married Camille Ballowe, August 12, 1942 (div. 1960); married Gail Atkinson, 1964: education: Western State Teachers College, Kentucky, 1933–1935.

John Paul Twitchell, founder of ECKANKAR, the Ancient Science of Soul Travel, was born in Paducah, Kentucky, in either 1908 or 1912. His life prior to the founding of ECKANKAR is difficult to trace because he created a new biography for himself in the mid–1960s, an account that has obscured the details of his life. It is known that after college he returned to Paducah. In 1942 he enlisted in the navy and married that same year. He remained in the navy through the war but resigned after the war ended. He moved to New York City, where he became a correspondent for *Our Navy* magazine. He moved to Washington, D.C., at the end of 1945.

In 1950 Twitchell joined the Self-Revelation Church of Absolute Monism, an independent congregation begun by former pupils of Swami Yogananda's Self-Realization Fellowship. He and his wife lived on the grounds, and Twitchell edited *The Mystic Cross*, its periodical. However, in 1955, Twitchell was asked to leave the church by Swami Premananda and he and his wife separated.

That same year, 1955, Kirpal Singh, founder of the Ruhani Satsang, a Sant Mat movement teaching the yoga of the sound current, made his first visit to the United States. Twitchell was at that time initiated by Kirpal Singh. While a disciple of Kirpal Singh's, Twitchell became involved with L. Ron Hubbard and the Church of Scientology. He was among the first to attain the level of "clear" in Scientology, and he worked on the church staff.

In the early 1960s he moved to Seattle and worked for the *Seattle Post-Intelligencer*. He also met his future wife, Gail Atkinson, a librarian. In 1963 he introduced her to Kirpal Singh, and she was initiated into the Ruhani Satsang. In 1964 Twitchell married Gail and moved to San Francisco, where he emerged as an independent teacher of *shabd yoga*. In his early classes he emphasized the concept of bi-location, the ability of a person's consciousness or spirit to separate from the body.

In 1965 he declared himself the Living ECK Master and launched ECKANKAR. The remaining years of his life were spent in building his organization and expounding his teachings. His efforts were advanced by the publication of two books: *The Tiger's Fang* (1967), a personal account of his alleged travels in the inner world, and *In My Soul I Am Free*, a biography by noted psychic author Brad Steiger. Other books flowed from the headquarters ECKANKAR had established in Las Vegas: *All About ECK* (1968); *Stranger by the River* (1969); *The Flute of God* (1970); and *The Far Country* (1970). Twitchell also began a periodical, *The Mystic World*.

Twitchell taught that all life emanates from God, the SUGMAD, by way of the ECK currents, which are perceived by the soul as the Sound of ECK and the Light of Nuri. Under the guidance of the Living ECK Master, the soul can detach itself from the body and travel to the higher realms of the SUGMAD.

Twitchell claimed that he was the 971st ECK Master and the descendent of an unbroken line of the Order of the Vairagi, a lineage that predates recorded history and includes Plato, Pythagoras, and Lao Tsu. Twitchell claimed that he received the rod of power from Tibetan ECK Master Rebazar Tarzs.

Twitchell's teachings were called into question in the late 1970s when it was discovered that a significant portion of *The Far Country* had been plagiarized from two works by Julian Johnson, who like Kirpal Singh had been a disciple of Sawan Singh. Also, Twitchell had taken articles from the 1960s in which he had acknowledged his indebtedness to Swami Premananda, Kirpal Singh, L. Ron Hubbard, and Meher Baba and reprinted them as chapters of his books. However he replaced the names of his real teachers with those of ECK masters Rebazar Tarzs and Sudar Singh. He also seems to have invented his trips to study in India, for no record of his having left the country has been uncovered.

Twitchell died in 1971. On October 22, 1971, Darwin Gross, a long-time disciple, claimed reception of the rod of power and was acknowledged as the 972nd Living ECK Master. Ten years later, however, Gross (who in the interim had married and divorced Twitchell's widow) relinquished his role as a Living ECK Master and was succeeded by Harold Kemp in October 1981. Soon after his resignation, Gross was officially cut off from the ECKANKAR organization, which no longer recognizes him as a genuine ECK teacher.

Paul Twitchell, *Eckankar, the Key to Secret Worlds* (New York, 1969).

——— , *Stranger by the River* (Las Vegas, Nev., 1970).

——— , *The Spiritual Notebook* (Menlo Park, Calif., 1971).

——— , *The Flute of God* (Menlo Park, Calif., 1971).

——— , *Eckankar, Compiled Writings*, volume I (San Diego, Calif., 1975).

Brad Steiger, *In My Soul I Am Free* (New York, 1968).

"Eckankar, A Hard Look at a New Religion," *SCP Journal* 3, 1 (September 1979).

David Christopher Lane, *The Making of a Spiritual Movement, The Untold Story of Paul Twitchell and Eckankar* (Del Mar, Calif., 1983).

EOP, 950.

VILATTE, Joseph René (January 24, 1854, Paris, France—July 8, 1929, Versailles, France); education: College of St. Laurent, Montreal, 1876–79; McGill University, Montreal, 1880–82.

Joseph René Vilatte, the first man to bring independent Catholicism to the United States, was born in France to a family who were members of the Petite Eglise, an independent Catholic Church that arose during Napoleon's conflict with the papacy. By the 1850s the church had almost disappeared from the Paris vicinity, and Vilatte was raised a Roman Catholic. As a young man, he entered the Community of Christian Brothers in Namur, Belgium. Partly to escape military duty, he migrated to Canada and entered the College of St. Laurent to begin studies for the priesthood.

Vilatte's studies for the priesthood were interrupted when his faith was disturbed by hearing apostate priest Charles Chinquy. He left Montreal and retired to Bourbonnais, Illinois, where he lived with the Clerics of St. Viator. He continued his contact with Chinquy; he also corresponded with lapsed priest Hyacinthe Loyson, who had formed the schismatic Gallican Catholic Church in France.

When he began to work again in 1884, he appeared as an independent Presbyterian missionary to French-speaking Belgian immigrants near Green Bay, Wisconsin. Possibly at the suggestion of Loyson, Vilatte approached Episcopal Bishop John Henry Hobart Brown of Fond du Lac and proposed that he cooperate with Vilatte in building an "Old Catholic" church in Green Bay. In 1885, with Brown's support, Vilatte traveled to Switzerland; on June 6 and 7, he was ordained deacon and priest by Old Catholic Bishop Eduard Herzog.

With Episcopal support and financial aid, the mission prospered and three parishes emerged. Vilatte authored a *Catéchisme Catholique* and took on an assistant. Vilatte began to think about becoming a bishop, but he was caught between the desire of Bishop Charles C. Grafton, who had succeeded Bishop Brown in 1888, to control the Green Bay mission, and the advice of the European Old Catholics for Vilatte to separate from the Episcopal Church. Grafton indicated that any attempt to separate would lead him to withdraw financial support.

Vilatte perceived that his future lay in his securing the episcopacy, and he approached both the European Old Catholics and the Russian Orthodox Church with that goal in mind. He finally opened correspondence with Mar Julius I, Metropolitan of the Independent Catholic Church of Ceylon, Goa, and India, a small Latin-rite body in communion with the Jacobite patriarch of Antioch. In the summer of 1891 Vilatte sailed for Ceylon. Almost a year later he was consecrated by Mar Julius, on May 29, 1892.

Vilatte returned to Green Bay and raised his parish church to the status of a pro-cathedral. For the next six years he struggled to make a success of his Old Catholic diocese. Frequently in debt, he attempted, unsuccessfully, reunion with Rome. Then abruptly in 1898, he left Green Bay to his assistant priest and began the life of a wandering bishop. Contacted by a group of Polish Catholics who refused to join the Polish National Catholic Church, he consecrated their leader, Stephen Kaminski. On May 6, 1900, during a long visit to Europe, he consecrated Paolo Miraglia-Gulotti, who had formed the independent National Italian Episcopal Church in Italy.

In 1907 Vilatte settled in Chicago. He met William Henry Francis Brothers, the prior of an Old Catholic community that had come under the patronage of Bishop Grafton, and ordained him to the priesthood. However, the future Old Catholic bishop and Vilatte soon parted company.

In 1915 Vilatte founded his own jurisdiction, the American Catholic Church, and on December 19, he consecrated its first bishop, Frederick E. J. Lloyd. The young church grew slowly during the war years and the aging Vilatte finally turned the church over to Lloyd in 1920. The church in turn gave its retiring leader the title Exarch. His only remaining episcopal act was the consecration of George Alexander McGuire in Chicago on September 22, 1921, as the first patriarch of the African Orthodox Church.

Soon after the McGuire consecration, Vilatte returned to France. In 1925 he renounced his independent career and made his submission to Rome; he lived quietly at the Cistercian Abbey of Pont-Colbert near Versailles. According to one account, shortly before his death, Vilatte ordained two of the Cistercian novices and eventually raised one to the episcopate. No records survive, however; when he died, he was buried with the requiem mass for laymen.

Joseph René Vilatte, *Catéchisme Catholique* (Green Bay, Wisc., 1886).

——— , *The Independent Catholic Movement in France* (London, 1907).

——— , *Mode of Receiving the Profession of the Old Catholic Faith from One Newly Converted* (Chicago, 1919).

——— , *A Sketch of the Belief of the Old Catholics* (Green Bay, Wisc., 1889).

Gregory Tillett, *Joseph René Vilatte; A Bibliography* (Sydney, 1980).

William M. Hogue, "The Episcopal Church and Archbishop Vilatte," *Historical Magazine of the Protestant Episcopal Church* 34, 1 (March 1965), 35–55.

Bertil Persson, *A Collection of Documents on the Apostolic Succession of Joseph René Vilatte with Brief Annotations* (Solna, Sweden, 1974).

Paul G. Schultz, *The Background of the Episcopate of Archbishop Joseph René Vilatte* (Glendale, Calif., 1976).

Peter Anson, *Bishops at Large* (London, 1964).

VIVEKANANDA, Swami (Narendranath Datta) (January 12, 1863, Calcutta, India—July 4, 1902, Ramakrishna Math, Belur, India); education: Calcutta University, B.A., 1884.

Swami Vivekananda, founder of the Vedanta Society in the United States and the Ramakrishna Math and Mission in India, was born Narendranath Datta, into an aristocratic Bengali family. His father was a lawyer. Early in life, the young Narendra joined the Brahmo Samaj, a reform movement founded by Ram Mohan Roy, but yearned for a spiritual path that had a more affirmative approach to the Hindu religious heritage.

In 1881 he began his university studies. One day, while studying the poetry of Wordsworth in English literature class, the professor mentioned a priest at a nearby temple as having attained the state of blissful trance described by the poet. As a result of the class, Narendra traveled to Dakshineshwar, five miles north of Calcutta, and met Sri Ramakrishna. Though he remained in school, he also joined the group of disciples who had accepted Sri Ramakrishna as their guru.

Narendra's relationship to Ramakrishna was severely tested in 1884. That year he received his college degree, and at about the same time, his father died. The family was plunged into poverty; Narendra inherited some of the responsibility for caring for his family. Though facing hardships, he continued his work at the university and his association with Ramakrishna. Gradually he came to head the group of disciples and formally took charge after Ramakrishna's death. He located a house at Baranagore, Calcutta, into which the small band moved and which is today recognized as the beginning of the Ramakrishna Order.

In 1887 Narendra and the others took the vows of the renounced life (*sanyasin*) and became monks. They also accepted religious names. Narendra thus became Swami Vivekananda. The taking of vows became the beginning of an unstable period in the loosely organized group's life, and most divided their time between their house and wandering throughout the country. During Vivekananda's wanderings in 1892, he heard of the World Parliament of Religions to be held in Chicago the following year.

Vivekananda decided that it was his mission in life to go to the West with the message of Hinduism. He convinced others of his mission, and the money was raised to send him. He arrived in the United States in May 1893 and proceeded to Chicago, only to discover that he had not registered for the congress and it was too late to get the credentials to attend and address the assembly. He traveled to Boston where he met Dr. Theodore Wright of Harvard University, a speaker at the parliament. With Wright's assistance, he not only attended the parliament but spoke four times. He became the single most popular speaker at the gathering.

After the parliament Vivekananda lectured through the Midwest for almost a year before settling in New York City. He wrote his first book, *Raja Yoga*. After a side trip to London, he returned to New York, where in December 1895 he founded the Vedanta Society of New York. The next year he went to England as the first stop on a return trip to India. He arrived in his homeland in January 1897.

Vivekananda returned to India a hero. His triumph at the parliament and subsequent work in England and the United States had become known throughout India. He gathered the remnants of the group he had left behind and, along with a group of new followers, founded the Ramakrishna Math (monastery) and Mission. His new order emphasized Ramakrishna's uniting of the monastic life with social service, at this time still a radical idea in Indian religion. He purchased a site for the math at Belur. It was dedicated the following year, but even before it was under construction, Vivekananda began the first relief work by the mission just fifteen days after it had been formally organized in May 1896.

Vivekananda made one last trip to the West in 1899–1900. He then left the work to his assistants and returned to India where he lived out his final years at Belur, traveling on behalf of the mission throughout the country.

The Vedanta Society that he founded was the first organized Hindu work in the United States; it survives with centers in many United States cities.

Swami Vivekananda, *The Complete Works of Swami Vivekananda*, 12 volumes (Calcutta, India, 1965).

Sailendra Nath Dhar, *A Comprehensive Biography of Swami Vivekananda* (Madras, India, 1975).

Reminiscences of Swami Vivekananda by His Eastern and Western Admirers (Calcutta, India, 1964).

R. Ramakrishnan, *Swami Vivekananda, Awakener of Modern India* (Madras, India, 1967).

Romain Rolland, *The Life of Vivekananda and the Universal Gospel* (Calcutta, India, 1931).

DRB, 486–87.

EOP, 969.

WARNER, Daniel Sidney (June 25, 1842, Marshallville, Ohio—December 12, 1895, Grand Junction, Michigan); married Tamzen Ann Kerr, 1867 (d. 1872); married Sarah A. Keller, June 1874 (div.); married Frankie Miller, 1893; education: Oberlin College, Ohio, 1865, 1866.

Daniel Sidney Warner, founder of the Church of God (Anderson, Indiana), was born in rural Ohio. A year after his birth, his father sold his tavern and moved to a farm. Unfortunately, his father did not give up his excessive drinking. In 1863 Daniel served for a period as a private in the Union Army. At the end of his brief career as a soldier, he was a self-professed infidel. Then, in February 1865, he was converted at a protracted meeting sponsored by the Methodists. In the fall he enrolled at Oberlin College but did not finish the term. He enrolled again in 1866 but left after experiencing a call to preach. He withdrew to devote himself to private study. On the following Easter Sunday evening he preached his first sermon at a Methodist gathering.

In the end, he decided not to join the Methodist Episcopal Church. In October 1867 Warner was licensed to preach by the Church of God founded by John Winebrenner, which had, as a major tenet, a disavowal of all sectarianism. The next six years were spent in the pastorate in northwest Ohio. In 1873 he moved to Nebraska as a general missionary. In the midst of his two-year stay he returned to Ohio briefly to marry and in 1875 moved back to Ohio as the pastor of a church.

The turning point in Warner's career came in July 1877. He experienced the second work of grace, sanctification. He began to work with the members of the National Association for the Promotion of Holiness, for which he was heavily criticized by his fellow ministers of the Church of God. Despite opposition, he was assigned a circuit in the area of Canton, Ohio, in the fall of 1877. He soon resigned his circuit to preach sanctification and holiness. After he had preached a revival in Finlay, Ohio, that split the local congregation, Warner was tried and expelled from the Church of God.

Warner became a full-time holiness evangelist. In October 1878 he became associated with the Northern Indiana Eldership of the Church of God, a group that had broken with the same Church of God that had expelled Warner. He was appointed the assistant editor of their periodical, the *Herald of Gospel Freedom*. By March of the next year he was the co-editor and in 1880 became the sole editor. In 1881 the *Herald* merged with another magazine to become the *Gospel Trumpet*. Warner edited the *Gospel Trumpet* for most of the rest of his life. In 1881 he withdrew support from the National Holiness Association because of its recognition of "sects" in its constitution. In October 1881 he also withdrew from the Northern Indiana Eldership for the same reason. With five people at Beaver Dam, Indiana, he formed the Church of God (now generally distinguished from other groups with the same name by the designation "Anderson, Indiana"), the site of its current headquarters.

About the time that Warner withdrew from his Indiana colleagues, Warner's associate in the *Gospel Trumpet* parted company with him, leaving Warner financially strapped for many years. Also his wife had become convinced that true holiness demanded celibacy, and she left Warner and divorced him.

Warner devoted himself to evangelistic work. In 1886 he inaugurated the practice of using an evangelistic team and toured the churches with a group of musicians. He eventually married a member of the team. Music became an important part of his evangelistic work. He was a poet and wrote many songs, some of which were included in an early Church of God publication, *Anthems from the Throne*.

Warner died in 1895 at Grand Junction, Michigan, where the headquarters and campgrounds of the church had then been located.

Daniel S. Warner, *Poems of Grace and Truth* (Grand Junction, Mich., 1890).

——— , *Salvation, Present, Perfect, Now or Never* (Moundsville, W.V., n.d.).

——— , *Bible Proofs of the Second Work of Grace* (Goshen, Ind., 1880).

———, *The Church of God or What the Church Is and What It Is Not* (Anderson, Ind., 1885).

Andrew L. Byers, *Birth of a Reformation* (Anderson, Ind., 1921).

Barry L. Callen, ed., *The First Century* (Anderson, Ind., 1979).

Charles E. Brown, *When the Trumpet Sounded* (Anderson, Ind., 1951).

WATTS, Alan Wilson (January 6, 1915, Chislehurst, Kent, England—November 16, 1973, Sausalito, California); married Eleanor Everett, April 2, 1938 (annulled 1950); married Dorothy DeWitt, June 29, 1950 (div. 1963); married Mary Jean Froman, December 4, 1963.

Alan Watts, the major exponent of Buddhism in America during the mid-twentieth century, was born into a middle-class British family. As a child he was sent to boarding school, first St. Hugh's (1923–28) and then King's School, Canterbury. While at school he had his first encounters with Eastern religion through the works of Lafcadio Hearn and other Orientalists. Then he discovered the existence of a Buddhist lodge operating in England and in 1930 traveled to London to meet its leader, Christmas Humphreys. Humphreys introduced Watts to the writings of D. T. Suzuki, who had been translating Buddhist works into English. He also discovered Swami Vivekananda, the founder of the Vedanta Society (the first Hindu group in the West), and began to practice yoga. During his years at Canterbury, Watts rejected Christianity and wrote and published his first book on Zen, no copy of which has survived.

Watts did not go to a university. He left school in 1932 to work in his father's business, but continued his education through reading widely. He began to contribute articles to the Buddhist Lodge's periodical; in 1935 he wrote his first significant Buddhist work, *The Spirit of Zen*, a lay presentation of the more difficult material that Watts had absorbed from Suzuki. In 1936 Watts attended the meeting of the World Congress of Faiths in London, where he met Suzuki for the first time.

In 1938 Watts married the daughter of wealthy American Buddhist, Ruth Everett. He moved to New York City and associated with the First Zen Institute, founded by Sokei-an Sasaki, and began to teach.

The early years in America became a time of reevaluation of life for Watts. In 1940 he wrote a book, *The Meaning of Happiness*, in which he tried to interpret the East in the light of Christian experience. He also decided to give Christianity a second chance in his life; he enrolled at Seabury-Western Theological Seminary in Evanston, Illinois. He finished his theological work, and in 1945 he was ordained a priest in the Protestant Episcopal Church. The bishop appointed him chaplain at Northwestern University. During these years he wrote two works on Christian mysticism, *Behold the Spirit* and *Supreme Identity*.

Events were not going well for Watts, in spite of his popularity at Northwestern. In 1950 his marriage was dissolved, and he resigned from the ministry; he then lived in seclusion for a year, as he once again reevaluated his life. He emerged from his self-imposed exile in 1951 and moved to California as a faculty member of the newly formed American Academy of Asian Studies. His latent Buddhist tendencies reappeared to dominate the rest of his life.

In 1956 Watts published *The Way of Zen*, which was to become the major work introducing Americans to the practice of Zen Buddhism and which made Watts a popular lecturer. He began a period of writing and speaking as an advocate of Buddhism. Among his many books were *Beat Zen, Square Zen and Zen* (1956); *This Is It* (1960); *Psychotherapy East and West* (1961); *Beyond Theology* (1964); *The Book: On the Taboos Against Knowing Who You Are* (1973); and his autobiography, *In My Own Way* (1973).

In 1962 some of Watts's supporters organized the Society for Comparative Philosophy to facilitate his work while alive and carry on after his death. It began the *Alan Watts Journal* and continues to distribute his books and hold seminars and lectures on issues that have grown out of Watts's work.

Alan Watts, *An Outline of Zen Buddhism* (London, 1932).

———, *Beat Zen, Square Zen, and Zen* (San Francisco, Calif., 1959).

———, *In My Own Way: An Autobiography* (New York, 1972).

———, *The Spirit of Zen* (London, 1936; 2nd ed., 1955).

———, *The Way of Zen* (New York, 1957).

David Stuart, *Alan Watts* (New York, 1976).

Rich Fields, *How the Swans Came to the Lake* (Boulder, Colo., 1981).

WWW, VI, 426–27.

WEBB, Muhammad Alexander Russel (November 18, 1846, Hudson, New York—October 1, 1916, Rutherford, New Jersey); married Ella G. Weff.

Muhammad Alexander Russel Webb, the first American convert to Islam, began life as a Presbyterian. He found the church dull and restraining, and at the age of twenty, he simply walked away. He became a journalist and in 1873 purchased and managed his own newspaper. After three years he sold the paper and moved to Missouri. He joined the staff of the *St. Joseph Day Gazette* and later served as night editor of the *Missouri Republican*. During his years as a journalist he became a student of oriental religions and read widely in the new world of science that emerged in the late nineteenth century. Both only confirmed him in his religious skepticism.

In 1887 he was appointed United States consul in the Philippines. While living in Manila, he encountered and studied Islam and eventually accepted it as his religion. Having found a satisfying faith, he became a staunch advocate. He claimed, "It is the only system known to man which is strictly in harmony with religion and science."

He resigned his post in Manila in June 1892 and returned to the United States. On his way home he lectured in India. His three main lectures, "The Better Way," "Islam," and "Philosophic Islam," were published in a booklet in India. He settled in New York and established the Oriental Publishing Company. The first issue of *Moslem World*, a periodical, appeared the next spring. It continued for seven monthly issues (May to November).

Webb was the main representative of Islam at the World Parliament of Religions in Chicago in 1893. He spoke on "The Influence of Islam on

Social Conditions" and made a defense of Islamic social life in the face of attacks by Christian missionaries, who also addressed the Parliament. He also addressed the Parliament on "The Spirit of Islam."

During the remainder of his life, Webb emerged as the main spokesperson in America for the minuscule Moslem community. He opened a short-lived mosque in New York City. He wrote one book from an Islamic perspective on the Armenian war, *The Armenian Troubles and Where the Responsibility Lies* (1896). He authored numerous booklets on Islam including *An Outline of the Mohammedan Faith*; *The Five Pillars of Practice*; *Polygamy and Purdah*; and his major apology, *Islam in America*.

By the turn of the century, Webb had retired to Rutherford, New Jersey, where he lived quietly for the remaining years of his life. He was appointed Honorary Turkish Consul of New York by the Turkish Sultan, Abdul Hamid II, in recognition of his efforts.

After his death in 1916, Webb was forgotten. Unlike Buddhism and Hinduism, Islam has no current American group that can trace itself directly to the World Parliament of Religions or to the nineteenth-century efforts to convert Americans to Islam. Webb's role as a pioneer has received attention as scholars recognized the growth of Islam in the United States throughout the twentieth century.

Muhammad A. R. Webb, *Islam* (Bombay, India, 1892).

———, *Islam in America* (New York, 1893).

———, *A Guide to Namaz* (New York, 1893).

———, *Lectures on Islam* (Lahore, 1893).

———, *The Armenian Troubles and Where the Responsibility Lies* (Ulster Park, N.Y., 1896).

———, "The Influence of Social Conditions," in *The World's Congress of Religions* by J. W. Hanson (Chicago, 1894), 523–31.

Emery H. Tunison, "Mohammad Webb, First American Muslim," *The Arab World* 1, 3 (1945), 13–18.

Nadim Makdisi, "The Moslems of America," *Christian Century* (August 26, 1959), 969–71.

Islam Our Choice (Karachi, India, 1970).

WHITE, Alma Birdwell (June 16, 1862, Lewis County, Kentucky—June 26, 1946, Zarephath, New Jersey); married Kent White, December 21, 1887 (separated, 1910); education: Millersburg Female College, 1880–81, A.B.; University of Denver, A.M.

Alma White, founder and bishop of the Pillar of Fire, was one of eleven children born to a poor family in Kentucky. Her father was a tanner, and Alma joined her brothers and sisters in working in the tannery as a child. She developed aspirations to escape her situation by obtaining an education and becoming a teacher. She was encouraged by her family, and after a year at a local seminary, she obtained a teacher's certificate. Her first job was at a mountain school that had only a three-month session annually. She was also a religious child, having been raised in the Methodist Church by her mother. At the age of sixteen, she had a conversion experience at a Methodist revival meeting.

She spent the 1880–81 school year at Millersburg College, which enabled her to get a teaching post for a year at Paris, Kentucky. Then in

1882 she traveled to Montana and became a pioneer schoolteacher. She had been advised by her minister to marry a minister, because she had professed a call to the ministry at the time of her conversion. Her minister thought it would be more proper for her as a woman to express her "ministerial" desires through assisting a minister-husband. While in Montana she met and married a ministerial student and moved to Denver with him while he attended the university.

Working with her husband, who gave her leadership roles in congregational worship, satisfied her for a while. However, in 1893 she was sanctified; that is, she experienced what the Methodists called the second work of grace, the baptism of the Holy Spirit, which makes one perfect in love. After this experience, she felt unable to take a secondary role any longer and began to organize and conduct revival meetings on her own. Her efforts led to immediate trouble with the hierarchy of the Methodist Church. Because she was a woman, they were opposed to her work and in addition condemned the outbursts of emotional activity that accompanied her meetings. In the end, they saw her as another uncontrolled preacher working with the independent holiness associations. In 1901 she left the Methodist Church and formed the Methodist Pentecostal Union, which in 1917 was renamed the Pillar of Fire.

Alma became the bishop of the church; for a decade her husband assisted her. In 1909 he went to England; while there he decided he could no longer take second place to his wife. He withdrew from her church, settled in England, and eventually joined the Apostolic Faith Church, a British Pentecostal body.

Bishop White moved to Zerephath, New Jersey, where a tract of land had been donated to the church, and made that location her headquarters for the rest of her life. She put her total energies to work building the church. She traveled extensively, spoke frequently, and wrote many books. In 1921 she founded Alma White College at Zarephath, one of eight schools she started. She purchased two radio stations (in New Jersey and Colorado) and was among the first to begin a radio ministry. She authored more than two hundred books and several volumes of poetry.

As her history might suggest, Bishop White was an early advocate of women's rights. She actively recruited women ministers and edited *Woman's Chains*, one of several periodicals published by the church. She was also vegetarian. She was strongly anti-Catholic, a position that led her to one of her most controversial stances as an advocate for the Ku Klux Klan. She first encountered the Klan when they showed up at her church in Bound Brook, New Jersey, to stop an attack upon the building by what she described as a "Roman Catholic mob."

Bishop White died at the age of eighty-four after having built the Pillar of Fire into a national organization.

Alma B. White, *The Titanic Tragedy—God Speaking to the Nations* (Bound Brook, N.J., 1913).

——— , *The Story of My Life*, 2 volumes (Zarephath, N.J., 1919, 1921).

——— , *The New Testament Church* (Zarephath, N.J., 1929).

——— , *Why I Do Not Eat Meat* (Zarephath, N.J., 1938).

——— , *Guardians of Liberty*, 2 volumes (Zarephath, N.J., 1943).

Arthur Kent White, *Some White Family History* (Denver, Colo., 1948).
NAW, 3, 581–83.
DRB, 500–2.
WWW, II, 571.

WHITE, Ellen Gould Harmon (November 26, 1827, Gorham, Maine—July 16, 1915, St. Helena, California); married James White, August 30, 1846 (d. August 6, 1881).

Ellen Gould Harmon White, co-founder of the Seventh-Day Adventist Church, was born on a farm in rural Maine. She was named, in part, for her mother, Eunice Gould Harmon. Her family moved to Portland while Ellen was still a child, and her father worked as a hatmaker. Ellen's normal progress as a child was suddenly altered when, at the age of nine, she was hit by a rock. She remained unconscious for three weeks, after which she only partially recovered; reading made her dizzy. Also she was disfigured. When she reached the age of twelve, her parents gave up trying to keep her in school.

The Harmons were active Methodists. In 1842 Ellen had a conversion experience, and in June she was baptized (by immersion) and joined the Methodist Episcopal Church. During this same period, however, she and her family had heard William Miller speak and had become ardent Adventists, believing that Christ would return in 1843. In September 1843 the family members were disfellowshipped by the Methodists.

Ellen lived through the Great Disappointment, the failure of Christ to return visibly in October 1844, and stayed with the Adventists. In December 1844 she had the first of many visions in which she saw the Adventists marching to the City of God. She began to travel to various groups of Adventists in New England, relating her vision and exhorting them to remain true to their faith.

In Orrington, Maine, she met her future husband, an Adventist preacher, James White. At the time of their marriage both had been considering the issue of keeping the seventh-day sabbath—a concern presented to them in a pamphlet written by the Adventist minister Joseph Bates. A month after their marriage, they began to keep Saturday as the Sabbath. On April 3, 1847, Ellen had a vision in which she saw the Ten Commandments, with the fourth encircled by light. The vision confirmed the correctness of their new practice.

The Whites traveled among the Adventists, speaking and sharing their new views, and saw groups of sabbath-keeping Adventists emerge. In 1849 James began an Adventist journal, *The Present Truth*, and the following year, the *Review and Herald*, which remains to this day as the magazine of the Seventh-Day Adventist Church. In 1851 Ellen began her literary career with her first pamphlet, *A Sketch of the Christian Experience and Views of Ellen G. White*.

In 1855 the Whites moved their publishing concern to Battle Creek, Michigan, which would remain their center for many years. Shortly after the move, Ellen had a vision of the great conflict between the forces of good and evil. This vision led to her single most famous book, *The Great Controversy Between Christ and His Angels and Satan and His Angels.*

The Seventh-Day Adventist movement, of which the Whites were the recognized leaders, organized formally through a series of steps. In 1860 the name Seventh-Day Adventist Church was adopted. The publishing association was incorporated the next year. In 1863 a general conference adopted a constitution and formally organized the church.

Ellen spent the rest of her life traveling and writing on behalf of the church. Her visions continued throughout her life, and she is accepted by the church as having been called in a special manner as the messenger of the Lord. Her writings, though not considered equal to the Bible, are accepted as authoritative material by the church. Her role as a prophet and the "supernatural" element in her visions were questioned by several ministers and members of the church during the 1970s. The resulting controversy led to several ministers and leading members being disfellowshipped.

Ellen's voluminous writings were left to her estate, which still controls them. The royalties are paid to the church. In addition to many articles, she wrote more than twenty-five books and two hundred pamphlets.

Ellen Gould Harmon White, *Spiritual Gifts: My Christian Experience, Views and Labors* (Battle Creek, Mich., 1860).

———, *Life Sketches: Ancestry, Early Life, Christian Experience, and Extensive Labors, of Elder James White, and His Wife, Mrs. Ellen G. White* (Battle Creek, Mich., 1880).

———, *Life Sketches of Ellen G. White* (Mountain View, Calif., 1915).

———, *The Great Controversy Between Christ and Satan* (Washington, D.C., 1911).

———, *Patriarchs and Prophets* (Washington, D.C., 1890).

Francis D. Nichol, *Ellen G. White and Her Critics* (Washington, D.C., 1951).

Arthur L. White, *Ellen G. White, Messenger to the Remnant* (Washington, D.C., 1969).

René Noorbergen, *Ellen G. White, Prophet of Destiny* (New Canaan, Conn., 1972).

Ronald L. Numbers, *Prophetess of Health* (New York, 1976).

Walter T. Rea, *The White Lie* (Turlock, Calif., 1982).

DRB, 503–4.

DAB, 20, 98–9.

NAW 3, 585–8.

Seventh-Day Adventist Encyclopedia (Washington, D.C., 1969), 1584–97.

WWW, IV, 1004.

WILKINSON, Jemima (November 29, 1752, Cumberland, Rhode Island—July 1, 1819, Jerusalem Township, New York).

Jemima Wilkinson, the Publick Universal Friend and founder of a pioneering eighteenth-century religious community in the wilderness of western New York, was born into a Quaker family that had been among the first to join Roger Williams in the Rhode Island colony. She was one of twelve children. Her mother died when she was thirteen. Jemima became a devout Quaker and read the Bible to the point of memorizing much of it, as well as all the books in Quaker theology and history she could acquire.

Two events in 1776 changed her life. In August 1776 she was dismissed from the Society of Friends because of her attendance at the meeting of evangelist George Whitefield and her subsequent attraction for the New Light Baptists. Two months later she became ill with a "fever" that led to some delirium. When she recovered she was a different person. She claimed that during her period of illness she had actually died but had been sent back to deliver a message to humankind. She said she was no longer Jemima Wilkinson, but the Publick Universal Friend, her role on the mission from the divine. From that time forward, she did not answer to her given name, and her followers took pains to refer to her with the neutral term the *Friend* rather than *she*.

In the years immediately following her assumption of her new identity, she lived as an itinerant preacher in New England and the middle colonies. She soon had a growing following; regular preaching places were established in Rhode Island, Connecticut, and Pennsylvania. She used a building on the estate of Judge William Potter of South Kingstown, Rhode Island, as her headquarters.

Her message followed Quaker emphases. She preached repentance, the forsaking of evil, and the necessity of preparing for the future judgment. She advocated nonviolence (during the Revolutionary War), opposed slavery, dressed in plain clothes, and held up celibacy as the ideal (though she did not demand it of her followers). She adopted a short and somewhat masculine haircut and dressed in a long robe very similar to a clergyman's garb.

Followers were attracted to her, not by any unique theology but by her charismatic presence, her speaking ability, and the attribution of miraculous powers. Jemima was said to have healed the sick and to have prophesied and interpreted dreams. Some followers openly announced their belief that she was a messiah, though the Friend denied she possessed any divine powers and never accepted upon herself the messianic ascriptions of her disciples. She merely asked of her friends (followers), "Ye cannot be friends except ye do whatsoever I command you."

As early as 1785 the Friend conceived of a retreat for her followers so they could live their lives apart from the world. She sent one of them to western New York to secure land, and in 1788 a group began to clear a tract on the west side of Seneca Lake. Two years later the Friend joined what had become a settlement of 250 people. The colony was plagued from the beginning because of fraud in the sale of the land, their subsequent inability to secure clear title, and bickering about the division of land among the settlers. (There had been no intention to establish a communal living arrangement; all persons were to own land in proportion to their investments in the project.)

Finally, in 1794 the Friend moved farther west and established a second community, Jerusalem Township. She moved her poorer followers to this new settlement, where she resided in a house with her "faithful sisterhood," a band of celibate women who were her closest disciples. She spent the last days of her life ministering to the two communities of followers.

She finally succumbed to dropsy, from which she had suffered for several years; her body was buried in an unknown and unmarked grave. The society she created did not long survive her death; however, she is remembered as one of the first of America's religious leaders to offer a dramatic alternative to dominant religious patterns. She is also credited by historians with being a major force in encouraging the settlement of western New York.

Herbert A. Wisbey, Jr., *Pioneer Prophetess* (Ithaca, N.Y., 1964).

Mark Holloway, *Heavens on Earth* (London, 1951).

Arthur Bestor, *Backwoods Utopias* (Philadelphia, Penn., 1970).

NAW III, 609-10.

DRB, 512-3.

DAB, 20, 226-7.

WWWH, 581.

WILLIAMS, George (February 14, 1814, Thorp, Surrey, England—April 25, 1882, England; married Susannah Adelaid Louise.

George Williams—also known as the Prophet Cainan, the founder of the Church of the First Born, one branch of the remnant of the Morrisite Mormon group—began life in England as the son of a gardener. He was well into adulthood and married when he encountered the Mormon missionaries in the 1840s and joined the church in 1848. He became active in the Rotherham branch and in 1851 was ordained to the Aaronic priesthood. In 1855 he migrated to Utah and became a member of the Mill Creek Ward. He seems to have lived quietly in Utah for the next seven years, though he participated in the revival that swept the church in 1857 and was rebaptized, a sign of a new religious commitment.

During 1861 Prophet Joseph Morris established his settlement and the Church of Jesus Christ of Saints of the Most High. In June 1862 the settlement was attacked, and Joseph Morris killed. The followers scattered into Idaho, Montana, Nevada, and California. George Williams was not a member of the Morrisite movement; nor was he present at the settlement during the time of the attack. However, in the fall of 1862, he began to circulate a manuscript entitled "A Description of Interviews with Celestial Beings." The document related an encounter in April of 1862 in which God instructed him to begin preparing for life as prophet and leader of the Morrisites, who were called "The Church of the First Born the Holiest of All."

In subsequent revelatory encounters, Williams was ordained by two beings, Elias and Enoch, and identified as the reincarnation of the angel Cainan and of the Old Testament priest Melchisedec (or Melchizedek). From these revelations he began to be known as the Prophet Cainan. He initiated correspondence with the scattered Morrisite flock and made several trips to visit with them, though he continued to live in Salt Lake City.

In 1868 Cainan noted his intention to move to Montana, where a group of Morrisites who accepted his leadership had gathered. He appointed William M. James as head of the group in Deer Lodge Valley; Montana began to be seen as the center of the Church of the First Born. Then in 1869, unexpectedly and without explanation, Cainan moved back to England. On his way home, he stayed with some Morrisites in Council Bluffs, Iowa, who confirmed his prophetic role. This group migrated to Montana in 1872.

Cainan continued to lead the group for the rest of his life but did so by correspondence from England. For example, in 1874, when a division arose in the Deer Lodge community, he instructed the group in the creation of two stakes in such a way that the total community would not be destroyed. He also tried to build a European following. In 1868 he sent Soren Peter Guhl, a Danish-born follower, to build a Danish church. Instead Guhl went to Denmark, rejected Cainan, and built his own movement.

Cainan's health began to fail in 1880, and he died in the spring of 1882. The small band of followers in Montana continued well into the twentieth century.

George Williams, *Gems of Inspiration, A Collection of Sublime Thoughts by Modern Prophets*, compiled by J. R. Eardley (San Francisco, 1899).

C. Leroy Anderson, *For Christ Will Come Tomorrow: The Saga of the Morrisites* (Logan, Utah, 1981).

WINEBRENNER, John (March 25, 1797, Frederick County, Maryland—September 12, 1860, Harrisburg, Pennsylvania); married Charlotte Reutter, October 8, 1822 (d. May 20, 1834); married Mary Hamilton Mitchell, November 2, 1837 (d. May 22, 1888); education: Dickinson College, Carlisle, Pennsylvania, 1816.

John Winebrenner, founder of the Churches of God of North America (General Eldership), was born on a farm in rural Maryland and raised in the German Reformed Church (i.e., the Reformed church in the United States, now a constituent part of the United Church of Christ). Though initially opposed by his father, as a youth John developed an early inclination for the ministry and to that end he attended Dickinson College (though he did not graduate). In 1817 he moved to Philadelphia to study theology with Dr. Samuel Helffenstein, Sr., the pastor of Race Street Reformed Church, for the Reformed Church had not yet established a seminary.

Winebrenner studied in Philadelphia for two years, during which time he had a personal experience of regeneration under his revivalistically oriented tutor. In September 1820 he was ordained by the Reformed Synod meeting at Hagerstown, Maryland, and the following month he moved to Harrisburg, Pennsylvania, to become pastor of the Salem Reformed Church. His charge included preaching duties at three rural churches on a part-time basis.

In 1922 Winebrenner's first book appeared, *A Compendium of the Heidelberg Catechism*. That same year the trouble that had been growing slowly in his congregation in Harrisburg became public. A number of the leading members opposed Winebrenner's use of revivalistic techniques popularized by Charles G. Finney and known as "new measures." They particularly objected to women praying in public, praying for individuals by name in meetings, protracted meetings, the use of an anxious bench (for those under conviction of sin), and letting ministers from other denominations preach in the church's Sunday services. Though several attempts were made to find a compromise, the tension continued until April 1823, when he was denied entry into the church. This action by the vestry led to a split in the congregation, and Winebrenner continued to preach to his supporters.

The Reformed Synod of 1825 considered the issues of the Harrisburg situation and voted to support the church's vestry. Winebrenner cut his ties to the Reformed Church and, with his congregation's support, erected a church building in Harrisburg, Union Bethel Church. During these years of controversy Winebrenner had traveled widely in eastern Pennsylvania and Maryland and had preached at camp meetings and in Reformed Churches. People who had been converted under his ministry began to form congregations in fellowship with Union Bethel. From these congregations the Churches of God were formed.

During the controversy, Winebrenner was also changing his ideas and developing the perspective that was to dominate the Churches of God. He saw in the formation of Union Bethel and in the other congregations the opportunity to restore true primitive Christianity, which conformed to the biblical model and thus differed from the numerous "sects" that had in some measure departed from the apostolic church. He adopted the true name, the Church of God. By the time of his 1829 book, *A Brief View of the Formation, Government and Discipline of the Church of God*, he had become convinced that the true church was congregational in government, with elders and deacons designated as leaders. He also adopted a belief in immersion and was himself immersed by a United Brethren minister. He advocated foot washing as a third ordinance of the church. By 1830 the elders of the Church of God began to meet together; the "Eldership" emerged as an advisory body to facilitate cooperation among the Churches.

In 1830 Winebrenner resigned the pastorate of Union Bethel and for the rest of his life supported himself by writing and publishing. He published several revisions of I. D. Rupp's survey of American churches, *History of All the Religious Denominations in the United States* in the 1840s and 1850s. A *Prayer Meeting and Revival Hymn Book*, first printed in 1825, was his single most popular work, going through twenty editions before his death in 1860. The last decades of his life were spent as a preacher-at-large for the growing movement. His prestige allowed him strong support through the numerous controversies in which he became embroiled.

John Winebrenner, *A Brief View of the Formation, Government, and Discipline of the Church of God* (Harrisburg, Penn., 1829).

———, *Doctrinal and Practical Sermons* (Baltimore, Md., 1860).

———, *The Truth Made Known* (Harrisburg, Penn., 1824).

———, *History of All the Religious Denominations in the United States*, comp., (Lancaster, Penn., 1844).

Richard Kern, *John Winebrenner, 19th Century Reformer* (Harrisburg, Penn., 1974).

WWWH, 589.

WROE, John (September 19, 1782, Bowling, Bradford Parish, Yorkshire, England—February 5, 1863, Melbourne, Australia); married Appleby, 1815 (d. May 16, 1863).

John Wroe, the founder of the Christian Israelites, was the son of a worsted manufacturer and as a youth learned his father's trade. According to his autobiography, he was much abused and mistreated by both his father and his brothers. As a result of injuries, he had a humpback. He spent many years in deafness after a near drowning, though he was eventually cured. He had only one year of schooling and taught himself to write. As a young adult, he married and settled into business unhappily with his father.

In 1819 Wroe became so seriously ill that he feared for his life. The illness became the occasion for the nominally religious Wroe to begin serious reflection upon his spiritual state. Beginning November 11, 1819, Wroe experienced a series of visions in which he met and spoke with angels. One set of these visions created a desire in him to become a Jew, and he traveled to both Manchester and London seeking a rabbi. He was, however, unsuccessful in his quest.

In another vision he encountered Joanna Southcott, the visionary whose movement had spread across England. He took the vision as a sign that he should unite with the Southcottits, then under the leadership of George Turner. Wroe affiliated with the group at Bradford, which he impressed with his visions. Having seen other claimants to prophethood, the group at first resisted his assertions of leadership after Turner's death in 1821. Only in October 1822 did a majority of the ruling committee at Bradford accept his new role.

Having been accepted, Wroe moved quickly to consolidate his position. Earlier he had divested himself of his interests in his father's business and had hired himself out as a laborer with a wool-comber. He now began to travel to other Southcott groups and had great success in the north of England drawing meetings under his leadership. In April 1823 he traveled to Spain and then to Europe. In 1824 he chose Ashton as his new headquarters (though he continued to live in Bradford) and began to mold the distinctive movement he was to lead for the next four decades.

Wroe called his group Christian Israelites, and he imposed "Jewish" regulations upon them. He ordered them to observe fully the Mosaic laws. He prepared a uniform that they adopted, and the men ceased cutting their hair and beards. All abstained from tobacco and alcohol. Finally, he ordered them to learn Hebrew. The movement grew slowly through the 1820s but ran into trouble in 1830–31 when Wroe was involved in a scandal. Elders at Ashton accused him of illicit sexual encounters with several of the young female members. Wroe countered the accusations by transporting his printing press and headquarters to Wrenthrope and disaffiliating himself from the following at Ashton.

For the remainder of his life, Wroe concentrated upon building his following worldwide. In 1844 he sent the first representatives to the United States, where they organized a group in New York City. A few years later John L. Bishop arrived and organized what came to be known as the

Christian Israelite Church. The church spread across the United States from Massachusetts to Minnesota. Wroe came to the United States four times on his various world tours. Wroe's greatest success, however, was in Australia, and it was there he died at the age of eighty.

Only one congregation of the Christian Israelite church remains in the United States, located in Indianapolis, Indiana. Others of Wroe's followers joined the House of Israel headed by Benjamin Purnell, another prophet who came out of the Southcott lineage.

John Wroe, *The Life and Journal of John Wroe* (Ashton-under-Lyne, England, 1900).

———, *A Guide to People Surnamed Israelites* (Boston, 1848).

———, *Sermons Selected from the Scriptures* (Ashton-under-Lyne, England, 1880).

———, *The Faith of Israel* (Wakefield, England, 1843).

G. R. Balleine, *Past Finding Out* (New York, 1956).

J. F. C. Harrison, *The Second Coming, Popular Millenarianism 1780–1850* (London, 1979).

DNB 21, 1073–75.

YOGANANDA, Swami Paramahansa (Mukunda Lal Ghosh) (January 5, 1893, Gorakhpur, India—March 7, 1952, Los Angeles, California); education: Scottish Church College, Calcutta; Serampore College, Calcutta University, A.B., 1914.

The man known in the Western world as Swami Paramahansa Yogananda was born Mukunda Lal Ghosh to an affluent Bengali family living in the northern part of India, near the border of Nepal. Mukunda's father was an executive with the Bengal–Nagpur Railroad and was also a disciple of Lahiri Mahasaya, the reviver of kriya yoga in modern India. Mahasaya gave Mukunda's father one of the rare photos of himself, which became a treasured household possession.

As a child Mukunda would stare at the photograph and, on occasion, he would see the image of Mahasaya come alive. At the age of eight, he was healed by the photograph. He remembered a brilliant light coming from the picture and completely engulfing him. Only after his mother's death did he learn that Mahasaya had blessed him and predicted that he would become a yogi.

After finishing high school, Mukunda entered a hermitage at Benares, the Sri Bharat Dharma Mahamandal. While there he met Sri Yukteswar Giri, who was to become his guru (teacher). Yukteswar instructed him to enter college. He attended the Scottish Church College but transferred to Serampore College, an affiliate of Calcutta University, located in the town where Yukteswar lived. Thus Mukunda could both attend college and study with his guru. In 1914 he received his degree and took the vows of a monk in the Shankaracharya order, Giri (mountain) branch. He thus became Swami Yogananda (meaning "yoga is the path to bliss").

Yogananda had always had an interest in the education of youth; in 1917 he founded a school for boys at Dihika, Bengal. His efforts attracted the attention of the Maharaja of Kazimbazar; in 1918 he moved his school to Ranchi on a twenty-five-acre tract donated by the Maharaja. At his Yogoda Sat-Sanga Brahmacharya Vidyalaya, he taught not only the standard high school subjects but also yoga and meditation.

While Yogananda had shown a growing interest in the West, it took Yukteswar's insistence to overcome his reluctance and actually begin a mission to spread the teachings of yoga in the United States. The mission began in 1920 when Yogananda received an invitation to speak at an International Congress of Religious Liberals in Boston. He followed that meeting with three years of teaching in Boston and, in 1924, with a lecture tour across the United States. The response to his lecture tour was promising enough that centers were established and an American headquarters opened on Mount Washington Estates in Los Angeles. In 1923 he published a pamphlet, *Yogoda*, which contained his essential teachings and which went through numerous printings.

Prior to 1935 Yogananda called his work the Yogoda Satsanga Society, but that year he incorporated as the Self-Realization Fellowship. He prepared the lectures he had been giving to his students as a correspondence course that could be sent out weekly to his students around the United States. That same year he also made his last visit to India. He saw his guru again and was given the title *paramahansa* (literally, "supreme swan"), an indication that his guru recognized that Yogananda had reached the state of *nirbikalpa samadhi* ("irrevocable God-union").

Upon his return from India, Yogananda concentrated upon building the fellowship and writing his most famous book, *Autobiography of a Yogi*, published in 1946. In 1942 he opened the Church of All Religions in Hollywood and in 1950 the Self-Realization Lake Shrine and Mahatma Gandhi World Peace Memorial in Pacific Palisades, California.

Kriya yoga, which formed the central focus of Yogananda's teachings, is described as a scientific technique for God realization. The actual practice is revealed in teaching material given only to students of the fellowship but involves a psycho-physiological method by which, it is claimed, the blood is decarbonated and recharged with oxygen.

Yogananda was succeeded in leadership of the fellowship by Mr. J. J. Linn (also known as Rajasi Janakananda), who died in 1955. He in turn was succeeded by Sri Daya Mata. Major centers of the fellowship and the Church of All Worlds are in California, but smaller groups are scattered around the United States. The Yogoda Satsanga Society of India is also affiliated with the fellowship.

Swami Yogananda, *Autobiography of a Yogi* (Los Angeles, Calif., 1971).

———, *Yogoda* (Boston, 1924).

———, *Metaphysical Meditations* (Los Angeles, Calif., 1960).

———, *Whispers from Eternity* (Los Angeles, Calif., 1958).

Paramahansa Yogananda, In Memoriam (Los Angeles, Calif., 1958).

DRB, 536–8.

EOP, 1008.

YOUNG, Brigham (June 1, 1801, Whitingham, Vermont—August 29, 1877, Salt Lake City, Utah); married Mariam Works, October 8, 1824 (d. September 8, 1832); married Mary Ann Angel, February 1834.

Brigham Young, who became the leader of the largest group of the Church of Jesus Christ of Latter-day Saints after the death of founder

Joseph Smith in 1844, was born in Vermont but moved to New York at the age of three. The family's poverty led to frequent moves, which left little time for formal education. He married, began a career as a painter and carpenter, and, though not a very religious man, he joined the Methodist Episcopal Church. In 1829 he moved to Mendon, New York.

In 1830 he first became aware of the *Book of Mormon*. Both his father and his brother Phineas joined the Latter-Day Saints; in their company he visited the church at Columbia, Pennsylvania, where he spoke in tongues. He joined the church, and in 1832 he was baptized and ordained an elder. After his wife's death, he moved to Kirkland, Ohio, and used his carpentry skills to assist in the building of the temple. He remarried in 1834 and left soon afterward for his first missionary tour in the East.

Young showed himself a capable leader, and Smith named him to the Council of Twelve Apostles organized in 1835. In 1838 he accompanied Smith on the move to Missouri. His position in the church rose when one apostle was killed and another defected. When the governor of Missouri ordered the Saints out of his state, and Smith was arrested, the task of organizing the move to Illinois fell to Young.

After the settlement at Nauvoo was stabilized, Young went to England to head the British mission. During his brief stay, he saw the British edition of the *Book of Mormon* printed and the conversion of more than eight thousand people. England became the single largest source of new members.

In April 1841 Young left England to return to Nauvoo. Upon his arrival he was introduced to the idea of plural marriage by Smith. Though reluctant to accept the notion at once, he soon entered into it enthusiastically. He took his first plural wife, Lucy Ann Decker, on June 15, 1842. He married twice more in 1843, added four brides in 1844 and three in 1845. In 1846, the year of the migration out of Nauvoo, he married eight more women.

In 1844 Young went east to superintend Joseph Smith's presidential campaign. When word reached him of Smith's death, he returned to Nauvoo. Arriving in Nauvoo on August 6, he quickly persuaded the community to support the Council of Twelve Apostles, which he headed, over the various claimants to Smith's prophetic role. As the new leader of the church, he took a conciliatory role to avoid armed conflict. He negotiated and planned the exodus of church members from Nauvoo and personally led the first company of two thousand in February of 1846.

After a winter at Council Bluffs, Iowa, Young and over a hundred church members departed westward to find a new home. On July 24 Young saw for the first time the Salt Lake Valley and according to popular legend pronounced, "This is the place." He made the initial plans for a settlement and returned to Iowa to winter with the members still camped there. Over the winter he was sustained as president of the church. In May, with 1,200 followers he began the trek to Utah. The group arrived October 20, 1848. By the end of the year, five thousand people resided in Salt Lake City.

Young had emerged as both temporal and spiritual leader of the Salt

Lake Valley, and in 1849 he was named governor of the proposed state of Deseret. The next year Deseret was admitted as a territory of the United States but under the name "Utah." As leader of the church and governor, Young demonstrated his organizational genius; he oversaw a vast expansion program not only in Utah but throughout the Rocky Mountains and the Southwest. A missionary program throughout North America and Europe swelled the ranks of the church, and many of the new converts migrated to Utah. During Young's lifetime, over 350 settlements were begun by the more than 100,000 people who joined the church.

Young's career, however, was plagued by the polygamy issue. Once in Utah, the Saints practiced polygamy more-or-less openly, and in 1852 Young announced it as public doctrine. By the latest count, he married more than fifty women, of which twenty-seven were publicly acknowledged. The practice killed the idea of Deseret and led to the replacement of Young by a federally appointed territorial judge in 1858 (though Young, as head of the church, remained the most powerful man in the territory). He did not live to see the major efforts to eradicate polygamy in the 1880s and 1890s nor to hear his own church repudiate the doctrine, but he did witness the rise of federal power in Utah and the initial assaults on the Mormon marriage codes.

Brigham Young, *Journal of Discourses*, 26 volumes (Liverpool, England, 1854–86).

Leonard J. Arrington, *Brigham Young: American Moses* (New York, 1985).

———, *Great Basin Kingdom* (Lincoln, Neb., 1958).

Morris R. Werner, *Brigham Young* (New York, 1925).

Kimball Young, *Isn't One Wife Enough?* (New York, 1954).

Stanley P. Hirshson, *The Lion of the Lord* (New York, 1969).

DRB, 538–9.

DAB, 20, 620–23

WWWH, 602.

ZALMAN OF LADI, Rabbi Shneur (Elul 11, 5505 (1745), Liozna, Russia—Teveth 24, 5573 (1813), Piena, Russia); married Sterna Segal, 1760.

Rabbi Shneur Zalman of Ladi, founder of Chabad-Lubavitch Hasidism, was born in Byelorussia (in what is now the Soviet Union) from a long line of distinguished rabbis. He was given the best of early training in the Torah, Talmud, and Kabbalah (the mystical Jewish teachings) and was recognized as a child prodigy. At the age of twelve, he was sent to the center of Talmudic scholarship at Vitebsk, where he received a thorough grounding in traditional studies. At the age of fifteen he married the daughter of Rabbi Judah Leib Segal.

When he was twenty, he traveled to Meseretz, the Hasidic center in Poland, to study under Rabbi Dovber who had succeeded the Baal Shem Tov as head of the movement. In his two years at Meseretz he distinguished himself by his scholarly abilities.

Rabbi Zalman began his career as a rabbi by becoming the *maggid*, or preacher, in his hometown of Liozna in 1767. During the decade at Liozna, he developed the unique perspective on Hasidism that was to characterize the Lubavitch movement, and he began the revision of the *Shulchan*

Aruch, the handbook of Jewish law originally compiled by Rabbi Joseph Caro two centuries earlier. Zalman's *Shulchan Aruch* was his first major work. From 1773 to 1776, he headed the Liozna Academy, in which he trained his first disciples.

After a decade at Liozna, he transferred his headquarters to Ladi, which became the center for his mature work of spreading Chabad Hasidism. In 1799 he published his main work, the *Tanya*, which expounded his system.

Prior to the publication of the *Tanya*, there had been no regular method for the study of Hasidism; in creating his systematic approach, Zalman showed the influence of his scholarly background. His approach was termed *Chabad*, an acronym formed from the words *chockmah*, *binah*, and *daath*, the names of the first three realms, or *sephirot*, emanating from God in Kabbalistic understanding. Without losing the Hasidic mystical emphasis upon cleaving to God and joy in worship and service, Zalman wished also to preserve the more traditional Jewish approach to God through study and learning as well.

Theologically the Chabad had four unique ideas. Zalman emphasized God's individual (as opposed to His general) providence over all creation. He expounded the notion of God's continuous creation, the steady flow of life to the universe, and opposed the notion of God's self-limitation in place of which he proposed God's omnipresence. His radical approach to the understanding of God's presence in the cosmos led quite naturally to an appreciation for the reality of evil. Evil is not merely the nonexistent; evil was real and placed in the world by God to test humans for their ultimate good.

Major problems afflicted the Hasidic community in the years following Rabbi Dovber's death in 1772, the very period of Zalman's major accomplishments. He watched the Hasidic leadership fragment (with a number of Dovber's students spreading out to form their own dynasties) and experienced the emergence of the strong and organized opposition to the Hasidim from the traditional non-Kabbalistic Jewish rabbis, the Mitnagdim.

In 1798 the conflict with the Mitnagdim came to a head when Zalman was denounced as a traitor to the Russian government. He was arrested and taken to St. Petersburg and imprisoned. He impressed those placed in charge of his case and was released on express orders of the Czar. Two years later the whole event was repeated, but Zalman was ultimately vindicated.

Zalman's last days were spent in flight from Napoleon's armies. He became ill in the escape from Ladi and died in the small village of Piena, near Kurst. He was succeeded by his son, Rabbi Dovber (1778–1827); the lineage of leadership of the Chabad-Lubavitch Hasidism has been passed through the family to the present day. Rabbi Joseph Isaac Schneersohn, the head of the group, moved to Brooklyn, New York, in 1940. He took direct leadership of the small Lubavitcher community, which had been in existence since the 1920s, and built it into the only one of the many Hasidic groups to have centers across North America. The Lubavitch have been characterized by an aggressive approach to the Jewish community, which has resulted in their spectacular growth since World War II.

Gershon Kranzler, *Rabbi Shneur Zalman of Ladi* (Brooklyn, N.Y., 1975).

Naftali, Hertz Ehrman, *The Rav* (Jerusalem, 1977).

Challenge (London, 1974).

Ben Zion Bokser, *The Jewish Mystical Tradition* (New York, 1981).

Jacob S. Minkin, *The Romance of Hasidism* (New York, 1935).

APPENDIX I:
RELIGIOUS FAMILY TRADITIONS

Individuals in this volume founded or led one particular sectarian or alternative religious body. They also helped shape a religious tradition. Below they are listed under the various religious families. The attempt has been at inclusive listings; thus those prominent in more than one tradition are listed in both. (For example: Clarence Jordan was a Baptist who founded a commune.)

ADVENTIST
William Miller
Benjamin Purnell
Charles Taze Russell
Joseph Franklin Rutherford
Joanna Southcott
George Storrs
Ellen Gould Harmon White
John Wroe

BAHA'I
Abdu'l-Baha
Baha'u'llah
Shoghi Effendi Rabbani
Charles Mason Remey

BAPTIST
Johann Conrad Beissel
Clarence Jordan
Robert T. Ketcham
John Franklin Norris
Daniel Parker

BUDDHIST
Paul Carus
Anagarika Dharmapala
Dwight Goddard
Ernest Hunt
Shigatsu Sasaki
Nyogen Senzaki
Soyen Shaku
Daisetz Teitaro Suzuki
Alan Wilson Watts

COMMUNAL
Eberhard Arnold
Adin A. Ballou
Johann Conrad Beissel
Father Major Jealous Divine
Thomas Lake Harris
Jacob Hutter
Eric Jansson
Clarence Jordan
William Keil
Johannes Kelpius
Ann Lee
Christian Metz
John Ballou Newbrough
John Humphrey Noyes
Robert Dale Owen
George Rapp
Cyrus Read Teed
Jemima Wilkinson

FREE THOUGHT/ RATIONALISM
Felix Adler
Abner Kneeland
Joseph Lewis
Robert Dale Owen
Elihu Palmer
Charles Lee Smith

HINDU
Sri Aurobindo
Pierre Bernard
Paramahansa Muktananda
Swami Paramananda
A. C. Bhaktivedanta Swami Prabhupada
Sai Baba of Shirdi
Sri Ramakrishna
Swami Sivananda
Swami Vivekananda
Paramahansa Yogananda

HOLINESS
William Booth
Phineas Franklin Bresee
Charles Price Jones
Martin Wells Knapp
Lightfoot Solomon Michaux
Phoebe Worrall Palmer
Benjamin Titus Roberts
Frank W. Sandford
Orange Scott
Albert Benjamin Simpson
Daniel Sidney Warner
Mollie Alma Birdwell White
John Winebrenner

ISLAM
Mirza Ghulam Hazrat Ahmed
Timothy Drew (Noble Drew Ali)
Georgei Ivanovitch Gurdjieff
Hazrat Inayat Khan
Samuel L. Lewis
Meher Baba
Elijah Muhammad
Muhammad Alexander Russell Webb

JEWISH
Felix Adler
Israel Baal Shem Tov
Arnold Josiah Ford
Joel Sol Goldsmith
Wentworth Arthur Matthew
Rabbi Nachman of Breslov
Shneur Zalman of Ladi

LUTHERAN
Elling Eielsen
Eric Jansson

MAGICK
See WITCHCRAFT.

MENNONITE/BRETHREN/ QUAKER
Jakob Ammann
John Herr
Elias Hicks
John Holdeman
Jacob Hutter
Alexander Mack
Menno Simons
Christian Metz
John H. Oberholtzer
George Rapp
Caspar Schwenckfeld von Ossig
Jemima Wilkinson

METHODIST
William Booth

Lorenzo Dow
James O'Kelly
Phoebe Worrall Palmer
Benjamin Titus Roberts
Peter Spencer

MORMON
Rulon Clark Allred
Alpheus Cutler
Otto Fetting
Ervil Morrell LeBaron
Joel Franklin LeBaron
Joseph Morris
Joseph White Musser
Sidney Rigdon
Joseph Smith, Jr.
James Jesse Strang
Charles Blanchard Thompson
George Williams
Brigham Young

NEW THOUGHT/ CHRISTIAN SCIENCE
William Walker Atkinson
Nona Lovell Brooks
Father Major Jealous Divine
Mary Baker Eddy
Warren Felt Evans
Charles Sherlock Fillmore
Mary Caroline "Myrtle" Fillmore
Ursula Newell Gestefeld
Joel Sol Goldsmith
Ernest Shurtleff Holmes
Emma Curtis Hopkins
Phineas Parkhurst Quimby
Frank B. Robinson
Augusta Emma Simmons Stetson
Elizabeth Lois Jones Towne

OLD CATHOLIC
William H. F. Brothers

Carmel Henry Carfora
Michel Collin
Irving Steiger Cooper
Duc de Landas Berghes
Frederic Ebenezer John Lloyd
George Alexander McGuire
Arnold Harris Mathew
Aftimios Ofiesh
George W. Plummer
Joseph René Vilatte

PENTECOSTAL
Asa Alonzo Allen
Eudorus N. Bell
William Marrion Branham
Florence Louise Crawford
William H. Durham
J. J. Roswell Flower
Garfield Thomas Haywood
George Went Hensley
Grady R. Kent
Joseph Hillery King
Kathryn Kuhlman
John Graham Lake
Gordon Lindsey
Aimee Semple McPherson
Charles Harrison Mason
Eugene Crosby Monroe
Francisco Olazabal
Charles Fox Parham
W. J. Seymour
Richard G. Spurling, Jr.
Ambrose Jessup Tomlinson
Homer A. Tomlinson

PRESBYTERIAN
John Graham Machen

PSYCHIC/OCCULT
George Adamski
Edna A. Wheeler Ballard
Guy W. Ballard

Elbert Benjamine
Luke Dennis Broughton
Thomas H. Burgoyne
Edgar Cayce
Edwin John Dingle
Gloria Lee (Byrd)
Olney H. Richmond
Baird Thomas Spaulding
Emmanuel Swedenborg

ROSICRUCIAN

Johann Valentin Andrae
Max Heindel
Johannes Kelpius
Harvey Spencer Lewis
George Winslow Plummer
Pascal Beverly Randolph

SANT MAT (SIKH)

Jaimal Singh
Kirpal Singh
Sawan Singh
Seth Shiv Dayal Singh
John Paul Twitchell

SHINTO

Bunjiro Kawate
Miki M. Nakayama

SPIRITUALIST

Emma Hardinge Britten
Andrew Jackson Davis
Arthur Augustus Ford
Ann Leah Fox
Catherine Fox
Margaret Fox
Thomas Lake Harris
George W. Hurley
John Ballou Newbrough

Robert Dale Owen
Emmanuel Swedenborg

THEOSOPHY

Alice LaTrobe Bateman Bailey
Annie Wood Besant
Helena Petrovna Blavatsky
Emma Hardinge Britten
Irving Steiger Cooper
Max Heindel
William Quan Judge
Charles Webster Leadbeater
Henry Steel Olcott
Harold W. Percival
Nicholas Roerich
Rudolf Steiner
Katherine Augusta Westcott
     Tingley

WITCHCRAFT and
MAGICK

Aleister Crowley
Gerald Brousseau Gardner
Samuel Liddell Mathers

MISCELLANEOUS

Frank Nathan Daniel Buchman
George David Cummins
John Nelson Darby
John Alexander Dowie
Henry Drummond
Joseph C. Dylks
Frederick William Grant
Edward Irving
James Warren Jones
Adolph E. Knoch
Watchman Nee
L. T. Nichols
Mokichi Okada
Yoshikazu Okada

APPENDIX II:
LISTING BY BIRTHPLACE

UNITED STATES

ALABAMA
| Joseph Lewis | June 11, 1889 | Montgomery |
| John Franklyn Norris | Sept. 18, 1877 | Dadeville |

ARKANSAS
| Asa Alonzo Allen | Mar. 27, 1911 | Sulfur Rock |
| Charles Lee Smith | 1887 | Near Ft. Smith |

CALIFORNIA
Irving Steiger Cooper	Mar. 16, 1882	Santa Barbara
Gloria Lee (Byrd)	Mar. 22, 1926	Los Angeles
Samuel Leonard Lewis	Oct. 18, 1896	San Francisco

CONNECTICUT
Lorenzo Dow	Oct. 15, 1777	Coventry
Emma Curtis Hopkins	Sept. 2, 1853	Killingly
Elihu Palmer	Aug. 7, 1764	Canterbury

DELAWARE
| George David Cummins | Dec. 11, 1822 | Smyrna |

FLORIDA
| Eudorus N. Bell | June 27, 1866 | Lake Butler |
| Arthur Augustus Ford | Jan. 8, 1897 | Titusville |

GEORGIA

George Willie Hurley	Dec. 9, 1865	Texas Valley (near Rome)
Charles Price Jones	Feb. 17, 1884	Reynolds
Clarence Jordan	July 29, 1912	Talbotton
Grady R. Kent	Apr. 26, 1909	Rosebud
Elijah Muhammad	Oct. 10, 1897	Sandersville

ILLINOIS

Gordon Lindsey	June 18, 1906	Zion

INDIANA

Garfield Thomas Haywood	July 15, 1880	Greencastle
James Warren Jones	May 13, 1931	Near Lynn
L. T. Nichols	Oct. 1, 1844	Elkhart
Seth Cook Rees	Aug. 6, 1854	Westfield
Ambrose Jessup Tomlinson	Sept. 22, 1865	Near Westfield
Homer A. Tomlinson	Oct. 25, 1892	Near Westfield

IOWA

Edna A. W. Ballard	June 25, 1886	Burlington
Elbert Benjamine	Dec. 12, 1882	
Pierre Bernard	1875	Leon
Charles Fox Parham	June 4, 1873	Muscatine
Charles Mason Remey	May 15, 1874	Burlington

KANSAS

Guy W. Ballard	June 28, 1878	Newton

KENTUCKY

William Marrion Branham	Apr. 6, 1909	Burkesville
Nona Lovell Brooks	Mar. 22, 1861	Louisville
Edgar Cayce	Mar. 18, 1877	Hopkinsville
William H. Durham	1873	
Benjamin Purnell	Mar. 27, 1861	Greenup City
John Paul Twitchell	Oct. 22, 1908?	Paducah
Mollie Alma Birdwell White	June 16, 1862	Lewis County

LOUISIANA
William Joseph Seymour	May 2, 1870	Centerville

MAINE
Ursula Newell Gestefeld	Apr. 22, 1845	Augusta
Ernest Shurtleff Holmes	Jan. 21, 1887	Lincoln
Frank Weston Sandford	Oct. 2, 1862	Bowdoinham
Augusta Emma Simmons Stetson	Oct. 12, 1842	Waldoboro
Ellen Gould Harmon White	Nov. 26, 1827	Gorham

MARYLAND
William Walker Atkinson	Dec. 5, 1862	Baltimore
John Gresham Machen	July 28, 1881	Baltimore
Peter Spencer	1779	Kent County
John Winebrenner	Mar. 25, 1797	Frederick County

MASSACHUSETTS
Dwight Goddard	July 5, 1861	Worcester
Abner Kneeland	Apr. 7, 1774	Gardner
William Miller	Feb. 15, 1782	Pittsfield
George Winslow Plummer	Aug. 25, 1876	Boston
Katherine Augusta Westcott Tingley	July 6, 1847	Newburyport

MICHIGAN
Otto Fetting	Nov. 20, 1871	St. Clair
Martin Wells Knapp	Mar. 27, 1853	Clarendon
Olney H. Richmond	Feb. 22, 1844	St. John's, Clinton County

MINNESOTA
Charles Sherlock Fillmore	Aug. 22, 1854	St. Cloud

MISSOURI
Adolph Ernst Knoch	Dec. 12, 1874	St. Louis
Kathryn Kuhlman	May 7, 1907	Concordia
Joseph Franklin Rutherford	Nov. 8, 1869	Morgan County

NEW HAMPSHIRE

Alpheus Cutler	Feb. 29, 1784	Plainfield
Mary Baker Eddy	July 16, 1821	Bow
Phineas Parkhurst Quimby	Feb. 16, 1802	Lebanon
George Storrs	Dec. 13, 1796	Lebanon

NEW JERSEY

Harvey Spencer Lewis	Nov. 25, 1883	Frenchtown
Henry Steel Olcott	Aug. 2, 1832	Orange

NEW YORK

Phineas Franklin Bresee	Dec. 31, 1838	Franklin Township
Andrew Jackson Davis	Aug. 11, 1826	Blooming Grove
Ann Leah Fox	1814	Rockland County
Joel Sol Goldsmith	Mar. 10, 1892	New York City
Elias Hicks	Mar. 19, 1748	Hempstead Township, Long Island
Eugene Crosby Monroe	May 20, 1880	Sherman
Phoebe Worrall Palmer	Dec. 18, 1807	New York City
Paschal Beverly Randolph	Oct. 8, 1825	New York City
Benjamin Titus Roberts	July 25, 1823	Cattaraugus
Frank B. Robinson	July 5, 1886	New York City
Baird Thomas Spaulding	May 26, 1872	Kohocton
James Jesse Strang	Mar. 21, 1813	Scipio, Cayuga County
Cyrus Read Teed	Oct. 13, 1839	Moravia
Charles Blanchard Thompson	Jan. 27, 1814	?
Muhammad Alexander Russell Webb	Nov. 18, 1846	Hudson

NORTH CAROLINA

Timothy Drew	Jan. 8, 1886

OHIO

Mary Caroline "Myrtle" Fillmore	Aug. 6, 1845	Pagetown
John Holdeman	Jan. 31, 1832	New Pittsburg, Wayne County
John Ballou Newbrough	June, 5, 1828	Near Springfield
Daniel Sidney Warner	June 25, 1842	Marshallville

OREGON
Florence Louise Crawford	Sept. 1, 1872	Coos County
Elizabeth Lois Jones Towne	May 11, 1865	Portland

PENNSYLVANIA
Frank Nathan Daniel Buchman	June 4, 1878	Pennsburg
John Herr	Sept. 18, 1782	Lancaster County
Robert Thomas Ketcham	July 22, 1889	Nelson
John H. Oberholtzer	Jan. 10, 1809	Near Clayton, Berks County
Sidney Rigdon	Feb. 19, 1793	Piny Fork
Charles Taze Russell	Feb. 16, 1852	Pittsburgh

RHODE ISLAND
Adin A. Ballou	Apr. 23, 1803	Cumberland
Jemima Wilkinson	Nov. 29, 1752	Cumberland

SOUTH CAROLINA
Joseph Hillery King	Aug. 11, 1869	Anderson County

TENNESSEE
Charles Harrison Mason	Sept. 8, 1866	Near Memphis

UTAH
Joel Franklin LeBaron	July 9, 1923	Laverkin
Joseph White Musser	Mar. 8, 1872	Salt Lake City

VERMONT
Warren Felt Evans	Dec. 23, 1817	Rockingham
John Humphrey Noyes	Sept. 3, 1811	Brattleboro
Orange Scott	Feb. 13, 1800	Brookfield
Joseph Smith, Jr.	Dec. 23, 1805	Sharon
Brigham Young	June 1, 1801	Whitingham

VIRGINIA
Lightfoot Solomon Michaux	Nov. 7, 1884	Newport News
Daniel Parker	Apr. 6, 1781	Culpepper County

UNKNOWN
Father Major Jealous Divine   circa 1880?   Georgia?
Joseph C. Dylks
George Went Hensley   1870s?

OTHER COUNTRIES

ANTIGUA
George Alexander McGuire   Mar. 26, 1866   Sweets

ARMENIA
Georgei I. Gurdjieff   Jan. 13, 1872   Alexandropol

BARBADOS
Arnold Josiah Ford   1890s?
Harold Waldwin Percival   Apr. 15, 1868   Bridgetown

CANADA
Joseph James Roswell Flower   June 17, 1888   Belleville, Ontario
Catherine Fox   1839?   Bath, Ontario
Margaret Fox   1833?   Bath, Ontario
John Graham Lake   Mar. 18, 1870   St. Mary's, Ontario
Aimee Semple McPherson   Oct. 9, 1890   Ingersoll, Ontario
Albert Benjamin Simpson   Dec. 15, 1843   Cavendish, P.E.I.

CEYLON
See SRI LANKA.

CHINA
Watchman Nee   Nov. 4, 1903   Swatow, Kwangtung
                                                     Province

DENMARK
Max Heindel   July 23, 1865

ENGLAND

Alice LaTrobe Bateman Bailey	June 16, 1880	Manchester
Annie Wood Besant	Oct. 1, 1847	London
William Booth	Apr. 10, 1829	Nottingham
Emma Hardinge Britten	1823	London
William H. F. Brothers	April 7, 1887	Nottingham
Luke Dennis Broughton	April 20, 1828	Leeds, Yorkshire
Aleister Crowley	Oct. 12, 1875	Leamington, Warwickshire
Edwin John Dingle	Apr. 6, 1881	Paignton, Devonshire
Henry Drummond	Dec. 5, 1786	The Grange, Hampshire
Gerald Brousseau Gardner	June 13, 1884	Blundellsands
Frederick William Grant	July 25, 1834	London
Thomas Lake Harris	May 15, 1823	Fenny Stratford, Buckingham
Ernest Hunt	Aug. 16, 1878	Hoddesdon, Herts.
Charles Webster Leadbeater	Feb. 16, 1854	Stockport, Cheshire
Ann Lee	Feb. 29, 1736	Manchester
Frederic Ebenezer John Lloyd	1859	Milford Haven, South Wales
Samuel Liddell Mathers	Jan. 8, 1854	London
Joseph Morris	Dec. 15, 1824	Burwardsley, Cheshire
Joanna Southcott	Apr. 25, 1750	Tarford, Devonshire
Alan Wilson Watts	Jan. 6, 1915	Chislehurst, Kent
George Williams	Feb. 14, 1814	Thorp, Surrey
John Wroe	Sept. 19, 1782	Bowling, Bradford Parish, Yorkshire

FRANCE

Michel Collin	1905	Beachy
Arnold Harris Mathew	Aug. 6, 1852	Montpellier, Heraulh
Joseph René Vilatte	Jan. 24, 1854	Paris

GERMANY

Felix Adler	Aug. 13, 1851	Alzey
Johann Valentin Andrae	Aug. 7, 1586	Herrenburg, Württemburg
Eberhard Arnold	July 26, 1883	Königsberg
Johann Conrad Beissel	Mar. 1, 1690	Eberbach, Palatinate
Paul Carus	July 18, 1852	Ilsenburg

William Keil	Mar. 6, 1812	Prussia
Alexander Mack, Sr.	July 1679	Schriesheim, Palatinate
Christian Metz	Dec. 30, 1794	Neuwied
George Rapp	Nov. 1, 1757	Iptingen, Württemburg
Caspar Schwenckfeld von Ossig	1489	Ossig, Silesia
Richard G. Spurling, Jr.	1858	

HUNGARY

Rudolf Steiner	Feb. 27, 1861	Kraljevic

INDIA

Sri Aurobindo	Aug. 15, 1872	Calcutta, Bengal
Hazrat Inayat Khan	July 5, 1882	Baroda, Gujarat
Meher Baba	Feb. 25, 1894	Poona
Paramahansa Muktananda	May 16, 1908	Dharmasthala
Swami Paramananda	Feb. 5, 1885	Banaripura, Bengal
A. C. Bhaktivedanta Swami Prabhupada	Sept. 1, 1896	Calcutta, Bengal
Sai Baba of Shirdi	1856?	Hyderabad
Sri Ramakrishna	Feb. 18, 1836	Kamarpukur, Bengal
Jaimal Singh	July 1839	Ghuman, Punjab
Sawan Singh	July 27, 1858	Mehmansinghwala, Punjab
Seth Shiv Dayal Singh	Aug. 25, 1818	Agra, United Provinces
Swami Sivananda	Sept. 8, 1887	Pattamadai
Swami Vivekananda	Jan. 12, 1863	Calcutta
Paramahansa Yogananda	Jan. 5, 1893	Gorakhpur

IRAN

Abdu'l-Baha	May 23, 1844?	Teheran
Baha'u'llah	Nov. 12, 1817	Teheran

IRELAND

John Nelson Darby	Nov. 18, 1800	Westminster
William Quan Judge	Apr. 13, 1851	Dublin
James O'Kelly	Oct. 1735?	

ISRAEL
Shoghi Effendi Rabbani   Mar. 1, 1897   Akka (Acre)

ITALY
Carmel Henry Carfora   Aug. 27, 1878   Naples
Jacob Hutter   Moos, South Tyrol
Duc de Landas Berghes   Nov. 1, 1893   Naples

JAPAN
Bunjiro Kawate   Sept. 29, 1814   Kandori, Urami
                                                          Village

Miki Macgawa Nakayama   June 2, 1798   Sammaiden, Yomato
                                                          Prov.

Mokichi Okada   Dec. 23, 1882   Tokyo
Yoshikazu Okada   Feb. 27, 1901   Tokyo
Shigatsu Sasaki   1882
Soyen Shaku   1859
Daisetz Teitaro Suzuki   Oct. 18, 1870   Kanazawa

LEBANON
Aftimios Ofiesh   Oct. 22, 1880   Mohiedhthet

MEXICO
Rulon Clark Allred   Mar. 29, 1906   Chihuahua
Ervil Morrell LeBaron   Feb. 22, 1925   Colonia Juarez,
                                                          Chihuahua
Francisco Olazabal   Oct. 12, 1886   El Verano, Sonora

NETHERLANDS
Menno Simons   1496   Witmarsum,
                                                          Friesland

NIGERIA
Wentworth Arthur Matthew   June 23, 1892   Lagos

NORWAY
Elling Eielsen   Sept. 19, 1804   Voss

PAKISTAN

Mirza Ghulam Hazrat Ahmad	Feb. 13, 1835	Qadian
Kirpal Singh	Feb. 6, 1894	Sayyad Kasran, Rawalpindi

POLAND

George Adamski	April 17, 1891	
Israel Baal Shem Tov	Elul 18, 1698	Akop

ROMANIA

Johannes Kelpius	1673	Halwegen, Transylvania

RUSSIA
See UKRAINE.

Nicholas Roerich	Oct. 9, 1874	St. Petersburg
Nyogen Senzaki	1876	Siberia
Shneur Zalman of Ladi	Elul 11, 5505 (1745)	Liozna

SCOTLAND

Thomas H. Burgoyne	Apr. 14, 1855	
John Alexander Dowie	May 25, 1847	Edinburgh
Edward Irving	Aug. 4, 1792	Annan
Robert Dale Owen	Nov. 9, 1801	Glasgow

SRI LANKA (CEYLON)

Anagarika Dharmapala	Sept. 17, 1864	Columbo

SWEDEN

Eric Jansson	Dec. 19, 1808	Bishopskulla
Emmanuel Swedenborg	Jan. 29, 1688	Stockholm

SWITZERLAND

Jakob Ammann	Feb. 12, 1644	Erlenbach, Bern

UKRAINE

Helena Petrovna Blavatsky	July 30, 1831	Ekaterinoslav (now Dnepropetrovsk)
Rabbi Nachman of Breslov	Nisan 1, 5532 (1772)	Medzibuz

APPENDIX III:
RELIGIOUS BACKGROUNDS

This appendix lists—where the information is available—the religious background of each founder of a new sect or cult. Where two or more religions strongly influenced a person, he or she will be listed more than once. Thus, in the case of a person who departed from the faith of childhood and/or early adulthood, he or she will be listed under the newly created cult as well. However, in the case of a sectarian variation, where the person merely created a new branch of a religious denomination, the listing is under that principal religious family. In the case of disseminators of Eastern religions—where no new religion was created but rather a religion new to American culture was transported to the United States—the listing occurs under the parent religion.

ADVENTISM
Charles Taze Russell

ANGLICAN/EPISCOPAL
Alice L. B. Bailey
Annie W. Besant
William H. F. Brothers
George David Cummins
John Nelson Darby
Henry Drummond
Charles S. Fillmore
Arthur A. Ford
Frederick W. Grant
Ernest Hunt
Charles W. Leadbeater
Frederic E. J. Lloyd
George Alexander McGuire
Arnold H. Mathew
Joanna Southcott
Alan Watts
John Wroe

BAHA'I
Shoghi Effendi Rabbani

BAPTIST
Eudorus N. Bell
William M. Branham
William H. Durham
Arthur A. Ford
Dwight Goddard
Garfield Thomas Haywood
George Willis Hurley
Charles P. Jones
Clarence Jordan
Robert T. Ketcham
Abner Kneeland
Kathryn Kuhlman
Charles H. Mason
Lightfoot Solomon Michaux
William Miller
J. Frank Norris
Daniel Parker
Sidney Rigdon

Frank B. Robinson
J. F. Rutherford
Frank W. Sandford
W. J. Seymour
Richard G. Spurling, Jr.
James J. Strang

BUDDHIST
Anagarika Dharmapala
Miki Maegawa Kakagawa
Shigatsu Sasaki
Nyogen Senzaki
Soyen Shaku
D. T. Suzuki

CHRISTIAN CHURCH (DISCIPLES OF CHRIST)
Adin Ballou
Edgar Cayce
Arthur A. Ford
James Warren Jones
Sidney Rigdon

CONGREGATIONAL CHURCH
John Alexander Dowie (Australia)
Mary Baker Eddy
Thomas Lake Harris
Ernest S. Holmes
John Humphrey Noyes
George Storrs
Katherine A. W. Tingley

FREE THOUGHT
Florence Louise Crawford
John Humphrey Noyes

FRIENDS (QUAKERS)
Elias Hicks

Seth Cook Rees
Ambrose J. Tomlinson
Homer A. Tomlinson
Jemima Wilkinson

HINDU
Sri Aurobindo
Swami Muktananda
Swami Paramananda
A. C. Bhaktivedanta Swami Prabhupada
Sri Ramakrishna
Sai Baba of Shirdi
Swami Sivananda
J. Paul Twitchell
Swami Vivekananda
Swami Yogananda

HOLINESS
Grady R. Kent
Aimee Semple McPherson
Charles H. Mason
W. J. Seymour

ISLAM
Abdu'l-Baha
Mirza G. H. Ahmad
Baha'u'llah

JEWISH
Felix Adler
Israel Baal Shem Tov
Joel S. Goldsmith
Joseph Lewis
Samuel L. Lewis
Nachman of Breslov
Zalman of Ladi

LUTHERAN
Johann V. Andrae (Germany)

Eberhard Arnold (Germany)
Johann Conrad Beissel
  (Germany)
Frank N. D. Buchman
Paul Carus (Germany)
Elling Eielsen (Norway)
Eric Jansson (Germany)
William Keil (Germany)
Johannes Kelpius (Germany)
Christian Metz (Germany)
George Rapp (Germany)
Emmanuel Swedenborg
  (Sweden)

MENNONITE
John Herr
John Holdeman
John H. Oberholtzer

METHODIST
A. A. Allen
William Booth (British)
Phineas F. Bresee
George David Cummins
Lorenzo Dow
Warren Felt Evans
M. C. "Myrtle" Fillmore
J. J. Roswell Flower
Ann Leach Fox
Catherine Fox
Margaret Fox
Garfield Thomas Haywood
William Q. Judge (Ireland)
Robert T. Ketcham
Joseph H. King
Martin Wells Knapp
Kathryn Kuhlman
John Graham Lake
H. Spencer Lewis
Aimee Semple McPherson
James O'Kelly
Francisco Olazabal
Watchman Nee

Phoebe W. Palmer
Charles Fox Parham
Benjamin T. Roberts
Orange Scott
W. J. Seymour
Charles Lee Smith
Peter Spencer
Augusta Stetson
George Storrs
Elizabeth L. J. Towne
Daniel S. Warner
Alma White
Ellen G. White
Brigham Young

MORMON
Rulon C. Allred
Otto Fetting
Ervil M. LeBaron
Joel F. LeBaron
Joseph Morris
Joseph White Musser
Charles B. Thompson
George Wiliams

ORTHODOXY, EASTERN
Helena P. Blavatsky
Georgei I. Gurdjieff
Aftimios Ofiesh
Nicholas Roerich

PENTECOSTAL
Gordon Lindsey
Wentworth Arthur Matthew
Eugene Crosby Monroe
Homer A. Tomlinson

PLYMOUTH BRETHREN
Aleister Crowley
Adolph E. Knoch
Watchman Nee

PRESBYTERIAN
Nona Lovell Brooks
George David Cummins
Edward Irving (Church of
    Scotland)
J. Gresham Machen
Elihu Palmer
Charles Taze Russell
Albert Benjamin Simpson
Muhammad A. R. Webb

REFORMED
Alexander Mack, Sr.
John Winebrenner

ROMAN CATHOLIC
Carmel Henry Carfora
Michel Collin
Duc de Landas Berghes
Arnold H. Mathew
Caspar Schwenckfeld von Ossig
Menno Simons
Joseph René Vilatte

SHINTO
Bunjiro Kawate
Mokichi Okada
Yoshikazu Okada

SIKH
Jaimal Singh
Kirpal Singh
Sawan Singh
Seth Shiv Dayal Singh
J. Paul Twitchell

SWEDENBORGIAN
Warren Felt Evans
Thomas Lake Harris

UNIVERSALISM
Adin A. Ballou
Thomas Lake Harris
Abner Kneeland

ZOROASTERIAN
Meher Baba

INFORMATION NOT
AVAILABLE
George Adamski
Jakob Ammann
William W. Atkinson
Edna A. Wheeler Ballard
Guy W. Ballard
Elbert Benjamine
Pierre Bernard
Emma Hardinge Britten
Luke D. Broughton
Thomas H. Burgoyne
Irving S. Cooper
Alpheus Cutler
Andrew Jackson Davis
Edwin John Dingle
Fr. M. J. Divine
Timothy Drew
Joseph C. Dylks
Arnold J. Ford
Gerald B. Gardner
Ursula N. Gestefeld
Max Heindel
George Went Hensley
Emma Curtis Hopkins
Jacob Hutter
Hazret I. Khan
Ann Lee
Gloria Lee
S. L. MacGregor Mathers
Elijah Muhammad
John B. Newbrough
L. T. Nichols
Henry Steel Olcott

Robert D. Owen
Harold W. Percival
George W. Plummer
Benjamin Purnell
Phineas P. Quimby
Pascal B. Randolph
Charles Mason Remey

Olney H. Richmond
William J. Seymour
Joseph Smith, Jr.
Baird T. Spaulding
Rudolf Steiner
Cyrus R. Teed

INDEX